CU00760506

Liberia's First Civil War

This book provides a comprehensive narrative history of Liberia's first civil war, from its origins in the 1980s right through the conflict and up to the peace agreement and conclusion of hostilities in 1997.

The first Liberian Civil War was one of Africa's most devastating conflicts, claiming the lives of more than 200,000 Liberians and sending shockwaves across the world. Drawing on a wide range of local and international sources, the book traces the background of the war and its long-term and immediate causes, before analysing the detail of the unfolding conflict, the eventual ceasefire, peace agreement and subsequent elections. In particular, the book shines a light on hitherto unseen first-hand Roman Catholic indigenous and missionary sources, which offer a rare intimacy to the analysis. Detailing the impact of Liberia's individual warlords and peacemakers, the book also explains the roles played by non-governmental agencies, national, regional and international actors, by the UN, ECOWAS and the Organisation of African Unity, as well as by nations with special interests and influence, such as the USA and other West African states.

This book's detailed narrative analysis of the Liberian conflict will be an important read for anyone with an interest in the Liberian conflict, including researchers within African studies, political science, contemporary history, international relations, and peace and conflict studies.

Edmund Hogan is currently Archivist of the Society of African Missions, of which he is a member. He has been a Lecturer for over four decades in universities in Ireland and across Africa, most recently as Professor in Church History and Patrology at Good Shepherd Major Seminary, Kaduna, Nigeria.

Routledge Studies in Peace, Conflict and Security in Africa

Edited by Cyril Obi, Social Science Research Council, New York, USA

For more information about this series, please visit: www.routledge.com/Routledge-Studies-in-Peace-Conflict-and-Security-in-Africa/book-series/RSPCSA

Liberia's First Civil War
A Narrative History

Edmund Hogan

Routledge
Taylor & Francis Group

LONDON AND NEW YORK

First published 2022
by Routledge
2 Park Square, Milton Park, Abingdon, Oxon OX14 4RN

and by Routledge
605 Third Avenue, New York, NY 10158

Routledge is an imprint of the Taylor & Francis Group, an informa business

© 2022 Edmund Hogan

The right of Edmund Hogan to be identified as author of this work has been asserted in accordance with sections 77 and 78 of the Copyright, Designs and Patents Act 1988.

All rights reserved. No part of this book may be reprinted or reproduced or utilised in any form or by any electronic, mechanical, or other means, now known or hereafter invented, including photocopying and recording, or in any information storage or retrieval system, without permission in writing from the publishers.

Trademark notice: Product or corporate names may be trademarks or registered trademarks, and are used only for identification and explanation without intent to infringe.

British Library Cataloguing-in-Publication Data
A catalogue record for this book is available from the British Library

Library of Congress Cataloging-in-Publication Data
A catalog record has been requested for this book

ISBN: 978-1-032-11304-3 (hbk)
ISBN: 978-1-032-11305-0 (pbk)
ISBN: 978-1-003-21930-9 (ebk)

DOI: 10.4324/9781003219309

Typeset in Bembo
by Taylor & Francis Books

Contents

Acronyms

AB SMA Archives, Cork, Ireland
ACDL   Association for Constitutional Democracy in Liberia
ACS   Society for the Colonisation of Free People of Colour (American Colonization Society)
AECAW   A Episcopal Conferences of Anglophone West Africa
AFJN   Africa Faith and Justice Network
AFL   Armed Forces of Liberia
AFP   Agence France-Presse
AICF   Action Internationale Contre la Faim
ALCOP   All-Liberia Coalition Party
AMI   Aide Médicale International
AP   Associated Press
ASC   Adorers of the Blood of Christ
AT SMA Archives, Tenafly, NJ, U.S.
BBC   British Broadcasting Corporation
BTC   Barclay Training Center (Barracks)
CIC   Commander in Chief
CRS   Catholic Relief Services
CSC   Holy Cross Brothers
CSJ   Sisters of St Joseph of Chambéry
CSSp   Congregation of the Holy Spirit
ECOMOG   Economic Community of West African States Monitoring Group
ECOWAS   Economic Community of West African States
ELBC   Eternal Love Broadcasting Corporation
ELCA   Evangelical Lutheran Church in America
ELCM   Eternal Love Community Radio
ELTV   Eternal Love Television
ELWA   Eternal Love Winning Africa
GAO(U.S.)   General Accounting Office
GOL   Government of Liberia
ICRC   International Committee of the Red Cross
IFMC   Inter-Faith Mediation Committee
IGNU   Interim Government of National Unity

IHRLG International Human Rights Law Group
INN International Negotiation Network
INPFL Independent National Patriotic Front of Liberia
INS Immigration and Naturalization Service
LAC Liberia Agricultural Company
LAMCO Liberian-American/Swedish Mining Company
LAP Liberian Action Party
LCC Liberian Council of Churches
LCHR Lawyers Committee for Human Rights
LDF Lofa Defence Force
LICORE Liberian Coalition for Relief, Resettlement and Reconstruction
LIMCO Liberian Mining Company
LINSU Liberian National Students Union
LNC Liberia National Conference
LNRCS Liberian National Red Cross Society
LNTG Liberian National Transitional Government
LPC Liberia Peace Council
LRRRC Liberia Refugee Repatriation Resettlement Committee
LTRC Liberia Truth and Reconciliation Commission
LUP Liberia Unification Party
LWR/CWS Lutheran World Relief / Church World Services
MMM Medical Missionaries of Mary
MMMA Archives of the Medical Missionaries of Mary
MOJA Movement for Justice in Africa
MSF Médecins Sans Frontières
MSF (B) Médecins Sans Frontières Belgium
MSF (F) Médecins Sans Frontières France
MSF (H) Médecins Sans Frontières Holland
NDPL National Democratic Party of Liberia
NPFL National Patriotic Front of Liberia
NPFL-CRC National Patriotic Front of Liberia- Central Revolutionary Council
NPP National Patriotic Party
NPRAG National Patriotic Reconstruction Assembly Government
NRC National Readjustment Commission
NULT National Union of Liberian Teachers
OAU Organisation of African Unity
OFD Office of U.S. Foreign Disaster Assistance
OPEX Operational Experts
PAL Progressive Alliance of Liberia
PPP People's Progressive Party
PRC People's Redemption Council
Propaganda Fide - Sacred Congregation for the Propagation of the Faith
REACT Revolutionary Action Committee
RS Regional Superior
RUF Revolutionary United Front

SCF   Save the Children Fund
SDB   Society of St John Bosco (Salesians)
SECOM   Special Elections Commission
SMA   Society of African Missions
SMC   Standing Mediation Committee (ECOWAS)
SRSG   Special Representative of the Secretary General
TPR   Temporary Protected Status
UFSI   Universities Field Staff International
UL   University of Liberia
ULAA   Union of Liberian Associations in the Americas
ULIMO   United Liberation Movement of Liberia for Democracy
ULIMO-J   ULIMO faction under Roosevelt Johnson
ULIMO-K   ULIMO faction under Alhaji G.V. Kromah
UN   United Nations
UNDHA   United Nations Department of Humanitarian Affairs.
UNDP   United Nations Development Program.
UNDRO   United Nations Disaster Relief Organisation
UNFPA   United Nations Population Fund
UNHCR   UN High Commission for Refugees
UNICEF   United Nations International Children's Emergency Fund
UNOMIL   United Nations Observer Mission in Liberia
UNSCOL   United Nations Special Coordinator's Office
UP   Unity Party
UPI   United Press International
UPP   United People's Party
USAF   U.S. Airforce
USAID   U.S. Agency for International Development
VOA   Voice of America
WCC   World Council of Churches
WFP   World Food Programme

Introduction

From its foundation in 1847 until late in the 20th century the small Republic of Liberia created scarcely a ripple on the consciousness of the West African region. Internationally it was known – if at all – as a legacy of slavery in the U.S. and for its Ship Registry[*]. Formed by freed slaves from the U.S. who dominated a mix of indigenous ethnic groups, Liberia did not feature in the Scramble for Africa, which commenced in 1884, when large swathes of the continent were colonised by predatory European powers. Even within its own borders, apart from periodic tribal disturbances, the upheavals that convulsed West Africa in the post-colonial 1950s and 1960s eluded Liberia. The only tie that Liberia had to the wider world was with the U.S. – a relationship that brought little benefit to Liberia but substantial political, commercial and military rewards to the 'mother country'. Thus, to observers of Africa in the last quarter of the 20th century Liberia appeared as a quaint anomaly – an aspiring 'little America' planted on African soil. And yet during the last two decades of that century into the 21st century, this apparently tranquil country was to spawn one of Africa's most devastating civil wars.

The following pages trace the background to Liberia's civil war, identifying its causes and describing its course. In these tasks it uses a wide variety of sources, local, regional and international. In particular, it makes use of extensive first-hand Roman Catholic indigenous and missionary sources, which not only add much to the analysis but give an intimacy which otherwise might be missing in a scholarly account. It contains a detailed account of the roles played by national, regional and international actors, by the UN, ECOWAS and the OAU, as well as by nations with special interests and influence (primarily the U.S. and ECOWAS member states). The roles played by non-governmental agencies, local and international are also assessed. Central to the study of this signature African civil war is the portrayal of Liberia's peacemakers and warlords.

---

[*] The Liberian Ship Registry, the second largest worldwide, is administered from the U.S. by a private U.S.-owned company. The Registry's statutes are enshrined in Liberian law. The Registry was established in 1948 with the assistance of Edward Stettinius, former U.S. Secretary of State. Liberia derives 8% of its gross national product from the Registry.

This book takes the approach of interpretative narrative. One of the earliest manifestations of the writing of history was the chronicle – the listing and dating of significant events chronologically, with little attempt to explain or interpret them. Narrative history, in its earlier forms, tended to maintain the chronological sequence but presented history in a story format that gains much of its momentum from the depiction of individuals, scenarios and purposes. In more recent times, while narrative history retains its story context, there is a more rigorous commitment to securing the accuracy of facts. Moreover, the attribution of meaning to the events recounted, is a central concern. In the present book, while the story format is maintained and the accuracy of the facts is attended to, the principal challenge is to seek answers to fundamental questions about the war. For example: 1. How was it that a relatively stable West African Republic descended into a chaos which was to endure for almost 14 years? 2. What was the nature of this war, the manner of its conduct and the factors which sustained it? 3. What were the influences which eventually brought it to a close? 4. Finally, what was the legacy of this civil war and what lessons might be learned to assist future peace-making.

In this book there is no distinct section or chapter that addresses these questions. The interpretation is inherent in the trajectory of the narrative, in the manner in which events are described, and in the way that questions are posed, and answers given. There is one further point in relation to the approach. It is hoped that the capacity of the narrative form to stimulate the faculty of imagination will produce some sense of what the war meant for those living in its midst and for those regional and international players drawn in.

> At the bottom of the heart of every human being, from earliest infancy until the tomb, there is something that goes on indomitably expecting, in the teeth of all experience of crimes committed, suffered, and witnessed, that good and not evil will be done!
>
> Simone Weil, 1909–43

Note on Sources

> In our estimation, yours was the richest collection of newspapers, magazines and other documentary sources on human rights and public affairs in contemporary Liberia held anywhere outside Liberia.
>
> Amos Sawyer to S. John Murray, Society of African Missions, Tenafly New Jersey, USA, November 1989

Many studies of the Liberian civil war have appeared over the years, written by journalists, retired military men, politicians and academics. While this study makes use of these and a wide range of other published and unpublished sources, it also has had access to an important source not previously plumbed. Catholic missionary agencies from Europe and America working in Liberia throughout the civil war witnessed at first hand the enfolding of events. Accounts of their experiences are contained in the voluminous documentary material preserved in the archives of these agencies. The material consists not only of administrative correspondence, reports, diaries and memoirs but also records of the extensive electronic communications between the missionaries in the field and their various headquarters, in Ireland, Italy, Spain, England, India, the U.S. and the Vatican. The missionary agency with the largest deployment of personnel over the years – and primarily responsible for the establishment of Liberia's Catholic Church – is the Society of African Missions (SMA), founded in the mid-19th century. Its various archives – in Ireland, Rome and the U.S. – are a treasure trove of information on Liberia. Perhaps the most important SMA archival holding on Liberia's civil war is that of the SMA community at Tenafly, New Jersey. Among those who accessed it during the civil war was Professor Amos Sawyer whose comment on its excellence is cited at the heading of this note.

Among several other missionary archives available to this author were those of the Adorers of Blood of Christ (Ruma, Illinois), Franciscan Missionaries of Mary (Rome) and the Medical Missionaries of Mary (Ireland). Missionary congregations that supplied information and documents included the Salesians (England), Holy Cross Brothers (Canada), Sisters of St Joseph of Chambéry and Christian Brothers (English Province). The library of the University of Indiana with its comprehensive Liberian newspaper collection, and the resources of London University's School of African and Oriental Studies were of inestimable value. Finally, the author drew on correspondence with numerous missionaries, journalists, aid agency personnel and other individuals who observed the civil war at first hand. To these and all who opened their doors and their hearts and minds to me during the ten years of writing this book, I am profoundly grateful.

Edmund M. Hogan, October 2021

Section 1
Prelude

1 Remote causes of Liberia's revolution

The earliest seeds of Liberia's civil war are to be found in the wake of the American Revolution (1775–83) when a new liberal climate led to a rapid rise in the number of liberated slaves. The failure of those promoting emancipation to embrace the freed slaves as social equals led in subsequent years to large numbers of unemployed and impoverished Blacks whose poverty and exclusion led to disruptive and, increasingly violent, behaviour. In 1820 outrages against wealthy Whites led the Virginia State Legislature to propose the repatriation of freed slaves, of which there were then estimated to be some 250,000.[1] The idea of repatriation was not new. Early in the 18th century Quaker and Protestant missionaries proposed it as a form of restitution for enslavement or in the hope that the returnees might be a civilising and Christianising influence for Africa. But now, in the 19th century, less worthy motives became evident. There was still a religious and philanthropic dimension which took concrete form in 1816 with the foundation of the Society for the Colonisation of Free People of Colour (ASC). However, it is unlikely that the ASC would ever have made an impact without the financial support and active involvement of important politicians and citizens of the Union, most notably in the South, who were driven by a determination to remove the menace of rampaging freed slaves in their midst. It was largely due to their influence that the U.S. Congress of 1819 passed a bill for assistance in financing and implementing such repatriation schemes.[2]

The first actual attempts at repatriation dated from 1820 and were inauspicious. However, over the following decades, a number of settlements established firm roots, despite strong resistance from local tribes. In 1837, with tribal hostility intensifying, it became necessary for the settlements to band together, forming the Commonwealth of Liberia. By this time, also, support from the U.S. had diminished. Those Americans who had hoped repatriation might solve the problem of unsocialised free slaves now began to look elsewhere for solutions, while others who had intended the settlements to exercise a civilising and Christianising influence, despaired at the way in which settlers copied the system of privilege which had operated for so long in the Southern States. Denied the level of U.S. financial and military assistance previously enjoyed, and in danger of losing territory not only to the tribes but to their European colonial neighbours,[3] the settlers became convinced that a more formal and

DOI: 10.4324/9781003219309-2

independent political status was required. Thus, in 1847 all legal connections with the U.S. were severed. A year later Liberia declared itself an independent Republic with a U.S.-styled Constitution and immediately set about seeking international recognition. Few countries responded but late in 1848 Britain and France acknowledged Liberia's sovereignty, thus giving the Republic a welcome measure of stability. The U.S. withheld recognition until 1862.

The declaration of a Republic was followed by two decades of economic progress. This came from trade to which Americo-Liberians took with enthusiasm and no mean skill. The commodities traded were produced in privately-owned plantations, and included coffee, palm oil, rice, cinnamon and rubber. It is recorded that by 1870 Liberia had built some 50 small ships to trade overseas. A year later, with a view to enhancing commodity production, President Roye (1870–71) obtained, on very reasonable terms, an international loan of half a million U.S. dollars. But by the mid-1870s global production and greater overseas competition caused prices of the aforementioned commodities to drop sharply, while the emergence of large steamships rendered Liberia's entire fleet redundant. In addition, it transpired that the value of President Roye's loan was reduced by almost a half because of deductions and clauses stipulating advance repayments. Henceforth, well into the 20th century, repayments of the loan remained a heavy burden on Liberia's exchequer.[4]

From this time, unable to raise taxes in tribal districts and receiving only a trickle of the income previously available from philanthropic agencies, Liberia's parlous economic situation was compounded by the settlers' unwillingness to engage in agriculture, which was regarded as a symbol of their former servitude. Henceforth Liberia teetered on the brink of bankruptcy and relied on small loans, mainly from Britain and the U.S., to keep afloat.

Ultimately Liberia's poor economy and lack of development was a function of its social and political policies.[5] In 1930 its population was estimated as 12,000 of settler origin[*] and 1.2 million tribal.[6] Investing in the indigenous population remained anathema to the ruling elite, which saw loss of control over the tribal majority as tantamount to the Republic's destruction. Thus, it was that during the next 100 years Liberia witnessed the rigorous application of a double standard whereby the indigenous population was ruthlessly kept in its place, while Americo-Liberian families lived off whatever fat the land possessed. Tribal Liberians lived under a socio-legal system very different from that of the Americo-Liberians, in relation to taxation, land tenure, residence and movement, marriage and divorce, legal jurisdiction, and access to education and medical care. Neither could they vote or stand for election. The system also included the imposition of penal exactions, such as unpaid services to local

[*]   The Liberian settler population was not entirely homogeneous. It included Africans who had been rescued by the U.S. Navy, while aboard U.S.-bound slave ships, and brought to Liberia ('Congoes'). There were also oppressed Blacks from the British Caribbean colony of Barbados who migrated to Liberia with the assistance of the ACS ('Barbadians'). Arthur Barclay, a Barbadian migrant was to become the 15th President of Liberia (1904–12).

authorities and forced labour for export. There were also extra-legal exactions of money, food (rice) and 'services' which included unpaid work for government officials and Americo-Liberian families. Among abuses perpetrated was the system of 'pawning', whereby native children became part of the colonial household until they came of age. In many cases the children came to occupy the status of slaves, and slave-concubines in the case of females. This repressive social and economic structure was entrenched by the last quarter of the 19th century.[7]

The maltreatment of the indigenous population attracted international attention in 1929 leading, during the next five years, to a crisis which threatened the very existence of the Republic. The practice of slavery within the territory and the transport of slave labour overseas were among accusations levelled against Liberia. The League of Nations responded by establishing a Commission of Inquiry under Dr Cuthbert Christy. Its findings, published in 1930, confirmed that forcible transportation of labour was taking place. It also declared that while slavery did not exist in its classic form, it was being widely practised under a different institution, namely 'pawnism' or 'domestic servitude'.

The Commission's report provoked an outcry for the abolition of the Republic, particularly among philanthropic and humanitarian organisations in the U.S. and Europe. There were others who proclaimed that Liberia proved beyond doubt that Blacks were incapable of governing themselves. In the event, Liberia's President, Edwin Barclay, managed to stave off the Republic's demise by dismissing officials and politicians (including his own Vice President) implicated in the Christy Commission's report. Barclay also indicated Liberia's intention of carrying out the recommendations of the Commission, while appealing for expert advice from the League. During the following three years a 'Plan of Assistance' drawn up by 'Experts' gave a comprehensive blueprint as to how Liberia might be financed and administered.[8]

In 1932 calls for the suppression of the State were renewed when an uprising on the Kru Coast was said to have been caused by widespread reprisals taken against those who had given evidence to the Christy Commission. A League Commission was sent to investigate, after which there was further unrest, claimed again to have been caused by the further victimisation of witnesses. Meanwhile in May 1934, the League of Nations declared that its 'Plan of Assistance' had been rejected by Liberia. This led the U.S. and Britain to withdraw diplomatic recognition and, together with Germany., urge the League to take control over the Black Republic. It seemed probable that if Liberia was found guilty of reprisals against witnesses to Commissions, action might at last be taken. However, the League was unable to prove conclusively that reprisals had taken place and Liberia (albeit with some refinements so as not again to incur international wrath) gradually resumed its traditional social, political and economic policies towards its indigenous population.

During its first half-century Liberia's defence against internal and external enemies had been spearheaded by an unpaid settler's militia, part-time and compulsory for certain age groups. However, in 1908, when it became known that the British and French had further designs on Liberia's territory, a permanent military force was established, 'the Liberia Frontier Force' (LFF). Defence of the realm was not the only goal of this new body. Its remit also extended to pacifying the unruly tribal majority within its boundaries and collecting tax. The LFF was officered by Americo-Liberians with the assistance of seconded U.S. officers. The rank and file was drawn from the smaller tribes. The force was to discharge its military responsibilities with distinction. Threats from external forces were countered, while the hinterland, interior and troublesome coastal regions were largely subdued and made tax compliant by 1920.

It has been observed that while the LFF officer corps sought to mirror the approach of European colonial forces, the enlisted men were driven by the African tradition which 'conceptualised warfare as a raiding system that aimed to collect booty, to exact revenge, or to liberate pawns from servitude'.[9] It is probable that without the latter the pacification campaign would hardly have succeeded, as Liberia simply did not possess the resources to conduct a campaign according to the colonial model. What it meant in terms of relations between tribal communities and their Americo-Liberian masters was to deepen the already existing resentment. The ruthlessness of the unpaid, unfed soldiers, who had to live off the land, whose poorly trained officers were unable to exercise control,[10] left a deep imprint on tribal consciousness. Nor did this oppressive behaviour cease with pacification but continued unabated during the first half of the 20th century.

Liberia's economy changed little during the Republic's first hundred years.[11] The involvement of international firms in the exploitation of Liberia's rich resources of iron ore and land, was introduced under the Tubman regime (1944–71), although there had been one notable arrival in 1926, namely the Firestone Rubber Company.[12] Tubman's 'open door' policy was skilfully managed so that while it provided income for the government and the settler community and very basic wages for tribal employees, it never interfered with Liberia's traditional social, political and economic policies. Control over the country would not be yielded up either to Europeans or tribesmen. But if the whip-hand over the indigenous population remained, there were certain straws in the wind that augured ill for Liberia's elite.

Notes

1 Edmund M. Hogan, Catholic Missionaries and Liberia – A Study of Christian Enterprise in West Africa, 1942–1950, Cork University Press, 1981, 1–3.
2 Ibid, 3.
3 See George W. Ellis, 'Dynamic Factors in the Liberian Situation', The Journal of Race Development, Jan. 1911, vol. 1, no. 3, 257–258.
4 Felix Gerdes, 'The Evolution of the Liberian State - A Study in Neo-patrimonial State Formation and Political Change' (2013), http://edoc.vifapol.de/opus/volltexte/2015/5813/pdf/AP_Evolution_State_Gerdes_2013_1.pdf accessed 3 April 2021.
5 George Dalton, 'History, Politics, and Economic Development in Liberia', The Journal of EconomicHistory, vol. 25, no. 4 (Dec. 1965), 580–581.

6 M.D. MacKenzie, Journal of the Royal African Society, vol. 33, no. 133 (Oct. 1934).

7 Dalton, op.cit., 581.

8 MacKenzie, op.cit., 376–377.

9 Timothy D. Nevin, 'The Uncontrollable Force: A Brief History of the Liberian Frontier Force, 1908–1944', The International Journal of African Historical Studies, 44, no. 2 (2011), 275.

10 Ibid, 286.

11 Moeen A. Quereshi, Yoshio Mizoc, Francis d'A. Collings, 'The Liberian Economy', Staff Paper (International. Monetary Fund), vol. 11, no. 2 (July 1964), 285.

12 See Ibid, 286. 'For the next three decades Firestone became 'the dominant economic enterprise … providing most of the employment, income, exports, and government revenues.'

2 Proximate causes of Liberia's revolution

As Liberia moved towards the last quarter of the 20th century, it witnessed a widening gap between its rich, often corrupt, ruling elite and its disenfranchised indigenous population. This was a country where some 4% of the population controlled 60% of its wealth.[1] The level of dissatisfaction was steadily rising as it became more difficult for ethnic Liberians to make ends meet. This was stridently articulated by Liberia's small, educated intelligentsia which, ironically, was predominantly Americo-Liberian, formed of those sufficiently privileged to study overseas (principally in the U.S.) where they had acquired 'liberal views.' The most vocal in calling for reform were those who on returning to Liberia took up teaching posts in the University of Liberia (UL), the larger of Liberia's two institutions of higher learning.[*]

The call for reform also came from among Liberians resident in America – either those who had fallen foul of government, or those scions of the elite currently acquiring third-level qualifications. Finally, there was the UL student population taking its lead from liberal-minded teachers, the most articulate of which were often indigenous Liberians who had benefited from missionary education and won scholarships to the institution.

Calls for reform might have been less dangerous for the ruling True Whig party[2] had it not been for extraordinary happenings in the West African region in the previous two decades. In many countries, strikes, mobilisation of the masses and armed action had hastened the post-war process of decolonisation. And this was quickly followed by the violent overthrow of the first tranche of post-colonial civilian governments in Ghana, Nigeria, Ivory Coast, Guinea and Sierra Leone. Civil unrest, peaceful mass protest, or the violent alternatives of coup-d'état or putsch had brought about fundamental changes in many places. Why not in Liberia?

***

There can be little doubt that the Rice Riots of 14 April 1979 marked a watershed in Liberia's history, signalling the end of an era of relative tranquillity and the beginning of a descent into chaos. Although at the time it seemed the old order would quickly reassert itself – all previous challenges had been

---

[*]   Cuttington University, the second such institution, originated in 1889 as a College and Divinity school of the Episcopal Church. It was erected as a university in 1977.

DOI: 10.4324/9781003219309-3

summarily dealt with - it is now clear that the events of that day marked the crossing of a line from which there would be no going back.

The growing clamour of a small but vocal, educated grouping for a more equitable society need not have ended in the virtual destruction of the country. In many societies acceptance of change and a willingness to compromise ensures a transition that is relatively peaceful. But in Liberia the division lines were too deep. The mass of Liberia's small population[3], impoverished, powerless and illiterate, had been ruled for 133 years by a privileged oligarchy. Nor were there any external forces which might have overseen a transition to a more just society. Liberia counted for very little in the West African region. It was, in reality, a cobbled-together republic made up of small ethnic groups pushed to the coast by the more powerful tribes of the Gulf of Guinea, lacking cohesion and governed by an elite of freed American slaves which had easily imposed itself.

When, eventually, the savagery of Liberia's civil war began to impact on regional stability, it was too late. The only country which might have prevented the collapse was the U.S. which had strong historical links with, and current strategic interests in, Liberia. It was not to happen. America's foreign policy, focused on the threat of international communism, was not greatly concerned by Liberia's politics. For Liberia had always been firmly in America's camp and any change of regime was unlikely to change this, such was the dependence of Liberia's tiny economy on U.S. commercial investment and modest financial assistance.

The background to the disturbances of 14 April is inextricably linked to the emergence of two political movements. The Movement for Justice in Africa (MOJA), founded by three UL academics (Togba-Nah Tipoteh, Amos Sawyer and Henry Boimah Fahnbulleh), emerged in 1973. Its socialist-oriented program advocated 'nationalisation of major economic enterprises', 'redistribution of land' and 'punishment for corruption'. To achieve these objectives, it called for 'strikes and slow-downs' and other forms of public protest. As it happened, formed of teachers and academics, MOJA had little capacity for organising strikes or protests. Nonetheless its skilful articulation of grievances, delivered at meetings throughout Liberia, did much to raise political awareness and heighten the sense of injustice.

Liberal-minded Liberians in the U.S. were responsible for founding the 'Progressive Alliance of Liberia' (PAL) in the closing months of 1975. PAL's leader was Gabriel Baccus Matthews, an Americo-Liberian, with family political connections to the Tubman regime. Previously a government official, he had served as vice-consul in New York until dismissed in 1972. While in America Matthews had been strongly influenced by the ideas and methods of 'African socialism' − a movement that applied European socialist ideology to Africa, advocating 'grassroots mobilization and revolutionary direct action such as strikes and demonstrations.'[4,5] Not a formal political party (Liberia permitted only one party), PAL was essentially a movement seeking to organise a viable opposition to the government. However, it also had a sharp edge, seen in its willingness to convoke, and skill in conducting, militant protest campaigns and demonstrations. The steady return of PAL members from the U.S. and its opening of an office in the capital, Monrovia, in 1978, changed it from a popular but remote movement to a proximate political force.

***

William R. Tolbert had served for 19 years as Vice-President to William V.S. Tubman — Liberia's ruler for 27 years — before succeeding to the presidency in 1971. In the early stages of his tenancy, he had made a number of superficial gestures towards a more democratic form of government, but these quickly gave way to meaningless rhetoric about reform. An ordained Baptist minister, Tolbert liked to coin aspirational slogans, ('the Wholesome Functioning Society', 'Total Involvement of the People', 'Rally Time'), formulate pseudo-philosophical economic and political ideologies ('Humanistic Capitalism') and deliver frequent, lengthy, barely comprehensible speeches. All this could not conceal the fact that little or nothing had changed, that corruption and nepotism still prevailed and that Liberia's majority indigenous population continued to be largely powerless and discriminated against.

Outwardly, wishing to present a liberal face to the wider world, the Tolbert regime tolerated MOJA and professed to welcome PAL, allowing both movements to operate with relative freedom. In meetings across the country, they focussed on the fact that despite the export of rubber, timber and rich deposits of iron ore, 96% of Liberia's 1.8 million people were poverty-stricken. They also highlighted the deteriorating relations between the ruling elite and the indigenous population and claimed the loudly trumpeted efforts by former President Tubman and current President Tolbert to unite the country were ineffectual and plainly half-hearted.

***

As MOJA and PAL mobilised support, the Catholic Church continued its tradition of conducting its affairs quietly, confining itself to internal pastoral matters and showing little preoccupation with the increasing political tensions. That Church had first set down tentative roots in the first decade of the 20th century and had struggled to establish itself for over half a century.[6] More recently, however, through involvement in education and health care, it had at last entered a phase of expansion. Nonetheless of all the Catholic mission fields in West Africa, which included countries like Nigeria, Ghana, Ivory Coast, Togo, Sierra Leone and Senegal, Liberia had been the least successful, with less than 5% of the population belonging to a Church organised into a mere two dioceses and mainly staffed by overseas missionaries. The recent establishment of a major seminary (serving three other countries in the region) and the appointment of Liberians to replace the two European bishops, augured well for the future, but Catholicism still lagged far behind other Christian denominations.

At this time Bishops Michael Kpala Francis of Monrovia Vicariate[*] and Boniface Dalieh of Cape Palmas Vicariate were assisted by 21 missionaries of the international Society of African Missions (SMA), four members of the Congregation of the Holy Ghost, five native-born Liberian priests, and one

---

[*]   'Vicariate': a legal term in Church canon law, signifying a quasi-diocese. Further progress was required before a vicariate was accorded the status of a substantive diocese. Leaders of vicariates were, however, ordained bishops.

Ghanaian priest. In addition, there was a variety of teaching and nursing Brotherhoods and Sisterhoods drawn from a diversity of continents.[7]

There was little concern among Liberia's Catholic Church leaders or indeed among those in its West African Region about the darkening political situation. The agenda of an inter-territorial meeting of bishops from Liberia, Sierra Leone and the Gambia consisted of purely pastoral and administrative matters. Similarly, the minutes of a meeting of the two Liberian bishops during March 1979 gave no hint of the troubles soon to come, preoccupations being solely pastoral and administrative.

***

Numerous accounts of Monrovia's so-called Rice Riots of Saturday, 14 April 1979, have been written. Between 50 and 100 people were killed, and 400 injured; and widespread looting took place.[8] One of those who came face to face with the horrors of that Saturday was Kieran O'Reilly,[9] chaplain to Monrovia's largest hospital, the John F. Kennedy Medical Centre.

O'Reilly entered the hospital compound at 5.30 pm, just as the first casualties were being brought in. He found a large open delivery vehicle disgorging wounded while a growing, disconsolate and angry crowd milled about.

In the reception area O'Reilly witnessed:

> the most appalling procession of wounded and dying... men, women and indeed children. The all-pervasive sight was of blood — uncongealed pools on the floor, flowing profusely through open wounds onto tattered clothes, or oozing through partly sutured wounds.[10]

The horror of the situation was compounded by the presence of soldiers. O'Reilly 'held one young man who had been shot while a nurse attempted to insert a drip into his wrist'. Meanwhile, soldiers were demanding custody of the man, claiming that he had shot one of their number. The nursing staff courageously refused to comply and ordered the soldiers out of the treatment area. There followed loud argument, threats and shouting, until eventually the soldiers moved outside the compound. Added to the uproar was the constant blaring of sirens and hooting of horns heralding the arrival of more dead and wounded.

Several hours later, as he left the hospital, O'Reilly was accosted by a crowd 'hostile at the sight of a minister of religion'. Many of Liberia's leading politicians, responsible for the present carnage, it was pointed out to him, were also ministers of religion. It was true, as the scholar Paul Gifford points out, that the unhealthy relationship between government and organised religion had been 'part of the structure of dominance which existed since the formation of the Republic of Liberia in 1847'. Along with the True Whig Party and Freemasonry, Christianity was 'the third pillar on which the whole oppressive set-up rested'.[11] And this remained true at the time of the Rice Riots when President Tolbert was also Chairman of the Baptist Convention, his Vice-President, Bennie Warner, was Presiding Bishop of the Methodist Church, while Reginald

Townsend, National Chairman of the True Whig Party, was Moderator of the Presbyterian Church.

***

Some weeks later a detailed account of the Rice Riots reached the headquarters of the SMA's American Province in Tenafly, New Jersey. It was penned by the Americo-Liberian, Dr Amos Sawyer, co-founder of MOJA, currently Professor of Social Sciences at UL.[12] In his account Sawyer outlined how in December 1978 Mrs Florence Chenoweth, Minister for Agriculture, had recommended an increase in the price of rice 'to help farmers cover their costs and encourage greater productivity'. If enacted the price of a 100 lb bag of clean rice would rise from the present rate of $22 to $30. This increase in the cost of a staple food, when the average wage was about $50 a month, was bound to meet strong opposition. PAL claimed that the measure, if implemented, would benefit only a small group of mechanised rice farmers. An influential pamphlet opposing the measure was written by Dr Patrick Seyon of UL.[13]

Resistance gradually became organised, and on 24 March PAL sought permission to hold a demonstration.[14] This was denied, leading to a decision by PAL to commence a campaign of civil disobedience, to be inaugurated at its Gurley Street headquarters on Saturday, 14 April. On assembling there, the demonstrators would march to the Executive Mansion (residence of the president) to hold a public protest. The government duly banned the proposed gathering. This provoked increased local defiance and a determination by many other groups (including the Liberian National Students Union – LINSU) to defy the authorities. It was clear that a confrontation would take place.

According to Sawyer's account, before dawn on 14 April, police and soldiers established strong points throughout the city. But this did not prevent a crowd some 500 strong from gathering on Gurley Street by 9 am. Two hours later this had swelled into several thousand congregating in the vicinity of the PAL Centre, along Monrovia's main thoroughfare, Broad Street. Shortly after 11 am the police stormed the PAL Centre and arrested its occupants.[15] The PAL leadership, however, had already vacated the building. 'The first fatalities', Sawyer continued, 'occurred when Police Director, Mr Varney Dempster, shot into a crowd on Capitol Hill, leaving many wounded and at least one dead'. This was the signal for indiscriminate fire by the police. The confrontation continued throughout the afternoon, during which roadblocks were erected by demonstrators, government vehicles were set on fire and widespread looting took place.

The *New African*, a pro-government paper, gave its own version of the course of events not widely different from Sawyer's:

> It seems as if the police at first fired into the air after 200 young demonstrators ran along a street waving palm branches and shouting 'Freedom' and 'Revolution'. Then they fired tear gas into the crowd and subsequently there was a shot and a boy was hit in the leg. Indiscriminate shooting followed and ambulances and trucks rushed the dead and

wounded to hospital. By now there was an estimated 2,000 demonstrators hurling rocks at the police and considerable looting taking place ...[16]

According to Sawyer the 'complete breakdown of order' continued through Easter Sunday, 15 April, despite a government curfew. On that morning Monrovia 'looked a complete shambles, with the occasional looter and a few intoxicated soldiers holding up the few people on their way to those churches which held services'.[17]

Later that day President Tolbert spoke on national radio describing the disturbances as 'a situation never before witnessed in our history' and which had 'marred our national image...'[18] His administration, he said, was blameless. The prohibition on the demonstration had been justified because its staging was bound to lead to disorder.[19] And had not events proved him right! At every stage of the sequence of events on that day, Tolbert declared, it was the demonstrators who were culpable. And he had no doubt that in the melee which followed, casualties would have been significantly higher had not the government exercised exemplary restraint.[20]

Tolbert's description of the course of events followed (and indeed embellished) a template often found in the case of dictatorships defending atrocities. So also did his final remarks. He had, he declared, become leader 'by the grace of God' as well as by the 'freely exercised choice' of the people; and he was now urging the populace to 'surge forward with unshakable faith in God and full confidence in ourselves'. Moreover, while offering 'condolences to the bereaved' he was not merely 'assuring' them but was 'actually with them in prayer at this time of sorrow'.

Two days later, apparently feeling that the populace was sufficiently chastened by his earlier remarks, Tolbert's went on the offensive. Lame attempts at exoneration and exculpation were now replaced by strong assertions about the iniquity of those who had challenged his regime. The demonstrators, he told his radio audience, were 'criminally minded individuals' assisted by 'foreigners, evil and satanic men'.[21] Primarily culpable, he asserted, were Gabriel Baccus Matthews of PAL, chief ringleader, and his assistants, Dr Togba-Nah Tipoteh and Dr Dew Tuan Wleh-Mayson, both members of MOJA. Tolbert also implicated several named student leaders and, curiously, a rather obscure agricultural improvement organisation called Susukuu[22] (of which Tipoteh was Director General).[23]

On April 19 the government announced that the situation was now fully under control. The riot, it stated, had been 'an organised attempt on the part of PAL, LINSU ... and other groups, to overthrow the government, kill the president and establish a socialist regime'.[24] And these efforts had been 'assisted by foreign sources.' At a time when Communist influence in Africa appeared to threaten American interests the implication was that the 'foreign sources' were of that variety. Thirty-three named persons, including the leaderships of PAL, MOJA and student organisations, would now be sought out, arrested and charged with treason. Already Matthews, Fahnbulleh and several others had been arrested and charged with 'unlawfully, wickedly, maliciously and traitorously' planning to 'seize power and overthrow the legally constituted government of the Republic of Liberia'.[25]

In the days that followed there were further arrests in which LINSU representatives and their connections were especially targeted.[26] Clergymen who reproached the government were vigorously sought out. One notorious case was that of Dr Nya Kwiawon Taryor, an outspoken Methodist preacher and member of MOJA, who had fled into Guinea to escape arrest, but was detained by the Guinean authorities at the behest of the Liberian authorities. Reports in the newspapers and by word of mouth of such occurrences increased tension.

Tolbert's confidence and the growing belligerence of his response were undoubtedly linked to the staunch support received from President Ahmed Sekou Touré of neighbouring Guinea. Relations between the two countries had become close in 1978 when Tolbert brokered a rapprochement between erstwhile enemies Sekou Touré and President Félix Houphouët-Boigny of Ivory Coast.[27] Subsequently, on 23 January 1979 Tolbert and Touré had signed a mutual defence treaty. At the outset of the Rice Riots crisis Touré offered military assistance to help in maintaining order. Unsure of the loyalty of his army – Liberian soldiers were accurately reported to have joined the rioters in looting – Tolbert gratefully accepted. This force, which arrived within days, was immediately assigned to protection duties at the Executive Mansion, Government House* and the OAU Centre.**

The government's grip was further demonstrated on Friday, 20 April, when that 'cradle of dissent', UL, and also Cuttington University, were closed 'indefinitely' by government order. On the same day two student leaders in hiding let it be known that they were willing to surrender provided they were given a fair and speedy trial. At the weekend these symbols of total and abject defeat, accompanied by Church leaders to whom they had first surrendered, were received in formal audience by President Tolbert before being taken to prison. Other student leaders submitted shortly afterwards and were duly imprisoned pending trial for treason scheduled for 14 April 1980, first anniversary of the Rice Riots.

With the passing of the immediate crisis came a need for Tolbert to explain to Liberians and the wider world why exactly such a calamitous series of events had occurred in a supposedly well-governed country. The explanation that the 'attack on the state' had been principally orchestrated by three or four mild-mannered academics was increasingly difficult to sustain. To stem the growing incredulity Tolbert now began to portray the April riots as a plot by the Communist bloc to destabilise Liberia and establish a foothold in the region. The Soviet Union, Tolbert declared, had used corrupt, power-hungry, unpatriotic intellectuals, foreign agents and street rabble to achieve its purpose.[28] There were two groups of foreigners, he said, the first composed 'of those ... who do not favour our peaceful way of life, our stability and our free

---

*   House of Representatives, meeting place of Liberia's legislature.
**   See p. 15

enterprise system'. Among these were three staff members of the Russian Embassy in Monrovia who now had been asked to leave Liberia. The second group consisted of non-Liberian Africans living in Monrovia who simply 'took advantage of the situation and joined in the looting...' Added to their numbers were 'corner-boys, street rabble and the criminally minded intellectuals' (now relegated to last place).

***

One factor more likely to have contributed to the crisis than an alleged Soviet conspiracy was the extravagant preparation undertaken by the Tolbert regime for hosting the Organisation of African Unity's (OAU) 16th annual summit.[*] Due to be installed as OAU Chairman for 1979–1980 Tolbert was determined to make an impression on his peers. The cost of summit facilities amounted to some 15% of the country's GDP for 1977 (equivalent to 57% of government income). These facilities included a so-called 'Unity Village' in which the conference was to be hosted. A seaside development, it would contain an 'Africa Hotel' to house Foreign Ministers and other dignitaries, as well as 52 sumptuous villas for visiting heads of state.[29]

In a *New African* interview Tolbert felt it necessary to explain the presence of Guinean soldiers in the aftermath of the riots. Their arrival had created much surprise and not a little unease, described by some commentators as 'unpatriotic, un-nationalistic, and unwarrantable'.[30] And there was also regional interest and surprise. What exactly had been the role played by the Guineans in the Liberian crisis? What would Liberia be expected to give to Guinea in return? Tolbert sought to defuse speculation saying that when the rioting commenced President Sekou Touré had sent a delegation offering 'such assistance as might be needed to support the armed forces and police to quell the disturbance'.[31] Concerned by the reports of the unrest, this delegation, 'within the framework of our mutual Defence Pact', had brought along a small contingent of Guinean military which was then deployed to protect the Executive Mansion.

But few believed Tolbert's version of events. Inhabitants of Monrovia knew that the Guinean contingent had been by no means 'small', some independent sources placing it at 500–700 men.[32] Adekeye Adebajo in his history of the Liberian Civil War cites evidence that, rather than responding to an offer of help, it was Tolbert who had sought military aid from Guinea invoking their Mutual Defence Pact.[33]

***

The veneer of democracy behind which the Tolbert regime had sheltered for so long was further diminished as the weeks went by. Court proceedings against the accused were abandoned following a decision by a compliant legislature to grant the president emergency powers. These included authority to suspend *habeas corpus*, set up special courts, ban subversive organisations and conduct seizures and detentions without warrant.[34] Armed with such powers Tolbert addressed the nation in a long,

---

[*]   Tolbert was chairman of this organisation of 32 independent African countries from July 1979 until his death in April 1980.

rambling radio broadcast in which he again absolved the government of all responsibility for what had happened. Immediate action, he said, would be taken against foreigners who were not gainfully employed. These were to be sent home, while all vagrants were to be rounded up and sent to 'correctional Centres'.[35] He also warned ministers of the Gospel to 'preach in sincerity and truth and not to use the pulpit to sow disunity and disharmony'. Clearly the administration was uncertain about the attitude of the Churches and was anxious to get them onside. Liberia's Vice-President, Bishop Bennie Warner, had already expressed his disappointment that so few Church groups had issued statements of loyalty to the administration.[36]

***

On 25 April a 'letter of repentance'[37] addressed to President Tolbert, reported to have been written by Gabriel Baccus Matthews in his prison cell, appeared in the Monrovia press and, in pamphlet form, on city streets.[38] This self-deprecatory letter decried the 'lack of experience of young people' and urged youth to 'rely on the experience and wisdom of men such as you (President Tolbert)'. Matthews himself, the letter said, was now convinced that he and his supporters must 'thoroughly re-examine our methods' and he appealed to the 'fathering consideration' of President Tolbert for permission 'to utilize our energies in helping to carry out a meaningful program of national reconstruction ... under your direct supervision'.

Did Matthews write this supine letter? *The New African* – pro-government, it is true – had no doubt that he did, citing the views of some of his close friends. Nonetheless, although there were some doubters, the weight of the evidence points to the probability that he did.[39] Tolbert's response, also widely circulated, expressed the president's delight that Matthews had 'now come to understand that wisdom is the principal thing ...' and assured him that 'when it comes to the reconstruction of our country' it was his will that 'all the people' should participate; adding that 'in the process we must first of all reconstruct ourselves morally and spiritually'. These lofty paternalistic sentiments did little to dampen feelings.

***

The reaction of the Catholic Church to developments in the aftermath of the riots varied. Based in Cape Palmas (Maryland county), remote from the cockpit of the crisis, Brendan Darcy, Regional Superior[40] of the SMA's American members, felt that it was unlikely that the present unrest would 'have any immediate effect on our mission work'.[41] Vice-President Warner's verbal attack on the Churches for not standing behind the government was general rather than specific. And, in any event, the Catholic Church stood well with younger people who 'have no doubt as to where it stands in relation to the poor.'

One missionary who wasted little time in making his views widely known was the Irish SMA, Patrick Harrington.[42] His public profile, as head of the Catholic Secretariat and Lecturer in Anthropology at UL, gave him a platform to speak out. He also enjoyed the support of Liberia's two Catholic bishops. A regular and impressive broadcaster, Harrington gave a number of radio and televised addresses in the wake of the crisis. The tone of these gives an idea of the perceived place of Christian Churches in Liberian society. Evidently, they enjoyed a position of some eminence which enabled spokespersons such as Harrington to speak their minds in a manner which would never have been tolerated in those African countries which had recently gained independence from colonial rule.

Harrington made his first post-riot radio broadcast on 20 April. Its tone was authoritative, echoing current Vatican pronouncements in the invocation of papal social teaching. Speaking 'as a priest and pastor of the Church of Christ' Harrington perceived the roots of the 14 April riots in Liberia's social and economic 'imbalances'.[43] Inequality and lack of human rights, he continued, had led Church leaders such as Popes John XXIII, Paul VI and John Paul II to call for 'a passage from misery towards the possession of life's necessities, victory over social scourges, increased esteem for the dignity of others, and the will and desire for peace'.[44] Harrington concluded his broadcast with the reflection that true peace in society 'requires a just order ... wherein the dignity of every human being is respected and personal freedoms are guaranteed.'. This broadcast was not welcomed by the government, for when Harrington later submitted the text for publication in the printed media, the censor slapped a prohibition on it.

Yet despite a growing impatience the regime could not hope to silence or ignore the Churches. Shortly after this broadcast, Tolbert invited Church leaders to the Executive Mansion to seek their advice. Frank Hynes SMA who was present recorded how Tolbert 'begged' them to 'preach peace, harmony and concord'.[45] He also asked them to suggest how normality might best be restored. The response to Tolbert's request was given on 18 May in a paper titled: 'Views and Suggestions of Concerned Ministers of the Gospel'.[46] On what might be done to restore calm it urged that young people held in jail be released 'into the care of responsible citizens', that rents be controlled, prices for building materials and medicines be fixed, and those for water and light be reduced. The government responded by nominating a committee to study 'Conflicts of Interests'[47] and by proclaiming a national 'healing strategy', the first step of which was revealed on 26 June when a general amnesty for all interned PAL leaders was declared.[48]

How genuine was this so-called 'healing strategy'? There can be no doubt that after the initial repression the regime adopted a more conciliatory approach. But this was as far as it went. There was no intention of addressing grievances. All that had changed was the method of suppressing dissent. Tolbert hoped the amnesty would deflate opposition while his flattering appeal to the Churches for advice might prompt them to use their influence on his behalf.

There was, however, no intention by the True Whig Party to relinquish the stranglehold on power which it had maintained since 1878. At the same time, such was the strength of the opposition – both in the transparent justice of its cause and the calibre of its leaders – that fundamental change could not long be delayed. The fact that the momentum for change was resisted to the death, to the extent that opposition leaders were portrayed as criminal and treasonous, was a tragedy for Liberia. It opened the way for opportunists motivated purely by self-interest to harness that momentum and eventually plunge the country into a catastrophic civil war.

***

By August 1979 UL had re-opened and Harrington was able to report that its Politics and Sociology Department had ambitiously 'given assignments connected with April 14', while a move was afoot to establish a branch of Amnesty International on campus.[49] Clearly the teachers and their students had not been cowed. Nor were Liberia's activists and would-be politicians. In the same month MOJA persuaded Amos Sawyer to stand for the Monrovia mayoral election, a direct challenge to the True Whig oligarchy since all previous such elections had been uncontested. Various efforts were made to disqualify Sawyer from the contest and when these looked likely to fail, Tolbert postponed the poll. At much the same time the MOJA leadership began to discuss the possibility of organising the movement as a political party.

***

On 20 December, signifying at last a realisation that the political crisis would have to be formally addressed, Bishop Michael Francis issued the first of a series of addresses and pastoral letters. These bore a strong resemblance to the broadcasts and allocutions given by Harrington who likely assisted in the preparation of Francis' offerings. The bishop set out consciously to present the Liberian crisis in the light of Catholic teaching on the relationship of the state to its citizens. The talks and letters laid out this teaching with scholastic thoroughness, demonstrating how it derived logically from both natural and divine law. The formal, pedagogic flavour of these addresses (which must have gone over many heads in their listenership) is demonstrated in the following extracts taken from a radio talk entitled 'Charity the Bond in Society'[50]:

> Prop. 22. The State is the servant of man in the attainment of the material common good, which in turn is only a means to man's final end. The State is not its own end. Man is not made for the State but the State for man.
>
> Prop. 23, The State has the duty to protect the family and all organic and free societal structures as well as the regional corporate bodies which are subordinate to the State itself.

It should not be concluded from the foregoing that the Catholic Church was now preoccupied with the Liberian crisis. The minutes of a meeting of Bishops Francis and Dalieh on 1 January 1980, to which a number of leading clergy were invited, gives a good indication of the Church's concerns, showing that the current political situation and its implications for the conduct of Church affairs was not one of them. Evidently it appeared that a tolerable measure of stability had at last been restored after the upheavals of the previous year and that political changes, if they were to take place, would be accomplished within the existing political order − most likely in the context of legislative and presidential elections due in 1981.

Few within the Church realised that Liberia was poised on the precipice of a major upheaval. A report on a visit to Liberia between 4 January and 1 February 1980 by Cornelius Murphy (Provincial Superior of the SMA's Irish Province) suggests that this was the case. Murphy had met each of the Irish missionaries in his place of work and held meetings with both bishops and his American counterpart, Ted Hayden (also visiting). Murphy's comprehensive report makes no reference to the current political situation.

Nonetheless, missionaries on the ground were not unaware of a growing uneasiness about the future. Fuelling this unease was the increasing incidence of disturbances at political meetings and demonstrations. Sister Margaret Chambers of the Medical Missionaries of Mary, an Irish medical doctor and 'Leprosy Controller' at Liberia's Ministry of Health, adverted to these feelings. Writing to her Irish Superiors from Ivory Coast, to where she had travelled for a conference, she mentioned that apparently there had been 'more trouble in Monrovia on the day I left' and that 'even the government radio service announced it'. Her hope was that the government would 'try to fix things up and prevent further plunder'.

***

As the early months of 1980 passed, the fragile nature of the current political situation became more evident. Plainly there would be no return to the past. One significant development underlining this was the successful registration of PAL as a political party under the title People's Progressive Party (PPP). The PAL movement had sought this shortly after the release of its leaders in June 1979 in order to contest forthcoming legislative and presidential elections.[*] When a court disallowed its registration PAL threatened to take to the streets. Fearing a repetition of the Rice Riots Tolbert reluctantly conceded and on 8 January permitted the registration.[51] This was quickly followed by MOJA's successful application to register, again in order to contest the forthcoming elections. Plainly, Liberia would no longer be a one-party state ruled by an oligarchy. But how the future would play out was uncertain as the relationship between these parties and the True Whig party became progressively confrontational.

***

On 10 March 1980 a series of events occurred which was to draw the Catholic Church briefly into the forefront of political confrontation. On that day Liberia's Washington Embassy issued a press release reporting that its government had issued 'a writ for the arrest of Gabriel Baccus Matthews and other leaders of the PPP on charges of treason'.[52] This, the world was told, had followed 'a campaign of public intimidation and violence practiced by its parent organization, the so-called Progressive Alliance of Liberia'. Specifically, the press release claimed that the government had acted following a 'series of incidents … from the night of Monday, 3 March to 8 March, designed to destabilise the state'.

Coinciding with the Embassy statement Tolbert addressed the Liberian joint-legislature on the attempted coup. His fair-minded and forbearing regime, he said, had permitted the registration of opposition parties and organisation of the so-called Progressive Alliance of Liberia'. Specifically, the press release claimed the creation of channels that those with grievances could easily use. But this had been spurned. Matthews and his cohorts had rejected dialogue and gone

---

[*]   Legislative elections were scheduled for 1980 and a presidential election for 1981.

much further, planning an armed insurrection. Illegal roadblocks had been mounted and attempts had been made:

> to burn down the Telecommunications building, destroy the Gabriel J. Tucker Bridge, and sever vital communication links between the capital and other parts of Liberia, and also to isolate the nation from the rest of the world.[53]

The final step in this diabolical plot was to be the seizure of the Executive Mansion and the installation of Matthews in power.

News of these developments reached Tenafly in a letter from Darcy. Citing sources in Monrovia, he wrote that a public meeting at which Matthews had called for a general strike and the resignation of the president, had taken place at midnight on Capitol Hill. During the same night police reported the death of a PPP supporter when his home-made bomb had exploded. After this Minister for Justice Joseph Chesson announced that police raids had uncovered 'more bombs and bomb-making equipment'. Darcy had little doubt that the claims of a PPP bomb plot were manufactured.[54] Nonetheless the situation was grave. Even on the far distant Kru Coast, where he resided, 'extra troops and riot police' had been deployed and there were 'roadblocks everywhere'.

In Monrovia events took a dramatic turn on 8 March, the morning after the supposed coup. Disguised as a street trader, beard shaven, wearing dilapidated blue pants, ragged white T-shirt and torn canvas shoes, Matthews arrived at the gate of the Vatican Embassy, where he requested, and was granted, political asylum. The Embassy sought from the government guarantees of safe conduct and a fair trial.* After these were obtained, at eight o'clock on the morning of Monday, 9 March, accompanied by the recently arrived Papal Pro-Nuncio, Archbishop Johannes Dyba and Bishop Dalieh, Matthews was taken into custody at the Executive Mansion and handed over to the police.

Detailed coverage of the PPP arrests, Matthews' surrender, and disturbances in Monrovia and Kru Coast towns, was given on the BBC World Service by its West Africa correspondent, Elizabeth Blunt. It was clear that while the government had quickly got control of the situation, simmering unrest lay just beneath the surface. There was also a certain excitement among young, educated Liberians, especially the university students, that things were about to change radically for the better, that an unstoppable tide of reform, even a revolution, was approaching.

***

It was clear from the government's hysterical reaction to the PPP's midnight demonstration that the True Whig Party was fast losing its grip on

---

*   At the time of his flight to the Vatican embassy, Matthews had been excluded from the Baptist Church because of his political activities. He was particularly friendly with Fr Robert Tikpor, a senior Liberian priest.

power. Unable to adapt to the mood for democracy both within the region and the country, it struck out wildly at perceived enemies.[55] Its claim that Gabriel Baccus Matthews and other leaders of the movement for multi-party democracy had set out to kill President Tolbert and impose their will by force, not only rang hollow but was manifestly preposterous, and could only have been dreamt up by a government in the grip of a growing hysteria. Had the regime been capable of meeting the clamour for democracy half-way there might have been a slight prospect for peace and stability. As it happened, more venal and desperate citizens saw, and were about to seize, their chance to destroy the already tottering regime.

Notes

1 J. Gus Liebenow, Liberia Studies Journal, vol. X(1), 1982–1983, 3.
2 The True Whig Party dominated Liberia's one-party state from 1878 until 1980.
3 1.8 million in 1980.
4 Elwood D. Dunn, Amos J. Beyan, Carl Patrick Burrowes, Historical Dictionary of Liberia (U.S., 2001), 343.
5 While Matthews was influenced by ideology, he also exhibited a capacity for 'mercurial behaviour'(J. Gus Liebenow, Liberian Studies Journal, XIII, 2, 253), making frequent and often radical changes in direction. Whether this was opportunism, or a matter of temperament is open to question.
6 See Edmund M. Hogan, Catholic Missionaries and Liberia – a Study of Missionary Enterprise in West Africa, 1830–1950 (Cork University Press, 1977), 12–41.
7 These included Brothers of the Holy Cross, Christian Brothers, Marist Brothers, St John of God Brothers, Missionaries of St Paul, Franciscan Missionaries of Mary, Bernadine Sisters, Consolata Sisters, Sisters of Charity, Sisters of the Sacred Heart, Sisters of the Immaculate Conception, Holy Family Sisters, Adorers of the Blood of Christ and Medical Missionaries of Mary.
8 The government never released figures of the casualties, but estimates ranged from 50 to 300 killed and hundreds injured. See, Similih M. Cordor, Crises and Challenges; c.f. Liberia Truth and Reconciliation Commission, henceforth cited as LTRC, Consolidated Final Report, Chapter Five, 83.
9 Later to become SMA Superior General (2001–10). Subsequently was Bishop of Killaloe (Ireland) (2010–2014) and Archbishop of Cashel (Ireland) (2014–).
10 A.B. (Archives of the Society of African Missions, Irish Province, Blackrock Road, Cork), Eyewitness Account: Fr Kieran O'Reilly, 14 April 1979.
11 The Tablet, 30 June 1990, 7.
12 A.T (Archives of the Society of African Missions, American Province, Tenafly, NJ), see typed document (henceforth cited 'Sawyer's Report') dated 5 May 1979, appended to Hynes to Hayden, 8 May 1979.
13 See ibid.
14 A.B. New African, 16 April 1979.
15 A.T. LTRC, Consolidated Final Report, vol. 2, 134, makes no reference to arrests.
16 A.B. New African, 16 April 1979.
17 Sawyer's Report, 5 May 1979.
18 A.B. New African, 16 April 1979.
19 A.B. 14/923.530, 'Statement by the President of Liberia, William R. Tolbert Jr in the wake of civil disturbances in Monrovia'.
20 A.B. New African, 17 April 1979.
21 Sawyer's Report, 5 May 1979.

22 A non-political self-help movement in rural areas for people with farming or technical skills. It was financed by Church organisations (local and international).
23 Ibid.
24 Ibid.
25 Ibid.
26 Ibid.
27 Mark R. Lipschutz, Dictionary of African Historical Biography (Univ. of California Press, 1989), 288.
28 A.B. New African, 20 April 1979.
29 African Index, 1–15 July 1979. vol. 11, no. 13. See also Mark Tessler, UFSI Report, 1983/no, 17 Africa (MT-2-'83).
30 See Similih M. Cordor, op.cit., An Analysis of the Tolbert Administration 1971–1980, www.liberiaseabreeze.com/?p=2570, accessed, 20 June 2014.
31 New African, 20 April 1979.
32 See LTRC, Final Report, 'Human Rights Abuses during the Rice Riots and Doe Era', Chapter Five, 103, note 2.
33 Adekeye Adebajo, Liberia's civil war: Nigeria, Ecomog, and regional security in West Africa (U.S. and U.K., 2002), 23.
34 A.T. Sawyer's Report, 5 July 1979.
35 A.T. Ibid. C.f. Brendan Darcy to Ted Hayden, 7 May 1979.
36 A.T. Hynes to Hayden, 8 May 1979.
37 See A.B., 'Matthews Recants', pamphlet containing a photocopied version of the Matthews letter (dated 25 April 1979), a typed copy of same, and photocopy of President Tolbert's reply. c.f., New African, 26 April 1979 (in A.B. 14/923.530), newspaper cutting containing 'letter of repentance'; see also West Africa, 18 February 1980.
38 AT. G. Baccus Matthews, 'Letter of Appeal to President Tolbert'.
39 Jesse Z.G. Fahngon, in an obituary of Matthews, accepts that he wrote the letter (see The Perspective, 11 September 2007), www.liberiaitech.com/theperspective/2007/0911200701.htm, accessed 2 February 2016. See also Philip N. Wesseh, 'Liberia: The Fear of the Pending April 12 Demonstration – Taking a Note from Baccus Matthews' letter to the President', The Inquirer, 1 April 2013.
40 Responsible to the Provincial Council in Tenafly, New Jersey, for the welfare of all members of the American Province working in Liberia.
41 A.T. Brendan Darcy to Hayden, 7 May 1979.
42 Harrington was to become SMA Superior General (1983–95) and Bishop of Lodwar, Kenya (2000–10).
43 A.B. 14/923.530, Patrick J. Harrington, 20 April 1979.
44 This was a quotation from Paul VI's encyclical letter, Populorum Progressio, promulgated on 26 March 1967.
45 A.T. Hynes to Hayden, 8 May 1979.
46 A.B. Typed copy of the submission, dated 18 May 1979.
47 A.T. Harrington to Hayden, 13 August 1979.
48 Adekeye Adebajo, op. cit., 23.
49 A.T. Harrington to Hayden, 13 August 1979.
50 A.T. Radio talk given by Bishop Michael Francis at the National Intercessory Prayer Service, 29 December 1979.
51 See Adekeye Adebajo, op. cit., 23.
52 A.T. copy of press release of 'Statement by the Ministry of Foreign Affairs'.
53 President Tolbert's Address to the Joint Legislature', Press Release, 3 10 March 1990.
54 The Liberian Truth and Reconciliation Commission refers to a major government crackdown against Matthews and the PPP, but makes no reference to an attempt to overthrow the government. LTRC Consolidated Final Report, vol. 2, 216.
55 LTRC, Consolidated Final Report, vol. 2, 30 June 2009, 216.

Section 2
The Falling of the Axe

3 Dawn of the revolution – the 1980 coup

The overthrow of the Tolbert Regime – Liberia's first coup d'état during its 133-year history – took place bloodily at 1 am on Saturday, 12 April 1980. At 6.30 am the BBC World Service reported that during the night gunfire had been heard in the vicinity of the Executive Mansion. Shortly after 8.30 am the now rebel-controlled ELBC radio station announced to the world that the Tolbert regime, then in its tenth year, had been overthrown and that a 'Peoples Redemption Council' had taken power. During the next 24 hours news reports from local and international stations began to fill out the details. At 11 am the BBC reported that President Tolbert and his Executive Mansion guard (29 people in all) had been killed. Thereafter reports from a variety of stations confirmed the arrest of former government officials, including several ministers. By nightfall it was known that all PPP prisoners had been released, and almost a hundred officials and office-holders of the previous administration were to be tried for treason.

The coup had been carried out by a group of non-commissioned officers led by Thomas Quiwonkpa, Thomas Weh-Syen, Harrison Dahn, Harrison Pennue, J. Nicolas Podier, Nelson Toe and Master Sergeant Samuel Doe. Quiwonkpa later claimed to have devised the plan for storming the Executive Mansion, personally leading the dissident soldiers to the eighth floor where Tolbert was sleeping in his office. He also claimed that the first of several shots which killed the president was fired by Toe, who subsequently disembowelled his victim. In the following hours the 'People's Redemption Council' (PRC) was proclaimed, with 28-year-old Doe as chairman and head of state. The selection of Doe had already been arranged by the plotters and was based on his seniority.[1] Weh-Syen was named PRC vice-chairman and deputy head of state, Quiwonkpa became commanding general of the Armed Forces of Liberia while Sergeant Podier was appointed speaker of an interim national assembly, yet to be created.

Within hours of his death, along with others killed during the coup, Tolbert was buried in an anonymous downtown mass grave. Retribution against other members of the Tolbert regime was taken on Thursday 22 April. On that day 13 were shot dead, including Tolbert's brother, Frank, and Foreign Minister Cecil Dennis. Also executed were the regime's Justice Minister, Joseph

DOI: 10.4324/9781003219309-5

Chesson, Speaker of the House Richard Henries, Chairman of the True Whig Party E. Reginald Townsend and Chief Justice James A. Pierre. Hundreds of civilians and soldiers were filmed cheering the executions of these men who stood convicted of 'rabid corruption, misuse of public office, gross violation of human and civil rights and high treason'.[2] They had been convicted by a six-man military tribunal established by the PRC, sitting at the army's Barclay Training Centre situated about half a mile from the Executive Mansion. In all, 83 former ministers and officials were arraigned to appear before the tribunal which prohibited legal representation for the defence.

A graphic, if disturbing, account of the 13 executions was given by eyewitness Jack White of Time-Life News Service. They took place

> after Doe's first meeting with the foreign press at which he appeared in a ranger hat, camouflage suit and wearing a ceremonial sword, PRC information minister, Gabriel Nimley... stepped to the podium and announced in a matter-of-fact voice: 'Ladies and gentlemen, there will be executions at 2.30 pm'. Crowds of civilians and soldiers then gathered as workmen from the Liberian telephone company erected 5 telegraph poles to which the condemned would be lashed.[3]

While the work proceeded the 13 condemned men remained seated in a bus 300 yards from the killing grounds.

> As soon as the poles were up, the bus was driven to the shore of the Atlantic Ocean ... As the crowd jeered, nine of the condemned men were dragged out and shoved against the newly erected posts... For more than 20 minutes, several hundred soldiers milled around in front of the condemned men. Finally, a firing squad marched up and shot volley after volley into the condemned men. Former Foreign Minister Dennis stared stoically straight ahead as the soldiers missed him several times. Finally, a soldier stepped out of the crowd and killed him with a barrage of automatic fire. The remaining four were dragged from the bus and lashed to the posts. They died in a five-minute burst of automatic weapon fire in which the on-looking soldiers joined.[4]

***

On the night of the coup most of the priests and religious of the Monrovia Vicariate were gathered in the parish of St Anthony's, Gardnersville, some eight miles north of the city, to celebrate the silver jubilees[*] of Fr Kevin Scanlan, a former head of the American SMA, and that of Sister Evelyn Nagle (ASC) who had worked in Monrovia's Gardnersville suburb since 1973.[5] It was an impressive occasion with over 25 priests concelebrating a thanksgiving Mass.

---

[*]   25 years of priesthood or, in the case of religious sisterhoods, the 25th anniversary of final profession.

The only shadow over the celebration was the illness of Bishop Michael Francis. Although present he was unable to concelebrate and, untypical for him, his address to the gathering was 'very brief'.[6]

One of the young Liberian priests present was Edward Jackson. His wonderment (expressed in a letter written a few days later) that 'on 12 April we had our first ever coup'[7] was typical of the mood of young Liberians whose sense of alarm was tempered by excitement and hopes for a better future. The practical result of the coup for the festive gathering was that those who had come from up-country missions were unable to return because it was considered unsafe to travel. Jackson reported a lesser effect, namely the requisition of three mission vehicles by soldiers, one in Monrovia and two in Gbarnga. But these were soon retrieved and before the week was out, all had returned to their mission stations where life appeared to be back to normal.

***

In at least one respect the Liberian coup bore a resemblance to that of the previous June in Ghana when a group of junior officers, led by Flight-Lieutenant Jerry J. Rawlings, overthrew the existing military regime. In the wake of the Ghanaian coup, which ushered in a so-called 'Revolutionary Ruling Council', eight high-ranking officers, including three former heads of state, were executed.[8] Whether Doe and his associates were inspired by this coup is unknown.

It was a fact, however, that the ruthlessness shown by Master Sergeant Doe and his co-conspirators caused deep shock to many Liberians and expatriate observers. True there had been some violent incidents in recent times, principally the Rice Riots and their aftermath, but most Liberians regarded these as alien to Liberia's peaceful traditions. The events which were to occur in the weeks following the coup were to cause even greater dismay for while on the night it took place, in the heat of battle as it were, a certain loss of restraint might have been expected, the bloodthirsty actions of the following days could not easily be justified. Not only were members of the former regime publicly humiliated but they were subjected to show trials. Most reprehensible of all, their execution in the presence of cheering crowds was filmed and shown triumphantly to the world by the new regime's Ministry of Information.

The public jubilation in Monrovia and in many Liberian towns and villages when news of the coup was first announced was perhaps understandable, given the Tolbert regime's unpopularity. However, the spectacle of crowds enjoying the savagery inflicted on former members of the regime was deeply disturbing. Some of the Press coverage was equally disquieting. For example, the *New Liberian*, now speaking for the new regime, ran a picture of former Corporal Pennue, now a colonel, mimicking the hapless Tolbert when forces burst into his apartment, holding up his hands in surrender and begging for his life.

***

On the populous Kru Coast, far from Monrovia, there was bewilderment at the course of events but no great anxiety; rather excitement and expectation of better things to come. Brendan Darcy in Cape Palmas heard the BBC's 6.30 am report of gunfire and radioed[9] Frank Hynes in Monrovia to be told that even as they spoke shots were being fired. Later he heard the ELBC radio broadcast announcing the overthrow of the Tolbert government. At much the same time Bishop Dalieh arrived in person to say that the government was no more, and that Tolbert had been shot.[10]

Approaching 9 am Darcy visited the town to find normality prevailing with stores open and a brisk market underway. The people, he ascertained, had heard little or nothing about events in Monrovia. This was to change after 11 am when the BBC news bulletin announced that Tolbert was dead. Then the news spread like wildfire and people took to the streets, 'singing, chanting and waving palm branches.' Jubilant soldiers fired shots in the air while speedily and discreetly the stores closed. Nobody, Darcy observed, seemed to know much about the new head of state, one Samuel K. Doe, a Krahn from Grand Gedeh County. By 4 pm it was reported on radio that all County and Territorial Superintendents had been replaced by men from the new regime, all soldiers. And it was said that, while some incumbents had run away or had resisted, all were now safely under lock and key.

In Cape Palmas the handover of power had been seamless. Superintendent Cox, the senior official, was in the 'bush' and had left his good friend Captain Charles Cooper in charge. When the coup took place Cooper sent soldiers to fetch Cox. They escorted him back to Cape Palmas where he handed over his keys 'in gentlemanly fashion, without fuss, violence or confusion'.[11] But not all such handovers were conducted with such cordiality. Darcy learned that Superintendent J. Dominique Bing of Sinoe County had resisted when asked to hand over and had been shot dead.

The coup had taken place in the early hours of Saturday. On Sunday morning the mood in Cape Palmas remained relaxed. People were encouraged to hear that a number of leading civilians had been included in the new cabinet. No less a person than Gabriel Baccus Matthews had been appointed Minister for Foreign Affairs, Dr Togba-Nah Tipoteh was given responsibility for Economics and Planning, while Chea Cheapoo (PAL's legal counsel) was now the new Minister for Justice. They also welcomed an element of continuity with the former regime in the appointments to cabinet posts of Gabriel Tucker (Public Works) and Kate Bryant (Health), both ministers under Tolbert.

On Tuesday, the mystery surrounding the identity of the new head of state was somewhat dispelled when Doe addressed the nation on national radio. According to Darcy, the students of Cape Palmas were 'a little disappointed' when they heard his voice. He did not sound like a heroic leader. However, he was evidently a 'man of action' and among early actions taken by Doe, applauded by the students, was the abolition of the traditional 26 July public holiday (commemorating the declaration of a republic), and its replacement by a public holiday to be held henceforth on 12 April and known as 'Redemption Day'.

Indeed 'Redemption' was to become a favourite word in the new order of things, the regime's ruling body enjoying that name. There was certainly about to be redemption for the Liberian army, for one of Doe's earliest acts was to increase soldiers' salaries from $85 per month to $250.* And for the general populace there was the announcement of free education for all by the coming July. But the greatest cause of hope and optimism for the masses was the declaration that the price of rice and transportation – crucial demands by Tolbert's opponents – was to be reduced.

Many welcomed, too, the new leader's declaration of a week of prayer for the nation. Here, evidently, was a man with respect for religion, a man who humbly invoked the help of Almighty God in the great task facing him. And his decision, a few days later, to summon the leaders of the various Churches to the Executive Mansion in order to request their 'help' and 'advice', appeared to further underline his respect for the moral influence of religion and the wisdom of its ministers. In the hopeful atmosphere which prevailed few regarded such actions in a cynical light. Few interpreted them as revealing, more likely, fear and distrust of the power of the Churches and a desire to 'get them onside' – much as Tolbert had attempted in the wake of the Rice Riots.

***

As the first week came to a close Cape Palmas witnessed some acts of petty revenge against the Tolbert regime. The former Country Attorney, David A.T. Browne was arrested and accused of 'high treason, rampant corruption and misuse of public office'. Many people thought he would face the firing squad. However, as opposition to the coup evaporated, vindictive actions against former members of the Tolbert regime became less frequent. The new government was now strongly entrenched, enjoying a wide measure of public support. Stability if not normality appeared to have returned to Liberia.

The coup, it must be said, did give rise to sharp anxiety among one group. In Ganta, where United Methodist missionaries ran a large hospital specializing in the treatment of leprosy, there was fear of repercussions after Vice President Bennie Warner, their 'Presiding Bishop', was deposed from his political office. Warner (accompanied by his wife and family) had the good fortune to be attending a Conference in the U.S. at the time of the coup.[12] It was widely felt that had he been in Monrovia he would have suffered the same fate as other leading members of Tolbert's cabinet.[13] The fact that Dr Togba Nah Tipoteh, a prominent United Methodist, had been appointed a government minister went some way towards calming fears. Nonetheless most expatriate Methodist missionaries in Ganta fled Liberia and only returned several months later when a new 'Presiding Bishop', Arthur F. Kulah, was told by the PRC that it had no quarrel with Methodists.[14]

***

The reaction of Liberia's regional neighbours to the coup initially tended to be hostile. Foreign Minister Matthews was refused entry to Nigeria to attend an economic summit of the OAU. And Liberia received no invitation to an

---

*   It must be admitted that prior to this, salaries of rank-and-file soldiers were markedly low, reflecting 'their low status in Liberian society for most of the century' (J. Gus Liebenow, Liberia Studies Journal, op. cit., 11).

ECOWAS* Defence Ministers meeting. The exclusion of Liberia from an ECOWAS Heads of State summit in Lomé caused Doe to recall his ambassadors from Abidjan, Freetown and Lagos and declare a suspension of Liberia's obligations to the organisation. Part of the reason for anti-Doe sentiment was the bloody nature of the coup. The hostility was also nurtured by the fact that Tolbert had been a popular African leader who had impressed by his hosting of the June 1979 OAU summit.

Siaka Stevens of Sierra Leone, Doe's most outspoken opponent, had been a close friend of Tolbert's with whom he had created the Mano River Union. Tolbert had also been close to Houphouët-Boigny of the Ivory Coast and, as mentioned, had helped to heal a rift between the Ivorian president and Ahmed Sekou Touré of Guinea. Moreover, Tolbert's son, Adolphus, murdered in the aftermath of the coup, had been married to Houphouët-Boigny's adopted daughter. Thereafter Liberian dissidents could find a welcome in the Ivory Coast. Adekeye Adebajo in his book on the Liberian civil war notes the hypocrisy of several of these African leaders who themselves had come to power through bloody coups, who lacked democratic credentials and whose violations of human rights were notorious.[15] However, whatever might be said about their attachment to democratic methods and their human rights record, it must be said that at least Stevens, Sekou Touré and Houphouët-Boigny had attained power peacefully.

Eventually Doe was to find a supporter and ally in Guinea's Sekou Touré who brought together leaders from Ivory Coast, Togo and Sierra Leone to discuss reconciliation and eventually secured agreement to Liberian representation at the July 1980 OAU summit. It must be said that there were strong economic reasons for Sekou Touré's change of heart. The Guinean port of Conakry could not export Guinean iron ore and other commodities without access to Monrovia's Freeport and the ocean-going port of Buchanan.[16] Nor was the reconciliation whole-hearted, causing Doe to look elsewhere outside the region and the continent to ensure his regime's survival.[17]

***

Reaction to the coup in the wider world was generally muted. The Soviet Union and other Eastern-bloc countries, as well as Cuba and Libya, welcomed the development. In many Western countries, however, the overthrow of the Tolbert regime was regarded as yet another in a long list of *coups d'état* afflicting emerging African nations since the 1960s, bloody in nature and with less to do with the improvement of living conditions than with tribal conflicts and hunger for power. Nonetheless, because of America's historic ties with Liberia, symbolized in the current era by the presence there of strategic U.S. radio and telecommunication installations, U.S. newspapers, at least, tended to pay more attention, reporting the coup and expressing revulsion at its savagery. The brutal overthrow of a legitimate regime had occurred not in some scarcely civilized

---

*   Economic Community of West African States, founded by 16 West African countries in 1975.

remote African country but in the homeland of America's closest African ally. In the weeks immediately following the coup this sense of revulsion, conveyed to the new regime by the American embassy, played a part in stemming the bloody tide of political executions on which the Doe government had so enthusiastically embarked.

As the first weeks passed some attempts were made, mainly in the American press, to analyze the significance of the coup. Tolbert, *The New York Times* declared, 'had made efforts to root out corruption, but ... power continued to reside largely with the 45,000 descendants of American slaves ... a mere 5% of the total population'.[18] He had also tried to broaden the one-party system by allowing opponents to organize Liberia's first opposition party. But his reforming zeal had weakened, and his tolerance had paled after the Rice Riots. This, according to the *Times*, had set the scene for the coup. So also had out-rage within Liberia at Tolbert's lavish expenditure on the 1979 OAU summit.

Smith Hempstone, a distinguished syndicated columnist and later U.S. ambassador to Kenya, took a different view in the *Chicago Daily News*,[19] holding the U.S. responsible for much of what had happened.

> The U.S. has given Liberia its flag, currency, cuisine and constitution. Its capital is named after an American president. America has educated many of its leaders and developed its economy. For its part Liberia has sided with the U.S. in two global conflicts and provides the U.S. with two strategic commodities, iron and natural rubber... Liberia's Con-stitution, written by a Harvard law school professor, states that the country was founded 'to provide a home for the dispersed and oppressed Children of Africa...' Liberia has fallen far short of its goal and *its failures have been ours*[20].

What attracted widespread attention in the U.S. media was the information that on the night of the coup Foreign Minister Cecil Dennis, one of the 13 later executed, had sought asylum in the U.S. Embassy but had been refused.

***

In the days immediately following the coup the Catholic Church had privately pleaded with the regime for mercy towards those arrested and, this having failed, sought Christian burial for those executed. But again, this fell on deaf ears. Its first public reaction came in an ELBC TV broadcast delivered by Patrick Harrington on 21 April.[21] A carefully crafted talk, it gave a cautious welcome to the sentiments expressed by the new head of state, describing as 'responsible' a promise made in the first week to restore civil and human rights, and to provide food, health care, shelter and edu-cation for the poor. However, he warned that words must be followed by deeds, otherwise the new regime would never gain the trust of the people.

***

The attitude of the new regime to broadcasts such as Harrington's and other attempts at intervention by the Churches, was illustrated in its reaction to the paper submitted in response to Doe's request for help and advice. The document was presented some three weeks after the coup by the Reverend J. Edwin Lloyd, a Liberian Baptist who previously was the Tolbert-appointed chief chaplain to the armed forces.[22] Addressing the current security situation, it asserted that because members of the armed forces were still 'molesting citizens', all soldiers should be recalled to barracks. By the same token those who 'violated people's rights and property should face the appropriate military discipline'. Even less likely to enthuse the new regime was the document's criticism of the absence of a 'long-range plan' for economic recovery and a political future.

> Citizens, residents and foreign investors need to know… No one wishes to exist in a vacuum; neither can one make any plans for oneself or one's family in the darkness.

Furthermore, reminding the head of state of a promise made in the first days after the coup, to reform the Constitution and return Liberia to civilian rule, it asked when the Commission on Constitutional Reform would be established, whether a multi-party system was to be expected and if plans for a general election existed?

The regime greeted this 'advice' with a frosty silence. But shortly afterwards the Reverend Lloyd – whose choice to represent the Churches was unfortunate given his links to the Tolbert regime - was arrested and interned; and by July strong but unconfirmed rumours were sweeping Monrovia that he had died in custody. As it turned out, he was to spend two years in custody.

***

How did the U.S. view the overthrow of a legitimate government which had facilitated its foreign policy to the extent that no African country was ever likely to do in the future? For now, governing this state in one of the most volatile regions of the world, where vital U.S. interests were at stake, was a rogue regime, formed of a rump of non-commissioned officers led by an almost illiterate 28-year-old Sergeant. Was America to give recognition to this new state of affairs? Doe was not unaware of this critical question. In his very first radio broadcast, two days after the coup, he took care to be introduced as the incumbent Chairman of the OAU, the position held by Tolbert at the time of his death. In the event, the U.S. administration took the view that, as long as America's vital interests were not undermined, recognition might be accorded. Indeed, such was the inexperience of Liberia's new rulers and their complete lack of statecraft skills, the U.S. might in effect govern Liberia to its own advantage by supplying what was needed. If the survival of the Doe regime depended upon U.S. military, economic and technical assistance, then, according to the adage 'he who pays the piper calls the tune'.

In making the decision to support Doe's regime, the U.S. administration was fully cognizant of its nature. A report by the State Department's Bureau of Public Affairs[23] left no doubt of the new Liberia's fundamentally undemocratic character and its distain for those very values which underpinned the U.S. Constitution. It recorded that, in the new dispensation, the 1847 Constitution was suspended,[24] martial law imposed, and all legislative and executive power vested in an unelected 28-member Council which, under its chairman, ruled by decree. Regarding the judiciary, the traditional system was now superseded by a People's Supreme Tribunal composed of seven judges appointed by Doe. In addition, there was a Supreme Military Tribunal for political crimes against the state.

Notwithstanding the character of the new regime, official U.S. policy essentially remained as it always had been, namely, to maintain and strengthen the close ties between the two countries. In the second half of the 20th century these ties had been evident in a strong Peace Corps* presence and by military assistance programs. There was also a mutual defence pact signed in 1959 which was followed in the next decade by the construction of a telecommunications relay station that transmitted diplomatic and intelligence traffic between Washington and some forty embassies on the African continent. A Voice of America transmitter, broadcasting to all of Africa, the Middle East and parts of southwest Asia, came next. Finally, the U.S. constructed an OMEGA navigational station near Monrovia. Four hundred and 27 metres high this, the tallest structure in Africa, enabled ships and aircraft to calculate continuously their positions in the Eastern Atlantic and along Africa's west coast. The U.S. also had important commercial and financial interests in Liberia. The Firestone rubber plantation, which had opened at Harbel in 1926, was the largest of its kind worldwide. Bethlehem Steel had a 25% interest in Liberia's major iron ore mine, LAMCO. Revenues from these companies amounted to 52% of Liberia's total tax take. Chase Manhattan Bank, Chemical Bank and Citibank all had local branches or affiliates in Liberia. In addition, Liberia was a principal stopping point for Pan American Airways while a Pan Am subsidiary had a management contract for the International Airport.

It was understandable that after the debacle with revolutionary Iran in 1979,** Washington might have been anxious to avoid being caught in Liberia on the wrong side of a popular revolution. Therefore, in the immediate aftermath of the coup and in the months that followed, U.S. officials had adopted a cautious, wait-and-see approach. Showing disapproval at the methods employed by the coup perpetrators (rather than at the deed itself), Doe was urged to avoid a bloodbath. When this was ignored the State Department expressed displeasure and reduced the flow of financial aid. It also offered no protest when the IMF and World Bank imposed stricter borrowing conditions on the new regime. In contrast to the U.S., the Soviet Union, Cuba, Libya and Eastern bloc countries reacted warmly to the new regime, leading Doe to dispatch officials to these countries in the early days of PRC rule. But, ultimately, for the Americans

---

*   Dating from the Kennedy presidency in 1961, this was a government-sponsored volunteer movement addressing social and economic issues in poorer countries.

**   Some 60 Americans were taken hostage in 1979 and held for 444 days. A rescue attempt was unsuccessful and claimed the lives of eight American servicemen.

strategic considerations took precedence over moral. Against the background of the Cold War and the danger – however remote – that Liberia might fall into the Soviet camp, Washington sent Assistant Secretary of State for African Affairs, Richard M. Moose[25], to Monrovia in June 1980 to meet Liberia's new head of state. After the visit, Moose recommended, not simply a return to former levels of support but an increase in U.S. economic and military aid.[26]

***

Whatever about the external - and often negative - evaluations of the Doe Regime made at the end of its first year there was little self-doubt among those now in government. On 12 April 1981, Liberia's first 'National Redemption Day', Foreign Minister Henry Boimah Fahnbulleh Jr., erstwhile Professor of political science at UL gave a speech marking the coup's first anniversary.[27] The revolution, he told his listeners, had rescued Liberia from 'oppression, political and social violence, narrow-mindedness… and impending doom', and had given the country a stability it had never before enjoyed.[*] As for the rank and file soldiers who now ruled Liberia, they were 'instruments of the will of the poor and dispossessed'.

Fahnbulleh also took the opportunity to display his skill as a political scientist when outlining an approach to future foreign policy. Henceforth relations with the international community would be based on self-interest, not ideology. And at the core of this 'self-interest' would be 'self-reliance.

> No power bloc will ever have more interest in us than we have in ourselves … For too long we have been puppets holding onto the apron strings of foreign masters who only throw us crumbs to barely keep us alive from day to day.

Nonetheless the pursuit of self-reliance did not mean an end to foreign investment. For the new government had already made it clear that it 'recognized the importance of protecting important business enterprises.' Firestone, LAMCO and the other multi-nationals need not worry. And the international community might further be re-assured by the granting of a general amnesty to political prisoners and political exiles, a decision, he declared, which would earn Liberia 'singular distinction in the eyes of the world'.

***

Fahnbulleh's address – with its flashes of academic brilliance and rhetorical flourishes – took only second place to that of head of state Doe. On the occasion of his first address to the nation, delivered two days after the coup, Doe had pledged a return to civilian rule. Now on Liberia's first Redemption Day he repeated that pledge and gave details of modalities and scheduling. The

---

[*]   Despite social, political and economic inequalities, Liberia had been a relatively stable country since the Republic was declared in 1847. The Doe regime, on the other hand, was scarcely a year old and, born in blood, was already beginning to look over its shoulders for enemies who might supplant it.

first step would be the establishment of a Constitutional Commission charged with drawing up a draft constitution which, after a period of review, would then be put before the people. The final step, following its approval, would be the election of a civilian government. This would take place in the summer or fall of 1984.[28]An additional feature of the process, suggesting to some observers more sinister intentions, was to be the PRC power of veto 'over specific aspects of the proposed constitution'. The purpose of this, Doe said, was to safeguard the revolution. And lest anyone might doubt the PRC's good intentions, its choice of commission members should dispel such misgivings. The commission chairman was to be none other than the co-founder of MOJA, Dr Amos Claudius Sawyer. Other appointees, all notable men and outspoken critics of corruption and inequity, would include the veteran activist and pamphleteer Albert Porte* and the lawyer-journalist Tuah Wreh.[29]

One sour note was struck during the anniversary celebrations. Already the Churches had been subject to official frowns on account of their failure to wholeheartedly endorse the new regime in the 'advice' paper presented to the president and in the content of some broadcasts by churchmen. A further example of this recalcitrance was brought home sharply to the regime on the first anniversary of the coup. On that very formal occasion, in the presence of Doe and other leading figures, Arthur F. Kulah, Vice President Warner's successor as 'Presiding Methodist Bishop' but of a very different disposition**, took the theme for his homily from the scriptural verse: 'Arms that liberated must not enslave us'. He followed this by announcing that 'like the children of Israel, we too are afraid'. Doe took strong exception to this, telling clergy a week later that they should 'preach about Christ and lead their flocks to the throne of grace rather than engage in politics'.[30]

***

Whatever the protestations on Redemption Day 1981 that better times had arrived, there was little evidence of any significant change on the ground. In fact, much less than striving towards the creation of a 'self-reliant' society, the energies of the Doe regime seemed to be focused firmly on seeking more external aid. On 25 and 28 September Fahnbulleh was on the floor of the UN General Assembly appealing for assistance. His pleas did not go unheard, the Assembly calling on all member states and the 'specialized agencies' of the UN to 'contribute generously to the reconstruction, rehabilitation and development of Liberia'.[31]Moreover, it requested the UN Secretary-General to oversee an

---

*   Albert Porte had been a thorn in the side of the last four Presidents, while Tuah Wreh had suffered 'constant abuse for his exercise of free speech ...' (Liebenow, J. Gus, 'Liberia, the Dissolution of Privilege'[Issues 39–41 of UFSI Reports, American Universities Field Staff]).

**   During Easter 1979, after the Rice Riots, he preached a sermon that focused on 'those in prison and oppressed by poverty and hunger'. And in the wake of the 1980 coup d'état he had expressed his horror at 'the bloodshed, looting and lawlessness that followed' (Levi C. Williams, The History of the United Methodist Church in Liberia (Outskirts Press, U.S., 2014), 117–118).

international assistance programme involving UN agencies already active in Liberia. Finally, the Resolution requested the Secretary-General 'to dispatch a mission to Liberia with a view to holding consultations with the government on the assistance it needs…' With such a willing international community, it appeared, the dedicated pursuit of self-reliance seemed less attractive.

Notes

1 Africa-Asia, June 1985, 'Quiwonkpa breaks his silence'.
2 A.T. press cutting, Jack White, Citizen (Time-Life News Service).
3 A.T. Press cutting, 'Liberians Cheer as Firing Squad shoots Thirteen', African Mirror, July 1980 (published in U.S.).
4 Ibid.
5 A.T. Edward Jackson to Ted Hayden, 29 April 1980.
6 Ibid.
7 Ibid.
8 A.T. Press cutting. Leon Dash, Washington Post, 21 April 1980.
9 The Catholic missions kept contact with one another by means of a private radio-telephone network.
10 A.T. Darcy to Edward Biggane, 30 April 1980.
11 Ibid.
12 Wisely, he remained on in the U.S., relocating to Oklahoma.
13 Williams, Levi C., A History of the United Methodist Church in Liberia (Outskirts Press, Inc., U.S.), 107–108.
14 MMMA (Archives of the Medical Missionaries of Mary, Drogheda, Ireland). Mgt. Chambers to Sister Jude, 17 May 1980, and 3 June 1980.
15 Adekeye Adebajo, op. cit, 32.
16 Ibid.
17 West Africa, 12 September 1983, 2097.
18 13 April 1980.
19 'Failure of the Liberian oligarchy reflects on its American parent'.
20 Author's italics.
21 A.B. Transcript of this and other broadcasts by Harrington, and Bishop Michael Francis, in A.T. and A.B. (14/923.531).
22 See A.B. 14/923.531, Con Murphy SMA, 17/7/1980, 'Memo of information' provided to him by Harrington. The attachment to the Memo was signed 'Sub-committee on Issues', dated 10 May 1980.
23 Published in December 1981, it covered the first 14 months of the Doe regime.
24 With some minor exceptions.
25 Held this office 1977–81.
26 See Adekeye Adebajo, op. cit, 34.
27 West Africa, 4 May 1981, 963ff.
28 Ibid.
29 J. Gus Liebenow, 'Liberia, Dr Doe and the Demise of Democracy', Part 1: 'The Anatomy of Subterfuge' (31/8/1984, USFI Reports, Issue 17).
30 Paul Gifford, The Tablet, 30 June 1990, 7.
31 At its 103rd Plenary Meeting, on 17 December 1981, entitled: 'Assistance for the Development of Liberia'.

4 Revolutionary fervour diminishes

In April 1982 celebrations to mark the second anniversary of the coup were very different from those of the previous year.[1] Much had happened in the intervening 12 months to dampen enthusiasm for the revolution. In the first place a number of executions had taken place, including that of Thomas Weh-Syen, deputy head of state, accused of plotting to kill Doe, Quiwonkpa and Podier. Nelson Toe, the man who reportedly had disembowelled Tolbert, died with him. Secondly, the self-confidence of the leaders was now giving way to nervousness and insecurity a token of which was the imposition of a daily curfew between 1 am and 6 am. Apart from sourcing international aid, the elimination of real or imagined threats from within now appeared to be the principal preoccupation of the regime. That this should have been so is not surprising when it is borne in mind that Doe, like many other West African heads-of-state, was driven by a thirst for power rather than the pursuit of an ideology. What resulted was a 'patrimonial' or 'big-man' state, based on force rather than consent, with foundations which were inherently unstable.[2] Thirdly, resignations and dismissals of leading cabinet members added to the sense that all was not well. One of those who resigned was Dr Togba-Nah Tipoteh who took his leave in August 1981 while visiting the Ivory Coast, citing human rights abuses by the regime. As a co-founder of MOJA he had been embraced by the Doe regime and appointed to senior ministries. But soon the military leaders found themselves ill-at-ease with this well-educated, American-trained Professor of Economics turned politician, and began to accuse him of being a 'socialist'.[3] Particularly unsettling for the population at large had been the dismissal of Gabriel Baccus Matthews from his post as Foreign Minister, and his sudden reinstatement in March 1982 as Director General of the Cabinet. Little of this made sense, apart from pointing to mysterious and deep divisions within the regime.

Yet this was only one side of the picture. On the other there were some positive features. For example, a number of educated outsiders remained in cabinet, including Dr Fahnbulleh. Also continuing in public office was Dr Amos Sawyer, Chairman of the Constitution Drafting Commission. At his post, too, as Chairman of the National Investment Commission, was Professor Dew Tuan Wleh-Mayson, formerly of MOJA. In addition, some genuine

DOI: 10.4324/9781003219309-6

political reconciliation appeared to be taking place following the release of political prisoners and the general amnesty granted to political exiles.

The amnesty had led some prominent opponents of the regime to return from exile. Doe appointed a number of these to positions in government and semi-state corporations. Dr Bernard Blamo, erstwhile Minister for Education who had fallen out with the regime, returned and was given charge of the National Port Authority. Another exiled opponent, Ayun Cassell, a senator during the Tolbert regime, became Deputy Minister for Commerce, Industry and Transportation. And then there was the re-emergence of Dr Tipoteh, in London to launch his book titled *Democracy – The Call of the Liberian People* – at which he was expected to publicly attack the Doe regime. Instead, he declared he wanted 'to respond to Doe's call for a new society' and that his book was 'a concrete manifestation of this, presenting 'a viable plan of action for self-sufficiency in food production'.[4]

Despite Liberia's difficulties, which had dampened the mood of celebration on the coup's second anniversary, the U.S. administration seemed reasonably satisfied with developments. Doe's renewal of his offer of an amnesty to Liberians in exile, had made a good impression in Washington. So also did his declaration that he and his comrades had not taken power to perpetuate military rule and had 'no intention to outlive our usefulness'.[5] Washington was sufficiently impressed to send a congratulatory message and an invitation to visit President Reagan.

Relationships between the regime and the U.S. administration were to be further consolidated in August 1982 when head of state Doe paid a two-week official visit to Washington. By all accounts, Doe and Reagan got on well with the former leaving his host in no doubt that his country was now firmly on the road back to civilian rule.[6] The U.S. administration would have been further gratified to learn that within a year Liberia had expelled the Russian ambassador, closed the Libyan People's Bureau and renewed diplomatic relations with Israel, ruptured for a decade.[7]

Further evidence suggesting Liberia was on the road to stability came with the interagency mission promised by the UN Secretary-General after Liberia's appeal for assistance in April 1981. The mission had sat down with the government during its visit and together drew up what exactly was needed to tackle Liberia's problems. And with a view to making this programme of assistance a reality it was agreed the United Nations Development Programme would assist the Liberian government in organising a round-table conference of donors to be held in 1983.

***

One constituency which Tolbert had found difficult to subdue was that of third-level students. These, mostly drawn from UL, had been in the vanguard of opposition to the Tolbert government and generally welcomed the coup. However, optimism soon gave way to doubt and, as the realisation dawned that there had been little real change, student activism again began to surface. In January 1982 this resulted in a significant confrontation. Suspecting that the students were being manipulated by opponents with political ambitions Doe banned all forms of student political activity until the return of civilian rule in 1985. Student leaders responded by appealing for a reconsideration of the ban. When their request for a meeting was refused, they released the text of their appeal to the general public. The government acted swiftly. Within a matter of days most of the student leaders were under lock and key. And then, brought before a Special Military Tribunal, six were found guilty of treason and sentenced to death by firing squad. Doe's intention might well have been only to teach the students a lesson, for on the eve of the scheduled executions he granted them clemency, an act which drew large numbers of Liberians onto the streets of Monrovia singing his praises.

Frank A. Settle, an American visiting Liberia to give educational workshops on behalf of the United Methodists, asserts that the mainline Christian Churches played a key part in persuading Doe to stay his hand.[8] While his claim may be exaggerated, it was nonetheless true that the Churches certainly were an unwelcome irritant for the head of state during this episode; and in a manner not previously experienced. For on 3 January 1981 a critical decision had been taken by the Episcopalians, United Methodists, Presbyterians, Lutherans, Baptists and Roman Catholics – all Churches with an international dimension – to form what henceforth was known as the Liberian Council of Churches (LCC).[9] From this time on, instead of dealing with individual Churches or churchmen, political leaders had to deal with a formidable, united, well-organised and articulate grouping. In the present case, when the warrants to arrest the student leaders were issued, the LCC persuaded the miscreants to surrender, promising to give them protection. They then had escorted them to the authorities and thereafter, throughout the trial process, had remained as close to the students as military surveillance would allow.

Other constituencies claiming to have influenced Commander-in-Chief Doe to stay his hand included the Liberian Marketing Association, the Traditional Chiefs, the American ambassador and various other diplomatic representatives. All felt sure that they had been listened to. But it would be wrong to underestimate Doe's instinctive cunning which enabled him to survive much longer than many had predicted. He was well aware that the execution of students would bring local revulsion and a violent reaction from Liberia's student population. Even more so, he knew he would have had to face international outrage at a time when he was becoming increasingly dependent on the international community to fund his regime. By publicly invoking the pleadings of the LCC and the others who had made representations, Doe was enabled to save face and avoid a bloody and calamitous episode.

***

As the third anniversary of Liberia's coup approached there was increased local and international interest in the projected return to civilian rule. The corner stone of the Redemption Day celebrations was the presentation of a draft constitution to the People's Redemption Council by the Sawyer-led drafting commission. A special elections commission (SECOM) had already been formed, tasked to organise a referendum on the constitution and oversee subsequent elections for a civilian legislature and president. And now a detailed timetable for the return to civilian rule existed. The political parties would be permitted to organise and register with SECOM after Redemption Day 1984. Campaigning would commence the following November and continue until two days before the election, scheduled now for 20 January 1985.

Although the draft constitution was published with much fanfare, there remained an underlying anxiety among the populace that the military leadership might not fulfil its pledge to return Liberia to civilian rule. Professor Mark Tessler[10], an eyewitness to this period, explained its source in a University Field Staff International report. In the wake of the 1980 coup, not only had the soldiers taken control of government but they had also seized the homes and possessions of the former elite. Senior members of the new regime now went around wearing 'expensive three-piece suits, rather than military uniforms', no longer living with their men in barracks but choosing instead to live in the palatial residences they had requisitioned and in which they had installed their families. 'Top political figures with luxury housing, chauffeur-driven cars and other perquisites of high office, might not easily return to barracks life'.[11]

There were other reasons why the current ruling elite might be reluctant to yield power to civilians. The prevalence of corruption on a grand scale among the old elite had been one of the great grievances of those who opposed the Tolbert regime. But the level of corruption, if anything, was higher now among the new elite. Henry Boimah Fahnbulleh, who stayed with the regime when others had left, grew uncomfortable with this venality. Eventually in July 1982 he was dismissed from his post as Foreign Minister supposedly because of 'ideological differences' with the government, but in reality, because he had expressed misgivings about the regime's integrity. In a speech given in December 1982 Fahnbulleh, now in exile, asked how was it possible that 'government officials who want to live in air-conditioned, split-level mansions in Monrovia's suburbs and who want to ride in the latest-model car', could be expected to genuinely build a new society?[12]

Many observers were also expressing doubts as to whether Doe possessed the capacity, if he so wished, to lead Liberia back to civilian rule. Among signs of Doe's incapacity during the first three years of his tenure were a number of grandiose schemes suggesting that the head of state had lost touch with economic realities. One proposed scheme was the building of a new capital. Nigeria had created a new capital. Why not Liberia? The existing capital, Monrovia, Doe explained, did not correspond to the revolutionary spirit of the nation because of its 'colonial legacy'.[13]

What was plain was that instead of governing, Doe appeared to be concentrating his energies on staying in power, preserving his God-given, 'Bigman' patrimony. And he was accomplishing this with no small measure of success. His grandiose schemes served as effective distractions from the realities of life. Appealing to the vanity of citizens, they hid the fact that Doe was living from day to day, attempting desperately to keep the populace in order. In a word, he had little intention of, or capacity for, addressing any of the real problems facing the country. When he did enter the public arena, it was usually in the context of stamping out opposition, uncovering coups (mostly imaginary), eliminating perceived political rivals, or promoting bizarre schemes to gain public approval. Yet behind his erratic behaviour there was a determined concentration to maintain his position, matched to a natural cunning which kept him ahead of those who might drive him from power. Not only did he outwit his political opponents within Liberia but he managed to retain the support of the US administration and the international community. Thus, was he able to survive much longer than one would have expected for an uneducated, enlisted soldier.

***

In the old Liberia it was customary that religious intercessory services formed part of the celebration of significant national events. This custom was retained by the new regime. The third anniversary of the coup provided the LCC once again with an opportunity to make its views known directly to the government. It will be remembered it was in the course of delivering such a service on Liberia's first Redemption Day that the Methodist bishop, Arthur F. Kulah, angered the head of state.[14] On the current occasion, Archbishop Michael Kpala Francis led the service. Taking for his theme 'Charity – the Basis of the Just Society', he claimed to observe 'a certain tiredness' throughout the country at the lack of progress. Not all of it, of course, he told his listeners, was the fault of government. A global economic slump since 1980 had had its effect. But the battle against corruption had not yet been won despite a series of strong measures taken by head of state Doe. And he issued a warning. Revolutions, he said, tended to occur because of the 'materialistic selfishness' of incumbent regimes; while revolutionary regimes which lack the contrary spirit of 'self-sacrifice', rarely succeed.

The leaders of the PRC, again, could hardly have been happy with this address although its respectful tone might have gone some way to mollify feelings. However, Francis' allocution was delivered not as leader of Liberia's Catholic Church but as LCC vice president. The regime did not know what to make of this recently established body composed of Liberia's major international Churches. But getting what might prove to be an important, influential, body on side (rather than shooting its messenger) appeared to be a safer course to follow.

***

The process of return to civilian rule designed by the regime had provided for a National Advisory Assembly to convene in Gbarnga in the autumn of 1983. This august body was to meet for a period of two months to review the draft constitution, after which it would make recommendations to the PRC. The first convention to elect delegates took place in Bomi county in May 1983, conducted with aplomb and typical of what was to occur throughout Liberia.[15]

> It was attended by 31 individuals, representing the 14 major clans of the area, while the secret ballot elections were supervised by a 6-person technical committee. The two delegates elected were, respectively, the

secretary general of the Liberian Baptist Missionary and Educational Society and a classroom teacher at a local mission school.[16]

The last convention was held in Monserrado County during the second half of July.

***

Fears that the military might yet find ways to derail the process lingered in the background. There were certain straws in the wind which warned of trouble ahead. For example the stipulation in the draft constitution which required the future president to be at least 35 years old, and which would have excluded Commander-in-Chief Doe (who was only 28 at the time of the coup), had been followed by a declaration by the head of state that, in fact he would shortly be 33-years old and would have reached 35 years before the new civilian government was installed. This suggested that, despite protestations to the contrary, he intended to run for the presidency.[17] Further support for this conclusion came from the fact that he appeared to be undermining the position of potential rivals. Fahnbulleh together with Hilary Dennis, the latter a popular member of the Americo-Liberian community, were likely to be presidential candidates. But Fahnbulleh had been forced into exile while Dennis had been imprisoned and sent for trial on charges of embezzlement.[18] Another man of national stature with leadership potential from the Americo-Liberian community was Winston Tubman, nephew of former President William V.S. Tubman.[19] Having distanced himself from Tolbert and the True Whig party prior to the coup, Doe had appointed him ambassador to the United Nations. Later he became Minister for Justice, but more recently had been dismissed from the cabinet allegedly because of his connections with Dennis.

Further evidence of Doe's intention to run was seen in a March 1982 decree requiring government employees seeking political office to resign their posts by the end of April. This was seen as an attempt 'to smoke out potential opponents' and deprive them of 'a base from which to pursue their aspirations'.[20] Among those who resigned were Gabriel Baccus Matthews, Oscar Quiah and Marcus Dahn, all leaders of PAL during the Tolbert era and currently involved in progressive party politics.

Perhaps a more formidable candidate for the presidency, should he choose to run, was Doe's co-conspirator, General Thomas Quiwonkpa, the well-respected head of the armed forces. Popular with army rank and file he had eschewed the conspicuous material rewards reaped by most of his fellow-conspirators, even speaking out against colleagues for abandoning the revolutionary spirit which had inspired the April 1980 coup.[21] Another well-qualified candidate was MOJA activist and chairman of the constitutional commission, Amos Sawyer. But he had given no signal of an interest in the post and, instead, seemed happy to return to academic life.

***

Against the expectations of Liberia's many critics, the Doe administration succeeded in meeting the new deadlines which it had set. On 3 June 1984, a referendum on the draft constitution was held and on 20 July an affirmative result was announced. There followed within a week the dissolution of the PRC and the installation of a civilian transitional government (although there were doubts as to its truly civilian character). Among those commentators who observed events in Liberia and wrote about it later was the distinguished political scientist, J. Gus Liebenow[22]. He was struck by the extent to which the mood among external observers changed when this flurry of activity took place. Greatly encouraged, British newspapers, including *The Times, The Guardian* and *The Telegraph*, and the American *Washington Post*, 'hailed Liberia's first bold step towards civilian rule and progress towards constitutional democracy'.[23]

But, as Liebenow observed, in fact Liberians soon found that they had been the subjects of a 'well-orchestrated charade'.[24] Doe had no intention of relinquishing power. The fact that he had never assumed the title of 'President' had been taken by many as a sign he was genuine in his declarations about a return to civilian rule. Coup leaders in other countries en route to becoming dictators usually declared themselves 'President' as soon as they seized power, the most recent example being Colonel Lansana Conté of Guinea who had led a coup within a week of the death of Sekou Touré. In his first year Doe had allowed himself to be called 'Commander-in-Chief', 'Head of State' or 'Chairman of the PRC' but was best pleased with the title 'Master-Sergeant'. Early in the second year he began to favour the titles 'Commander-in-Chief' or 'General,' although he began to appear more frequently in civilian attire. The conferral of an honorary doctorate degree from the University of Seoul, South Korea, in 1982, led to a new designation in government press releases and government-controlled newspapers. He had now become Doctor Doe. Appearing, according to Liebenow, 'in smartly tailored three-piece business suits ... the frail Master Sergeant had become a rather paunchy bureaucrat...with the demeanour of any other modern African head-of-state'.[25] But he still appeared to reject use of the title 'President'. This, however, was an illusion soon to be shattered. On 20 July, when Doe dissolved the PRC and instituted the Interim National Assembly, he assumed the title of 'President'. From now on he was to guard the title jealously.

***

Few were surprised when, on the day following the lifting of the ban on politics, 27 July, Doe declared himself a candidate for the presidency, despite a statement on the previous day that he had no interest in politics.[26] He was nominated by the powerful Liberian Marketing Association and the Traditional Chiefs. The former, consisting mainly of Liberia's market women, was an influential body which Doe had carefully cultivated from the time of the coup. Their protests were claimed to have been a factor in causing Doe to stay his hand over the execution of the six student leaders in January 1982. Equally powerful were the traditional chiefs. Doe had also done much to foster this constituency, creating new territorial administrative units in response to their overtures.

Doe's failure to resign his positions as head of the transitional government and Commander-in-Chief was ominous, for it flew in the face of the new constitution which required those seeking election to resign official positions. The fact that he made his declaration from the strategically placed Shiefflin military barracks[*] surrounded by Liberia's military chiefs was also symbolic. Moreover, despite the dissolution of the PRC the Special Military Tribunal remained in place.[27]

Thus Doe rode rough-shod over the constitution with the full encouragement of his military colleagues. Those who had tried to cry halt had been put out of commission. By this time, too, most of those who might have been expected to challenge for the presidency had been executed, forced into exile or rendered politically impotent.

***

As already noted, tensions within the PRC had quickly developed in the wake of the coup. Doe persisted in promoting and appointing Krahn to senior positions in the army and government, ignoring Gio and other large ethnic groupings. (One smaller ethnic group also favoured by Doe was the Mandingo. But this was to prove a poisoned chalice in later years when the Krahn were no longer in the ascendancy). The executions of Weh-Syen and Toe in August 1981 were the first in the elimination of those who conceivably might have threatened Doe's position. It was only a matter of time before Quiwonkpa, highly popular with the army and the civilian population, would be removed. Well-regarded within Liberia and overseas, he was credited with representing the true spirit of the PRC in his willingness to fight corruption and in the simplicity of his lifestyle. It must also, of course, be borne in mind that he had been a leading figure in the assassination of Tolbert and the subsequent slaughter on the beaches of Monrovia, the brutality of which shocked the world and for which he seems never to have expressed any regret. Nonetheless he now lived in modest barrack quarters, refusing to move into the Executive Mansion, had done much to restore discipline within army ranks and had tried to put a stop to the seizure of property by PRC members and military. He was also outspoken on the need to honour the PRC pledge to return Liberia to civilian rule. In October 1983 relations with Doe deteriorated sharply when Quiwonkpa began to insist that neither should run for political office in the forthcoming elections.

Scarcely a month later Doe informed Quiwonkpa of his intention to relieve him of his command and appoint him Secretary General of the PRC. Sensing that much more than a redeployment was in store for him Quiwonkpa refused the appointment. Doe reacted by dismissing him from the army and from the PRC. There were many protests at this; a number of leading Liberians called for the restoration of the respected and popular general to his position. But Doe fearful, among other things, of Quiwonkpa's potential as a political rival, had other plans. Learning that he was about to be arrested on charges of organising a coup, Quiwonkpa hastily went into hiding along with his aide-de-camp, Prince Yormie Johnson, and one Charles McArthur Taylor. It is probable that the latter

---

[*]   Situated half-way between Monrovia and Harbel (and the adjacent Firestone Rubber Plantation).

took this course less out of loyalty to Quiwonkpa than from the fact that he was about to face trial on charges of embezzlement. As proof that there had been a genuine plot the Doe regime paraded arrested soldiers before the television cameras where they confessed their crimes.

Quiwonkpa was tried *in absentia* by a Special Military Tribunal in June 1984 along with nineteen 'co-conspirators', three of which testified against their fellow-accused. Quiwonkpa's disappearance created much embarrassment for the Doe government. It was believed he had made his way to the Ivory Coast and then to the U.S. At the time Doe was contemplating a second visit to the U.S. to meet President Reagan and fully intended to ask for Quiwonkpa's extradition if he could be found. The visit had been scheduled for December 1983 but was postponed by the Americans on the grounds that President Reagan would be receiving the Chinese Prime Minister. Rescheduled for January 1984, it was again cancelled, and no further date was fixed, indicating that, among other reasons, the White House was uncomfortable at the circumstances leading up to Quiwonkpa's disappearance.

Major-General Nicholas Podier was another of the 1980 coup leaders who fell foul of his leader. Made deputy head of state after Weh Syen's execution, he was arrested with nine others on 28 August 1984 and charged with plotting to over-throw the regime. The circumstances surrounding his arraignment were bizarre. His uncle, former Justice Minister Isaac Nyeplu, who was being sought, gave himself up and appeared on television implicating his nephew in the alleged plot. Podier, he said, had sought his collaboration in ousting Doe. Others implicated by Nyeplu included well-known Interim National Assembly members and Amos Sawyer. All were charged with treason. The detention of the UL Professor, an internationally respected champion of democracy, caused outrage. However, on 13 October events were to take a further bizarre turn when Doe announced that he was setting all the plotters free, on the grounds that their trials, which were bound to be lengthy, would delay Liberia's return to democracy.[28]

***

The January 1982 confrontation between the Doe Regime and Liberia's student constituency, described above, had revealed government determination to crush student dissent. Events during August 1984 showed that in the interim little had changed. On the twenty-second day of that month, at about 3.30 pm with classes over for the day, Brother James Newberry CSC[*] of St Patrick's High School, an institution adjacent to the University of Liberia (UL), was putting items on a notice board when the air was filled with rifle fire. Going to the second floor of the building from where he had a clear view, he saw soldiers moving onto the UL. campus where students, in large numbers, were gathering for a mass rally to demand the immediate release of Amos Sawyer and other alleged coup-plotters; and to protest the 'thwarting of the democratic process' by the regime.[29] From his vantage point Brother James witnessed groups of students being pursued by soldiers who kicked and beat anyone they

[*]   Holy Cross Brothers Canadian.

could lay hands on. Next the soldiers blocked off exits and corralled the students, holding them at gunpoint, beating and kicking them and tearing clothes from their backs. In the confusion and amid continuing sounds of gunfire, some succeeded in climbing over the wall into St Patrick's compound where they hid.[30] Later, when the students had been driven off campus, they observed the soldiers looting the buildings.[31]

Government reaction to these events was to declare the university closed and claim that there had been very few casualties since most of the soldiers had used blank ammunition. Those killed, Defence Minister Gray D. Allison said, speaking on radio and television, had been hit by stray live bullets fired into the air. Reaction within the student community to the campus invasion took some days to develop. Then, on 29 August, bills began to appear on walls all over Monrovia declaring Friday, 31 August, 'a Day of Mourning for the Martyrs of Bloody Wednesday'. The bills, signed by the self-styled 'Students Revolutionary Committee', a clandestine grouping, claimed to give details of 'the brutal invasion' of the UL Campus. The invasion, the bills explained, had been carried out when Interim[32] President Doe ordered Minister Allison and Chief-of-Staff, Henry Dubar, to move against the protesting students. The unit sent in was 'made up of French-speaking Ivorian Krahn who had no relatives in Liberia'.[33]

In the weeks following this statement the Revolutionary Committee lay low as government did all in its power to identify the 'culprits'. Finally on 7 November, shortly after Sawyer was released from custody without charge, a pamphlet began to circulate under the title: '*REACT* is Back'. *REACT*, in effect, was the newssheet of the same subversive Students Revolutionary Committee and had appeared on campus very occasionally in previous months despite strenuous efforts on the part of the university authorities to suppress it. This pamphlet was to be the first in a series of five on the topic: 'Why Doe cannot be President'. The last of the series,[34] issued on 16 January 1985, was a self-congratulatory tract mocking the government's unsuccessful efforts to uncover the identities of its authors. In no way mollified by the release of Sawyer, the tone of the 7 November pamphlet was even more incendiary than that issued in the immediate aftermath of the campus invasion. Its main thrust was to expose Doe's manipulation of the political process so as to prevent a genuine return to civilian rule. Claiming it had impeccable inside sources, *REACT* depicted Doe as a venal, grasping tyrant, living like the notorious Caligula of Roman antiquity. The attack was deeply personal and vicious. Details of mistresses and concubines living in houses rented by the state were given.

Other leading members of the regime were also pilloried. A particular target was Jenkins Scott, Minister for Justice, 'who had reminded the public that corruption was so rampant even the judges and lawyers were taking bribes.' *REACT* wanted to assure Minister Scott that he 'did not have to go that far to find out about corruption. In his own department, the stealing of government money was as broad as daylight'.

Another leading member of the regime subjected to close and venomous scrutiny was George Boley, Minister for Presidential Affairs. And Doe's wife did not escape the poison pens of *REACT*.

> First-Lady Nancy Doe has purchased the old IMC yard in Dimla at the cost of three million dollars, using a sizable portion of children's playground funds. She is also engaged in other sophisticated construction works, such as a palace on Airfield road and a similar structure (underground) on Niabo Road in Zwedru, Grand Gedeh County.[35]

As well as claiming to expose the venality of the Doe regime, *REACT* focused on its incompetency, evident in its failure to identify the membership of the Student Revolutionary Committee and its journalists. A complete issue of *REACT* was devoted to this topic, addressed, as usual to 'The People, Youth and Students of Liberia'.

***

Efforts by the regime to combat dissent and root out opposition had already, on 21 July, led to the promulgation of a new Decree (No. 88A), focusing on publications and broadcasts critical of government.[36] Ostensibly this decree was 'to prevent any individual, group of individuals or organisations from creating disharmony, spreading rumours, lies and disinformation or from undermining the security of the State'. In practice it was used as an instrument to intimidate newspaper editors, journalists and anyone who expressed even the mildest reservations about the head of state and his government. Many prominent newspaper men of an independent disposition were to be arrested and sentenced under its provisions, including Kenneth Y. Best and Rufus M. Darpoh of the *Daily Observer* and Momolu Sirleaf and C. William Allen of *Footprints Today*.[37] It was this instrument which was employed against those suspected of being behind *REACT*. On 3 December one Ezekiel Pajibo, aged 25, a student in the UL Science faculty and acting president of LINSU, was arrested with six others under the terms of Decree 88A, on suspicion of being a member of the Directorate of the Student Revolutionary Committee. Two other senior members of the LINSU secretariat, Christian G. Herbert and Wuo G. Tappia, were arrested on the same suspicion. A Catholic from the Kru Coast, Pajibo was well known to many of the missionaries, both in his home region and in Monrovia.

On 18 December LINSU issued a 'position statement' on the arrests and the statute under which they had taken place. It was claimed that a stencil found on Pajibo at the time of his arrest had nothing to do with the Revolutionary Committee or its clandestine publication. Instead, it was directly related to LINSU's policy, formulated after the campus invasion, which sought the restoration of the right to form a students' council at the university. As LINSU acting president, it maintained, Pajibo was in fact organising a campaign for the restoration of a students' council at the time of his arrest, while the documentation found on him was a draft position paper to be put to a student gathering. The statement went on to claim that not a shred of evidence had been produced to prove links with 'clandestine publications' and demanded that government should either speedily charge and try the three leaders or release them unconditionally. Giving its view of what it termed the 'infamous Decree 88A', LINSU quoted from the editorial of Monrovia's *Daily Observer* of 14 August: 'Many pressmen have expressed fears and grave doubts as to their ability to continue their work without endangering their personal safety and livelihood.' LINSU also called on the U.S. to intervene, noting that the present dictatorship in Liberia relied on the U.S. for survival.[38] With not inconsiderable courage the statement had six signatories.

Meanwhile, Pajibo and those arrested with him had being airlifted from their Monrovia prison to Belle Yalla, the much-feared maximum security prison in the remote north of the country.[39] Here reports filtering out claimed they were being 'subjected to regular beatings, interrogation at gun-point, starvation diets and mock executions'.[40] Calls for the release of Pajibo and his companions were not confined to Liberia. International civil rights groups and Catholic support groups were to the forefront. Amnesty International adopted those in captivity as 'political prisoners of conscience' within its 'Urgent Action Network'. *About Liberia,*[*] an SMA-sponsored news journal for Liberian students in the U.S., produced a special issue on the 'unlawful detention and torture of Ezekiel Pajibo'. And there were individual appeals for clemency, such as that of Monica Neff of Junction City, Kansas, who had met Ezekiel at a Students Conference in 1982 and corresponded with him regularly thereafter.[41]

The LINSU arrests had little effect on the activities of the Students Revolutionary Committee. *REACT* continued to appear, claiming the recently installed president of the University, Dr Joseph Getehmnah Morris, had 'tipped off government security forces that Ezekiel Pajibo … was responsible for organizing the student masses.' Nor was the student body cowed in the absence of its leader, convening and conducting mass meetings in the UL auditorium 'in order to adopt a common position in their struggle for a democratic university way of life'. It also declared that unless a commission of inquiry was established 'to investigate the ugly incident of 22 August, students would not agree to return to classes should the university re-open. Instead, they would mount 'a national and international campaign to isolate the University of Liberia, to dishonour any and all degrees granted by UL and to immediately halt all financial or material (overseas) aid'.

Notes

1 Hene Johnson, Africa Now, May 1982, 67.
2 John Kilcoyne, 'The role of the Catholic Church during Liberia's Civil Crisis, 1990–1997', Middlesex University and Missionary Institute, London, May 1999, 9.

---

*   About Liberia was edited by James Butty (see note on p. 54 below). It was recognised for its objectivity by the ULAA which awarded Butty the Charles C. Gbenyon Award on 29 June 1987.

3 See ibid. Also West Africa, 24 March 1986, Matchet's Diary, 606.
4 Africa Now, May 1982.
5 Leon Dash, The Washington Post, 17 June 1982.
6 Michael Massing, Best Friends: Violations of Human Rights in Liberia, America's Closest Ally in Africa, May 1986 (A Fund for Free Expression Report, New York), 11.
7 J. Gus Liebenow, Liberia Studies Journal, vol. X, 1, 13.
8 The Christian Century (United Methodist Journal) 12–18 August 1982.
9 Paul Gifford, The Tablet, 30 June 1990, 7.
10 He had been commissioned to write a report on Liberia by the reputable U.S.-based University Field Staff International agency.
11 Tessler, UFSI Reports, no. 2.
12 Ibid, no. 3.
13 West Africa, 5 July 1982, 1740.
14 See pp. 35
15 Ibid.
16 Ibid.
17 Tessler, UFSI Reports, nos 8–9.
18 These charges appeared to have been trumped up. He was acquitted.
19 See John Clifford Caspar, 'Tragic Pragmatism: Liberia and the United States, 1971–1985', M.A. thesis, North Carolina State University, 2012.
20 Tessler, UFSI Reports, no. 9.
21 Edward Lama Wonkeryor, Liberian Studies Journal, XI, 1 (1986), 35–36.
22 Professor Liebenow played a central role in founding the Liberian Studies Association (and its academic journal) based in Indiana University.
23 See, J. Gus Liebenow. 'Liberia, Dr Doe and the Demise of Democracy', Part 1: 'The Anatomy of Subterfuge' (31 August 1984, USFI Reports, Issue 17).
24 Ibid.
25 Ibid.
26 Ibid.
27 Liebenow, J. Gus, 'Liberia, the Dissolution of Privilege'(1980–1981, UFSI Reports, Issues 39–41).
28 The New York Times, 14 October 1984.
29 A.T. Brother James Newberry to Phil Armstrong, 25 September 1984.
30 Ibid.
31 Ibid.
32 'Interim', until elected. Commonly in the media Doe was referred to as 'interim president'.
33 A.T. 'Statement by the Directive of the Executive Bureau REACT' (Revolutionary Action Committee), 29 August 1984.
34 Titled, 'In Search of "React"'.
35 11 October 1984.
36 LTRC, Media and Outreach in the LTRC Process [vol. 3, Appendices], 10–11, 46.
37 See Momo K. Rogers, 'Liberian Press under Military Rule', Liberian Studies Journal, XXI, 1 (1996).
38 Footprints Today, Monday, 27 August 1984, 1.
39 About Liberia, January 1985. Ezekiel Pajibo, 'Urgent Action Update – Unlawful Detention and Torture'.
40 Ibid.
41 A.T. Letter signed by Monica Neff, Kansas Life Community, 618 N. Adams, Junction City, KANSAS 66441.

5 Return to civilian rule

If relationships between the Doe regime and Liberia's students sharply deteriorated during 1984, those with the Liberian Council of Churches were also on a downward, though less precipitous, slope. It will be remembered that shortly after the 1980 coup Bishop Francis (as he then was) and the Catholic Secretariat's Patrick Harrington had responded by forcefully outlining Catholic teaching on good governance, human and civil rights, and social and economic justice. Subsequently, under the umbrella of the LCC, Francis continued to comment on such issues. It was in this capacity that he delivered his unwelcome homily to the PRC on the third anniversary of Redemption Day, mentioned above.* But at this point Francis could not be described as a 'thorn in the side of the regime'. Perhaps the more vocal Bishop George Browne, leader of the Episcopal Church and first president of the LCC, might have been more deserving of that description. Although vice-president, Francis tended to confine public utterances to his annual Lenten pastoral letters. Not that the regime was at all satisfied with the attitude of the Catholic Church which, with most other LCC member Churches, was withholding wholehearted endorsement and support. And a particular distrust applied to some of the activities of the Catholic Church. For example, there were deep suspicions within the PRC that the Church might have been involved in the disappearance of Thomas Quiwonkpa in November 1984, a suspicion which, as will be seen later, was to prove well-founded.

In the second half of 1984, reacting to the deterioration in relations between government and students and increasing worries about a return to civilian rule, relations between the LCC and the Doe regime changed from being barely cordial to being confrontational. This was heralded by the manner in which Archbishop** Francis, now chief spokesperson of the LCC and soon to become its president, became noticeably more forthright in criticisms of the regime. On the Sunday following the UL campus invasion Francis was the first signatory to a LCC letter, read in all Christian churches, which condemned the recently announced Decree 88A and castigated the government's handling of the students.[1]

---

* See p. 41.
** The Monrovia jurisdiction was elevated to the status of Archdiocese in December 1981, with Michael Francis as Archbishop.

DOI: 10.4324/9781003219309-7

From this time on Francis, acting for the LCC, continued to issue press releases, letters and statements, condemning civil and political rights violations and calling on the government to honour its promises. In fact, the independent-minded and frequently silenced *Daily Observer*, in its New Year edition for 1985, reflected its satisfaction at the LCC's refusal to be silenced by conferring on Francis the title 'Man of the Year'. Weeks later the newspaper itself was again silenced following the placing of a front-page story concerning interim President Doe at the bottom of the page rather than in headline position.

***

Because of the unpopularity of his regime Doe had virtually no possibility of winning the presidential prize in a fair election. Accordingly, success depended upon his ability to eliminate or exclude his electoral opponents and silence criticism. Having dealt effectively with students and the press, and picking off one by one potential political rivals, he now turned his attention to the mainline Churches. At a dinner for the Diplomatic Corps on 17 January he launched an outright attack on the LCC. Recalling the purpose of decree 88A – to combat disharmony and disinformation – he accused 'the press, the bishops and certain politicians' of having failed (or being unwilling) to embrace the decree. Rather, in their opposition to it they had chosen to become 'spokesmen for those who do wrong in society'. And he wondered why the Churches, so vocal against the PRC, had remained silent in the wake of the Rice Riots of 1979 and during earlier periods when governments had acted oppressively. Henceforth, he declared, he would not permit bishop, priest or pastor to 'use the pulpit to issue anti-government statements or engage in acts that would create conflict and confusion in society'.[2]

The LCC prepared a robust response to these accusations and threats, mandating Archbishop Francis to deliver it in person. However, in a letter refusing Francis' request for an audience, Doe again complained that his regime had 'not received the desired sympathy, understanding and co-operation' it deserved. And he appeared particularly annoyed by the request for an audience. In the past, 'rather than seeking appointments for discussion and dialogue', the LCC had 'chosen instead to use the press, leaflets and pulpits to air its differences with government'.[3] How surprising it was now, after the government had exposed 'LCC actions and attitudes publicly, that it should come seeking an audience'![4]

Snubbed by the regime, the LCC leaders next decided to put their version of the facts into the public domain by publishing a 'clarification', ostensibly for the benefit of the six LCC member-Churches, but in reality aimed at a wider audience. The 'clarification', signed by representatives of these mainstream Christian denominations, gave details of the exchange of letters between interim President Doe and Archbishop Francis and then set out to refute Doe's criticisms one by one. While the LCC regarded the purpose of Decree 88A as 'laudatory', it found its methods and techniques 'unacceptable'. The 'clarification' also rejected outright the accusation that the Churches had become spokespersons for 'those who do wrong in our society'. By the same token it asserted that while the separation of Church and State was truly a worthy principle, Doe's innuendo that the Churches were seeking to 'break the dividing line between religion and politics' must be rejected. The head-of-state's criticisms on this point were based on a false assumption, namely 'that there was no application of the Word of God to the area of politics.'

The 'clarification' also addressed Doe's accusation that the Churches had failed to speak out in the past on social issues and that its present outspokenness was politically motivated. This was declared patently untrue. The Churches had always spoken out when injustices were perpetrated and had been quite outspoken in condemning government's actions during and in the aftermath of the Rice Riots. In this the authors of the 'clarification' were being somewhat disingenuous, ignoring the fact that up to the last few years of the Tolbert presidency a number of the mainline Churches had been in effect organs of True Whig dominance.

***

In February 1985, his term as U.S. Provincial completed, Ted Hayden was appointed to Washington DC as Director of the SMA Social Concerns Department, with a mandate to promote Liberian human rights issues. A key element in this task was the publication of the news sheet *About Liberia* but there would also be direct advocacy. He set about his task with characteristic energy. On 25 March he informed his successor as Provincial Superior, Sylvester John Murray[5], of the steps already taken. He had visited members of Congress and 'talked extensively' with the staff of the congressional sub-committee on Africa.[6] In addition he had prepared a brief report on the Liberian situation for members of Congress and their staff.

Clearly were Hayden to become a lobbyist highlighting the Doe regime's violations of human and civil rights and pressing the U.S. administration to change its current policy - as was his intention - this could have serious implications for his SMA confreres working in Liberia and in fact for the Liberian Church. Already *About Liberia* was running this risk. Hayden was under no illusions that the Doe regime would become aware of his activities. Addressing the issue he told Murray that Doe's January speech to the diplomatic corps had already shown the regime regarded the LCC as hostile. The fact that it had not acted more militantly against these mainline Churches to date was probably due to their international character. Hayden had already discussed the danger of SMA advocacy at Washington with those most directly involved during a recent visit to Liberia[7] – with Archbishop Francis, Bishop Dalieh, and his missionary confreres in the firing line. They had not discouraged him, and he felt comfortable in proceeding. His advocacy was to have repercussions on the relationship between the Catholic Church and the regime, but not as lethal as some might have feared.

***

On 7 March 1985 a hearing of the U.S. House of Representatives sub-committee on Africa heard testimony from Liberian Patrick L.N. Seyon[8], former vice president at UL.[9] The hearing was in preparation for a submission to the Appropriations Committee charged with setting the U.S. subsidy allocation to Liberia for the following year. Although in post-coup Liberia Seyon was appointed a member of the

Constitutional Commission, he soon came to be recognised as an opponent of the regime. In June 1981 when Doe discovered yet another coup plot (the third within a year) Seyon was among those arrested. Tried by military court, no evidence could be produced against him, and he was declared innocent and released. However, Seyon had been badly beaten and took a long time to recover.[10] In the aftermath of the campus invasion of August 1984 he was among a number of UL staff dismissed as enemies of the government. Fearing worse he took refuge in the U.S., where he was now a visiting scholar at Harvard.

Seyon's testimony focused on the U.S. government's rationale for giving aid to the Doe administration. This, according to administration spokesmen, was to ensure political stability and a prompt return to civilian rule. But Seyon doubted whether such laudable objectives would ever be accomplished. Many things had happened and were happening in Liberia which called the U.S. strategy into question. For example, much U.S. aid had been spent on the Liberian army, despite the fact that Liberia was at peace with its neighbours. And now the new military resources were being used to deprive people of their fundamental rights. As examples of this, Seyon cited the introduction of Decree 88A, and subsequent arrest and detention without trial of Dr Amos Sawyer, Ezekiel Pajibo and many others, also the campus invasion, the silencing of an independent press, and the elimination, one by one, of potential political rivals. On this latter point he described the manner in which Sawyer, who arguably posed the greatest threat to a Doe electoral victory, was excluded. On 12 February the Doe-controlled Interim Assembly had banned Sawyer from political activities pending an audit of his handling of the funds of the Constitutional Commission which he had headed. Another obstacle inhibiting the formation of political parties other than Doe's own, was the requirement imposed by the Elections Commission of a $150,000 registration fee for applicant political parties – this in a society where the per capita annual income was about $400. Seyon concluded his testimony by declaring that the U.S. objective of using its aid packages to achieve free and fair elections and a return to a democratically elected civilian government, was being thwarted at every turn.[11]

Seyon's testimony was only one of several. Not surprisingly, in the light of testimony such as Seyon's, the subcommittee recommended the following restriction on aid to Liberia. $94.4 million might be given for the next fiscal year but this would be dependent upon 'a successful completion of free and fair elections on a multi-party basis in October 1985, and a return to full civilian, constitutional rule as a consequence of such elections.'[12]

***

Hayden was by no means the only lobbyist pleading for a reduction in U.S. military aid to Liberia. On 17 March Jucontee Thomas Woewiyu, President of the Union of Liberian Associations in the Americas (ULAA),* appeared before the Appropriations Committee, making the same point. It must be said, however, that American-based Liberians were by no means united. On the one

---

★   ULAA, founded in 1974, comprised some 20 chapters throughout the US.

hand there were those who backed the Doe regime and, on the other, a much larger opposition with its own divisions and subgroups. In his testimony, Woewiyu, who had come on scholarship to Cornell's and later studied in Rutgers, concentrated on the regime's human rights violations, expressing little confidence that a return to civilian rule was ever likely to take place. Woewiyu, who was on first-name terms with Hayden, was to play a significant and arguably sinister role in Liberia's civil war in the years to come.

***

On 2 April 1985 yet another assassination plot was uncovered. This time it was genuine. On that day Colonel Moses Flanzamaton, a Krahn bodyguard of the interim president, opened fire on Doe's jeep. The president was unhurt, but two bodyguards were wounded. The attempt occurred at a time when a number of Doe's praetorian guard had been arrested and imprisoned for financial irregularities. Flanzamaton, it seems, was about to be arrested on a similar charge. Detained after a dramatic three-day search, Flanzamaton was executed by firing squad. Doe took advantage of the assassination attempt to arrest several possible opponents in his bid for the presidency, including Counsellor Tuan Wreh and Harry Greaves of the Liberian Action Party, Dr Edward Kesselly of the United Party and Gabriel Baccus Matthews of the United People's Party. And although strong protests from the American Embassy soon led to their release, other political opponents continued to be excluded from the election process. Amos Sawyer, leader of the Liberian's People's Party and clearly Doe's strongest opponent, remained banned from politics, while the party's deputy leader, Dusty Wollokollie, was jailed on charges of speaking ill of the head of state.[13]

***

In June 1985 Doe's equanimity was further disturbed with the surfacing of Quiwonkpa in the U.S. Despite a reward of $10,000 for his capture dead or alive when he went into hiding in November 1983, Quiwonkpa had managed to make his way out of Liberia. In so doing he had been helped by Fr Robert Tikpor of the Catholic diocese of Monrovia. A friend of Quiwonkpa's, Tikpor had presided at his wedding, and both remained close. Quiwonkpa had spent the first night of his disappearance in Archbishop Francis' residence (some sources say that this was unknown to the archbishop, but this would have been unlikely) and then had received shelter at the Catholic mission in Ashmun Street, hiding there with his wife in an attic-room by day and a bedroom at night. Fr Augustine Fahnbulleh[14], attached to Ashmun Street, made several journeys to the Sierra Leone border during which he became known to the soldiers manning checkpoints. When he attempted the journey with a nun and a priest in the back seat some six weeks after Quiwonkpa's disappearance, the car was waved through. The passengers in the back seat were, in fact, Quiwonkpa and his wife. In Sierra Leone they were received by a Holy Ghost priest who gave them shelter until a flight to the United States could be arranged. Although granted a pardon by Doe sometime later, Quiwonkpa had chosen to remain in hiding.

Quickly following on news of Quiwonka's re-appearance came the publication of an interview which he gave to one James Butty, a former UL student leader who had been sought by the government and was spirited out of Liberia by Hayden. Published in the journal *Africa-Asia*, Quiwonkpa denied he had plotted to oust Doe; and, in a passage which gives a chilling insight into discourse in the Executive Mansion, went on to explain why Doe wanted him dead:

> Doe had wanted to kill me for three good reasons: (1) I am the only person alive from the group that staged the first coup, apart from Harrison Pennue and David Kemeh. If Doe can get rid of me, he will have all the power to himself; (2) Because I was against the idea of the army remaining in power after 1985. (3) Doe did not want me to keep asking him about the whereabouts of 12 people arrested by his death squad for allegedly plotting to overthrow the regime.

***

Responding to the growing chorus of international criticism from human and civil rights organisations and from the press in the U.S. – even *The Wall Street Journal* had its say[15] – Doe decided to mount a diplomatic offensive.[16] In the last week of May 1985 a delegation, which included three government ministers, flew into Washington. In the days that followed, meetings were held with U.S. administration officials including Assistant Secretary of State for African affairs, Chester Crocker.* Defence Minister Allison met his U.S. counterpart, Casper Weinberger, at the Pentagon while Information Minister Karpeh was hosted on a Voice of America broadcast where he praised Washington's support for the Doe regime. The delegation met too with critics of the regime and others known to be monitoring Liberia's human rights record.

As already described, much of the criticism of the Doe regime circulating in the U.S. centred on the military invasion of the UL campus. The Liberian government, it was said, had refused to properly investigate the allegations that there had been many deaths. Nor had the regime been prepared to co-operate with any external inquiry. It was not surprising that the Liberian delegation should be pressed on this issue. This drew the admission that students had been injured by bullets, that there had been beatings and rapes, but also the consistent denial that there had been any loss of life. Administration officials, in turn, took the opportunity to assure the delegation that the U.S. had acted in a non-partisan fashion in Liberia's political affairs.[17] In particular they rejected President Doe's claim that the U.S. was hell-bent on removing him from Liberia's political life. At briefings, held after meetings with the delegation, administration officials also roundly rejected claims by Doe's opponents in

---

* Held this office during the Reagan presidency (1981–1989). Crocker was the author of the policy of 'Constructive engagement with South Africa' which replaced the confrontational approach of the Carter administration. Subsequently he championed the policy of 'quiet diplomacy' towards the Doe administration.

America that Washington was keeping him in power; and fended off criticism of its military assistance program, maintaining that this was predominantly directed towards the provision of military housing and training facilities.

Doe's diplomatic offensive also included press statements and interviews declaring Liberia was engaged in a life-or-death struggle against communism and socialism. A further initiative was the launch, on the fifth anniversary of Doe's accession to power, of a monthly magazine entitled *Sunrise*. This glossy publication highlighted the government's achievements and focused extensively on the virtues of Liberia's interim president.* A further initiative in the search for international credibility was the placing of articles in international journals. For example, *West Africa* published an article by Jonathan S. Reffell (from the Liberian Embassy in London) declaring that the U.S. Department of State had 'commended' the Liberian government on its human rights record.[18] The reference here was to the 'Country Reports on Human Rights Practices' which the State Department was legally bound to submit to Congress each year. This latter claim raised some eyebrows. A spokesman for the U.S. Embassy in Liberia, commenting on Reffell's assertion, declared the report was 'a declarative account of human rights practices as determined by U.S. embassies abroad', and did not 'commend, censure nor confer ratings on the human rights practices of any country'.[19]

How successful was Liberia's diplomatic offensive? One group which remained unconvinced was the Congressional Black Caucus, comprising black members of the U.S. House of Representatives, which telexed Doe on 3 August 1985 to deplore the 'deteriorating human rights situation' and to express their 'grave concern' over the arrests of students and political leaders and their 'detention in military prisons without formal charges or trial'.[20]

The U.S. House of Representatives was also unconvinced. The testimony presented during the March hearings had raised deep concerns while Liberia's diplomatic offensive had done little to offer reassurance. Subsequently, in July, the arrest of one Ellen Johnson-Sirleaf – well-publicised in the U.S. – appeared to confirm the March testimonies, heightening unease within Congress about the Reagan administration's Liberia policy. A Harvard-educated Americo-Liberian, and Minister for Finance in the Tolbert administration, at the time of her arrest Johnson-Sirleaf had already acquired something of a reputation as a financier, business leader and, more recently back in Liberia, as an upcoming politician. A strident critic of the Doe regime, her arrest followed allegations that in a speech delivered in the U.S. she had referred to Liberian government officials as 'idiots'.[21]

Johnson-Sirleaf's arrest led to an international outcry which was immediate and sustained.[22] Protests came from four West African heads-of-state while Congress passed a resolution calling for the suspension of U.S. aid to Liberia until her release.[23] This uproar, together with congressional criticism of

---

*   Despite its first issue's laudatory tone, this journal, edited by Rufus Darpoh, soon fell out of favour with the regime and was suppressed.

America's Liberia policy, compelled the Reagan administration to take action. Edward Derwinski[24] was dispatched to Liberia with instructions to acquaint President Doe first-hand with the rising tide of opinion against his regime. Derwinski's mission, however, proved abortive, Doe claiming to be campaigning in a remote part of the country and unable to meet him. The Reagan administration responded by ordering the suspension forthwith of $25.5 million in economic support already earmarked for Liberia.

Doe portrayed this measure as an outrage, perpetrated by a nation to which signal service had been rendered for well over a century. Liberia, he said, was not prepared to countenance this 'foreign interference' in its internal affairs; and if the U.S. was now acting in a hostile fashion Liberia would seek friends and protectors elsewhere. To this end the Foreign Minister would now embark on a trip to Libya to discuss the modalities of a closer relationship. However, indicative of the extent to which Liberia was dependent on the U.S., the suspension of aid soon created a major economic crisis and the prospect of social unrest. Doe responded by abandoning his threats and acquiescing to U.S. demands. In late September over two dozen political prisoners were released, including Johnson-Sirleaf. A day later the suspended funds were released by the U.S. Treasury.

***

On 15 October some 900,000 of Liberia's 2 million citizens went to the polls to choose a new president and legislature. The latter was to consist of a Senate of 26 seats and a House of Representatives of 64. By election day three parties other than Doe's National Democratic Party had surmounted the formidable obstacles placed in their way by SECOM and made it onto the ballot papers: the Unity Party, the Liberia Unification Party and the Liberian Action Party (LAP). In the presidential election Doe was opposed by Jackson Doe, Edward Kesselly and Gabriel Kpolleh.[25] The results would be announced by SECOM within 15 days.

Despite threats to boycott the elections, mainly from opposition parties unable to secure registration, large numbers turned out to vote. When the results were announced interim President Doe was declared winner with 51% of the vote, causing, according to Archbishop Francis (privately) 'a gloom which was not tempered by the oft-repeated statement in government media that the result was God-ordained'.[26] In the legislature elections Doe's party captured 73 of the 90 seats. Of the remaining elected members many refused to take their seats and those who did were expelled from their parties. Even before the results were announced there were widespread allegations of fraud. Independent observers and foreign journalists were said to have uncovered a number of irregularities including 'multiple voting at some military polling places' as well as a compulsion on voters in numerous villages to state their preferences in the presence of soldiers'.[27] Nonetheless election day was said by at least one overseas observer to have been 'by all accounts, the first genuine election in the nation's history'.[28] But many other reports were damning, claiming that the poll was 'marred by allegations of widespread fraud and rigging'. Indeed, several independent observers believed that the LAP candidate for the presidency, Jackson Doe, who was placed second, had in fact won the contest. Doe had offset this, it was said, by having the ballots counted in a secret location by handpicked staff.[29] On the whole those declaring the poll to be fraudulent outnumbered those who maintained that despite shortcomings it was fair. And eventually the former view came to predominate both in the popular mind, the local and international press and among historians. It was also the view of the U.S. Congress, expressed in its resolution No 367 of 18 September 1985.[30]

Whatever about the outcry against the poll's validity at the time, Samuel Doe was duly inaugurated as first president of Liberia's Second Republic on 6 January 1986. Aware that he was under international scrutiny the now substantive president adopted a conciliatory tone, proclaiming a wish for national reconciliation as well as a willingness to work with the opposition. And, as he had done when he first seized power, he nominated several opposition members to his cabinet. He also freed eighteen prominent political prisoners and a journalist. Persuaded by these gestures some opposition members who had refused to take their seats in the legislature, including Tuan Wreh, founding member of LAP, changed their position. But Doe's apparent benevolence was merely cosmetic. There was no genuine desire to share power or introduce a democratic form of government.

***

On 12 November 1985 a genuine coup attempt was mounted by the Gios and Manos of Nimba County led by Quiwonkpa. On that day, at the head of a small group of well-armed soldiers, Quiwonkpa crossed from Sierra Leone into Liberia and made his way unopposed to Monrovia where he seized the national radio station. Quiwonkpa had calculated on the mass of the people coming out onto the streets in support; and on the non-Krahn elements in the armed forces mutinying. In the period of uncertainty which followed the radio broadcast there was some rejoicing in the streets, but this was to be short-lived. Doe reacted swiftly, summoning reinforcements from Camp Schieffelin – mainly Krahn – and together with the presidential guard capturing by noon most of the insurgents, re-taking the radio station and re-establishing order in the streets. Quiwonkpa evaded capture for a few days but eventually was arrested and summarily executed, his body mutilated and dismembered. There followed a grotesque and ghoulish parade of his body parts through the streets of Monrovia, reminiscent of the Paris mob bearing the dismembered bodies of royalty into the streets during the French revolution.

The failed coup gave Doe the opportunity to deal decisively with anyone who threatened his position. Despite calls for restraint from the American ambassador, purges were conducted in Monrovia and in Nimba County, mainly against Gio and Mano. Particular attention was paid to those who were known to have demonstrated in favour of the attempted coup. Wildly varying estimates of between 400 and 3,000 people were executed.[31] The scale of the slaughter of Gio and Mano was such as to suggest that eventually they would unite against the regime and that Doe's days were therefore numbered.[32] Among those imprisoned were the leaders of the three opposition parties which had participated in the elections (Jackson Doe, Kesselly and Gabriel Kpolleh). Doe also availed of the opportunity to return Johnson-Sirleaf to prison. Other well-known Liberians jailed included Byron Tarr, LAP secretary-general, Isaac Bantu, a journalist and correspondent and, once again, Momolu Sirleaf, publisher of *Footprints*. There is no evidence that any of those arrested had any involvement in the coup.[33]

***

Initially the U.S. administration made little effort to respond to the chorus of criticism which followed Liberia's elections. In fact, the State Department's first statement on this subject did not come until 10 December and only then before a session of the Senate subcommittee on Africa when Chester Crocker declared that things were by no means as bad as had been represented. It was true, he said, that the election had been marked by 'shortcomings', but there were also many 'noteworthy aspects'.[34] For example, four political parties had taken part, there had been press coverage of opposition campaigning and the election had been conducted in an orderly fashion, despite some minor incidents. His sub-text was that the 'quite diplomacy' of the State Department and its embassy staff in Monrovia had played a part in securing these favourable results. And Crocker went on to characterise the outcome as an imperfect beginning of an experiment in democracy, 'a benchmark for future elections.'

Crocker told the hearing that the policy of 'quiet diplomacy' (non-confrontational, behind the scenes dialogue) also had been in effect employed in the wake of the failed Quiwonkpa coup. When the Doe regime vented its fury on all conceivable opposition, the Reagan administration had protested privately, while Ambassador Vernon Walters, in a telephone call to President Doe, urged caution and the State Department's Bureau of Human Rights called for restraint. Crocker failed to add that little notice was taken of such pleas. He concluded that if the U.S. administration had not intervened, quietly and behind the scenes, the ravages wrought might have been much worse. It must be said that Crocker's defence of U.S. policy did not impress the hearing, for by its close on 18 December a resolution was unanimously adopted urging the administration to punish the Doe regime for its failure to conduct free and fair elections and for its flouting of the democratic process in other respects.[35] But this resolution was not binding on the U.S. administration, nor would it have much impact.

Crocker was to appear again before the congressional subcommittee on Africa in January 1986 and, although more willing to accept that excesses had occurred in the wake of the Quiwonkpa coup, he made it clear that administration policy would not change.[36] Following this hearing the House voted a resolution, similar to that passed by the Senate subcommittee, linking U.S. aid to the performance of the Liberian government. The chief arm of the administration dealing with Liberia, the State Department, responded to these resolutions by reducing the aid amounts for 1986, although it was felt by some observers that 'the exigencies of the Gramm–Hollings Act* may have played an even more important role than human rights in bringing about these reductions'.[37] That Act, passed in 1985, required mandatory budget restrictions to reduce federal government borrowings to manageable levels.

***

The half-hearted attempts by the U.S. administration to impose restraint on the Doe regime, evident among other things, in the swiftness with which the suspended \$25.5 million aid package was restored in September 1985** when only a part of the conditions imposed had been met, was interpreted by Doe as weakness. No opportunity to pursue his agenda was missed. And when excesses reached such a point that a reluctant U.S. administration again insisted on restraint, the regime knew in its heart that token gestures would be enough. What was foremost in U.S. administration thinking was the value of Liberia to America's strategic interests. And the corollary to this was the conviction that the Doe leadership was most likely to ensure the stability of the relationship. Moreover, Doe was seen as a weak leader who could be controlled through his desperate need for economic and military assistance. Provided his abuse of human and civil rights remained beneath a certain threshold – commensurate with that to be found among neighbouring regimes in West Africa – the U.S. need not interfere.

Notes

1 About Liberia, 14 February 1985.
2 A.T. Text of President Doe's address to Church leaders, dated 17 January 1985.
3 Made by letter on 24 January 1985.
4 A.T. Doe to Francis, 28 January 1985.
5 Known to his confreres as 'S. John Murray' to differentiate him from another John Murray.
6 The staff, he pointed out, were 'the ones who actually draft the legislation'.
7 He had visited between 17 January and 4 February 1985.
8 Seyon wrote the influential pamphlet opposing the increase in the price of rice in 1979.
9 His gave his testimony the title: 'The Threat to Democracy in Liberia'.
10 LTRC, Consolidated Report, Chapter 5, 'Human Rights Abuses during the Rice Riots and Doe era', 1995, 105.
11 According to Seyon between 1979 and 1983 military assistance from the U.S. had increased by 846% to \$12.7 million.
12 The Wall Street Journal, 23 March 1987, 'Better Ways to Allocate Foreign Aid' (Harry J. Shaw).
13 See Massing Report, Best Friends, Violations of Human Rights in Liberia, America's Closest Ally in Africa, May 1986 (A Fund for Free Expression Report), 14.
14 A Liberian priest ordained for the Archdiocese of Monrovia.
15 28 May 1985.
16 Eddie Momoh, West Africa, 3 June 1985, 1096–1097.

*   The Gramm-Rudman-Hollings Act, provided for automatic spending cuts to take effect if the President and Congress failed to reach established targets.
**   When Johnson-Sirleaf was released.

17 Ibid.
18 6 May.
19 Richard J. Gilbert, Counsellor for Public Affairs.
20 West Africa, 'Dateline Africa', 19 August 1985, 1719.
21 Ibid., (Tunde Agbabiake, in Monrovia, 'Doe defends Sirleaf's arrest').
22 The New York Times, 26 August 1985.
23 Michael Massing, op. cit., 18.
24 Appointed Counsellor to the State Department by President Reagan.
25 The New York Times, 16 October 1985.
26 Report to Extraordinary Council, Liberia, June 1986.
27 Massing, op. cit., 21.
28 Ibid.
29 The Los Angeles Times, 25 July 1986 (Scott Kraft – Los Angeles Time Service).
30 Survey of Activities, vol. 99, 652. https://books.google.ie/books?id=4B7O51eI_R-oC&pg=PA582&lpg=PA582&dq=survey+of+Activities' accessed 20 March 2020.
31 Adekeye Adebajo, op.cit., 30. See also Adekeye Adebajo, Building Peace in West Africa (Liberia, Sierra Leone, and Guinea-Bissau), (Occ. Papers Series, U.S. and UK, 2002), 46. He estimates the number of Gios and Manos killed at 3,000.
32 Heneryatta Ballah McNair, 'Ethnicity, Politics and Social Conflict: The Quest for Peace in Liberia', Penn State McNair Journal (2003), 10, 63.
33 See Massing op. cit., 23.
34 Hearing before the Senate subcommittee on African Affairs, 99th Congress, 1st session, 10 December 1985, 41.
35 Resolution 271, 18 December 1985 passed/agreed to in Senate, The Congressional Record, for 18 December 1985 (S. Res. 271).
36 January 1986.
37 See, Michael Massing, op. cit., 51.

6 Economic crisis and increasing international scrutiny

It will be recalled that reacting to Liberia's fraudulent elections and the post-coup reprisals both houses of the U.S. Congress passed resolutions calling for the suspension of American aid unless all political prisoners were released, freedom to organise political parties was accorded, a truly representative civilian government was formed, and genuine efforts were made to achieve national reconciliation. President Doe appeared to respond to this stern warning in March 1986, lifting a ban on the activities of professional and student organisations and restoring *habeas corpus*.

This response went some way to deflating American and international criticism. But such measures did not lead to any significant relaxation of tension on the ground. For in the same month, three influential Liberian political parties, the Unity Party, the Liberia Unification Party and the Liberian Action Party formed a 'Grand Coalition' and began to campaign for new elections.[1] They were quickly joined by the students and by elements of the independent press. A return to violence on the streets was not long in following. Teachers had been on strike since 10 March 1986 to protest against the non-payment of salaries for several months. Eight days later a student demonstration, demanding that the salaries be paid forthwith, was confronted by armed police. *The Sun Times* carried reports that over a hundred students suffered beatings and gun-shot injuries.[2] The Ministry of National Defence countered that no student, or any other citizen or resident, had been shot at during or after the demonstration though whips and rattans were used to disperse them. Whatever the details of the encounter,[3] the incident underlined the reality that far from bringing peace and stability the arrival of a so-called civilian government had heightened Liberia's sense of crisis.

***

Doe, who had not been seen in public since his inauguration, was becoming increasingly isolated, distrustful now not only of political opposition but of the civil service and the army. The latter institution had not been paid for months. Nor was democratic expression of political dissent to be tolerated. A mass rally by the Grand Coalition, scheduled for 21 March 1986, was declared illegal two days before it was due to take place.[4] A month later, Amos Sawyer was to

DOI: 10.4324/9781003219309-8

break his silence for the first time since taking refuge in the U.S.* The occasion was the 18th annual academic conference of the Liberian Studies Association. Taking for his topic 'the making of the Liberian Constitution',[5] Sawyer told his audience that while Liberia had in truth a democratic Constitution, the current government was unwilling to implement it. And that was the long and the short of it!

***

As for criticism of U.S. administration policy – coming mainly from American and international civil and human rights organisations – at least one source of contention was shortly to be resolved early in April 1986 when Chester Crocker visited Liberia and met all party leaders – something which hitherto U.S. embassy officials had refused to do. But this heralded no change in policy. The Doe regime was certainly under greater scrutiny than in the past, yet aid continued to be disbursed, not on the same scale as before, but sufficient to prop up the regime. Military assistance, too, continued to be given, although the administration downplayed its significance insisting it was confined to providing housing for soldiers and making the Liberian armed forces a more disciplined and better-trained body.

***

On 6 June 1986 advocates of the 'quiet diplomacy' policy had every reason to feel vindicated. On that date, having been under sustained pressure to do so from the U.S. administration, President Doe granted an unconditional pardon to all persons alleged to have participated in the Quiwonkpa coup. Among those released was Ellen Johnson-Sirleaf. A few days later the Grand Coalition sat down to reconciliation talks with the ruling National Democratic Party of Liberia. The talks had been urged on the parties by the U.S. while the Liberian Council of Churches had been accepted by both sides to oversee the process. President Doe not only had agreed to participate but he now emerged from seclusion to proclaim Liberia's greatest needs were 'reconciliation and reconstruction'; and that he personally would lead a crusade to achieve them.

However, this initiative was to run into trouble within a matter of days when the LCC abandoned its mediation role.[6] It did so, a letter to the Grand Coalition explained,[7] when its representatives 'had come to the president with proposals for an agreed agenda. Enraged by these the president had given it as his 'considered opinion that the LCC was biased and one-sided, favouring the other parties ... and should stop its mediation in this process of reconciliation forthwith'.[8]

Although the breakdown of the talks appeared to mark the end of any hope of reconciliation, there was at least one positive development which suggested that all might not be lost. In his 1986 Redemption Day speech President Doe took his crusade for 'reconciliation and reconstruction' a step further, inviting exiled Liberians, 'to return home and contribute their quota towards the

---

* He had been banned from all political activities since February 1985 and, after suffering an arson attack on his house, had fled to the U.S. on 21 April 1986.

progress and development of our country'.[9] Weeks before, he had already signalled his readiness to welcome them by granting appeals for clemency by two
exiles, former Vice-President Bennie D. Warner and former Army Chief of
Staff, Henry Koboi Johnson. Now he was reminding Liberians, whether at
home or abroad, that the country belonged to them, 'from Cape Mount to
Cape Palmas, from the highest mountain to the lowest plain...'[10] And to show
that this was not hollow sentiment, he declared that he would recommend to
the National Legislature the amending of the contentious Decree 88A because
Liberia was under 'a constitutional government', and this meant that now 'a
great deal of fear had been removed and Liberians were living in peace'.[11]

Among exiled Liberians who responded to President Doe's appeal was the
quixotic Gabriel Baccus Matthews. According to a Liberian embassy press
release in Washington, Matthews, on his return to Liberia, called for 'dialogue,
reconciliation and national development'.[12] He also spent an hour with the
president during which he expressed his 'preparedness to work in the interest of
the Liberian nation and its people'.[13] Another mentioned in the embassy press
release was Johnson-Sirleaf, recently granted clemency by President Doe.
During the past three weeks she had met twice with the president pro-tem of
the Liberian Senate, John G. Rancy, telling him that 'all patriotic citizens ...
were ready to honour and obey the national laws as prescribed by the constitution, and that there was a need for continuous dialogue among all political
leaders in order to achieve national development'.[14]

Johnson-Sirleaf, was not impressed by claims that she was clamouring for
reconciliation and national development. *The Mirror* of 31 June 1986 quoted her as
saying that the stumbling block to true reconciliation had been the government. It
was the government not the opposition, she said, that had effectively broken off
the last attempt at reconciliation – the all-party talks mediated by the LCC. And it
was up to the government to 'recommence those talks.'

***

On the streets of Monrovia there was little genuine sign of reconciliation. 18
August witnessed violence when riot police attacked a group of women
returning from a prayer service for opposition leaders in detention held at the
First Methodist Church.[15] The meeting had been organised by the wives of the
three main opposition-party leaders* who had been arrested on 5 August on
charges of contempt and consigned to the notorious Belle Yalla prison in
remote Lofa county. They had first been brought to court on 1 August, for
representing themselves as a 'Grand Coalition' without securing the legal
recognition required for such an entity. Fines of US$1,000 each had been
imposed which the leaders refused to pay. The grounds offered by the regime
for attacking the prayer meeting was that the gathering, consisting of about 500
people, apparently had violated an order prohibiting people from walking in
groups.[16] During the meeting worshippers had been told that the wives would

*   Jackson F. Doe (LAP), Edward B. Kesselly (UP) and Gabriel William Kpoleh
    (LUP).

present a petition to the Supreme Court and were invited to join with them. Also attacked on the same occasion were the homes of Johnson-Sirleaf and that of her mother both of whom were returning to their Congotown residences from the prayer service.

The three leaders were released some ten days later when the fines were paid, mainly by anonymous donors.[17] They then attended a prayer service of thanksgiving – the government did not interfere – taking the opportunity to re-assert their commitment to eradicate human rights abuses, especially those relating to detention. Among promises made was one to close down the Belle Yalla prison. A few days later, manifestly still a Grand Coalition, they gave a press conference in which they spoke at some length about that prison where 'many innocent people had been killed or subjected to conditions which made survival impossible'.[18] They also alleged the presence of mass graves in its vicinity containing the bodies of the executed.[19]

***

A week after the attack on her home, Johnson-Sirleaf again fled Liberia. She surfaced some days later in New York stating that she had gone into exile because her home had been ransacked and the chairman of Doe's National Democratic Party of Liberia party (Keikura B. Kpoto), had threatened her life.[20] J. Emmanuel Bowier, Liberia's Washington Embassy spokesperson, told *The New York Times* that his government was unaware that Johnson-Sirleaf had left the country and that, in any event, twelve men had been arrested for attacking her house. Kpoto was less accommodating. Contacted by the *Times* he ridiculed the notion that he had threatened Johnson-Sirleaf's life and accused her of 'cheap politics to advance her political standing'. The attack on her home, he had no doubt, had been carried out 'by disgruntled demonstrators who were angered when she failed to attend a rally'.[21]

***

1 September 1986 saw the *Daily Observer* back on the streets of Monrovia after an absence of 20 months. Perhaps the most outspoken of the independent Liberian newspapers, the *Observer* had a long history of conflict with successive Liberian governments. In 1953, faced with imminent suppression, its then editor, the renowned Albert Porte, bravely faced down the authorities with a blistering editorial in defence of freedom of the press, explaining how difficult it was to steer an even course between the desires of the people and those of the government.[22] Now, in 1986, after over a year of silence, the current editor (Kenneth Y. Best, a nephew of Porte) chose to re-print the 1953 editorial, commenting that little had changed in the interval. Clearly the *Daily Observer* was not about to change its colours, stubbornly resolving to preserve its independence.[23] And now back on the streets the *Observer* was again pledging itself to its duties as an independent newspaper, 'determined to continue ferreting out the truth and reflecting public opinion…without fear or favour'. Its rallying cry would be that of the recently deceased Porte who had preached for more than 50 years the doctrine that 'the surest safeguard of state security is more freedom and liberty'.

***

Nonetheless the *Daily Observer* and other independent newspapers continued to be persecuted and the intensifying gloom over Liberia was compounded by news in mid-December that after forty-five years of service Pan-American World Airways was suspending flights to Liberia from 1 February 1987.[24] This was truly a bad blow to morale since Pan-Am's four flights weekly into Liberia's Robertsfield International Airport, accounted for 38% of the airport's income. In the same week came news that the official allocations for U.S. foreign aid in 1987 signalled a 50% cut over the previous year.[25] This reduction did not reflect a change in U.S. policy towards Liberia. Other African countries also receiving a significantly reduced aid allocation included Niger, Mauritius, Madagascar, Chad and Botswana. Closer to the U.S., Jamaica and the Dominican Republic also suffered large reductions. The principal cause was not dissatisfaction at the manner in which assistance was being used. Rather it was a result of the Gramm-Rudman-Hollings Act[*] which led to a 34% cut in expenditure amounting to $1 billion for the fiscal year 1987. As the U.S. could not afford to reduce aid to countries such as Israel, Egypt and Pakistan, there was little left to conduct foreign policy elsewhere.[26]

***

In the opening week of 1987 Liberia was to be momentarily distracted from its economic and political woes by the visit of U.S. Secretary of State, George P. Shultz. Despite the significant budgetary-imposed reduction in financial assistance to Africa, the exigencies of the Cold War still required vigorously conducted diplomatic initiatives towards that continent. To this end Shultz set out on an eight-day visit to 'six African countries with close ties to the West', including Liberia. This was the first time the Reagan administration, subject to much negative comment on account of its policy towards apartheid South Africa, had sent a Secretary of State to Africa.[27] The purpose of the visit was primarily to stiffen resistance to the Soviet Union's strategic ambitions, although Shultz was also expected to promote the free market economy, defend U.S. policy towards South Africa and raise the issue of human rights while in Liberia and Kenya. Liberia was one of the most important African countries for the U.S., hosting the Omega navigation station serving sea and airborne traffic in the eastern Atlantic as well as all U.S. diplomatic traffic for West Africa; hosting, too, a Voice of America transmitter covering all of sub-Saharan Africa. Moreover, Monrovia was the headquarters of U.S. Intelligence for the region, while Robertsfield airport – with Liberian agreement - was designated for the rapid deployment of U.S. forces. Finally, Liberia was the location for important U.S. commercial interests, not least the rubber producer, Firestone, with its vast plantation near Harbel. Secretary of State Shultz's visit at the very least was necessary to ensure that such assets remained secure.

Shultz arrived days after the announcement of the results of December municipal and legislative by-elections, the first testing of the waters since the

---

[*]   See note, p. 59.

October 1985 poll. The turnout had been poor, described by the *Daily Observer* as a 'vote of no confidence'. Three days before the election SECOM had changed the rules and Doe's NDPL party won almost all the seats. One of those who had been expected to contest the elections – seeking a Senatorial seat – was Gabriel Baccus Matthews who after returning from exile and apparently making a temporary peace with the regime, had succeeded in registering his United People's Party (UPP) party. However, shortly before the poll Matthews had withdrawn from the contest, following a statement from the SECOM chairman that any candidate who succeeded in the election but refused to take his seat would be imprisoned or fined punitively. Thus, the government, which controlled SECOM, sought to undermine the chief tactic of the opposition in its efforts to secure new elections, namely the continuing boycott of parliament by those opposition leaders elected in the October 1985 poll.

The failure, again, of free and fair elections to transpire led commentators to speculate that Shultz would take a hard line with the regime. Already the White House for once had defied its own policy of 'quiet diplomacy' and, through the State Department, had issued a public rebuke to the Doe government.[28]

Some leading members of the Liberian opposition appeared to have been flattered by the arrival of such a high-ranking American delegation and held their fire. The Shultz visit fondly reminded them of other Secretaries of State such as Edward Reilly Stettinius who had come in 1945, William Rogers of the Nixon administration – Nixon himself had come when he was vice president to Eisenhower – and, more recently, Henry Kissinger of the Ford administration. But others, far from over-awed, were not afraid to accuse the U.S. of complicity in the current collapse. In advance of the visit, after paying due deference to the long association between the two countries, the *Daily Observer*, again sailing dangerously close to the wind, spoke frankly.[29] Although Liberia had received more than $400 million of U.S. aid since 1980 its economy was in tatters. It was true that the actions taken by the U.S. administration in the face of rigged elections and human rights violations had forced the regime to release political prisoners, permit the re-opening of some newspapers, and enter reconciliation talks. But taking everything into account the *Daily Observer* was compelled to the conclusion that there had been little real improvement.

As it turned out, Secretary of State Shultz's visit proved a disappointment although the government, understandably, hailed it a turning point in relations with the U.S. The opening phase of the visit – the entire affair took place on 14 January and lasted a mere six hours – proved a fiasco. After arriving at Robertsfield to a 17 gun-salute, Shultz convened a press conference at the American Embassy only to find the event boycotted by most of the journalists and photographers. They, apparently, had taken umbrage at the insistence of U.S. security agents that a sniffer-dog should inspect their equipment. Nor had they been impressed to see the sniffer-dog in question conducted on a chain by the only black man in the delegation, a Mr Harris.[30] The only members of the media to remain at the conference were a correspondent from the *Daily*

Observer (there because it was felt in press circles someone should relay to the Liberian people what was occurring), a BBC representative and a journalist from the New China News Agency. The conference was something of a 'damp squib', apart from the fact that it was learned that Mr Harris was an explosive expert at the U.S. State Department while the sniffer-dog, a two-year-old named 'Alco', had undergone nine weeks training for his speciality. One official from the State Department earnestly imparted the intelligence that dogs were now more effective than explosive detectors. The customary entertainment for Mrs Helena Shultz – treated to a grand performance by the National Cultural Troupe during a luncheon in her honour hosted by Mrs Eva Blamo, wife of Foreign Minister J. Bernard Blamo – created a sense of normality. So too did the 'grand dinner'.

At the airport Shultz had told President Doe that Liberia 'must make changes in its economic policy', and that the U.S. regarded the reconciliation process as of the greatest importance.[31] When he again spoke of political reconciliation at the dinner, President Doe replied, with a pained expression, that Liberia was the 'only African country without political prisoners' and went on to criticise U.S. policy towards South Africa and Namibia. But it was only later, when Shultz emerged from his seventy-five minutes of talks with the president, that it became apparent those looking to America for help in Liberia's deepening crisis were to be disappointed. Instead of biding his time before his scheduled forty-minute meeting with eight opposition leaders, Shultz announced to the world that the Liberian political situation had significantly improved, that 'genuine progress' had taken place. And he called on the political opposition to abandon its boycott of parliament, adding that it was his impression the 1985 election had been 'quite open' and that only the 'vote-counting process' had raised concerns.

Shultz's meeting with the Grand Coalition and other opposition leaders saw him presented with a ten-page document outlining Liberia's problems and suggesting how the U.S. might best help.[32] There is no evidence that this made any impression on the Secretary of State. If anything, his remarks during his visit and afterwards served to deepen the divide on Liberia between the Reagan administration and Congress.[33] In the U.S. one of those quickest off the mark in calling Shultz to order was Michael Posner, executive director of the Lawyers Committee for Human Rights. Writing in *The New York Times* he described Shultz's assertion that there was a free press in Liberia 'bewildering' and his general conclusions as 'gross distortions' of the reality. Whichever way one looked at it, according to Posner, Doe's was simply a 'brutal regime'! Within Liberia, too, Shultz's press conference statement that Liberia 'had a free press, an elected government and no political prisoners', caused dismay.[34] Objectors pointed out that while five newspapers were still appearing, a further two recently had been suppressed, the *Sun Times* and *Footprints*.

Doubtless the U.S. administration's benign approach towards the regime was reinforced by fears that Doe might look elsewhere for support. And there was evidence that this was not beyond the bounds of possibility. In a rare press conference, held on 19 January 1987, after the appearance of strange-looking armoured vehicles on the streets of Monrovia, President Doe gave details of a recent visit to the Republic of Romania where he had secured from his 'friend' President Ceausescu 'a few pieces of equipment to defend the Executive Mansion and some strategic areas of the country'.[35]

One positive result of the Shultz visit was an agreement that the U.S. should dispatch a delegation of experts to advise the Liberian government on economic matters. Doe announced that the delegation's purpose would be to help to produce a working document to overcome Liberia's economic problems. The American understanding of the proposed delegation's role was very different; it would be far more intrusive, 'running the economy of Liberia for the indefinite future' and 'having the authority to co-sign all government cheques.'[36] Ostensibly this control would not be absolute, for while the American experts would act on the 'level of deputy government ministers, President Doe would still retain final control over decisions'. But the sub-text was that the Liberian president, dignity preserved, would readily endorse the delegation's proposals.

Another team due to arrive in Liberia in April was from the International Monetary Fund (IMF), coming for 'routine inspection and consultation'. The IMF had already rejected giving further loans to Liberia, currently some $160 million in repayment arrears. That decision had been taken when, shortly before an IMF audit team was due to arrive in Monrovia, 'a mysterious fire in the finance ministry had gutted the 11th floor, where all the records were kept'.[37]

***

February 1987 brought to light startling new information on Liberia's economy and on the effectiveness of overseas aid. This emerged as the U.S. Congressional Foreign Affairs Subcommittee on Africa prepared to hold hearings on economic assistance authorisations for 1987 and 1988.[38] U.S. economists who had just returned from Monrovia were quoted as saying that the public sector was being looted. And categorical evidence, rather than anecdotal, of the depth of the crisis was provided when Senator Edward Kennedy published a summary of an audit of Liberia's use of U.S. assistance – both economic and military – for the period 1980–86, complied by the U.S. General Accounting Office (GAO).[39] The audit found that of the $434 million contributed during this period, some $84 million had gone missing. Damning also were the conclusions that 'U.S. economic and food assistance to Liberia' had 'faced a high risk of diversion and/or misuse since 1980'. Significantly, too, the audit declared that the U.S. administration had been reluctant, for foreign policy reasons, 'to enforce certain conditions designed to promote fiscal and economic reforms.'[40] Curiously, the auditors found no evidence of misuse in military assistance programs.[41] However the explanation for this was that U.S. military personnel closely supervised the building of soldiers' accommodation – on which most of the military aid was spent.

Kennedy had requested a copy of the GAO audit as early as June 1986 in response to representations by various justice and human rights groups in the

U.S. that the Liberian government was engaged in widespread corruption. Now he was declaring that 'General Doe had used his position to enrich himself and his associates at the expense of the American taxpayer', adding that severing the U.S.–Doe support line was long overdue and that unless the U.S. moved decisively it ran 'the risk of losing not simply our friendship with Liberia, but also our significant interests in the country'.[42]

Kennedy's declarations provoked a sharp response from Emmanuel Bowier of the Liberian embassy. He told *The New York Times* that he doubted whether Kennedy's summary was 'a true report,' adding defiantly, 'we in Liberia are tired of these threats. The U.S. cannot dictate what our priorities should be'.[43] The relationship between Liberia and the U.S., he added, was 'not based on an individual's opinions and will survive long after Senator Kennedy and President Doe are no longer around'. And he invited Kennedy to come to Liberia 'to see for himself how we run our government'. In the meantime, the Senator should realise that 'Liberia is not a plantation or factory that he or anyone else can close down by simply dismissing the employees and declaring bankruptcy...'

Kennedy's attack on administration policy towards Liberia, coming within a month of Secretary Shultz's positive assessment of the Doe regime, attracted considerable attention. The *New York Times* referred to dissident voices 'rebuking George P. Shultz for flying in the face of the facts.'[44] In the light of the damning GAO report these voices had now grown louder. And U.S. officials had told *West Africa* that because of the audit the Reagan administration 'now faced an uphill battle in getting congressional approval for the recommended assistance package for Liberia'.[45]

***

Faced with a barrage of criticism of its Liberian policy, administration officials were critical of the GAO report, questioning some of its statistics and finding its conclusions misleading.[46] One official said that while in the past there had certainly been embezzlement of funds, 'currently we don't see tremendous problems as far as the misuse of funds given them'.[47] The point was made that not all of the assistance went through the hands of the Liberian government. Another official stated that 'most of the developmental assistance... whether agricultural, educational, or health care' was 'pretty well handled...' And a third rather patronisingly explained that although Liberia was now 'being run by people who are unsophisticated and uneducated', the U.S. had 'expended a lot of time in trying to steer them down the right road'. In addition, most of Liberia's 'human rights' problems seemed to have been overcome and there was 'pretty good freedom of the press', probably more than almost any place in Africa'.[48] Patently, the Reagan administration had circled the wagons on its Liberia policy.

The astute *West Africa* staff writer, Eddie Momoh, who had predicted in January 1987 that Doe would be compelled to sack several of his ministers, was proven correct in April when the president conducted a major cabinet reshuffle, removing four and appointing three new ministers. One of the latter was Emmanuel Bowier, the voice of Liberia's Washington Embassy.[49] This young journalist had vigorously defended the Doe regime against its many critics in America, including Edward Kennedy, Bob Berkeley[50] and Ellen Johnson-Sirleaf. It was Bowier who had responded to Kennedy's call for the cessation of all aid to Liberia. And his loyalty to his president was never to waver, at least until November 1990, when civil war had taken a grip.* Doe's reshuffle directly followed the formalisation of the agreement with the U.S. for the supply of economic advisers to assist the Liberian government. It was now agreed that seventeen 'specialists' or 'experts' would be sent. Momoh regarded the reshuffle as a pre-emptive strike against the influence of such a group. Through it the president had succeeded in installing his key supporters in the country's main financial ministries and institutions as a countermeasure to the 17 experts. The new appointees would be able to keep an eye on the U.S. team and its designs. This again proved an accurate assessment of what was to happen.

Notes

1 J. Gus Liebenow, 'Liberian Political Opposition in the Post-Election Period', *Liberian Studies Journal*, XIII, 2 (1988), 246–247.
2 20 March 1986.
3 The LTRC makes no mention of this.
4 Ibid.
5 West Africa, 21 April 1986, 825.
6 Daily Star (Monrovia), vol. 1. no. 195, 28 June 1986.
7 The letter, dated 25 June 1985, was addressed to the chairman of the coalition, Dr Edward Kesselly. It was signed by Archbishop Michael Francis and four leaders from other denominations.
8 Daily Star (Monrovia), 28 June 1986; See also The Standard, vol. 1, no. 71. 28 June 1986.
9 Ibid.
10 Ibid.
11 Ibid.
12 Liberian Information Centre, Embassy of the Republic of Liberia, Washington, 24 July 1986.
13 Ibid.
14 Ibid.
15 The Sun Times, 19 August 1986.
16 Ibid., 20 August 1986.
17 Daily Observer, 1 September 1986.
18 Ibid., 3 September 1986.
19 The LTRC refers to the appalling conditions endured by prisoners during the Doe era. 'Conditions of detention were abysmal: overcrowding, little or no sanitation, and generally no medical treatment. Prisoners were routinely flogged with rattan switches and pieces of steel belt radial tire… Verbal and physical abuse, harassment,

---

*   On 30 May 1990, as rebels approached Monrovia the New York Times reported, 'Among those who have not been seen here and believed to have fled the country is one of the president's closest friends and collaborators, J. Emmanuel Bowier, Minister for Information… The Information Ministry seems rudderless since Mr Bowier left for Washington as part of a delegation that sought to explain the fighting to American officials.'

and intimidations to extort money from prisoners were the norm' (LTRC Consolidated Final Report, vol. 2, Chapter 5, 92).

20 The New York Times, 21 September 1986.
21 Ibid.
22 Daily Observer, 1 September 1986, 4. The original title of the newspaper was the Liberian Observer.
23 Ibid.
24 Daily Observer, Tuesday, 16 December 1986.
25 The Washington Post, 16 December 1986.
26 Ibid.
27 The New York Times, 4 January 1987 (David Shipler).
28 West Africa, 12 January 1987, 86.
29 14 January 1987.
30 Daily Observer, 15 January 1987.
31 The New York Times, 15 January 1987.
32 See copy of this document in A.T.
33 See David B. Ottaway, The Washington Post, 15 January 1987.
34 See David Shipler, The New York Times, 16 January 1987.
35 The press conference in the Executive Mansion took place on 19 January 1987. He visited Romania in October 1986.
36 The Washington Times, 2 April 1987.
37 The New York Times, 10 May 1987 (James Brooke).
38 About Liberia, February 1987, no. 38. (James Butty, SMA Social Concerns department, Washington).
39 The GAO audit findings show that $16.5 million of commodity assistance support had not been accounted for since 1984. It also found regular unauthorised withdrawals of funds totalling $1.7 million in 1986 and diversion of $12 million in economic support funds. See, Kendall Wills, The New York Times, 22 February 1987
40 See, About Liberia, February 1987, no. 38.
41 Ibid.
42 The New York Times, 22 February 1987.
43 22 February 1987.
44 Ibid.
45 West Africa, 26 January 1987, 179.
46 Don McLeod, The Washington Times, 2 April 1987; cf., Insight, 30 March 1987.
47 Ibid.
48 Ibid.
49 West Africa, 6 April 1987, 648.
50 Author of the Lawyers Committee for Human Rights Report.

7 Popular support for the regime falters, but backing from the Reagan Administration continues

The University of Liberia (UL) had been a cockpit of unrest and dissent for over a decade. As during Tolbert's final years, UL was also to prove a constant thorn in the side of the Doe regime, and efforts to extract it had never succeeded. Expulsions, imprisonments, the imposition of fines, closure of the institution, violence – all had been employed to silence Liberia's intellectual elite. Now, on 5 April 1987, the university was again shut down, on this occasion by UL president, Joseph Getehmnah Morris.[1] This had followed a three-day strike by academic and ancillary staff who had not been paid for three months.[2]

Relations between university and regime were to plummet further two days later, on Wednesday 7 April, when the head of the UL philosophy faculty, Fr James Hickey SMA, was arrested and deported. A missionary of the American SMA Province – a naturalised American, born in Ireland – Hickey had graduated from the Catholic University in Washington, DC before coming to Liberia in 1965. There he had served as principal of Our Lady of Fatima College, Harper, and taught at St Paul's seminary, Gbarnga, before joining the UL philosophy faculty as lecturer in 1981. Within days the story of his deportation was to become international news, widely portrayed as an attack by the regime on Liberia's academic community and on its missionaries. The SMA's capacity to communicate its message, together with Hickey's ability to articulate his case, both in words and in writing, did much to secure this outcome.

The bizarre sequence of events – indicative among other things of the timidity of the regime in dealing with an international religious body – which led to Hickey's deportation is well documented. At 6.30 pm on the day of his detention Hickey was marking student essays at his Sinkor residence when he was interrupted by the arrival of three immigration officials who politely served him with a summons to appear immediately before the Immigration Commissioner. Taken to the Immigration Office, there was no sign of the Commissioner nor of any senior official, not until 11 am on the following morning when at last Hickey was brought before the Commissioner's deputy who told him he was to be expelled for activity incompatible with his status as an alien. Two officials then appeared bearing his passport and an Air Afrique ticket and with orders to place him aboard the 1 pm flight to New York. However, some minutes before the flight was due to leave, the deportation was aborted, and

DOI: 10.4324/9781003219309-9

Hickey was returned to Monrovia. Meanwhile Archbishop Francis, notified of Hickey's detention, received a letter from the Ministry of Justice stating that Hickey was guilty of violating Section 7.1 (h) of Liberia's 'New Alien and Nationality Law', a provision relating 'to the preservation of neutrality towards other nations.' Consequently, 'having abused the privileges accorded him', he was now to be declared 'an undesirable alien' and should leave 'the country within 36 hours'. During those 36 hours the Minister for Foreign Affairs received a succession of letters, some pleading, others protesting, all seeking a reversal of the decision. These came from Archbishop Francis, the Liberian Council of Churches, the Episcopal Conference of Anglophone West Africa, and Archbishop Panciroli, Apostolic Pro-Nuncio to Liberia. Meanwhile, the U.S. Consul passed on a communication from the State Department to the effect that Hickey's detention was already 'on the floor of Congress' and was being followed with 'serious concern'.

But all to no avail, for on Friday, 10 April, accompanied to the airport by a small convoy of security officials, priests, sisters and laity, Hickey boarded a plane at Robertsfield bound for New York. On the same day Liberia's Ministry of Justice sent a message to the U.S. State Department declaring that Father Hickey was 'an undesirable alien' and that the decision to expel him was 'predicated upon his continuous advocacy of issues or matters that do not lead to the nation's desire for peace and understanding'.[3]

One is tempted to a perverse sympathy with the Ministry's statement and with what was now, owing to the outpouring of criticism, the regime's predicament. It must be said that as a lecturer at UL Hickey was outspoken about the ills of the regime and its impact on society. These unfriendly remarks were made in the context of teaching sociology. However, the border lines between scientific social observation and partisan political comment can sometimes be wafer-thin and in the white-hot heat of UL discourse there might well have been occasions when Hickey over-stepped the line. There is no doubt that any attempt to engage in a critique of government policy by an expatriate in the neighbouring, newly independent West African states would not have been tolerated and would have been quickly labelled as unacceptable meddling in politics. But Liberia had never been colonised in the manner of other West African territories. By the same token, neither did it enjoy any of the advantages which a colonial past might have brought, such as a sophisticated educational system, a public service tradition, or economic infrastructure. Lacking the self-confidence of a Nigeria, a Ghana or an Ivory Coast, Liberia was a small, poor, republic on the periphery of the Gulf of Guinea. In choosing to deport Hickey this weak and inept republic was setting itself up against a self-confident international Catholic Church, and an America not only highly sensitive to the rights of its citizens overseas but replete with the necessary diplomatic and media resources to defend them.

***

Reaction in the U.S. to Hickey's expulsion was swift. Among the first off the mark was Neal Allen of the northern New Jersey newspaper, *The Record*, local paper of the SMA community in Tenafly.[4] Samantha Sparks of the *National Catholic Reporter,* America's most widely read Catholic newspaper, wrote of 'the growing dismay among congressional lawmakers' at current U.S. policy towards Liberia.[5] And she quoted Hickey's reaction to Secretary Shultz's remark that the 1985 election had been conducted fairly which 'had incensed the people of Liberia'. Hickey, it was clear, far from resting after his ordeal, was coming out fighting.

April 16 saw the Catholic Church in Liberia further stamp its foot in reaction to the Hickey expulsion. On that day Archbishop Francis announced that all of its institutions – clinics, schools and its signature hospital in Monrovia – would be closed on Wednesday of the following week as an 'expression of gratitude to Fr James C. Hickey'.[6] At much the same time, the Director of Liberia's Public Affairs Bureau responded to fears voiced by the academic staff at UL, consequent on the Hickey deportation, that academic freedom would be curtailed and foreign nationals on the staff expelled. Academic freedom, he declared, would be respected and the 'rights of aliens' would be upheld. At the same time, he warned UL staff against 'poisoning the minds of students.'[7] Nor was there any question of the government's 'mapping out certain professors for victimization', a further matter for concern among UL staff. They could be assured that they would have no cause for fear if they discharged their duties with integrity.

Back in the U.S. Hickey's remained highly visible, speaking about the background to his deportation and suggesting reasons why it might have been ordered. He told Karen Sullivan of the *Bergen Record* that after the campus invasion of August 1984, he had unsuccessfully 'urged his colleagues at subsequent faculty meetings to demand an investigation'.[8] Also, 'on occasions during his lectures, he had incorporated examples of government actions that were contrary to constitutional law'. He told her, too, he was determined to go to Washington D.C. where he would 'provide information about Liberia's national condition and his deportation'.

Hickey also was to be heard on the BBC World Service, a station closely monitored in Africa, rehearsing the reasons which might have prompted his deportation. In class he had expressed 'doubts concerning the legitimacy of the 1985 general elections and the invasion of the university in August 1984'.[9] He had regarded that invasion as 'outrageous' and regretted the failure of the government to 'conduct any investigation to clear the air'. He also told the interviewer that he had been warned by students to be careful about what he was saying as there were 'favourers of government who were carrying stories.' But he denied ever having said anything directly 'rude' about President Doe or the Krahn tribe. It must be admitted that whatever Hickey might have said in the UL classroom, the boldness of his post-deportation performance left little doubt as to why exactly the regime might have wanted him removed.

***

Meanwhile the first rumblings of dissent at the projected arrival of U.S. financial experts (known as 'the Opex team') to manage Liberia's economy, began to be heard. In July (1987) *West Africa* reported that some cabinet ministers regarded the agreement 'as a virtual surrender of Liberian sovereignty', or as an act of 'neo-colonialism' by the United States.[10] One of those who saw in the agreement an absolute lack of confidence in his capacity to fulfil his duties was Robert C. Tubman (younger brother of Winston Tubman) who had just been demoted from his post as Minister for Finance to that of Minister for Labour for challenging some of the regime's excesses. Another, equally unhappy with the challenge to his efficiency and integrity, *West Africa* reported, was Minister for Finance John G. Bestman. Liberian civil servants, however, appeared to welcome Opex, hoping that it might prevent corrupt cabinet ministers from raiding government coffers. And American officials continued to downplay the punitive nature of the new arrangement.

At the same time, the U.S. government agency responsible (USAID) was having difficulty in recruiting suitable experts for Opex. Out of some 60 requests made to companies, only five replies had been received. The proposals made by these firms were impressive when detailing the qualifications of the experts offered, forceful in outlining the fees they would expect, and clear on the overall purpose for which they were tendering – bringing efficiency to Liberia's fiscal management and revenue collection. But they were extremely weak on how exactly these objectives would be accomplished.[11] In fact the tendering process proved to be so unsuccessful that in August USAID revealed that the implementation of the scheme would have to be postponed until February 1988.[12]

***

As the decade moved into its closing years, seeing himself increasingly threatened, Doe rarely moved out of the Executive Mansion. When he did, he tended to go to areas where he was assured of a welcome, principally to his own tribal heartland of Grand Gedeh County. It was from here, at the end of November 1987, following a three-day closed-door meeting with citizens of Nimba and Grand Gedeh Counties, that he made another impassioned plea for Liberian exiles to return home 'with an open heart to join the government in building the nation'. But at the same meeting he claimed that Ellen Johnson-Sirleaf, still in exile, was raising funds to overthrow his government.[13] The effect of his conciliatory approach was further eroded by a front-page story in the *Standard*,[14] that his protégé and trusted ally, Emmanuel Bowier, the fiery former spokesperson at the Washington Embassy, recently elevated to the Ministry of Information, Culture and Tourism, now stood accused of embezzling a sum of $85,000. Never at a loss for words, Bowier had issued a press release saying he would prefer to let the public judge the matter rather than the *Standard*. That newspaper, he informed the public, owned by ex-Chief Justice Cheapoo,* whose trial for impeachment was impending, had in its last three issues, 'attempted to discredit the Minister for Justice, the Minister for

---

*   See p. 28 above

Presidential affairs, and himself'.[15] Plainly, Bowier's ability as a street-fighter had not been dented by the accusations levelled against him.

***

By the end of the year USAID had finally managed to recruit its Opex team which was duly dispatched to Liberia on New Year Day 1988. As well as stabilising Liberia, the U.S. administration hoped the measure would placate, or even silence those irate lawmakers in America, such as Edward Kennedy, who wanted a cessation of all assistance until free and fair elections were held. The Opex team had been contracted from a single company, the New Jersey-based Louis Berger International Inc., for a sum of $6.5 million and was to work under the supervision of retired USAID official, Frank Kimball. According to the terms of the contract Opex was to be assigned to all the main ministries and to the National Bank, the Bureau of Customs and Excise, the Civil Service and the National Agricultural Marketing Company. The contract was to run for one year, at the end of which USAID must justify its extension for a further year to America's lawmakers. The Opex team's arrival coincided with the departure of the IMF resident representative in Monrovia. As mentioned earlier, no IMF assistance had been given since January 1986, and there appeared to be little or no prospect of Liberia, with an annual gross domestic product of about $1 billion, repaying the $260 million owed to the institution.[16]

***

Minister Bowier was again in the news in mid-March 1988, having survived the accusations of embezzlement, explaining how a new plot against the government had been discovered and how its mastermind had jumped from the 6th floor of the Executive Mansion in the presence of his interrogators.[17] The man in question was one Joe Robert Kaipaye, a Liberian who was said to have served in the U.S. Marines. Nineteen people were being held in connection with the plot. Two weeks later Bowier again made the headlines after imposing further bans on *The Sun Times* and *Footprints Today*. In so doing he attracted the ire of the UL Student Union president, now Anthony Kesselly, who expressed his 'surprise' and 'disappointment'. Bowier, he said, had been a militant student while at UL, parading around the campus 'preaching justice, freedom and other noble ideas'.[18] His present action 'cast a cloud over all UL students'.

***

By mid-1988 reports about the fortunes of the Opex team began to circulate. For the regime, it was business as usual. *The Washington Post*'s foreign service correspondent, Blaine Harden, recorded that in the six months since the team had come, 'Doe and his close associates had found a variety of ways to skirt American-imposed spending controls'. Letters had been signed by President Doe and others in the Executive Mansion authorising extra-budgetary expenditures for the purchase of Mercedes automobiles. Further unsupervised and unauthorised payments had been made to building contractors who, in turn, paid kickbacks to Liberian officials. One disgruntled Opex expert had said that the level of extra-budgetary expenditure was high and that he and his colleagues were 'powerless to do anything about it'.

Among such expenditure was a sum of $750,000 for President Doe's attendance at the OAU's annual meeting held in Addis Ababa in April. The State Department, for its part, was no longer sanguine about the success of the initiative. *Africa Confidential*,[19] in its issue of 21 October 1988,[20] cited a recent report to Congress from the State Department which 'admitted the Opex team's failure to curb extra-budgetary expenditure and establish fiscal discipline'. In fact, Doe, it was reported, had failed to meet the Opex team. And more than 40% of government expenditure remained 'outside the general budgeting and accounting processes.' By the end of 1989 the Opex team had gone home. Its final report on the 'Liberia Economic Stabilization Support Project', admitted failure.[21]

***

On 13 July 1988 Liberia woke up to news of an attempted invasion from the Ivory Coast by a group of dissidents headed by Major General J. Nicholas Podier, Doe's former deputy and one of the alleged coup-plotters freed by Doe in October 1984.[22] Podier, it was announced, along with five others, had been intercepted and killed by Liberian soldiers. A curious feature of the invasion, announced by the government sometime later, was the involvement of two Americans, one an ex-U.S. Army sergeant from Baltimore who had served in Vietnam.

The truth about this coup attempt – the ninth announced by the government in eight years – appears to have been somewhat different. After falling out with Doe in 1986 Podier had gone into exile in the Ivory Coast and had sought help among the exile community there to oust his former leader. Failing to gain sufficient support he had then embarked on a reconciliation process, which gained momentum in late 1987 and early 1988. Eventually Podier was advised by regime members to return quietly to Liberia, assured of his safely. Podier persuaded two Americans, both of whom had business interests in the region, to accompany him, with the prospect of engaging in joint business enterprises. But all three were arrested once they crossed the border. According to *Africa Confidential* 'Podier was taken to the Executive Mansion where he was tortured and dismembered', while the two Americans, made to put on military uniforms, 'were tortured and imprisoned in the Monrovia's Post Stockade prison and pressured to "confess"'.[23]

***

August 1988 witnessed an upsurge in student unrest. As already recounted, relations between the regime and Liberia's school-going and undergraduate populations, had begun to deteriorate within a year of Doe's ascent to power. When reforms promised failed to materialise academics and student leaders were among the first to voice their discontent. Doe regarded these as the voices of disloyal subversives who must be carefully watched. In particular he was to harbour an intense resentment towards his articulate, university-trained critics, such as Gabriel Baccus Matthews, Amos Sawyer and Johnson-Sirleaf. They were able to outwit him in argument, not because they were more intelligent but because as Americo-Liberians they had been privileged to receive an education. And because of their education they enjoyed a privileged position in Liberian society. Student leaders, he felt, were the creatures of these subversive intellectuals, primed and placed in the first line; in time they would inherit high positions in Liberian academic and political life. Against such people his own lack of education and privilege was cast into sharp relief.

Already in 1983 Doe had made attempts to address this situation, first seeking an honorary degree and when this was not forthcoming, requesting a series of private tutorials preparing him for the award of a BA degree in political science, with 'international relations' as his speciality. The incumbent president, Dr Mary Antoinette Brown Sherman, had resisted these overtures, something which in the following year contributed to her removal. Her successor, President Joseph Morris, arranged for a team of tutors to visit the Executive Mansion for the purpose of teaching the president. This raised the eyebrows of many faculty members, although they did not formally protest. The Student Union, however, objected on the grounds that the president had not completed his high-school education, had not received the necessary certification from the Department of Education to entitle him to university training, and had never sat for a university entrance examination. Subsequently each graduating class let it be known that it would boycott the conferring ceremony should President Doe be granted a degree. An Executive Mansion grant of $50,000 to sponsor an MA programme in politics at UL, did nothing to defuse objections.

By 1988 President Doe had not yet received a degree. In June of that year trouble broke out in a Bomi high school over the election of its Students Union President. The students alleged vote-rigging by the school authorities who, in turn, refused to release the ballot boxes. There followed outbreaks of violence leading to the imposition of a fine on all students. They refused to pay, an act which led to the arrest of some twenty. Further protests followed until in mid-August the school was damaged by fire. This relatively small disturbance in Bomi county was to have repercussions for the whole educational sector when President Doe issued an Executive Order banning all student politics.

The government's hard line, manifest in the introduction of the new Executive Order, created consternation at UL, leading to a declaration by the Student Union that it was unconstitutional. Incensed at this defiance President Doe summoned the UL president and six student leaders to the Executive Mansion. There he ordered the students to write a letter of apology, failing which they would be expelled by the UL president. The leaders rejected the demand, and their decision was endorsed by a mass meeting, after which 21 student leaders were expelled.[24] Further protests by students led to police intervention and rioting on the UL Campus which spread to the city, followed by the appearance of military on the streets and the setting up of road-blocks. Trustees closed all UL colleges with the exception of the schools of law and medicine. Despite government efforts to re-establish order and re-open the university, the student body refused to submit until the Executive Order was revoked.[25] This was not to happen.

***

September 6 saw the commencement of the treason trial of those involved in the so-called Podier coup of early July. These were the 40-year-old American, Vietnam War veteran James Henry Bush and Curtis Elmer Williams, a printer from Jersey City, along with Mike Jackson, a self-exiled Liberian who lived in the Ivory Coast.[26] The indictment said that they had been led by Podier and Humphrey Moore, a former Liberian soldier, across the Liberian–Ivory Coast border on 10 July 1988. The incursion, according to the indictment's version, appears to have been something of a shambles.[27]

What exactly was Doe trying to achieve by this legal process? The trial of two Americans for plotting the overthrow of Liberia's government was bound to attract international attention and seems to have been intended to tell the world that Liberia was under siege from both within and without, and that the U.S., instead of defending its great ally, was complicit. Whether Bush and Williams had any case to answer is extremely doubtful. Certainly, the notion that these two men were engaged in a scheme to overthrow the Liberian government seems highly improbable.

***

At this time, nervous and sensing future danger, the Doe regime was taking new measures to consolidate its position. In August, the Liberian Legislature gave favourable consideration to a petition by citizens to 'amend the constitutional provision limiting the presidential office to two six-year terms.'[28] Doe, it seemed, now intended to be president for life. Moreover, the only units of the army now permitted to bear arms were the Executive Mansion Guard and the First Battalion based at Scheifflen, near Monrovia. Both units, trained by Israeli and U.S. army personnel, were commanded and populated almost exclusively by members of the Krahn ethnic group to which Doe belonged. Charles Julu, the tough and intensely loyal commander of the Executive Mansion Guard, had already been cited as responsible for many killings in the Lawyers' Committee for Human Rights Report, in the wake of the 1985 coup attempt.[29] Dislodging Doe would not be easily accomplished.

***

The closing months of 1988 saw the submission to UL of a thesis authored by President Doe and entitled 'A Survey of U.S.-Liberia Relations'. It was presented in partial fulfilment of the requirements for a bachelor's degree in political science. The thesis, dedicated to his father and mother and to the peoples of Liberia and America, expressed the hope of 'a new kind of relationship' which would prove 'mutually rewarding to the legitimate hopes and aspirations of our two nations'. Its central argument, as outlined in the abstract, was to 'ferret out what has gone wrong with Liberia's relations with the United States'.

Doe's thesis claimed that the purpose of the 1980 coup was not 'to wreak revenge upon Americo-Liberians ... clearly demonstrated by the inclusion of Americo-Liberians, as well as all the various ethnic groups of Liberia, in positions of trust in government and cabinet'. Concerning the legitimacy of the revolution the thesis, following the time-old precedent, claimed that it derived from God.

This historic Revolution was designed by God (how can 17 men overthrow a hegemony which dominated the nation for more than a century?)
to help restore the rights of all our citizens and to ensure their participation
in the nation-building process.[30]

Referring to America's role in Liberia's God-given destiny, the thesis
maintained that as the U.S. was in large part responsible for the country's
underdevelopment ('because, over the years, she has kept this nation at arm's
length') Liberia now expected America 'to play the principal role in assisting
us to realize our development objective'. Liberia needed 'the financial and
technological support of America'. And, regardless of its problems, the author
was 'convinced that with America's unsurpassed technology, capital and resi-
lience', Liberia could 'speedily resolve these problems once she musters the
requisite commitment'.

Much of the body of the thesis dealt with problems of 'national development' and how the U.S. might assist Liberia's president and head-of-state in his
God-given task. Most importantly Liberia required from America cancellation
of debts incurred. Had not President Doe 'written several letters to the American government' on this issue without result![31] As to why the U.S. might
respond positively, the thesis had no hesitation in reminding readers of Liberia's
fidelity down the years and America's failure to reciprocate, quoting at some
length a critique of the U.S. published by Professor Elbert Dunn.*

The thesis concluded with an optimistic, evangelical, rallying cry, invoking
the spirit of Dr Martin Luther King, citing 'Democracy' as the holy grail and
the 'Constitution' as the means to acquire it – all under the title 'Unity for
Victory'. At the heart of the message was the author's absolute belief in the
core values of America's civilisation, namely 'the pursuit of true democracy
through a sacred observation of the laws enshrined in its constitution'. Whether
such sentiments, uttered by a man whose actions manifestly were in another
direction, cut any ice with the audience for which they were intended is
doubtful.

***

Meanwhile, controversy about the Podier July coup attempt continued to
rumble on. Amnesty International published information which was in conflict
with the Liberian government's version. It claimed that the two American
nationals and the Liberian arraigned and convicted, had come to the Ivory
Coast on a business trip and were entirely without political motivation. While
imprisoned in the Post Stockade prison, both had been handcuffed, beaten, and
deprived of clothes. Moreover, according to the Amnesty account, General
Podier had not been killed during the attempted invasion (which the government had claimed) but was slain by soldiers after being arrested at Robertsfield
airport.[3233]

---

*   Dunn was believed to be the leader of the group of academics giving Doe private
     tuition (Africa Confidential, 21 October 1988, vol. 29, no. 1).

In America the Congressional Black Caucus was active in seeking the release of Bush and Williams, sending letters to President Doe and the U.S. State Department. For his part the Mayor of Atlanta City, Andrew Young, sent a telex to President Doe appealing for their release. And there was information that Chester Crocker had met with the Liberian Foreign Minister, J. Rudolph Johnson at the State Department and, although not requesting the release of Bush and Williams, had expressed the hope that they would be 'given due process under Liberian laws.'[34]

The issue was resolved on 15 November when President Doe announced the release of Bush and Williams. Minister Bowier explained that President Doe had received letters of apology from both and his action in releasing them should be interpreted as 'a manifestation of good will toward President-elect Bush'. However, the former U.S. Attorney General, Ramsey Clark, who had been retained to defend Bush and Williams, denied that the men had confessed. According to him they had simply explained what had happened and denied any intention to commit a criminal act.[35]

***

'We hope and pray that the year 1989 will bring a thunderous response from those at home as well as those abroad'. These words, taken from President Doe's BA degree thesis, were to be fulfilled in a sense altogether different from that intended by their author in the closing month of 1988. The other months of the year had been marked by an intensification of the regime's efforts to stifle dissent, tighten its grip on power and present Liberia to the outside world as a reputable, progressive, and well-ordered democracy. On one notable occasion, the Catholic Church was to fall within its sights for supposedly violating the latter, presenting Liberia in 'a bad light' to an international audience. This occurred when, on 11 June 1989, a crowd stampeded at an international football match between Liberia and Malawi at the Samuel Kanyon Doe Sports Complex in Monrovia. Later that day a news bulletin on the Catholic Church's radio station, ELCM, described what it termed this 'major tragedy' and its aftermath:

> Hundreds of persons were injured or killed just prior to the Liberia-Malawi soccer match this afternoon. ELCM News visited the St Joseph Catholic and John F. Kennedy hospitals in Sinkor and saw several injured and dead. The stampede occurred as a result of misinformation which circulated in the crowd that one of the several floodlight pylons was about to collapse. As the rumour spread the crowd panicked and stampeded, causing a collapse of the fence around gates numbers 10 and 11...

On the following day, claiming that the broadcast had damaged 'the image of Liberia', the Ministry of Information closed down ELCM, revoked its license and decommissioned its frequency. This led to a sustained outcry from the Churches, political parties, Liberia's press union, as well as organs of the independent press.[36]

Archbishop Francis told a large Sunday congregation in the cathedral that, as proprietor of the station, he had been given no prior warning of the closure, which he denounced 'as an attempt by some government officials to create confrontation with ... peaceful and law-abiding citizens.' ELCM radio was closed, he said, 'because it speaks nothing but the truth; gives both sides to every story and brings to light what is hidden'. Then, adding insult to injury, he announced that 'those who decided the fate of the station' had received their education in Catholic schools'. So saying, he held up the letter informing him of the ELCM closure, signed by Postal Minister Morris M. Dukuly, a former alumnus of the Catholic St Patrick's High School.[37]

The political opposition too wasted little time in joining the chorus of protest. The Liberia Unification Party, whose leader, Gabriel Kpolleh, was in prison declared it 'most reprehensible ... that the executive branch of government has once again arrogated unto itself powers that the constitution clearly reserves to the Judiciary'.[38]

Irritated by this flurry of criticism, Minister Bowier – looking somewhat embattled for the first time in his public career – released details of the background to ELCM's closure.[39] It had been prompted, he said, by the failure of ELCM management to produce a copy of the news script broadcast on the day of the incident, which included the information that 'several persons were crushed to death'. As a result, the government 'was constrained to put out a public notice that refusal to comply would lead to the indefinite closure and withdrawal of license'. The failure of the station to respond to this notice had led to its closure.

Minister Dukuly, who had been pilloried by Archbishop Francis, also sprang to the government's defence. Condemning the archbishop's 'personalization of the issue', not without good reason, he told a press conference that he had 'nothing against religious institutions' and that although he had graduated from a Catholic institution, his tuition was paid for by his parents. In any case, he continued, the decommissioning of ELCM's frequency and closure of the station had nothing to do with such matters. At the 'root of the problem' was ELCM's refusal to cooperate with the Information Ministry'.[40]

This incident again underlined the very different nature of Church-State relationships in Liberia from what prevailed in most of the newly independent West African countries. As already mentioned, during the 140 years of True Whig Party dominance, political leaders frequently were also Church leaders. One result of this was the extreme deference shown to the Churches by government and vice versa. So deeply ingrained was this that after the 1980 coup, when a very different political leadership came to the fore, a strong residue of undue deference remained. Being seen to listen to the Churches, to 'look up' to them, to 'seek guidance' and get them 'on-side', was regarded as an important priority by the new regime. The fact that now Churches were led by people with no political power might have made the government's task less daunting. However, the formation of the LCC, led by the international Churches – less likely to be politically compromised – was an obstacle to government ambitions. Conflicts between Churches and Regime therefore were of much more consequence than what might be expected elsewhere in West Africa. Thus, as one author noted, in Doe's Liberia there existed a paradox in Church–State relations. 'While government reaction was often hostile, there seemed ultimately to be the acceptance that the Church was too influential and perhaps too useful to be overly censored'.[41] It was therefore not surprising that in the same year as the Catholic radio station was closed the Catholic Church's new Polytechnic college, named after Don Bosco, was opened by Vice President Harry Moniba 'with due praise for the work of the Church in Liberia'.[42]

Notes

1 A former diplomat and ambassador, he was president between 1984 and October 1987.
2 West Africa, 6 April 1987, 685.
3 Bergen Record, 17 April 1987.
4 The Record, 10 April 1987.
5 1 May 1987.
6 Ibid, 16 April1987.
7 The Overseas Press Bureau, Ministry of Information, 'Rev Father Hickey's deportation: why government did what it did'.
8 17 April 1987.
9 Daily Observer, Joe Mulbah, 28 April 1987.
10 West Africa, 27 July 1987, 1457.
11 Ibid.
12 About Liberia, No 44, August 1987 (Ezekiel Pajibo).
13 Suntimes, 1 December 1987.
14 26 November 1987.
15 Suntimes, 1 December 1987.
16 The African Letter, 16–31 December 1987.
17 The Los Angeles Times, 31 March 1988.
18 Daily Observer, 19 April 1988.
19 Africa Confidential, established in 1960, and edited by a series of distinguished editors (Richard Kershaw, Stephen Ellis and Patrick Smith) is a highly regarded fortnightly newsletter on Africa.
20 Vol. 29, No. 21.
21 Louis Berger International, INC, Arthur Young & Company, Robert R. Nathan Associates, The Aries Group, 'Final Report on the Liberian Economic Stabilization Support Project' (December 1989).
22 Podier was also one of the coup plotters of April 1980. By this time almost all his comrades had died violently.
23 Africa Confidential, 21 October 1988 (vol. 29, no. 1). Other accounts of the coup attempt can be found in Jeremiah T. Kugmeh, 'Hold Bota's Mouth: A Stirring Account of Liberia at War', West Africa: The Legacy of the 1980s (W. Africa Pub. Co. Ltd, 1900, 33ff; Augustine S. Cheah, Survival Beyond Belief, The Rape of a Nation, 32ff.
24 Africa Confidential, 21 October 1988 (vol. 29, no. 1).
25 Ibid, 30 August 1988.
26 Daily Observer, 5 September1988.
27 Ibid.
28 Africa Confidential, 21 October 1988 (vol. 29, no. 1).

29 Ibid.
30 Liberian–US Relations. A Thesis by Samuel Kanyon Doe. University of Liberia, 1988, 6 (copy in AT).
31 Appended to the thesis was a list of 'Important Dates in Liberian-U.S. Relations'.
32 West Africa, 7–13 November 1988, 2116.
33 The LTRC Consolidated Final Report makes no reference to Podier's death.
34 Ibid.
35 James Brooke, The New York Times, 16 November 1988; The Washington Post, 17 November 1988.
36 Daily Observer, 19 June 1989.
37 The Herald, Vol. 2 No 25, 22–28 June 1989.
38 In a press release published in the Daily Observer, 19 June 1989.
39 The News, vol. 1, no. 39, 22 June 1989.
40 Ibid.
41 John Kilcoyne, op. cit., 29 (quoting Yekutiel Gershoni, 'The Paradox of Church-State Relations in Liberia', Liberian Studies Journal, X, 1 [1982–1983], 67–83).
42 Ibid.

Section 3

The Advent of Charles Taylor

8 Enemies of the revolution cross into Liberia and liberation from tyranny is proclaimed

It was in the last month of 1989 that the hammer blow, which always threatened, finally struck the Doe regime. On 24 December a number of armed men crossed the Ivory Coast border into Liberia. The group, styling itself as the National Patriotic Front of Liberia (NPFL), was led by one Charles McArthur[*] Taylor. Early estimates of its size varied greatly, from 15,000 to a mere 200. In fact, the initial number was far smaller. A report based on extensive research published four months later by 'Africa Watch' (an arm of the New York-based International Human Rights organisation) gave details. Prior to the incursion, in mid-December 1989, members of the Mandingo ethnic community in Nimba County (bordering on Ivory Coast) had reported 'suspicious activity' to local government officials and to the Minister for the Interior. Both Superintendent Daniels of Nimba County and the Minister had rubbished these reports, the former giving an assurance to Vice-President Moniba that the citizens of Nimba would never 'subvert the government'.[1] Less than a week later, between 24 and 26 December the insurgency commenced:

> The first attack by the rebels, conducted mainly with knives, machetes, and some small arms, took place at the border town of Butuo and was aimed at securing firearms. The attack was premature and unplanned but was forced on the rebels when they received news of the arrest of a small number of colleagues in Monrovia. In the Butuo attack an undetermined number of soldiers and immigration officials were killed (not more than 16) and their arms captured by the rebels. The insurgents, numbering probably no more than 40, then took cover in dense forest. Their next attack was at Karnplay on January 1 and the third at Loguatuo on 2 January. From then on, the picture is less clear.[2]

Early reports portrayed the rebels as a disparate group 'linked to Taylor through their common objectives', augmented by a number who sought revenge for

[*] Taylor, born an Americo-Liberian, was to change his middle name from 'McArthur' to 'Ghankay' (meaning 'warrior' or 'the bold one' in Gola) as a means of gaining indigenous credentials.

DOI: 10.4324/9781003219309-11

the massacre of Gio and Mano civilians after the Quiwonkpa coup. Although a raggle-taggle assortment, the group did have a hard core of men who, like Taylor, had spent time in Libya where they were given some training in the use of firearms. Taylor's initial role appears to have been that of quartermaster, 'instrumental in acquiring arms and providing training for some of the rebels.' However, he also had made efforts to organise them, 'unifying the scattered forces', and gathering them under the umbrella of an imposing title - the National Patriotic Front of Liberia.[3]

***

Who was this Charles Taylor? The third of ten children, he had been born into an Americo-Liberian family on 28 January 1948. In 1972, like many of Liberia's privileged class, he went to the U.S. for his undergraduate education, studying economics at Bentley College, Waltham, Massachusetts. Taylor was politically active, joining the Union of Liberian Associations in the Americas and taking part in protests against the Tolbert regime. It is not known exactly when he married but by the time of the 1989 insurgency he and his wife, Tupee, had two U.S.-born children.[4]

It was at the invitation of President Tolbert, anxious to enlist some of his well-educated critics, that Taylor returned to Liberia in January 1980 'to observe government programs at close hand'.[5] During his visit the coup over-throwing the Tolbert regime took place. Taylor, according to his wife (who was now living in Pawtuckett, Rhode Island, with her children), became a friend and admirer of General Thomas Quiwonkpa and also gained the trust of Samuel Doe, in consequence of which in June 1980 he was given the post of Director General of the General Services Administration. In October 1983, accused of embezzling in excess of $900,000, Taylor fled Liberia denying the charges and saying, 'he had learned that Mr Doe planned to arrest and do away with General Quiwonkpa and his associates for plotting against the govern-ment'. This might well have been the case, but the prospect of facing charges for embezzlement might have loomed larger in his decision to abscond. Seven months later, in May 1984, while visiting acquaintances in Somerville, Massa-chusetts, Taylor was arrested on a Liberian extradition warrant to face charges of embezzlement. During the extradition hearings he claimed that he had fallen out with the Doe regime because of its abuse of human rights. But U.S. Magistrate Robert J. DeGiacomo overruled this defence.[6]

When the extradition process was nearing completion, on 1 September 1985 Taylor disappeared from prison and his subsequent movements were unknown until he re-appeared at the Liberian border in December 1989 leading an insurgency against the government. In sum, it could be said that Taylor was 'a product of the political ferment in Liberia of the late 1970s and early 1980s for whom personal ambition, not ideology, was the deciding factor'.[7] And Taylor was well-equipped to pursue this ambition, possessing intelligence, personality, and determination as well as a formidable capacity to wage war by military and diplomatic means.[8]

***

Knowledge of what was going on in Nimba County was sketchy beyond its borders. Fr Anthony (Tony) Jennings, an Irish SMA, based in Buchanan (Grand Bassa County), almost 140 miles from Nimba's administrative capital, Sanequellie, noted that rumours of incursions had been circulating during the closing weeks of December 1989. However, these attracted little notice among the Buchanan populace because President Doe had developed the habit of 'flying kites', especially when things were not going well.[9] When ELBC reported that the government of Liberia (GOL) army had driven back the invaders, and President Doe was threatening to invade the Ivory Coast in retaliation for the sanctuary afforded them, it seemed in truth this was another kite. However, after the Christmas period, when it became apparent that there had been more incursions and these had not been driven back, people further afield began to pay more attention. Doe's threat to 'blast Nimba County off the map if the rebels did not surrender', caused a wave of fear. Next came news of refugees fleeing Nimba County over the borders into Guinea and Ivory Coast.[10]

***

Early accounts in the international press saw the insurgency as yet another attempted coup, unlikely to succeed. Reportage concentrated on repressive measures taken by GOL against Mano and Gio living outside Nimba. And it was revealed that at this stage the large influx of disaffected tribesmen which Taylor had expected to join him was failing to materialise. It was this which led Taylor and his small band of no more than 200 men to rely on 'hit-and-run attacks on small villages, singling out Krahn. '[11] The Mandingo ethnic group – regarded by the rebels as loyal to Doe – was also targeted.

But the conclusion that the insurgency was unlikely to succeed was premature. After the initial skirmishes and setbacks Taylor's disparate group re-emerged from the bush and moved deeper into Nimba County, scene of vicious reprisals after the failure of the Quiwonkpa coup. The anticipated influx of Gio and Mano to Taylor's cause came soon after the dispatch of two GOL battalions, mostly Krahn, who instead of fighting the invaders descended on Gio villages summarily executing young men and looting and burning homes.[12] Many Gio, it seems, interpreted such actions as indicative of a determination to eliminate them, a conviction which was reinforced by the complete lack of wounded civilians in Nimba's hospitals.

Meanwhile, in Sanniquellie the GOL army claimed to be firmly in control, its commander, General Edward Smith, declaring that he was now conducting 'mopping up' operations.[13] However Monrovia's Mandingo population was receiving very different and alarming information from Nimba County to the effect that the rebels were targeting and killing members of their group.[14] How, they asked very publicly, if the government was in control could such atrocities occur? President Doe responded to these complaints on 30 January by summoning all Mandingo citizens based in Monrovia to the City Hall where he reassured them that there was no truth in these 'rumours' and that the situation in Nimba County was under control.[15] On the same day newspapers in Monrovia carried a story which appeared to support the President's assertion.

These reported that the mining of iron ore in Nimba County and its transfer south for export was proceeding as normal. Indeed, processing of the high-grade ore had progressed to such an extent that a massive shipment of 62,300 tons had just taken place from Buchanan port, destined for the 'Fos Sur Mer' plant in France, while a further 300,000 tons of shippable ore, had been stockpiled and was ready to go.

Despite such assurances, however, there were signs that the insurgency was making progress. Continuing GOL atrocities against the Gio community in Nimba suggested a growing number of rebel successes. These atrocities, widely and reliably reported, led President Doe – sensitive to international criticism – to dispatch Defence Minister, J. Boimah Barclay and GOL Chief of Staff, Henry Dubar, to Sanniquellie to caution the troops against 'harassing peaceful citizens.' Barclay assured a gathering of citizens and foreign residents that the government was not at war with the inhabitants of Nimba County and 'was doing everything possible to protect them from dissident attack'.[16] The atrocities, he claimed, had been perpetrated by insurgents dressed in GOL uniforms in order to blacken the name of the army. Barclay's caution to the gathering 'against harbouring dissidents' and to report their 'hideouts' demonstrated that the rebels were still a force. Further evidence that the rebel incursion had taken root came on 14 February, when a senior GOL official told a press conference that President Doe was 'still determined to ensure that the 1991 elections were held despite the insurgency'.[17]

The United Nations was keeping a watchful eye on developments and, in particular, on the problems of population displacement and food shortages. On 28 March a UN relief convoy left Monrovia for Nimba County with food supplies for an estimated 135,000 displaced persons. At the same time, following intelligence of fierce fighting near Ganta, Sageipie and Karnple, the U.S. embassy was advising all U.S. citizens in Nimba, with the exception of those in Tappita (where all was reported quiet), to leave without delay. But within hours came reports that rebel forces were now approaching Tappita and that there was fighting on the outskirts of the town. Fast on the heels of this came reports of a setback to the UN relief convoy which had been forced to suspend its plan to enter Nimba County because of government inability to guarantee its safety. On the same day, 29 March, the British Embassy advised all 'British, unrepresented Commonwealth and Irish nationals' to leave Yekepa.[18]

Further signs that the government was losing its grip came on 30 March when it imposed restrictions on journalists reporting the fighting in Nimba County. Henceforth all media institutions were ordered 'to confirm their stories with the Ministry for Information before publication'. This, it was said, had become necessary following the publication of incorrect and inaccurate information which caused 'fear and anxiety among citizens and residents in Nimba county'.[19]

***

Precisely at this time Taylor was taking to the BBC World Service airwaves beginning a long association which was to stretch well over a decade. Many of the interviews were conducted by the journalist Robin White. White had already won a reputation for the quality of his broadcasts on African affairs. His trenchant interviews with many African heads of state led, much later,[20] to the awarding of an MBE by the British monarch. Whether his interviews with Taylor might have contributed to that award is questionable. The view that the BBC World Service indulged Liberia's warlord and was outfoxed by him still has some currency.[21]

Three decades after the event White was to write about his initial contact with Taylor.[22] It was the insurgent leader who first called the BBC on New Year's Day 1990, at a time when the Focus on Africa programme was short of material. Taylor announced that he had invaded Liberia and was on his way to Monrovia to dethrone President Doe. White had never heard of Taylor or the National Patriotic Front of Liberia but, finding him 'plausible', decided to interview him. Suave, reasonable and articulate, almost immediately calling his interlocutor by his first name, Taylor addressed the killing of two Protestant missionaries, Rev. Thomas Jackson and his wife Jane, shot during fighting at Bahn City.[23] He had made contact, he said, to request an opportunity 'to set the record straight', and he was most grateful that the opportunity was being afforded him'. It was a very unfortunate situation', he told White, and of course the Liberian government was to blame.

> From our field report what happened was that GOL troops seized Mr and Mrs Jackson from their home and tried to use them as cover as our forces attacked…

And he had now ordered all flags flown at half-mast as well as a 24-hour ceasefire in commemoration of the Jacksons.

He also took the opportunity to tell the world that Guinean units were fighting alongside GOL soldiers. His own troops had killed many of them in Karnplay and Sannequillie and he suspected that Doe's current visit to Guinea was to ask for more assistance.

The mention of Guinean troops was bound to raise hackles among Liberians. During the Rice Riots of 1979 troops from Guinea had entered Monrovia seemingly at the behest of President Tolbert. Once Doe had taken power, he had been quick to condemn the Guinean interference. Now, it seemed, he was hand-in-glove with a 'former enemy'. Not surprisingly the government was quick to react. On 31 March Radio ELBC told its listeners that a recent visit to Guinea by President Doe had been geared towards finding a lasting solution to issues concerning the mining of iron ore from the mountain range which straddled both borders.[24] Separately, the government-controlled Liberian News Agency quoted Minister Bowier's denial that Guinean soldiers were fighting alongside GOL troops.[25] There is no independent evidence that there were ever Guinean troops in Liberia at this time.

There was also concurrently a flurry of GOL denials in the Liberian *Standard* of 30 March that the fighting had spilled over the Nimba County border into

Bong County'.[26] Radio ELBC told the nation that Bong County Superintendent, Venecious K. Vorkpor, had rubbished these reports saying that business activity was 'still going on fine'. A day later it quoted army Chief of Staff Dubar saying that his troops had successfully surrounded the rebels in Nimba County and it was now safe to travel to Ganta, Sanniquellie and Yekepa.[27] Beyond this line he claimed government troops were 'engaged in mopping up operations', mostly in the region of the Cocopa rubber plantation at Saclepea in Nimba County. Here, according to a separate GOL report the rebels had entered the plantation, 'lined up employees, and singled out and killed Krahn and Mandingo in the presence of the British manager'.[28] This atrocity was later described in some detail in a publication by 'Human Rights Watch'.[29]

***

Whatever about GOL claims about the progress of the insurgency, the humanitarian situation in Nimba County was becoming critical. The president of the Liberian National Red Cross, Rev. J. Edwin Lloyd*, was the first to propose peace talks. He appealed to the National Legislature to arrange for dialogue between 'the dissident Charles Taylor' and 'the legitimate President of Liberia, Dr S.K. Doe'.[30] Not surprisingly the legislature – creatures of the Doe regime – rejected the appeal out of hand, saying it was akin to being asked to 'negotiate with a thief who has burgled one's home'.[31] It also impugned the Reverend Lloyd's bona fides, suggesting that the appeal originated with Taylor who it claimed Lloyd had met clandestinely during a recent visit to the Ivory Coast. There is no evidence of any such meeting.

Given the repeated GOL statements that its army was largely engaged in 'mopping up' operations, some explanation had to be offered to its domestic and international audience for the failure to complete this process over three months. Discharging this task with some relish was Emmanuel Bowier. On 5 April Bowier held a widely-reported press conference in which he announced that the GOL army had surrounded the very forest where the 'mercenaries' were taking refuge but for humanitarian reasons was reluctant to use full military force.[32]

At much the same time Brigadier General Charles Julu of the Executive Mansion Guard, introduced on Radio ELBC as 'commander of troops carrying out mopping-up operations in Nimba county', was assuring the citizens and business community in the county 'that peace and harmony would be soon restored'.[33] Julu, who had been appointed ten days previously, gave this assurance during a meeting with prominent community members in Ganta.

But on the ground, there was little evidence that this was likely. On the contrary whatever reliable evidence came to hand pointed in the opposite direction. On 6 April Agence France-Presse noted that Julu's appointment represented the third change of command since the December incursion. It also cited the Liberian News Agency's statement that 'government forces ...

---

*   A courageous pastor, Lloyd had fallen foul of the regime in 1980 and was imprisoned (see p. 32).

intended to re-open the highway between Nimba and eastern Grand Gedeh county, currently blocked by rebels.' Significantly, up to this time there had been no government admission that this major highway had ever been closed. It also noted that in addition to his new command the ruthless[34] General Julu remained commander of the Executive Mansion Guard. His appointment gave a sense that the Doe regime was beginning 'to circle the wagons'.

***

At this time, Ted Hayden, now working out of Washington DC with the advocacy agency Africa Faith and Justice Network (AFJN),[*] was collecting information about the situation in Liberia. As well as being an advocacy organisation, AFJN was increasingly becoming a news agency providing up-to-date information on Liberia. Among those from whom Hayden sourced information (which he disseminated through the publication *Afjn Information*) was an unnamed senior official at the State Department, another was Chris Hennemeyer of the U.S. hierarchy's Catholic Relief Services, and there was also S. John Murray, his Provincial, who was in daily contact with Archbishop Francis. On 9 April Hayden learned from his State Department source that the rebels were making steady progress and now held the road from Ganta to Tappita. In addition he was told that some 66,000 Liberian refugees were now in the Ivory Coast, 100,000 had sought shelter in Guinea, while a further 60,000 were displaced within Liberia.[35] A week later Hayden was in touch with the Liberian ambassador to the U.S., Eugenia Wordsworth-Stevenson, who told him that there was still some fighting in Nimba county but that the government hoped 'to have it cleared up very soon'.[36] The government line on the insurgency was holding fast.

***

Hoping to distract from the darkening situation in the north-east of the country and to improve his international credibility, President Doe announced the release of a number of political detainees whose cases had been championed by international human rights agencies. Among those freed were Gabriel Kpolleh and Cepar Mabande, leaders of the outlawed Liberia Unification Party, convicted of treason in October 1988. Other magnanimous gestures were the restoration of its license and broadcast frequency to Radio ELCM, the Catholic station, and the withdrawal of the ban imposed in April 1988 on the independent newspapers, *Footprints* and *The Sun Times*.[37]

Emmanuel Bowier, unbowed, continued to insist on the solidity of the regime and its control of the north-east. Any reports to the contrary, he said, originated with those bent on bringing Liberia down and contained not a grain of truth. On 17 April, Agence France-Presse reported Bowier's verbal attack on a British diplomat who stated on the BBC World Service that GOL had virtually lost control of Nimba county. Bowier did not dispute the content of the interview. Instead, he attacked the inappropriateness of a professional diplomat posturing 'as

---

[*]   AFJN, founded in 1983, was a network of missionary congregations striving to bring missionary experience 'on the ground' to bear on U.S. policy toward Africa'.

a BBC correspondent'. The interview in question, given by British ambassador, Michael Edward John Gore, imparted the intelligence that Sanniquellie, Nimba's capital, had been captured by the rebels. 'A strange phenomenon', Bowier declared, 'where a diplomat becomes a news correspondent' and it was nothing short of 'interference in Liberia's domestic affairs.'[38]

***

At an Executive Mansion press conference on 25 April President Doe called upon the rebels to lay down arms within a period of two weeks, specifying two locations in Bong and Grand Bassa counties where this might take place. He also took the opportunity to tell the assembled journalists, some from overseas, that he would never negotiate with Taylor, 'a criminal and a wanted man'. Moreover, he emphatically denied reports that the rebellion had moved beyond Nimba County in the direction of central Bong county and eastern Grand Bassa county, dismissing the persistent reports that hundreds of civilians in those locations had fled before advancing rebels. Furthermore, he accused the press 'of promoting rebel activities through "false reporting"' and warned that any journalist who published or broadcast the rebel capture of a town 'would be compelled to prove it or be treated as a rebel'.

On the day following President Doe's press conference, Taylor telephoned the BBC World Service to tell the world what he thought of Samuel Doe and his ultimatum. Again using the royal 'we' and addressing White by his first name, he spoke as if they were both on the same side of the argument – knights together fighting evil – he, absolutely denying any desire to inherit the kingdom, but knowing that at the end he might be dragged screaming and struggling to the throne by an imploring populace.

WHITE: 'Mr Taylor, some time ago, you told me that you had no intention of becoming Liberia's next leader. Is that still your position?'

TAYLOR: 'The Liberian people, I tell you, Robin, they will eventually decide. I am not sure if they are going to let me get off the hook … I am not sure if they are going to let me have my way, regardless of what I think. I think they are going to hold me responsible for rebuilding their country and bringing lives back to normal'.[39]

***

In America Ted Hayden was keeping his Provincial up to date with the latest information available to him.[40] In the last days of April he had received a phone call from Amos Sawyer. Clearly events were moving fast. Sawyer told him that officials of the ruling National Democratic Party of Liberia (NDPL), with the knowledge of President Doe, had contacted the U.S.-based Association for Constitutional Democracy in Liberia (ACDL) of which Sawyer was a member, to ask it to use its good offices to bring about a settlement of the Liberian crisis. Now these officials wanted the ACDL 'to contact Taylor's Patriotic Front to bring them into the discussions.' Doe, Sawyer was convinced, was 'looking for some sort of safe passage out of Liberia'. The ACDL had responded to these overtures, seeking assurances that those speaking for the NDPL were doing so with real authority.[41] To put Sawyer's mind at rest on this, the NDPL officials had agreed to meet with President Doe on that very day to discuss the proposition of an interim government, and would phone him with the result. But no phone call came and when asked later by Robin White if he was about to broker peace talks in Washington Sawyer declared he had no authority to do so and 'did not have the leverage to bring Charles Taylor or President Doe to the table'.[42]

Taylor continued to make use of the BBC World Service, calling the station to challenge GOL reports about the course of the war, offering snippets of information about new GOL atrocities, reacting to coverage of the conflict in the international media, and speaking like the soul of reasonableness. His claims about the behaviour of GOL were difficult to prove or disprove but always sounded authoritative. Only on rare occasions did he overstep the bounds of credibility as, for instance, when he told of an arms accord between Liberia and Taiwan; and of a Taiwanese ship already on the high seas with a consignment of arms bound for Monrovia. Responding to the allegation on Radio ELBC on 30 April, the Taiwan embassy expressed amazement at the report.[43]

It now appeared that as the rebels closed in on the capital, nearing Robertsfield international airport, and the port town of Buchanan,* the fall of the regime was imminent. At least Taylor was telling the world it was so. In the last days of April, he told Agence France-Presse that his soldiers had advanced to within two hours of Monrovia and could strike at any time. He also said that between 3,000 and 5,000 civilians had been massacred by GOL forces in Nimba county while his own soldiers – some 3,000 strong – had killed the same number of government forces for the loss of between 300 and 500. Doe's forces, he said, had fled from Nimba leaving a trail of destruction in their wake. 'Skeletons, skulls, bones are to be found all over the towns and villages burned in north-eastern Liberia'.[44] And with his keen sense of the value of publicity, as well as studied righteous indignation, he invited journalists and television crews into Nimba County to 'show the world what that boy (Doe) did to that county'. Nonetheless, Taylor's public persona belied a nervousness which caused him to delay for the best part of a month before he was sufficiently confident to launch a further offensive, taking the towns of Kakata, Harbel and finally over-running the Firestone Plantation.

By the beginning of May a large number of expatriates, including businessmen, diplomats and missionaries, and half of the 5,000 U.S. citizens estimated to be resident in Liberia, had already left, and the regime's capacity to resist the tide of rebellion was quickly ebbing.[45] Buchanan, 60 miles from Monrovia, was being defended by 400 untrained army recruits while those at the front fighting the rebels were mainly young boys, press-ganged into the army, who fled at the first sound of gunfire.[46] On 1 May *The Washington Post* told

---

★ Although in recent years Buchanan has been designated a city, in this study it will be referred to as a town.

its readers of a chartered Pan Am flight and two Swiss-Air flights which had left two days previously containing Peace Corp volunteers, missionaries and dependents of diplomats. Some 350 Britons and nationals of other countries catered for by the British consulate, had also been flown to safely. The advice from the U.S. and British embassies to their citizens was to leave the country immediately.

Meanwhile efforts to resolve the crisis were emerging nearer home. On 2 May the government's mouthpiece, ELBC, broadcast a 'special programme' – the first in a series – hosted by one Paul Wieh and 'designed to focus on the search for peace in Liberia'. The programme was sponsored by a body calling itself the Joint Peace Committee of Citizens of Nimba, River Cess and Grand Gedeh counties.[47] The broadcast tiptoed along gently, conspicuously fearful of antagonising the belligerents.

> Charles Taylor has succeeded to some extent in sending out brothers against brothers in Nimba county. But he is a Liberian and those that are fighting with him are Liberians. Therefore, a possibility exists that whatever grievances or problems Charles Taylor may have experienced could be resolved peacefully in Liberia, but this cannot be done while fighting goes on. We call upon Charles Taylor in furtherance of the president's peace initiative to lay down his arms and go to the designated safety zones...

Some three weeks after declaring he lacked the leverage to bring Taylor to the table, Sawyer contacted Hayden with the news that NPFL leader had responded favourably to an ACDL proposal for a round-table conference, provided a truce was brokered and President Doe resigned. Those attending, tasked with setting up an interim government, would include the NPFL, the ruling NDPL and all other political parties certified in 1984 by the Special Elections Commission.[48] If such a meeting was held – and Sawyer thought it might take place in the Gambia – Taylor had signalled his agreement not to attend in person but to be represented. This was the first in a long line of such responses to peace-making proposals over the next ten years, with the NPFL leader seeming to accept (and creating a surge of hope that peace might be at hand) but placing conditions which were either unworkable or unrealistic.

Calls for peace talks, hitherto confined to Liberians at home or overseas, were now coming from the international community, with the U.S. taking the lead. These could be less easily ignored by the belligerents. Alarmed by persistent reports of GOL atrocities in Nimba, the U.S. administration, principal supporter of the Doe regime, was becoming progressively embarrassed. Deeply engaged with extricating U.S. citizens, businessmen, diplomats and their dependents, and recognising that the regime's military situation was deteriorating, the State Department began to urge dialogue with the rebels. Meanwhile, with its fortunes in decline, elements within GOL also appeared ready to embrace some form of negotiation.

To this end and with encouragement from the State Department, early in May a delegation of GOL ministers and 'prominent private citizens' travelled to Washington for talks with officials. Leading the group was Winston Tubman; also in the party was Posts & Telegraphs Minister, Morris Dukuly and Information Minister, Emannuel Bowier. A meeting was scheduled between Winston Tubman and Herman Jay Cohen[49], who had succeeded Chester Crocker as U.S. Assistant Secretary of State for African Affairs. The delegation was also to meet with members of the House International Relations Sub-Committee on Africa and with the ACDL.[50] However, from the moment of its arrival, although armed with illustrious credentials, doubts began to arise as to whether the delegation had the only credential which really mattered, namely, the support of President Doe.

***

On Wednesday 9 May President Doe held a news conference during which he announced the formation of a Human Rights Commission and declared that elections would still be held on schedule in 1991. He also extended the deadline for the rebels to give up their arms and announced the establishment of new reception centres to which they should go (changed from the previous list because of rebel advances). Doe's extraordinary offer, made from a position of terminal weakness, was characterised by some as the last blind wager by a deranged man.[51] Others saw it as a move by a cunning streetfighter to gain time.

And indeed, in some quarters there was beginning to be a feeling that a rebel victory was not as imminent as originally predicted. *AFJN Information* estimated that while Doe could not win on the battlefield, 'he could hold the city of Monrovia for a considerable period'. It also noted a recent lull in the fighting. Taylor seemed poised to take the Robertsfield international airport but had held back. Clearly there were good reasons why Taylor should seek a quick victory. For increasing doubts were being expressed in the U.S. about his democratic credentials and his suitability as a political leader. Why then did he hold back? The fact was that, as mentioned earlier, Taylor was less sure of himself than his public persona would suggest. Whatever lay behind this - whether it was military weakness, political uncertainty, or fear of outside intervention - there now appeared a definite nervousness in the rebel camp.

Some plausible but unconvincing, explanations for Taylor's failure to 'finish the job' came from Tom Woewiyu, now chief spokesperson for the rebels. Hayden had known Woewiyu and worked with him when President of the ULAA. Woewiyu told Hayden when they spoke by phone on 16 May that the NPFL had not taken Robertsfield international airport because the U.S. administration had asked them to hold off. And this request had been repeated more recently when Woewiyu had met Ambassador James Keough Bishop in Monrovia.

Clearly, as was the case among many Liberians and outsiders closely acquainted with Liberia, Hayden hoped that Taylor might actually be a knight in shining armour, an image which both Taylor and Woewiyu assiduously cultivated. Taylor was given the benefit of the doubt from such people in those early months. Hoping against hope that Taylor might fulfil their expectations, the capacity to be taken in by a cunning and ruthless man was further increased by Taylor's manipulation of the media. On almost all occasions he came across as eminently reasonable, as one who abhorred bloodshed and whose sole interest was to see a tyrant overthrown and a modern democracy installed. Others who had joined Taylor, such as Woewiyu, were also articulate and reasonable, portraying themselves as poles apart from the primitive, uneducated cadre which had led Liberia since 1980. It was in these circumstances, hoping against hope that Taylor would live up to his expectations, that Hayden gave some consideration to a suggestion from 'Tom Woewiyu' that he should visit Liberia to see for himself 'the areas held by the NPFL and what is happening there'.[52]

Woewiyu had told Hayden that 'it would be good' for him to go there, adding that he knew and trusted Hayden so he 'would be free to move about' and could then report whatever he saw. The reason for the invitation, according to Woewiyu, was the desirability of having 'an impartial person visit the territory held by the NPFL who could give an objective report'. Hayden was hesitant, saying that he was 'not interested in any … political involvement to remove Doe', and 'would not be associated with any particular political solution'. But Woewiyu replied that was precisely why he had issued the invitation. Whatever Hayden reported 'would be trusted not only by the NPFL but by other Liberians, including political leaders.' Eventually Hayden told him that he would not be able to decide without consultation with his superiors.

Evidently prepared to consider the proposition, but ultimately doubtful, Hayden discussed it with his Provincial Superior, S. John Murray, and both calculated the advantages and disadvantages of such a visit. Among advantages would be the fact that AFJN and other U.S.-based groups concerned with human rights in Liberia 'would have a first-hand account of what is happening in the NPFL-held areas.' On the other hand, the visit might also be perceived as giving 'Church backing to the NPFL'. This, in truth, was the principal 'disadvantage'. At the end of the day, both men wisely agreed that there were 'more minuses than pluses.' There is no record of Woewiyu's reaction, but one can surmise that it was one of disappointment at the slipping by of an opportunity to manipulate what he considered to be an impressionable American clergyman who happened to possess a high profile.

***

On 17 May information about the talks between State Department officials and the Liberian delegation in Washington reached SMA headquarters in Tenafly. It had been obtained by the industrious James Butty[*] from Paul H. Means,[53] 'an American public relations consultant employed by the Liberian delegation',

---

[*]   Butty was a student leader who fell foul of the Doe regime and had been assisted by the Catholic Mission to leave Liberia and come to the U.S. There, at the University of Minnesota, he acquired a degree in journalism and international relations.

who had attended the talks as an advisor.[54] The U.S. officials, according to Means, had proposed that there be immediate elections, conducted under international supervision. Alternatively, they suggested that Doe might resign and that an interim government might rule until scheduled elections in 1991. However, neither of these solutions was acceptable to the Liberian delegation.

In the end the State Department appeared to revert to an earlier position, namely that the matter would have to be 'sorted out' between Liberians; and that could only mean one thing, a military solution[55] Unable to make headway, the Liberian delegation concluded its business in the U.S. having been told authoritatively by administration officials and members of Congress that Doe was no longer acceptable. They would now return to Liberia, reluctantly and disappointed, with the unequivocal message from Washington that Doe must resign, an interim government must be formed, and elections must be held at the earliest possible moment. The delegation's parting message for the administration, delivered by Winston Tubman, sounding notes of sadness, resignation and not a little frustration, made it clear to observers that nothing had been gained. 'Of course, we know we are a small country and President Bush is busy with Eastern Europe, but the problem of Liberia has an older history than that, and it is a direct responsibility of the U.S.'.[56]

***

As the Liberian insurgency unfolded and began to intrude on the consciousness of the wider American public, curiosity developed as to exactly who was this Taylor, the charismatic, mild-mannered, modern, leader of the rebels, whose familiar Americanised tones could be heard regularly over the airwaves of the BBC World Service, like an evangelist, demonising the incumbent Liberian regime and preaching the virtues of peace, order and, above all, democracy. Delving into his past a rather different picture began to emerge of this Americo-Liberian who had first come to the Boston area as a young man to study economics. A lengthy article by Richard McKenzie published in the 21 May issue of *Insight*, a weekly magazine of *The Washington Times*, gave pause for thought. The Associated Press too offered a narrative which raised eyebrows. Various newspapers, mainly local and regional, picked up the story which created a minor sensation at the time.[57] Among the revelations were details of Taylor's dramatic escape from Plymouth prison while awaiting extradition to Liberia:

> On 15 September 1985, during recreation time, Charles Taylor … asked a guard to bend the rules and let him pass from the north wing to the east wing, saying he wanted to play cards with a friend. The guard was persuaded and left his post going to the recreation hall for a few minutes. During this time Taylor and his accomplices – two car thieves - using a hacksaw blade, sawed through the bars on a second-floor window, reached ground level, climbed a 10-foot fence by means of a rope made of bedsheets and hid in an adjacent wood. It was Taylor who planned the escape, offering bribes to other inmates for their cooperation. In the event he was the only one to elude re-arrest and was, indeed, according to Plymouth County Sheriff, Peter Flynn, the only

escapee in the history of the 153-old jail to successfully abscond. His flight from the environs of the jail was assisted by his wife and sister who waited in a car near a highway. They were subsequently charged for aiding and abetting, but never brought to trial.[58]

Shortly after his escape there was a reported sighting of Taylor in New York.

The trail then went dry until 1987 when there were reports [uncorroborated][59] that he had surfaced in Ghana. Little was known of what subsequently happened to him apart from the strong rumour that he eventually reached Libya where he was welcomed by the leader, Colonel Qaddhafi, who provided him with the means to raise a small force to overthrow the pro-American Doe regime.[60]

Notes

1 Daily Observer, 20 December 1989.
2 Ibid. The report quoted from Jean-Baptiste Placca, 'Liberia, Journey into the rebel stronghold', Jeune Afrique, 12 March 1990.
3 Ibid. See also, The Washington Post, 19 March 1990.
4 The account here is based on Matthew Brelis's profile published in the Boston Globe, Friday, 3 August 1990.
5 Ibid.
6 The New York Times, 14 July 1990; AFP, 15 April 1990; Boston Globe, 3 August 1990.
7 John Kilcoyne, op. cit., 13.
8 This capacity has been expertly explored by Yekutiel Gershoni in 'Military and Diplomatic Strategies in the Liberian Civil War', Liberian Studies Journal, XXII, 2 (1997).
9 Anthony Jennings, Personal Diary, 'Civil War in Liberia, 24 December 1989', 2.
10 Ibid.
11 The Independent (London), 29 January 1990.
12 Ibid.
13 Ibid.
14 Daily Observer, 30 January 1990 (article by Philip N. Wesseh).
15 Ibid.
16 Daily Observer, 15 February 1990.
17 Ibid.
18 BBC World Service, 29 March 1990 – 'Focus on Africa'.
19 Radio ELBC, 30 March 1990.
20 In 2000.
21 The Liberian Truth and Reconciliation Commission examined the influence of media reporting on events during the civil war. See LTRC, Consolidated Final Report, Volume Three, Appendices (Media and Outreach in the TRC Process), 'Criticism of the International Media', Title V153–157.
22 www.bbc.co.uk/news/world-africa-17845592. Accessed 1 February 2014.
23 FBIS-AFR-90–060, 28/3/1990. AB2703213890 (Paris AFP in French).
24 'Africa Watch' Report, April 1990 (New York, Washington, London).
25 Ibid.
26 Transcript of ELWA broadcast, 2 April 1990.
27 Ibid, broadcast of 3 April 1990.
28 Ibid.
29 Testimony of Abuses in Nimba County (May 1990), Part IV.

30 AFJN Information, transcript of Radio ELWA, "Legislature Rejects Dialogue with Nimba Rebel Chief', 4 April 1990.

31 Ibid.

32 FBIS-AFR-90–067, 6/4/1990 (AB0504175090 Dakar PANA in English).

33 FBIS-AFR-90–067, 6/4/1990 (AB0504212790, Monrovia Radio ELWA).

34 The LTRC reported that Julu led the atrocities in the wake of the 1985 Quiwonkpa coup. See LTRC, Consolidated Final Report, vol. 2, no. 147, 218.

35 A.T. Hayden to S. John Murray, 9 April 1990.

36 Ibid.

37 24 March 1990.

38 AFP, 16 April 1990.

39 FBIS-AFR-90–082, 27 April 1990 (AB2604183990 London BBC World Service, 'Focus on Africa').

40 A.T. Ted Hayden, to S. John Murray, 30 April 1990.

41 Ibid.

42 Ibid, Hayden to Murray, 1 May 1990 (10.30 am, conversation with Dr Amos Sawyer).

43 Radio ELWA, 301990: 'Taiwan Embassy Denies Report on Arms Accord'.

44 The Washington Times, Tuesday, 1 May 1990 (AFP, Monrovia).

45 Ibid.

46 Ibid.

47 AFJN Information, Monrovia, Radio ELWA, 2 May 1990 (transcript).

48 AFJN Information, Washington, 8 May 1990.

49 Cohen held this office during the Bush Presidency (1989–93).

50 Butty, AFJN Information, Washington D.C., 8 May 1990, 'A "Peace Mission" in the US'.

51 The AFJN subscribed to the section of broadcasts on Africa transcribed by the State Department.

52 A.T. Hayden to S. John Murray, 16 May 1990.

53 Paul H. Means appeared earlier as a spokesperson for the Opex initiative.

54 Ibid.

55 Ibid, 17 May 1990.

56 Africa News, 28 May 1990.

57 See, for example, The Boston Globe, in which Matthew Brelis described Taylor's dramatic escape from Federal prison. C.f, Patriot Ledger (MA), 17 May 1990 (based on a report by Richard McKenzie published in the 21 May issue of Insight and by an Associated Press account).

58 Matthew Brelis, Boston Globe, 3 August 1990.

59 Author's insertion in brackets.

60 The TRC Consolidated Final Report, vol. 2, 310, asserts that it was President Blaise Compaoré of Burkina Faso who introduced Taylor to the Libyan leader and convinced him that Taylor possessed the credentials to overthrow the Doe government.

9 Peacekeeping and mediation interventions emerge as the rebel conquest of Monrovia stalls

Situated in Ganta, within three miles of the Guinea border, a small community of Medical Missionaries of Mary Sisters maintained a Leprosarium and TB Rehabilitation Centre. By mid-March 1990 most schools in the town had closed because a large part of the population had fled. The Peace Corps had left in January, and most expatriate staff in the adjacent United Methodist hospital had also departed. Since the early weeks of the insurgency some 200 inhabitants from two nearby villages 'too scared to remain in their homes at night' had taken refuge in the Rehabilitation Centre. And by the first week of April numbers in the Centre had swollen to almost 600, with a steady influx of refugees.

Efforts to get patients and refugees to safety either over the border to Guinea or southwards to Gbarnga continued throughout April into May. But as roads were closed and travel to the border with Guinea became more hazardous the numbers evacuated dwindled. By mid-May the rebels first began to launch sustained attacks on the town. Contact between the Sisters – Enda Gallagher, a medical doctor and Bridget Murphy, manager of the Centre – and the MMM motherhouse in Drogheda, Ireland, was maintained through the mission radio network. Ganta fell to the rebels on 14 May, after which there was no further radio contact with the Sisters.

On Sunday 21 May, by which time all efforts to make contact with the Sisters had failed, rumours began to circulate in Monrovia that two Catholic missionary sisters had been killed in Ganta. The rumours originated, it seems, with a British embassy official.* Attempting to establish the truth, Archbishop Francis was told that the embassy suspected the 'Sisters had been killed during a fierce battle on the grounds of the Rehabilitation Centre between the government army and the NPFL.'[1] But four days later came news that the Sisters were safe. They had been taken away from Ganta by the rebels for a short time while the attack on government soldiers at the Centre took place but were

---

* 'The Superintendent of the Methodist Mission in Ganta told a British embassy staff member he had been informed that the Rehabilitation Centre was destroyed and the Sisters were among the people killed', see MMM Archive, Archbishop Francis to Sister Catherine Dwyer, MMM Superior General, 24 May 1990.

DOI: 10.4324/9781003219309-12

later brought back and had resumed their work.[2] Two years later another group of missing Sisters was to be less fortunate.

***

The fall of Ganta was followed within a week by the rebel capture of Buchanan. Before the civil war the Catholic mission there, named after St Peter Claver, had been thriving. Its central station and ten outstations boasted a membership of over 1,000. Apart from the daily work of evangelisation and pastoral care the mission ran a medical program and had schools in the town managed by Italian Consolata Sisters, as well as rural schools which the Fathers supervised. The Buchanan mission was growing with every prospect of a bright future. The civil war, which had now intruded with a vengeance, was to change all that. John Kilcoyne SMA, assistant pastor there, was to compile a record of that intrusion a few months after the event, by which time the town had become 'a front line in the increasingly brutal civil war.'[3]

Life in Buchanan, as mentioned, had first changed in April and early May, as government soldiers began systematic targeting of Mano and Gio residents. Again and again during those months Tony Jennings (pastor) and Kilcoyne were called upon to hide Mano and Gio families or spirit them out of the town. At the time the UN Disaster Relief Organisation (UNDRO) had designated the Catholic Mission as a feeding centre for refugees, and by mid-May hundreds were receiving food daily, 'many arriving with heart-rending stories of brutality, 'coming only with the clothes they were wearing...'[4] The crisis, the mission diary recorded:

> was reached on Saturday, 19 May. At about 2.00 pm news was received of an ambush near the Benson river bridge. This caused consternation in the town and within a matter of minutes the streets were deserted. At about 4.00 pm the gunfire began. Gradually it came closer and closer to us. The NPFL forces had arrived.

The missionaries spent the remainder of that day and the following morning on the floor of the mission house while fighting went on outside.[5] Then, at about 1.30 pm, 'several members of the NPFL arrived at our front door heavily armed.' Their leader was a Liberian called Elmer Johnson, said to have been formally a U.S. marine, and now military advisor to Charles Taylor. 'He said that they had come to evacuate us'.[6] Later that day Kilcoyne and Jennings were escorted inland to the Catholic mission at the Liberia Agricultural Company (LAC):, an 'incredible wild journey past numerous ambush sites...'

On 25 May Kilcoyne and Jennings, anxious to visit their old mission – even for a day – returned to Buchanan, escorted by NPFL soldiers under Johnson. On the way, Johnson pointed out the site of a massacre carried out by the army. According to his account, government soldiers had accused the villagers of helping the rebels and set about killing all the men, women and children they could find. There had certainly been a massacre. Kilcoyne described the sight.

The bodies remained piled under orange trees. The sight and smell of a mass murder, which had occurred two weeks previously, was numbing and I will never forget it. Later we would meet some survivors in LAC hospital, a number horribly injured.[7]

Buchanan had an eerie feel about it:

When we reached the town, we found it very changed. This time there were no GOL soldiers on the streets but NPFL everywhere. They had taken over the whole town including the port. We were escorted to the mission and got strict instructions not to leave the campus. Soon pick-up vehicles began to arrive manned by NPFL looking for rice (intended for the refugees). In all seven came. We had no option but to let them take it.[8]

What especially lingered in memory was the massacre at the village en route to Buchanan. But there had been atrocities on both sides and Buchanan, now in the hands of the rebels, had presented a dangerous and sorry spectacle with

NPFL fighters tearing around in stolen cars against a background of continuous gunfire. Few civilians were to be seen... On that day, too, we watched helplessly as the food we had stored for ourselves and the refugees was looted.

For ten consecutive days back in LAC requests to return to Buchanan were denied on the grounds of repeated government counterattacks and lack of an available escort. Most of Buchanan's citizens had taken refuge in the bush, many of them walking the 30 miles before streaming into the LAC mission compound. Finally, on 6 June Kilcoyne and Sister Paula, one of the Consolata sisters, got transport to Buchanan in an NPFL pick-up.

It was a dreadful journey. The road was thronged with people, tired and listless. As we approached the town bodies were strewn on the road. And in the town bodies littered the streets. A front-loader was being used to remove them, and where a body had been moved a stain remained on the road. The smell of death pervaded the streets against a background of continuous shooting. Our mission house and the convent had been looted. It was our lowest point.

Three weeks later and permanently back in Buchanan, Kilcoyne and Jennings began the work of making the mission house habitable. They also spent time comforting returnees to the town, 'mourning with the mourning and praying for the dead and maimed'.[9]

***

Gbarnga, 103 miles from Monrovia and about 68 miles south-west of Ganta, was another large town in the path of the rebel advance as it moved inexorably towards the capital. Here was located the headquarters of the Catholic diocese of that name, led by Bishop Benedict Dotu Sekey, as well as St Paul's inter-territorial[10] major seminary. One missionary who wrote frankly about the experience of these months in Gbarnga was Michael O'Leary, an Irish SMA, who at the time of the incursion was administering the diocesan Pastoral Centre. O'Leary's account deserves notice because it gives insight into the dilemma facing missionaries, whether they should remain at their posts or seek safety elsewhere.[11]

From 1989, while resident in Gbarnga, O'Leary had also taken on responsibility for St Mary's parish in Ganta. This required travelling some 80 miles there and back every Sunday to celebrate Mass for the parish community and minister to the MMM Rehabilitation Centre. As the rebels advanced southwards, so did travelling to Ganta mission become more hazardous. By Easter week (8–15 April) the situation had deteriorated to such an extent that O'Leary decided not to travel to Ganta for Easter ceremonies. It was a judgement that proved wise, as on that weekend there was an NPFL attack on the town.[12]

O'Leary's weekly trips to Ganta had introduced him 'to the pressures of the rebel episode' at a very early stage. Gbarnga, however, had been 'relatively unaffected.' But now the civil war began to impinge. The Pastoral Centre, which provided residential courses for people from outlying areas and other towns and counties, began to suffer and by the beginning of April had ceased to offer programs. At much the same time both the major seminary and Gbarnga's secondary boarding school (run by English Christian Brothers) sent their students home. The FMM sisters vacated their convent shortly after this. Following the closure of these institutions a total of seven missionary personnel remained in Gbarnga, two in the seminary, two at the Christian Brothers compound, two in the parish and O'Leary in the Pastoral Centre. The seven met regularly to discuss the deteriorating situation. One decision taken was to give refuge in the Pastoral Centre compound to all who sought sanctuary, and this was done. However, the last vestiges of a normal society disappeared from the town after a rebel ambush on a convoy in which a number of local people, taken as a human shield, were killed. This caused 'at least 50% of the popula-tion of Gbarnga to flee the town.'[13] Next, within days, came a serious outbreak of fighting in the vicinity of the mission, lasting several hours, which caused the remaining population to flee.

There followed a 'particularly trying time' for the missionaries who now found themselves in a town devoid of people apart from the refugees in the Pastoral Centre. What was being achieved by remaining? And how long could the already dwindling food provisions last? How would the refugees survive if the missionaries were no longer there? Remaining in order to protect mission buildings would be futile, for with the removal of the missionaries, all mission property would be looted. The discussion as to what was the best course intensified. Some argued in favour of departure, others against. Marooned in Gbarnga, the group, in O'Leary's words 'spent a lot of time coping with these questions' over the early weeks of May. The uncertainty and lack of unanimity exacerbated the strain endured by all. Wisely, all were to depart before the arrival of the NPFL and when a measure of stability was restored those able returned to their posts.

***

The rebel onslaught reached Bong Mine* on 6 June 1990. John Feeney, member of the SMA's American Province, in charge of the Catholic mission there, was not impressed by the new arrivals;

> The so-called Freedom Fighters immediately set about terrorizing the populace by driving recklessly through town and shooting indiscriminately in the air. A few people were killed on the first day, all members of the Krahn and Mandingo ethnic groups.[14]

Feeney, a tough, strongly built man from the West of Ireland, who kept a journal, was not intimidated.

> Peter Nyemah, an assistant catechist, his sister, Oretha, and her baby arrived at the Mission at 1.00 pm seeking sanctuary. They are of the Krahn tribe. At 7 pm they were joined by another Krahn, a draughtsman employee of the Bong Mine company by the name of Glann Tarr and a Kpelle man by the name of Gibson.

When the mother and child were able to go to safety Nyemah and Tarr remained behind and were to become 'guests' of the mission, hidden out of sight for the next nine months. They were among the lucky ones.

> By the second day a systematic search was organised for Krahn and Mandingo. When found they were immediately bound, tortured, and eventually put to death by having their throats cut, or killed by gunfire. Their houses were then looted, and all property confiscated.

***

From Monrovia the U.S. Embassy was now issuing 'Emergency Evacuation Procedures' for its citizens.[15] A covering note said there was no anticipation of a need to evacuate, and that the instructions were merely an exercise in contingency planning. But few had any doubt that the notification was issued against a growing and proximate threat.

In America 'Africa Watch', was calling on the Bush administration 'to strongly urge GOL and the NPFL to respect the integrity of the civilian population ... in keeping with the provisions of Article 3 of the Geneva Convention.'[16] A letter had

---

*   Bong Mine, located in Bong County some 70 miles from Monrovia, was reputed to be one of the world's largest iron ore holdings. Thyssen, a German company, commenced mining there in 1958. A town grew up around the mining complex. In this book the 'town' is referred to as 'Bong Mine.'

already been sent to Secretary of State, James A. Baker III, urging him to be more pro-active in calling for 'the humane treatment of prisoners held by both sides and for guarantees of their protection from reprisals.' In its submissions 'Africa Watch' made reference to recent killings in Monrovia and in particular the discovery, on 22 May of the bodies of ten persons, all named, belonging to the Mano and Gio ethnic groups. Evidently, 'Africa Watch' had detailed, up-to-date information, so much so that ignoring it might cause embarrassment to the administration. In fact, the statement already contained some new, potentially embarrassing, intelligence about U.S. military assistance to the government.

> In February, two U.S. military advisors accompanied the Liberian army as it sought to put down the rebel insurgency. The advisors were withdrawn after protests by human rights groups. However, reports reaching 'Africa Watch' indicate that, on May 15, a U.S. military advisor accompanied Liberian army commanders to Buchanan to assist in an investigation into reports of desertions.[17]

***

As curiosity about Taylor grew in the U.S., and information about his past became better known, doubts about his capacity to bring real change to Liberia began to grow stronger. To counter this Taylor, ably assisted by Tom Woewiyu, intensified his public-relations offensive. Woewiyu told *Africa News* that the NPFL had 'backing from every segment of Liberian society.'[18] And he referred to Taylor's statement of 1 January, saying that the NPFL was a 'non-sectarian, nationalist movement which believes in the right of every Liberian to equal protection and opportunity under the law.' But not all Americans believed in such protestations. Assistant Secretary of State Richard Schifter had told the House of Representatives Foreign Affairs Subcommittee as early as 21 February that the rebellion against Samuel Doe was 'a Libyan-supported effort to over-throw him.' Woewiyu agreed with the second part of this description, but absolutely rejected that there was any Libyan involvement. On the contrary the insurgency, he maintained, had been mounted by a mere 'coalition of grassroots citizens.' And proof that there was no Libyan backing could be seen in the fact that when the rebels first crossed the border they were armed with 'only a few hand weapons.' The abundance of weaponry which the rebels now enjoyed had come from fleeing government troops who abandoned their arms. Taylor him-self, speaking to international journalists in Abidjan on 28 April, had rubbished Washington's accusations of Libyan support.[19] However, as Liberia's Truth and Reconciliation Commission made clear in its detailed study of the matter there can be no doubt of the critical role of Colonel Qaddhafi in supporting the NPFL throughout its insurgency.[20]

***

At this time relief efforts in Liberia suffered a setback. Following an attack on its compound in Monrovia UNDRO cancelled its emergency food program for refugees and pulled out its expatriate personnel, eleven in number.[21] Associated

Press stated that in the attack a guard had been killed. But Hayden, quoting local sources in Monrovia, said that 'several persons seeking refuge' had been 'brutally murdered and others were abducted by uniformed soldiers.' The formidable Joyce Mends-Cole[22], the Liberian-born, Washington-based counsel to 'Human Rights Watch', confirmed this in testimony to the U.S. congressional subcommittee on Africa on 19 June.

> In the early hours of 30 May, government troops attacked the UNDRO compound, where over 1,000 Mano and Gio people had sought protection. A group of ten soldiers scaled the wall after killing a security guard … and dragged away 40 persons, bundling them into army vehicles after stripping them of their clothes and possessions. In the days following the attack, a number of bodies appeared in the streets identified by relatives as belonging to the group taken away from the compound.

A chilling account of the incident appeared on the following day under the heading 'Liberian troops massacre United Nations (UN) refugees' written by the London-based *Daily Telegraph*'s Charles Laurence in Monrovia. The motivation for the terrifying attack was clearly linked to tribal hatreds.[23] Later President Doe visited the compound to promise survivors 'his personal protection' and offering to take them to his mansion. But, after saying that he would deal drastically with the murderers, 'he was hissed and booed.'[24]

***

And now the emergency evacuation which, on 24 May, the U.S Embassy had thought most unlikely, was beginning to happen. On Friday 1 June *The Washington Post* told its readers that the U.S. was sending an evacuation flotilla and had ordered most U.S. citizens in Liberia to leave without delay.[25] The rescue flotilla consisted of the *USS Saipan*, a helicopter assault carrier, and five support vessels carrying a detachment of some 2,100 Marines.[26] Its orders were to 'stand by in international waters off Liberia, for the evacuation of U.S. citizens and other non-combatants if so required.' The embassy's evacuation message was broadcast over local radio stations and through other channels circulated in the 'emergency evacuation procedures.' The rebel force was now said to be within 25 miles of Monrovia with some forward elements within two miles. At much the same time Monrovia's *Standard* was reporting a rebel telex sent to Robertsfield international airport saying all employees should evacuate because an attack was imminent. Already, the previous Wednesday, Ghana Airways, the last of the commercial carriers flying into Liberia, had suspended flights.

***

In Monrovia Doe's behaviour was becoming more erratic. In the last week of May he had told a rally that he would resign if that would end the fighting.[27] A few days later he asked the National Assembly to sanction early elections and an interim government, only to be told first to fulfil his promise to step down. Then, on Friday 1 June, he declared he would not resign and would be 'the last person to leave Monrovia', confiding to a group of ambassadors, who had tried to persuade him to leave that 'tough times never last. Tough people do.'[28] Next he was begging all peace-loving nations including the U.S. 'to come to the aid of the Liberian people.'[29]

Close to his President in the Executive Mansion the still buoyant Emmanuel Bowier told the world, on 5 June, that Liberia's ruler would be keeping his promise of the previous Friday, 'to step aside at the next general election in 18 months.' He also announced a press conference on the morrow 'to show photographs of dead rebel leaders' and film demonstrating that government troops had the situation under control.[30] Clearly, within the circle of wagons there now was confusion, fear and signs of desperation. And there was little confidence that President Doe had any real intention of relinquishing power. Instead, his conciliatory statements were interpreted by many as ruses to gain time and diplomatic advantage. Others saw in his erratic behaviour evidence that he was not only losing control of his country but of himself.

***

Meanwhile the U.S. State Department was seeking an African country pre-pared to give asylum to President Doe. And there were reports that, poised for victory, the NPFL leaders were discussing among themselves who should lead the transitional government once the freedom fighters took the capital in three or four days. This information came from NPFL Secretary General, Moses Duopu, who said the NPFL executive, 'which included Charles Taylor', would meet in rebel-held territory to choose a leader. These reports led to some speculation that there might be differences developing within the rebel group-ing. Taylor had stated on several occasions that he did not seek the presidency. But in recent times he had spoken of 'a new government under his leadership.' However, hopes (or fears) that there were serious divisions in NPFL ranks, or that Taylor might be challenged or supplanted, were unfounded. Duopu, in fact, was a remote and lone voice. Moreover, he was not in Liberia with the rebels but rather in Ivory Coast safe from the conflict. His statement that the NPFL executive council 'would meet to decide who would be interim pre-sident until elections can be held', and that 'anyone interested in being head-of-state would have to lobby support from other members of the movement', was unlikely to endear him to those leading the fight. Nor were his assertions that he 'would challenge Mr Taylor over his political ambitions', and that he wanted 'the world to know' that he was 'going up there (Liberia)', and that he had been in contact with several U.S. diplomats in West Africa who were confident of his ability to clip Taylor's wings.[31]

***

Concern for the safety of U.S. citizens in Liberia was by no means the only issue causing the Bush administration anxiety. Officials, according to *The New York Times* of 2 June, were especially worried that 'important U.S. commu-nications installations outside the Liberian capital could be damaged.' As has already been mentioned, these virtually unprotected installations were vital to U.S. strategic interests in Africa. It was true Taylor had told Washington that

American property and citizens were not targets. But the administration was not convinced. The situation was too volatile, and the forces engaged too undisciplined. And while many in the U.S. looked kindly on Taylor, hoping he might become Liberia's liberator, the official U.S. attitude was coloured by suspicion. After all, here was a man accused of stealing large sums of public money. Here also was a man who had ended up in a U.S. prison, had escaped and was believed to have spent time in Libya. In the final analysis the State Department concluded, correctly, that Taylor's struggle was not, as he liked to profess, driven by a Mosaic mission to liberate his people but by a desire to become an African head-of-state of the 'Big-Man' variety.[32] At the same time, the State Department saw no need to seek his removal, believing that just as it had controlled his predecessor it could rein in Taylor whenever it saw fit.

***

And now in Monrovia there appeared the first signs of panic among expatriates as well as indigenes. The *Washington Times* of 5 June reported that 'over 50 embassy workers, missionaries and their families had taken refuge in Spriggs Payne airfield, about five miles from the capital's centre, amid fears of a bloodbath if the rebels took the city.' It also reported some 2,000 Gios and Manos 'jammed into the compound of St Peter's Lutheran Church in Monrovia.' There were increasing signs, too, of panic within the regime. Doe began to plead ever more earnestly for U.S. intervention, announcing that he had ordered his troops into barracks 'because of charges that they were killing members of the tribal groups who supported the rebels.' Henry Dubar, the Liberian forces commanding general, wanted U.S. Marines 'to save Monrovia' telling journalists that 'the armed forces of Liberia would not consider a Marine-landing an invasion … The presence of the Marines here', he said, would 'scare the rebels away.'[33]

***

With Taylor's forces now poised to attack, Monrovia descended into near chaos becoming inaccessible by air and road. Lee Cahill (Regional Superior of the Irish SMA's, responsible for their welfare) reported to his Irish headquarters that all SMA members were safe but were expecting the inevitable rebel onslaught within a matter of days.[34] Looking forward to a future under NPFL control, he felt that so far, the indications were 'favourable.' Mission personnel in towns overrun by the rebels had been treated fairly, which augured well for the future.

It was at this juncture that Taylor, heretofore mainly of interest to the U.S. media, began to enter the consciousness of the American political classes. Richard MacKenzie signposted this development in a *Washington Times* article of 5 June, revealing a growing curiosity in political circles about Taylor and an acknowledgement that he had arrived as an important player on the West African stage. It was his alleged support from Qaddhafi of Libya which was causing the greatest concern. The Bush administration was now convinced that the support Taylor was receiving from the Libyan dictator was part of an attempt to 'destabilise Black Africa.' A senior administration official had stated that it was not a question of whether we think he may be getting support from Qaddhafi; rather that is a matter of absolute fact. We know that Libyan money went into Taylor's coffers; and most of the people who were with him at the beginning were trained in Libya.[35]

And yet, the same official had to admit that Taylor had never openly expressed anti-American sentiments. 'Every American who has dealt with Taylor so far has found him not to be anti-American', although he was 'certainly not somebody we are going to welcome with open arms.'[36]

***

For whatever reason, the long-awaited assault on a surrounded Monrovia, expected by the end of the first week of June, failed to materialise. Instead, on the morning of 14 June, emerging out of the apocalyptic gloom, came a large crowd, colourfully clad and waving palm leaves. Winding its way through the streets of the city the procession moved out through the suburbs to the gates of the beachside U.S. embassy.

Responding to the demonstration Dennis Jett, Chargé d'Affaires at the U.S. embassy, appeared at the embassy gates to tell the crowd that President Doe must resign in order to bring peace to Liberia. And he recalled Doe's recent pledge that he was willing to make 'any sacrifice' for peace. Jett's words were greeted by loud cheering from the demonstrators. But another U.S. embassy official told a *Washington Post* correspondent, Neil Henry, that Doe had no intention of quitting. 'He says he is afraid about what would happen to the country … he is concerned about confusion'!

On the day following the peace march an apparently pathetic and delusional President Doe gave an hour-long interview to Kenneth B. Noble of *The New York Times*, complaining bitterly about Liberia's abandonment by the U.S., 'it's oldest ally on the African continent.' The uninterrupted string of victories by the rebels, he explained, should be 'rightly attributed to the government's fear of harming unarmed civilians.' Moreover, he could see no reason why he should yield to calls for his resignation. What crime had he committed! Were he to have broken the law, the constitution provided for impeachment by the Legislature! Yet no one had attempted such a step. Moreover, how could he be accused of human rights abuses given his love for the people and they for him! And yet he had been vilified in the U.S. press on this very matter.

***

It will be recalled that in early May 1990 Taylor had said that he would be prepared to send delegates to a 'round-table conference' brokered by the US-based Association for Constitutional Democracy in Liberia, conditional on Doe's exclusion from the process. Behind the scenes, the Liberian Inter-Faith Mediation Committee (IFMC) had been working independently for some time to set up such a conference. The Liberian Council of Churches was not directly involved. After its attempt at mediation in the wake of the 1986 elections had been rebuffed by the head-of-state, that body had displayed a more conciliatory attitude, seeking a rapprochement, or at least a *modus vivendi*, with the regime lest its members be prohibited from conducting their pastoral and evangelising ministries. Nonetheless a number of LCC Churchmen, acting as members of the IFMC, 'refused to be silenced.'[37] The most prominent were the immediate past president of the Baptist Convention and current president of the LCC, Rev. J.K. Levee Moulton and Archbishop Michael Francis. These were at the forefront of a new effort to broker a peace, although the prospect of success was slight.

Overwhelming pressure from the international community and particularly the U.S., for some form of negotiations, lent urgency to the IFMC efforts. Desperate to halt the onslaught by Taylor's forces, Doe had blown hot and cold about mediation, but eventually had little option but to consent. Militarily in the ascendant but with his lines of communication stretched, uncertain perhaps as to what might happen within the NPFL after victory, anxious to win U.S. favour (or prevent its intervention) and exhibiting again that hesitancy and nervousness which manifested itself at moments of crisis, Taylor also agreed. The round-table Peace Conference between the government and the NPFL, under the supervision of the IFMC, got under way in the U.S. Cultural Centre in Freetown, Sierra Leone, on 12 June. The IFMC members were the distinguished Baptist Reverend J.K. Moulton, Lutheran Bishop Ronald Diggs, Muslim Council Secretary General, Sheikh Kafumba Konneh and Archbishop Francis. The NPFL delegation was led by Enoch Dogolea and included Woewiyu, while the government was represented by Tangaba Jankaba of the Liberian senate, Minister Jenkins Scott and Emmanuel Bowier as spokesperson.[38] On the second day of the conference a press release announced the encouraging, and certainly surprising, news that both sides had approved an agenda for substantive talks.

What appeared to be further encouraging news came in a press release on 16 June announcing that after five sessions the gathering had gone into recess to allow the delegations consult with their respective principals. The IFMC, too, would consult with Doe and Taylor and the talks would resume on Monday, 25 June, at which time all issues advanced by the government and the NPFL would be 'further negotiated and resolved.'[39]

The supposedly positive atmosphere within the conference was in no small measure, owing to the many concessions that the government delegation was offering in the hope that the NPFL would agree to a compromise. A general amnesty to NPFL members and all anti-government forces was now on offer; also, the reinstatement of banned political parties and organisations and a commitment that President Doe would not run in the 1991 national elections. These inducements, placed on the table by the regime's delegation were, in fact, to have little effect. Archbishop Francis, less sanguine than most about the level of progress, wrote starkly to S. John Murray that, despite the public perception, no conclusions had been arrived at on any substantive matter.[40] The NPFL had demanded that the government president, vice-president and chief of staff resign before any ceasefire – a requirement that President Doe had rejected. The result was deadlock. Attached to the archbishop's letter was a photocopied handwritten document titled: 'National Patriotic Front of Liberia – Conditions for Ceasefire.' These amounted to a call for surrender, requiring not only the resignation of the president and his cabinet, but the transfer of full control over the armed forces to the NPFL. The government delegation had rejected these terms out of hand and made its own lengthy, if unlikely, series of counter proposals. To what extent the principals were involved in the conference is unclear, but it seems likely that neither played any active part. Both stood well back from the proceedings, Taylor satisfied that the international community would be impressed by his willingness to enter into negotiation, Doe satisfied that the conference was merely another throw of the dice which might signal a change of fortune or at least give him more time.

During the recess the IFMC members fulfilled their commitment to 'touch base with Mr Doe and Mr Taylor.' The latter, who they met in Tappita, gave assurances that the NPFL delegation would return to the talks. Back in Freetown the mediation committee also met Dr Abass Bundu, Secretary General of the regional Economic Community of West African Nations (ECOWAS), who had arrived some days before the talks were scheduled to re-convene. The involvement of ECOWAS was of substantial significance, signalling for the first time, that Liberia's crisis was no longer confined within that country's borders but was of regional concern. And ECOWAS had already taken an initiative, something which caused considerable surprise to the members of the IFMC committee, when Dr Bundu informed them that he had recently presented President Doe with a four-point plan for resolving the crisis, and even greater surprise to hear that he had accepted. The plan involved a ceasefire, an ECOWAS peace-keeping force, an interim government without Doe or Taylor and early elections. ECOWAS representatives, he told the mediation committee, were now on their way to put the plan to Taylor. A few days later Dr Bundu was able to tell the IFMC members that what appeared to be unconceivable had happened. Taylor, too, had accepted the ECOWAS plan.

Nobody was more surprised than Archbishop Francis. But within a week surprise had turned to disbelief and anger. Writing to Murray, expressing his astonishment at the ECOWAS claim of agreement by the two principals, he said 'nothing could have been further from the truth.' In the initial negotiation he recalled that the NPFL had 'demanded that Mr Doe should immediately step down and that Mr Taylor should head the interim government.' When the conference resumed on 26 July, despite the assurances given by ECOWAS that all had been agreed, the Taylor delegation refused to change its position. 'Inevitably there was an impasse, and the conference broke down.'[41]

***

On 4 July the incoming U.S. ambassador, Peter de Vos, met President Doe at the Executive Mansion with an offer to help him to leave the country, an offer which was disdainfully refused.[42] In Brussels, U.S. Secretary of State Baker confirmed that the U.S. was prepared to transport Doe out of the country 'if he wants it.'[43] And in Liberia the rebels renewed their offensive, capturing Careysburg, 25 miles north-east of Monrovia and site of the Voice of America transmitter. Next came reports that about 1,000 rebels were advancing on Monrovia's eastern suburb of Congotown while government troops had gone 'on a shooting and looting spree during the dusk-to-dawn curfew.'[44] On the following morning at least 17 bodies were found, while during the day soldiers, some of whom appeared to be intoxicated, 'fired into the air and harassed passers-by for money and cigarettes. Others roamed the city in stolen cars and pickup trucks loaded with U.S.-made M16 rifles.'[45] Government army chief of staff, General Dubar, now safely in Sierra Leone, told a journalist that 'a general should know when to retreat.' He had decided to 'ground arms', when he 'saw our people without light and drinking unsafe water.'[46] This was the man who on 3 April had declared that the rebels in Nimba County were surrounded. This also was the man who had triumphantly told journalists on 5 June that the former U.S. marine, Johnson (who had escorted Kilcoyne and Jennings from LAC to Buchanan), reputedly 'the brains behind Taylor's military campaign', had been killed in battle.[47] In this case the information was true. Johnson and his NPFL bodyguard had been ambushed by government soldiers near the Benson River, not far from Buchanan. His burial took place in the Catholic church compound at LAC, and Kilcoyne read the service. Afterwards Kilcoyne and Jennings met Taylor who told the priests he wanted the Catholic Church to stay in Liberia and continue its work. They found his words 'comforting and full of promise.' Time was to radically alter their perception of the man.

***

On 6 July *The Washington Post* brought news that 'a friendly African country' had told the U.S. State Department it was willing to give refuge to President Doe.[48] It also reported that on the previous Wednesday, 'Doe's most trusted commander', Lt General Charles Julu, head of his praetorian guard and chief-of-staff since the defection of Dubar, had fled to Sierra Leone.[49] Julu was to remain there until 1994 only to re-emerge with a vengeance as a disruptive and dangerous force, as will be seen later*. The rebel offensive was now in its fourth day, with government forces outnumbered and apparently losing whatever last shreds of discipline they possessed, 'shooting their way into stores, warehouses and restaurants during curfew hours in search of loot.'[50]

***

Yet Taylor's prediction, made days earlier, that Monrovia would fall during the 15 July weekend was not to be fulfilled. In fact, the rebel army, now on the northern outskirts of Monrovia for over three weeks, was meeting stiffer opposition than expected. Doe's forces − now only the hard core because of desertions and with their backs to the wall − were putting up a good fight.[51] One explanation for such determined resistance was the realisation by the soldiers − mainly Krahn − that in all likelihood they would be massacred, should the rebels take Monrovia. The Mano and Gio soldiers, for their part, were more interested in vengeance against the Krahn than in any political ideology or in making Taylor president. This, together with their lack of training, might have militated against an early success.[52]

***

*   See p. 260.

For Monrovia's inhabitants the situation was growing increasingly grim. The population had swelled to half a million; and all had been without water, sewage or electricity for over three weeks. An estimated 34,000 displaced persons sheltered at 21 refugee sites[53] in the care of a broad coalition of relief organisations, statutory and non-governmental, local and international. Catholic Relief Services (CRS), with substantial funding from the U.S. government, took the lead, feeding a total of 100,000 people daily in the capital, while Médecins Sans Frontières (MSF) assisted at St Joseph's Catholic hospital which was inundated with outpatients. The Department of Health's Redemption Hospital[54] on Bushrod Island, was the only other hospital functioning.

Monday 23 July brought reports from Associated Press that elements of Taylor's forces were approaching the Executive Mansion.[55] One group was headed by a senior rebel commander, Prince Yormie Johnson while a larger element, headed by Taylor, was fighting government troops six miles outside the capital.[56] Doe was now reported to be a virtual prisoner in his oceanfront fortress, 'with rebels besieging the capital and his 500-member guard (Israeli-trained Krahn) refusing to let him flee without them.'[57] Although firmly on the back foot, Doe continued to defy those who called on him to quit. His acting Information Minister, Paul Allen Wie,[58] held an impromptu news conference at the Executive Mansion against a background of loud gunfire. The president, he said, was as defiant as ever and had no intention of resigning. Doe himself, in heroic mode, declared that he was prepared to 'die for his country'; while in statesman-like mode, he responded to a call for his resignation from a group of black U.S. congressmen, declaring 'I cannot heed their advice … because it would introduce a dangerous precedent of outrageous rebellion and instability into the West African region.'[59]

***

The first and only death of a Catholic priest during the course of the civil war took placed on 26 July 1990. Fr Damian Kwashie, a Ghanaian from Keta Ho diocese, on loan to the diocese of Cape Palmas, died of bullet wounds in Greenville, Sinoe County.* On the following day Taylor, broadcasting on his own rebel radio located in Gbarnga, declared that Liberia was now under his control and that a new government had assumed authority.[60] Introduced as 'President of the National Patriotic Front of Liberia', he proclaimed the dissolution of the Doe government and its replacement by the National Patriotic Reconstruction Assembly Government (NPRAG).

***

And now came news of the most dreadful act of violence to occur during the six-month civil war. On Sunday 20 July several hundred refugees, mostly

---

*   Liberia formally acknowledged Fr Damian Yawo Kwashie's tragic death on 8 May 2009 when he was posthumously awarded the 'Order of the Star of Africa.' The citation noted 'his distinguished and meritorious service to mankind, especially to the people of Liberia.'

Gio and Mano, sheltering in St Peter's Lutheran Church in Monrovia, were massacred by government soldiers.[61] Ten days after the massacre the State Department, citing what it considered 'credible sources',[62] confirmed the killings saying there had been 200 civilian deaths and 70 to 80 injured.[63] But the scale of the massacre was to prove much larger.

The massacre had taken place first on the ground floor and later on the upper floor where hundreds of refugees were sleeping. Soldiers ordered some women with their children, who tried to flee, to stand aside. Other soldiers then fired on them. Next soldiers began searching for those who had managed to hide. These were rounded up and most were shot. Journalists visiting the scene later reported that 'the entire floor was thick with blood and bodies were huddled under pews where people had tried to hide. Bodies of boys, aged 7 or 8, were draped on the church altar.' Survivors said 'the soldiers butchered the men with knives and machetes and shot women and children with machine guns.' Reporters saw 'dead women lying on the floor, children still wrapped in shawls on their backs, while the church crucifix had been thrown to the ground and bullet holes riddled the ceiling.' In all, according to Liberia's Truth and Reconciliation Commission and other sources over 600 people died in the massacre. The government's reaction was predictable. Doe announced that certainly there had been a massacre but it was perpetrated by rebels wearing Liberian army uniforms; and was conducted in order to discredit the government before the international community.

As news of the massacre spread, calls for U.S. intervention redoubled. But the administration held firm to its policy of 'quiet diplomacy' and non-intervention. *The Washington Post*'s David Hofman reported the reaction of the State Department's deputy spokesperson, Richard Boucher. 'The administration believes it is not our role to intervene, to engage in peacekeeping, or to impose a government or political system on Liberia.' The conflict, he said, was a colonial war between indigenes and Americo-Liberians, a matter for the region to solve. All types of intervention were ruled out by administration officials, except humanitarian aid and action to evacuate President Doe, should he wish to leave the country.

***

Elvira High, staunch Lutheran and doughty secretary to S. John Murray, the SMA American Provincial – she had been secretary to four of his predecessors – tracked reaction to the St Peter's Church massacre within the Lutheran Church worldwide. Deeply conscious of the great Lutheran tradition of risking all to expose evil – encapsulated in the courageous and saintly Dietrich Bonhoeffer during World War II – she validated that tradition within the limited scope of her daily occupation. Her pastor, the Rev. Charles Austin of Ridgefield Park, provided her with the statement of the Lutheran World Federation on the massacre, which she transmitted for dissemination through the Africa Faith and Justice Network (AFJN) network.[64] The statement called upon the UN and its member nations 'to do everything in their power to bring the present hostilities to an end...' and demanded a special sitting of the UN Security Council.

Elvira High was also able to provide additional information about the St Peter's Church massacre, sourcing her information from Dan Olson of the Evangelical Lutheran Church in America (ELCA), who had just exited Monrovia.[65] Approximately 2,000 displaced persons had taken refuge in the church compound, prominently displaying Red Cross flags both on the church and perimeter wall. There could have been no doubt in the minds of the soldiers that this was a refugee Centre. On the day before the massacre soldiers had 'entered the compound … and interrupted an outdoor worship service.'[66] On that occasion several people were taken away for interrogation and, in the confusion, one person was killed, and others wounded.[67]

One Lutheran voice calling loudly for UN intervention was Bishop Herbert W. Chilstrom of the ELCA. Speaking in Chicago he urged the UN Security Council 'to address the situation immediately…'[68] Within the U.S. Congress Representative Howard Wolpe, Chairman of the House subcommittee on Africa, noted that there had been repeated calls to bring the Liberian crisis to the Security Council.[69] Wider international political reaction to the massacre was one of horror and outrage and a feeling that something must be done without delay. Ambassadors to the UN from France, West Germany, Belgium Spain and Italy − but not the U.S. − called for an emergency session of the Security Council, while UN Secretary-General Javier Perez de Cuellar voiced 'horror and dismay.'[70]

This pressure had some effect for, on the last day of July, the Bush administration announced it was giving consideration to seeking a UN Security Council meeting calling for a ceasefire.[71] Clarification as to the nature of the administration's stance came later on the same day when Thomas R. Pickering, U.S. ambassador to the UN, said that although he had not sought a Security Council meeting he would support a Liberian request for one.[72] On one level it is difficult to conceive why the government might have wanted such a meeting, given that the St Peter's Church massacre was indisputably conducted by its troops. On another level the Doe regime might have been grateful for any type of intervention to stave off its seemingly inevitable demise.

As it happened, an administration spokesperson was able to announce that such a request actually had been received by the UN and the proposed meeting was scheduled for 'later that day.' The fact that the Security Council meeting had been sought by Liberia and not the U.S. allowed the Bush administration to maintain its policy approach to the Liberian crisis − the call for a Security Council meeting was not of its making and the U.S. would continue to pursue its policy of 'quiet diplomacy', insisting that Africans should solve Africa's problems.

Notes

1 Ibid.
2 Catherine Dwyer to Archbishop Francis, 25 May 1990.
3 A.B. John Kilcoyne, 'Account of the Civil War in Buchanan', December 1990.

4 A.B. Buchanan Mission Diary, 19 May 1990.
5 For a graphic account of the fall of Buchanan see A. Jennings, Personal Diary, 9ff.
6 A.B. Buchanan Mission Diary, 19–22 May 1990.
7 Ibid, 25 May 1990.
8 Ibid.
9 A.B. John Kilcoyne, 'Account of the Civil War in Buchanan', December 1990.
10 Serving Liberia, Sierra Leone and the Gambia.
11 He wrote on the request of his Provincial Superior while resting in Cork. His account in A.B. is dated 16 July 1990.
12 One of many brief assaults before the sustained attack in the second week of May.
13 Michael O'Leary, 'Liberia, the Pastoral Centre and the Rebel Invasion of 1990', 16 July 1990.
14 A.T. John Feeney, 'Journal of a Missionary', 10–11.
15 A.T. US Embassy, 24 May 1990.
16 'Africa Watch', Press Release, 24 May 1990.
17 Author's italics.
18 Africa News, 28 May 1990, 'Who are those Guys'?
19 See Washington Times, 6 June 1990, quoting an AFP report.
20 See, LTRC, Consolidated Final Report, vol. 2, 149; 310–312; LTRC Final Report, Volume III, Title VII, 7.
21 A.T. Hayden to Murray, 31 May 1990.
22 Later, senior UNHCR co-ordinator for refugee women and for many years a renowned peace activistand human rights promoter.
23 See also Human Rights Watch, 'Waging War to Keep the Peace', Reports, June 1993, vol. 5, issue no. 6.
24 Charles Laurence, Daily Telegraph (London), 4 June 1990.
25 Patrick E. Tyler, staff writer, quoting Sondra McCarthy, State Department spokesperson, wrote the story.
26 Washington Times, 1 June 1990.
27 AFJN Information, Associated Press release, 1 June 1990.
28 Washington Times, 1 June 1990.
29 Ibid, 5 June 1990.
30 Daily Telegraph, London 6 June 1990.
31 Washington Times, 1 June 1990.
32 Ibid.
33 Record of telephone call to Cork, from Lee Cahill, 4 June 1990.
34 Ibid.
35 Washington Times, 5 June 1990.
36 Ibid.
37 Paul, Gifford, The Tablet, 30 June 1990.
38 See Emmanuel Dolo, Ethnic Tensions in Liberia's Identity Crisis, (New Jersey, 2007), 89.
39 Ibid.
40 A.T. 18 June 1990 (from Freetown).
41 A.T. Francis to S. John Murray, 8 August 1990.
42 This pool report by Associated Press was published in The Washington Post on the following day.
43 The Washington Post, Thursday, 5 July 1990.
44 Ibid.
45 Ibid.
46 Ibid.
47 Chicago Tribune, 7 June 1990.
48 The Washington Post, 6 July 1990.
49 Ibid.

50 Ibid.
51 Thomas Hayden, AFJN Information, 20 July 1990.
52 See Ibid.
53 Ibid.
54 Redemption hospital was originally a public out-patients clinic. By 1982 it had become a 50-bed hospital. MSF became involved in the 1990s.
55 Bergen Record, 23 July 1990 (carrying pooled AP report from Monrovia).
56 The Detroit News, 31 July 1990 (David Butty).
57 Chicago Tribune, 23 July 1990 (Associated Press, Monrovia), Section 1, 5.
58 See p. 184 below.
59 Ibid.
60 Daily Telegraph, London, 28 July 1990.
61 Detroit News, 31 July 1990; Irish Times, 31 July 1990.
62 Mark Matthews, The Sun, 1 August 1990.
63 The Washington Post, 31 July 1990.
64 A.T. Elvira High to S. John Murray, 2 August 1990.
65 Ibid, containing Memo from ELCA Board of World Missions (signed by Dan Olson, Program Director for West Africa); ibid., 2 August 1990.
66 See A.T. Elvira High, 2 August 1990, 'Conversation with Dan Olson.'
67 Ibid.
68 Irish Times, 2 August 1990.
69 The Washington Post, Wednesday, 1 August 1990, 'US moves for ceasefire'; 'UN Security Council Meeting Studied' (David Hoffman).
70 Press cutting in A.T., The Washington Times, (n.d.) (Michael Roddy, Reuters, 'Hundreds Massacre in Monrovia Church').
71 Ibid.
72 The Sun, Wednesday 1 August 1990 (Mark Matthews).

Section 4

The Intervention of ECOWAS

10 ECOWAS peacekeeping force arrives

The spate of coups d'état in the West African region which had followed the granting of independence in the 1950s and 1960s and the increasing worldwide publicity given to human and civil rights abuses in the newly emerging states was causing the Organisation of African Unity (OAU)[*] to reconsider its 'sacred principle of non-interference in the internal affairs of member states.'[1] Ultimately this re-consideration was to pave the way for intervention in the Liberian civil war. Ironically the first step in this conversion occurred at the extravagant OAU summit chaired by President Tolbert in Liberia in July 1979, when a group of experts was commissioned to draft an 'African Charter of Human and Peoples Rights.'[2] The final version of this historic document was approved at a meeting of OAU Ministers at Banjul, Gambia, in January 1981. The Charter, which paved the way for intervention where human rights had been breached, was a manifestation of a general desire to make the OAU a more effective body. It was accompanied by plans for an African defence force and for a Security Council-type body that could react swiftly to emergencies.

***

Concern about the situation in Liberia within the 16-nation regional body ECOWAS[3], had first been given formal expression at a summit of Heads of State held in Banjul, Gambia, on 30 May 1990. At that meeting a five-member Standing Mediation Committee (SMC), comprising Nigeria, Ghana, Mali, Gambia and Togo, was set up and mandated to bring peace to Liberia.[4] It was this body which developed the 'ECOWAS Plan' for the resolution of the crisis. This involved dispatching an ECOWAS peacekeeping force, securing a ceasefire and disarmament of the factions, and establishing an interim government, pending elections for a substantive president and legislature. Critical to the plan was the provision that the leaders of the warring factions would be ineligible to stand for the presidency.

The SMC's first efforts to obtain a ceasefire through persuasion, conducted during the third week of June, mainly by Abass Bundu, ECOWAS Secretary General, had been singularly unsuccessful, despite assurances to the contrary given by him to the IFMC at the time. No genuine co-operation was forthcoming from

[*]   The Organisation of African Unity, founded in 1963 by 32 independent African countries. It was replaced by the African Union (AU) in 2002.

DOI: 10.4324/9781003219309-14

the belligerents. However, with the evident failure of the IFMC to broker peace and the abject failure of other peace initiatives, ECOWAS now began to play the leading role.

On July 6, realising that stronger methods were required, the SMC took a decision, pending ratification by an ECOWAS leaders' summit, to send a multinational peace-keeping force to Liberia. This force, given the title Economic Community of West African States Monitoring Group (ECOMOG), would be mandated to 'keep peace, restore law and order and ensure that a ceasefire agreed to by the warring factions was respected.' Beyond establishing and monitoring a ceasefire the SMC planned to convene a national conference of 'political parties and other interested groups', tasked with setting up a 'broad-based interim government', from which the leaders of the various warring factions would be excluded. This was to be followed within a year by free and fair elections to produce a substantive government.[5] The ECOWAS involvement was primarily prompted by fears of regional instability which might follow widespread population displacement within and beyond Liberia's borders.[6]

* * *

It was at this point that another major figure in Liberia's civil war first attracted worldwide attention. On 5 August the BBC World Service reported that a senior rebel commander, 38-year-old Prince Yormie Johnson, was alleged to have 'personally executed a Liberian citizen on Friday, 3 August, as he pleaded for his life.'[7] The victim, wearing a Red Cross bib, had been arrested for selling rice vouchers on the street. He was then handcuffed to CRS worker Jacques Mountouroi who happened to be passing by. After that Johnson launched into a tirade, accusing the man of profiteering from rice sales, saying the vouchers were for free distribution. Naming him 'traitor' and declaring he would make an example of him, showing the world how profiteers were dealt with in Liberia, Johnson fired a burst from his AK-47 rifle causing the man to collapse to the ground, wounded. Turning to the relief worker, Johnson told him he was fortunate to be 'a foreign diplomat.' Then he dispatched the pleading Liberian with a burst of gunfire.[8]

In the normal course such occurrences would not have raised eyebrows, since the summary execution of civilians on the streets of Monrovia was not uncommon. However, in this case a western journalist had witnessed the incident and filed the story that day, along with a photograph of the killing. This image was beamed around the world, quickly becoming a symbol of the brutality of the Liberian civil war.

There was information too, from the State Department, that Johnson, 'a key aide to Mr Taylor', had fallen out with his leader several weeks previously and that 'followers of the two rebel leaders had clashed, both sides suffering casualties.'[9] Effectively second-in-command of the force which invaded Liberia in December 1989, Johnson 'wanted to oust Mr Doe, but did not want Mr Taylor to succeed him.'

Who was this Prince Yormie Johnson who had taken Mamba Point and seemed poised to overrun the Executive Mansion? The journalist Isaac Bantu published a detailed profile for *AFJN* under the headline 'The Man: Captain Prince Johnson, Second Armed Rebel Leader.'[10] This headline suggested that, although both shared the objective of toppling Samuel Doe's dictatorship, Charles Taylor was no longer the sole military commander. Johnson, it seemed, had his own force, under his own command, independent of Taylor. Subsequently this was shown to be true.

Bantu's profile of the 'Second Leader' must be read with some caution as he was later to emerge as a Johnson loyalist. Johnson, he wrote, was a Gio who came from Lower Nimba County. He had joined the Liberian army in 1971 and formed part of a special task force during the Tolbert regiment. A man with a tough reputation, he was one of a group of soldiers who refused to obey the order to shoot demonstrators during the Rice Riots of 1979. After the riots, he was among soldiers rounded up and detained at the notorious Belle Yalla prison camp in Lofa County. There, on the instructions of Minister for Defence Bernard Holder, they were reportedly 'whipped 100 lashes' for disobeying orders. During the several months of detention, before his escape from Belle Yalla, Johnson was radicalised and converted to the idea of overthrowing the Tolbert regime.

After the 1980 coup Johnson was assigned to the army's 2nd Battalion and promoted first to the rank of Lieutenant and later to that of Captain. An admirer and supporter of General Thomas Quiwonkpa, he was overlooked by the Doe regime in the aftermath of Quiwonkpa's dismissal from the People's Redemption Council in October 1983. After Quiwonkpa's abortive coup attempt in November 1985, Johnson went into hiding. Subsequently his whereabouts were unknown until December 1989 when he was one of those who crossed the Ivory Coast border into Liberia with Charles Taylor. Bantu, revealing his pro-Johnson sympathies, declared that Johnson had been irritated by Taylor's broadcast that he was now President (and that his wife was Minister for Health). Since that time, a power struggle was in the offing and he would 'prevent Taylor from becoming president.'[11]

***

The disagreement between Johnson and Taylor impinged on the Catholic mission first in Bong Mine when, on 28 June, Prince Johnson's breakaway faction attacked the occupying NPFL, driving them out of the town. John Feeney described what happened.

> The attack came at night and evidently the NPFL was no match for the newcomers. We were treated to a whole night of gunfire. On the morning of the 29th there was an unnatural calm in the area and fear was all pervasive. One of the invaders told me that they had killed 137 of the NPFL and its collaborators the previous night and 37 this morning. That was probably a gross exaggeration, but independent witnesses have told me that there are many corpses strewn all through the town...[12]

Within a week Johnson and his fighters had left Bong Mine, moving towards Monrovia. The previous night a number of his Gio fellow tribesman had spoken with him about reconciling with Taylor. He responded by accusing them of being collaborators and had them executed on the spot. With Johnson gone, Feeney took the opportunity to visit his vacated camp.

> What a terrible sight! The bodies of six young men bound, shot, bloated and covered with flies, were thrown under a clump of banana plants for all to see. They were the bodies of some of the group who had asked Johnson to make peace with Taylor. Their seven companions were buried in a common grave nearby.

By 16 July Taylor's NPFL fighters were back in Bong Mine, 'harassing people and demanding food and money.' They were also causing problems for the distribution of rice by the committee of Christian pastors. They rendered the distribution only partially effective by using a mixture of blunt force and stealth to steal a significant proportion of the rice.[13]

***

As moral pressure for some form of international intervention built and since its most likely and most obligated source, the U.S., had consistently refused, attention tended to focus on ECOWAS. Its peacekeeping force (ECOMOG) had already been formed, although no decision had yet been taken on its dispatch. It must be said that not all sixteen members of ECOWAS were favourable to intervention. One dissident voice was that of President Félix Houphouët-Boigny of the Ivory Coast, whose goddaughter, Désirée 'Daisy' Delafosse, had been married to President Tolbert's unfortunate eldest son, Adolphus, murdered during the coup. Another dissident voice, also suspected of supporting Taylor, was that of Blaise Compaoré, President of Burkina Faso. Compaoré was married to Houphouët-Boigny's 'daughter', Chantal (foster sister of Désirée de la Fosse). Compaoré consistently opposed the notion of a peacekeeping force and was suspected of providing Taylor with military support.[*] But ECOWAS's larger players were running out of patience. Belligerent signals from Nigeria's President Ibrahim Babangida were now being reported on Lagos radio.[14] And there were signs that Ghana's leader, Flight Lieutenant Jerry Rawlings, was also beginning to lose patience. On 1 August he had warned that West African governments would consider certain 'action' if rebels or government troops failed to allow foreign nationals safe passage out of the country.[15] This declaration came after members of a group of 163 Ghanaians, brought back from Liberia by ship, had spoken of beatings and even killings of compatriots both by rebel and government soldiers. And hundreds of Ghanaians and over 3,000 Nigerians still remained trapped in Liberia. Another voice urging action was President Museveni of Uganda, current chairman of the OAU.[16]

***

---

[*]   These suspicions were well-founded. See, LTRC, A House with Two Rooms, Final Report, Volume III, Title VII, 7; LTRC, Consolidated Final Report, vol. 2, Chapter Two, 149; 308, 310.

In Monrovia open warfare had now broken out between Taylor's forces and those of Prince Johnson, the latter fighting under the banner of the Independent National Patriotic Front of Liberia [INPFL] and getting the worst of it. Taylor told foreign correspondents he had 'deliberately trapped Johnson's forces between his army and GOL forces.'[17] He would now 'destroy them' and then 'advance towards the Executive Mansion and capture President Doe.' And it seemed that the first part of this plan was already succeeding when rebels loyal to Johnson withdrew from key positions, and only a handful were visible in those areas of central Monrovia captured from government troops a few days previously.[18]

With Johnson subdued, albeit temporarily, one would have expected Taylor to expedite his final assault on Monrovia, but he delayed. No longer his suave self, but speaking in a nervous and rather uncontrolled fashion at a press conference in Firestone he announced that 'the final battle for Monrovia' would not begin 'until more civilians had been evacuated.'[19] In the same statement he warned Nigeria that 'Liberians would fight to the last against any ECOWAS intervention', declaring he intended to mobilise some 300,000 people to oppose this proposed 'new form of colonization.'

Taylor had good reason to sound unsettled at this press conference. Johnson's INPFL, though outnumbered and retreating, was putting up a good fight and absorbing much of the NPFL's energy. The breakaway force would not easily be annihilated. And now it was looking possible and even likely that the threatened ECOWAS intervention might receive the formal backing of the international community through a United Nations (UN) resolution. On the previous day Assistant Secretary Herman Cohen had said that 'within a matter of days if not hours' the UN would be taking an initiative aimed at ending the civil war in Liberia, although the dispatch of U.S. troops would not be part of that initiative.[20]

Back on the front line, Taylor appeared caught in a race against time. Just as he was about to secure the prize of victory, it seemed about to be snatched from him, first by Johnson and now by ECOWAS. It was probable that an ECOWAS summit would sanction the dispatch of the peacekeeping force and that this would occur sooner rather than later, since preparations were already advanced. Broadcasting from headquarters in Yekepa, Taylor was now appealing to 'all Liberians for a full mobilization in order to fight any foreign intervention.' And he had no doubt that the prospect of an ECOWAS peace-keeping force had been 'orchestrated in order to keep President Doe in power.'

***

The popular reaction in Buchanan to the news of an imminent ECOWAS intervention reflected Taylor's fears. Jennings described the report that ECOWAS was planning to intervene in the civil war as 'disturbing.'

> The countries mentioned are Nigeria, Sierra Leone, Guinea and Ghana. Most people think this would be a disastrous move since most of these states are friends of Doe.[21]

This reaction was not altogether surprising when it is borne in mind that Buchanan had been under NPFL control since the closing week of May and despite the deteriorating discipline of the occupying troops, the people depended for survival on rice provided by the NPFL leadership. There was also the incessant propaganda to which Buchanan's inhabitants were subjected. Moreover, at this comparatively early stage of Taylor's involvement many people still had not made up their minds about him and were hopeful that he would bring to an end, once and for all, the hated Doe regime.

***

At dawn on Sunday, 5 August, over two hundred U.S. Marines helicoptered from the offshore flotilla to evacuate some 300 American citizens taking refuge in the embassy and at the Voice of America and Satellite communications compounds.[22] The decision to undertake this 'Operation Sharp Edge' had been taken by President George Bush, Sr, while meeting with advisers to consider the Persian Gulf crisis.[23] It provided Doe with a momentary hope that he might be saved by American intervention, only to be quickly dispelled by a firm White House insistence that the deployment was 'a humanitarian act to protect and preserve the lives of U.S. citizens.'[24]

The decision to send in the marines had been taken following a threat, issued on the previous day by the volatile Prince Johnson, to kidnap American citizens and other foreigners. He had told journalists that he had ordered his men 'to start arresting foreigners on Monday, 6 August, starting with Americans, Britons, Indians and Lebanese.'[25] His rationale, he said, was to 'create an international incident' in order to provoke U.S. intervention.

The decision to evacuate U.S. citizens and foreigners was vindicated on 6 August when, true to his word, Prince Johnson fulfilled his threat to take hostages. At least eight foreigners were reported to have been detained, including three Britons, two West Germans, a Dutchman, an Argentine and a U.S. citizen. These and a further 11 non-Liberian Africans were presented to a group of reporters by an animated Johnson who announced that his INPFL 'would attack U.S. marines protecting the U.S. embassy, unless a U.S. or West African peace-keeping force intervened to end the country's civil war.'[26]

***

In the midst of anxiety and confusion, St Peter's Lutheran church, already a monument to hatred, had now become a monument to darkness. There had been no attempt to recover the dead refugees, to bless them, or bury them. A reporter who visited the ghastly scene on 8 August witnessed 'putrefying bodies, some jamming the windows where they were shot trying to escape.'[27] Another reporter made attempts to establish the numbers of those who had died. A priest had told him a week previously that he had 'counted more than 200 bodies on the ground floor and more than 400 women and children upstairs.' And diplomats had told him that, on the advice of 'a number of doctors', they were requesting permission from Doe's forces to burn down the building 'to prevent an outbreak of cholera, or plague, or Lassa fever, diseases likely to be caused by hundreds of decomposing bodies.'[28]

***

In Ireland the SMA Provincial Council[29] was meeting to consider the situation of its members caught up in the civil war. Care for these men, some traumatised by their experiences, was uppermost in their minds. Some had managed to leave the country, taking refuge over the border in Ivory Coast or Sierra Leone before making their way back to Ireland. Others were still in Liberia, mostly displaced; only a handful in remote areas managed to stay at their posts. The meeting decided that when the civil war ended – its end seemed imminent either through a Taylor victory or ECOMOG intervention – a gathering of all Liberian-based confreres would be convened 'to discuss and tease out the whole experience undergone by them.' But apart from overcoming shock and trauma, there were other issues to be dealt with. There had been differences of opinion among confreres on various issues, exacerbated and often caused by the tensions of war. Typically, these had concerned matters of life and death - when to evacuate a mission, when to go into hiding. And there had been differences of opinion, too, about the warring parties. Some were more encouraged by Taylor than others. Some were more hopeful than others that this was a good man who would end Liberia's cycle of tragedy.

The SMA's American Province was also closely monitoring the situation. Seven members still remained in Liberia. John Feeney, isolated by the war, was at NPFL-controlled Bong Mine north of Monrovia. With the prospect of ECOWAS intervention prompting an outraged response from Charles Taylor against 'outside interference', Feeney decided that as an 'outsider' it was dangerous to write a diary in English; henceforth, he would confide his thoughts to his diary in the Irish language.[30] With him was Bishop Sekey of Gbarnga diocese, who had been visiting Bong Mine Catholic mission when the road was cut. Also with him, but hidden from view, were the two Krahn 'guests', whose discovery would have led to their deaths and endangered his own life.

***

On 7 August a fateful ECOWAS meeting, hosted by Sir Dawda Jawara, current chairman, was held in a seaside hotel at Kotu, west of Gambia's capital, Banjul. In attendance were the presidents of Nigeria, Ghana, Sierra Leone and Guinea, and senior ministers from Togo and Mali. Representatives from Burkina Faso and Ivory Coast – the two nations supportive of Taylor - were noticeably absent suggesting there was a certain inevitability about the meeting's outcome. Early reports indicated agreement to send the already formed peace-keeping force to Liberia within a week, with a mandate to evacuate foreign nationals and, if possible, impose a ceasefire.[31] In fact the meeting went further, deciding, unambiguously, to impose a ceasefire and install a provisional government.[32] Despite its shortcomings, this was a momentous step, for it was the first occasion[33] on which an African inter-country political organisation had abandoned the time-honoured principle of non-intervention in the internal affairs of a member state. One result was the release of the hostages taken by Johnson on the previous day, done on learning that a peacekeeping force had at last been authorised and commissioned.[34] Taylor, for his part, was galvanising his supporters to resist 'foreign intervention.' At the University of Liberia's Fendell campus on the outskirts of Monrovia and under NPFL control, 'tens of thousands of supporters' came out to demonstrate against any intervention, chanting 'no Taylor, no Government' and 'Doe must go' and carrying placards declaring 'Liberia will be the graveyard of foreign aggressors.'[35]

The first week of August, too, saw the closure of the French embassy and the evacuation of the Italian ambassador although, hoping to weather the storm, the embassies of America, West Germany, Britain, Spain and Morocco remained open. The British ambassador, Michael Edward John Gore, *The Washington Post* reported, was 'said to be keen not to abandon ship before his American counterpart.'[36] Evoking an image of British eccentricity, the report added that Gore, a keen ornithologist, used the name 'Osprey' when communicating with other embassies.[37]

***

On Friday 10 August Feeney decided to take a stand against NPFL interference in the distribution of rice.

> My sixty-eighth birthday. When I got to the rice depot this morning there were no committee members present but lots of soldiers. I am tired of their shenanigans so I clashed with them. I eventually got results from the commanding officer whom I called. Things went much smoother for the rest of the day, and we distributed 581 bags of rice.

Four days later he was considering withdrawing from the Rice Distribution Committee.

> I may now give up the humbug of the rice distribution because all the others who are involved in the project comply with every request of the NPFL regardless of how unreasonable it may be. I do not begrudge them some rice but when they demand a bag of it so that their girlfriends can sell it in the market, I see no reason to give it to them.[38]

Back in Ireland there was growing concern for a Sister Joan Margaret Kelly from Dublin, a school principal in Voinjama, near the Guinea border, who had stayed on alone in her school in the hope of preventing its destruction. A member of the St Joseph de Chambéry order, she had built the school with funds from the Irish civil servants' trade union. A formidable lady, she was sister-in-law to an equally formidable Irish left-wing politician[39] and was not disposed to seeing her well-equipped school destroyed without making a stand.

August 11 saw the inevitable evacuation of patients from, and closure of, St Joseph's Catholic Hospital.[40] It had been one of only two hospitals operating in the city. Two days later, Archbishop Romeo Panciroli, Vatican Pro-Nuncio to Liberia (who had taken refuge in the Spanish embassy on 2 August) and Manuel de Luna, the Spanish ambassador, were evacuated, part of a small group which waited on the beach in a tropical storm before being taken to the ship by helicopter.[41]

News about the circumstances leading to the closure of the Catholic hospital, now in NPFL-controlled territory, reached an international audience on 17 August.[42] The evacuation, supervised by Belgian doctor, Johann Heffinck of Médecins Sans Frontières, and by Spanish John of God Brothers who managed the hospital, had taken place after rebel fighters threatened to seize patients linked with the beleaguered Samuel Doe.[43] On that day a convoy of some 30 vehicles carried badly-wounded patients through rebel-held territory to the Lutheran Phebe hospital near Gbarnga, some 125 miles distant, where the fighting had ceased. The official reason given for the evacuation was that the hospital was being shelled by government troops. It would not have been politic to give the true reason, namely that it occurred shortly after a group of NPFL soldiers entered the hospital 'in search of a former politician they knew was being treated there.' When the hospital staff refused to cooperate the soldiers departed empty-handed, but 'threatened to return later.'[44]

***

There could be no doubt that the continuing NPFL onslaught – now a mile from the Executive Mansion – had been prompted by reports that ECOMOG was about to sail from its assembly point off Sierra Leone. Estimated at about 2,500 soldiers, there was intelligence from diplomatic sources that the force would 'move into Liberia within a week to enforce a ceasefire.'[45] The largest contingents – two 880-strong battalions – would be from Nigeria and Ghana, with smaller units from Guinea, Sierra Leone and Gambia.

Standing in the way of ECOMOG in the fulfilment of its mission, the NPFL forces posed the greatest obstacle. A graphic, colourful but ultimately chilling account of Taylor's army appeared in the English *Sunday Times* of 12 August, written by Matthew Campbell, at that time embedded with rebel forces outside the Executive Mansion in central Monrovia.

> To call Liberia a slaughterhouse is misleading. In abattoirs the killing of animals is done with a degree of humanity; here human beings are dispatched with chilling bestiality. Travelling with the rebels' motley spearhead of 50 men is a terrifying bizarre experience. Some are kitted out for battle in women's wigs and dresses. Their few vehicles resemble New York subway carriages, adorned with spray-painted graffiti such as 'Here comes dead body trouble' and 'No surrender, no retreat.'

The government forces, it must be said, were of a similar disposition, evidenced in the random slaughter of perceived tribal enemies on the streets of Monrovia, the planned murders of the refugees in St Peter's Lutheran Church and countless atrocities in the interior. And the forces of Prince Johnson, though more restricted in opportunity, were quickly catching up in the contest for viciousness.

***

Now that a peace-keeping force was to be sent, international relief agencies which had withdrawn from Liberia began to make plans to return. The UN announced on 9 August that its 'relief officials' would return 'as soon as some order is restored', adding that it already had designated a Special Co-ordinator who was waiting for an instruction to begin his work.[46] Other agencies signalled a similar intention once the peacekeeping force had been dispatched. An estimation of the scale of the relief required was given in a 'Situation Report' released by the Office of U.S. Foreign Disaster Assistance on 15 August.[47] It estimated that between 15,000 and 25,000 people had been killed, with 300,000 displaced within Liberia and 450,000 taking refuge in Ivory Coast, Sierra Leone and Guinea. The bulk of the 1989 harvest had been lost and expectations for a better result in 1990 had been damaged by the prolonged conflict. So far, the U.S. government had allocated some $25 million for relief, private agencies in the U.S. were contributing $90,000, while the international community had allocated $8 million.

***

While much of its energy was concentrated in organising military intervention, ECOWAS still continued with its so far unsuccessful diplomatic initiatives. For some time now President Jawara, liaising with the SMC of which he was head, had been working might and main to convene a meeting of the various parties to the war. Finally, he was able to announce that this would take place in Banjul on 21 August and that the leaders of both factions (Taylor and Johnson) had agreed to attend.[48]

For two men about to meet each other and negotiate the settlement of a civil war – at least according to the ECOWAS version – relations between Johnson and Taylor took a curious turn on 14 August when Tom Woewiyu triumphantly announced that NPFL forces had killed Johnson in an ambush on Bushrod Island, north of Monrovia.[49] Johnson's body, he said, had been taken to rebel headquarters at the Firestone plantation east of the capital. Moreover, not only had Johnson been eliminated but 'his people' had been 'wiped out', which meant that the NPFL could 'now go back to fighting Doe and his foreign troops.' Woewiyu also told journalists that he, not Charles Taylor, would be flying to Banjul – courtesy of the U.S. government – to attend the peace negotiations. Evidently, this diplomatic initiative, like those which had gone before, was already unravelling. Shortly afterwards a man 'identifying himself as Johnson' called the BBC in London to deny that he was dead. 'Taylor is a liar. I am alive', he emphatically declared. The U.S. State Department's Margaret Tutwiler, quickly off the mark, doubted Woewiyu's claims saying that 'a reliable report' had been received that Johnson was seen alive. All doubt was expelled on the afternoon of 18 August when Johnson hosted a press conference in Monrovia, where he 'laughed off' reports of his demise.[50]

***

Early on the morning of 24 August came dramatic news that the long-awaited West African peace-keeping force (ECOMOG) – consisting now of 4,000 troops instead of the 2,500 initially projected – had set sail from Free-town, breaking the historical caveat within African politics that prohibited military intervention in the affairs of another state.[51] In the weeks leading up to

ECOMOG's dispatch, the NPFL leader had twice failed to honour promises to attend peace conferences, the most recent of which had been scheduled for Banjul on 21 August. It was now clear that the diplomatic efforts of ECOWAS and the Interfaith Mediation Committee must take second place and that *force majeure* alone could bring an end to the fighting.

***

Woewiyu was first to react to the dispatch of ECOMOG, interviewed by the BBC's Robin White on the Focus-on-Africa programme. Like his chief, Woewiyu was quickly on first-name terms with his host and assuring him that the NPFL would resist the ECOMOG force, should it land:

> No Robin, we are not bluffing, and I think the world will see whether we, the Liberian people, are truly dedicated to protecting our sovereignty or not. We didn't begin fighting in order for a group of other Africans to band together and start some military adventurism to dominate our sovereignty, so we will fight to the last man.[52]

Despite these threats the first ships carrying the force appeared off Monrovia's Freeport that evening. They were confronted by a battle raging between NPFL forces, seeking to occupy the port and prevent a landing, and Johnson's INPFL which still occupied the area. In the event Taylor failed to drive Johnson out. On the following morning, led by Ghanaian General, Arnold Quainoo, the first elements of the ECOMOG force came ashore, where they were warmly welcomed by a triumphant Prince Johnson.[53] On the following day ECOMOG took control of the 100-acre Freeport and pushed NPFL forces back beyond this perimeter, using its superior armament which included mortars, automatic weapons and artillery. These were well-trained troops and, although Taylor's fighters put up stern resistance, they were steadily driven back to Clara Town, about two miles from the Freeport.[54]

General Quainoo told journalists he considered his role as that of 'peacekeeper' rather than 'peace-enforcer' and believed the NPFL would yield, once ECOMOG demonstrated its resolve and strength.[55] The overall ECOWAS strategy was to restrain the three factions, while an interim government would try to resolve political differences and prepare Liberia for peaceful elections. However, the fact that the NPFL had immediately launched an artillery attack on the landing force and strongly resisted ECOMOG's attempts to move beyond the Freeport, did not augur well for the success of the strategy.

The meeting at Banjul, scheduled for 21 August, eventually convened on 27 August, but without Doe, Taylor or Johnston, thus rendering any agreement immeasurably difficult to impose. Present were the leaders of Liberia's five opposition parties, Archbishop Michael Francis and two other members of the Inter-Churches Mediation Committee, as well as Winston Tubman.

***

Back in Liberia, smarting from setbacks suffered since the arrival of ECOMOG three days earlier, the NPFL now began rounding up Ghanaians and other West Africans whose nations had contributed to ECOMOG. Jennings recorded what happened in Buchanan.

> All Ghanaians including those who were now naturalized Liberians are rounded up. We go to the administration building where they are detained but are ordered out by the NPFL commander, Philip Sangar. The following day all Ghanaian women and children are transferred to Demonstration School and men to the Methodist School, Old Field. There must be a total of 1,500 altogether.[56]

A few days later all were 'put in a railway locomotive' and taken to Flamingo camp (an abandoned logging camp) deep in the bush of lower Nimba County and 110 miles from Buchanan. Ordained two years after the end of World War II and aware of the circumstances in which six million Jews had died, Jennings found resonances in this transfer, describing it as 'all very distressing.'

Kilcoyne, Jennings and Sister Carletta, as well as an AMI[57] medical team, were permitted to visit Flamingo camp. There they found 'about 2,500 Ghanaians' whose plight was 'dreadful', and future 'uncertain.'[58] Kilcoyne met with their leaders who requested 'we beg the NPFL leadership to release the naturalized Liberians because they posed no possible threat.' They hoped that the naturalised, if released, might be able to protect the property of the Ghanaian community.[59][*] But the request was rejected out of hand.

Later, in the last week of September, Kilcoyne managed to see Charles Taylor at NPFL headquarters in Buchanan. There again he pleaded for the release of naturalised Liberians and also asked that the entire group be moved nearer to Buchanan to permit families and friends bring food and clothing. Taylor promised to release the naturalised Liberians and to consider the relocation of the detainees.[60] A rather caustic note added later in the Buchanan mission diary remarks that although Taylor was very friendly and affable, he subsequently either forgot his promises or changed his mind. It also noted that the whole interview was filmed, clearly for publicity purposes. Kilcoyne recorded, too, that from the time of his meeting with Taylor the Flamingo camp authorities became less courteous. Throughout this period and despite difficulties of transport and the distances involved, the missionaries and parishioners, along with the aid agencies (CRS and Aide Médicale International) continued to visit Flamingo camp. The embattled Ghanaians were eventually released in February 1991, at a time when the NPFL was under sustained pressure from ECOMOG.

***

On 30 August 1990, Ted Hayden learned that Amos Sawyer, still in the U.S., had been receiving increasing pressure from Liberian political leaders assembled

---

[*]   'A very sad part of the story of this episode was that as soon as the Ghanaians had been rounded up other residents of Buchanan started looting their property' (Kilcoyne to author, 5 October 2018).

in Banjul, the Gambian capital, to accept the position of Interim Head of State.[61] On the following day Hayden told Murray that a new interim government, upon which there now was agreement, would consist of Sawyer as President, Bishop Ronald Diggs as Vice-President, and Winston Tubman as Minister for Foreign Affairs. There would also be an 'Interim Assembly' with three members nominated by each of the six political parties and two members from each of Liberia's thirteen counties.[62] The obvious drawback to this arrangement was that it had been negotiated without the attendance of Taylor or any NPFL surrogate. Yet on 2 September – the last day of the conference – an interim government was formally constituted.

And there was also progress on the ground. Hayden's State Department source told him that ECOMOG was meeting less resistance from the NPFL, people were now 'beginning to move around' within those parts of Monrovia controlled by ECOMOG, while relief organisations were again becoming active. The U.S. government, he said, felt the situation sufficiently stable to send food relief through the Freeport. In NPFL territory, however, there was little change. An entry in the Buchanan diary highlighted the continuing difficulties for those engaged there in relief work.

> At this point we are all feeling physically and mentally exhausted. We feel besieged and are constantly in fear of harassment by the NPFL. On Saturday, 1 September, some NPFL gunmen called on the mission and harassed us to take the mission radio which we had brought from Gbarnga. It was a devastating experience. We managed to keep the radio – at least for the time being.

Such occasions and feelings were to be part and parcel of life for those engaged in relief work in Greater Liberia for the next seven years.

And compounding the tension was a fear, bordering on hysteria, whipped up by NPFL propaganda, of what the arrival of ECOMOG might bring. In Buchanan a diary entry for 6 September reflected these anxieties:

> There is a terrible uncertainty and confusion about the ECOWAS intervention. This morning we hear that 2,000 ECOWAS soldiers have landed in Monrovia. Nobody knows their ulterior motives or objectives.

Notes

1 B. Hettne, ed., The New Regionalism and the Future of Security and Development, vol. 4, (Palgrave Macmillan, 2000), 126.

2 D. Pal S. Ahluwalia, Politics and Post-colonial Theory: African Inflections (London and New York, 2001), 93; see also, 'A Guide to the African Charter on Human and Peoples Rights' (Amnesty International, 2006); c.f., Christof Heyns, ed., Human Rights Law in Africa (Leiden, Netherlands, 2002), 81.

3 Economic Community of West African States.

4 Clearly, from the outline of a solution put forward by Dr Abbas Bundu in August 1990, the Ecowas plan had been in the making for some time.

5　Comfort Ero, 'ECOWAS and the Sub-Regional Peacekeeping in Liberia', The Journal of Humanitarian Assistance (Feinstein international Centre, 25 September 1995, http://sites.tufts.edu/jha/archives/66 - accessed 28 October 2012).

6　Ibid.

7　See also for an account of this incident, Alistair Sinclair (AP in Monrovia), The Record, 8 August 1990.

8　Ibid.

9　Agence France-Presse quoting State Department officials.

10　2 August 1990, AFJN Information, Washington.

11　Ibid.

12　A.T. John Feeney, 'Journal of a Missionary', 11.

13　Ibid,

14　FBIS-AFR-90–150, 3 August 1990 (AB0208151890 Accra Domestic Service).

15　Ibid. (AB0308135590 Paris AFP, 3 August 1990).

16　FBIS-AFR-90–151, 6 August 1990.

17　Ibid.

18　FBIS-AFR-90–150, 3 August 1990 (AB0208170290 London BBC World Service in English, 'Focus on Africa').

19　FBIS-AFR-90–151, 5 August 1990 (AB0408070090 Paris AFP in English).

20　The Irish Times, 4 August 1990.

21　A.B. Buchanan Coutumier, 5 August 1990.

22　The Washington Post, Monday, 6 August 1990.

23　Ibid.

24　Press Conference Statement, Marlin Fitzwater, White House spokesperson, explaining the operation.

25　FBIS-AFR-90–151, 6 August 1990 (AB0508064990 London BBC World Service).

26　The Irish Times, 8 August 1990.

27　The Sunday Times, 12 August 1990 (Matthew Campbell with rebel forces in central Monrovia).

28　The Washington Post, 9 August 1990 (Neil Henry).

29　Consisting of the provincial superior and three councillors.

30　A.T. 'Journal of a Missionary', 22.

31　Daily Telegraph, London, 7 August 1990.

32　The Irish Times, 8 August 1990.

33　In 1980–81, during a civil war, an African multinational force had been sent by the OAU to Chad. But this was more in the nature of an ad hoc intervention in comparison with the decision in January of the same year which addressed breaches of human rights by Charter and provided for intervention into the future wherever necessary.

34　FBIS-AFR-90–153, 8/8/1990 (AB0808120690 Paris AFP).

35　FBIS-AFR-90–152, 7/8/1990 (A130608171890 Paris AFP).

36　The Washington Post, 9 August 1990 (AP correspondent report, 8 August 1990).

37　Ibid.

38　A.B. 'Journal of a Missionary', 24–25.

39　Proinsias de Rossa, a leading member of the Irish Labour political party and later a founder member and leader of the 'Democratic Left' party.

40　Situated adjacent to the SMA Regional House and not far from the German and Nigerian embassies, at Tubman Boulevard, Congotown, Monrovia.

41　Catholic Review (New York), 23 August 1990.

42　Boston Pilot, 17 August 1990.

43　Ibid.

44　Ibid.

45　Ibid., 11 August (Ben Fenton, in Freetown).

46　The Christian Science Monitor, 9 August 1990.

47 Situation Report, no. 6, 15 August 1990.

48 The Irish Times, 18 August 1990.

49 Daily Telegraph, 18 August 1990.

50 Ibid.

51 The Irish Times, 24 August 1990.

52 FBIS-AFR-90–166, 27/8/1990 (4B2408173090, BBC World Service, 'Focus on Africa').

53 Ibid, BBC World Service, 'African News', 25 August 1990.

54 Ibid (A82508193290 Paris AFP, 25 August 1990, from Ghana News Agency, quoting Lieutenant Colonel Ayiku, commanding the Ghanaian contingent).

55 Herbert Howe, 'Lessons of Liberia: ECOMOG and Regional Peacekeeping', International Security, vol. 21, no. 3 (Winter, 1996–1997), 154.

56 A. Jennings, 'Personal Diary', 32–33. See also, John Kilcoyne, 'Memoir' written late 1990.

57 Aide Médicale International', an international humanitarian NGO.

58 Ibid.

59 Information supplied to author by John Kilcoyne, 5 October 2018.

60 Buchanan Mission Diary, 30–31 September 1990.

61 A.T. Hayden to Murray, 30 August 1990.

62 Ibid., Hayden to Murray, 31 August 1990.

11 The assassination of Liberia's President and the leader of its revolutionary coup

On Sunday 9 September 1990 came the astounding news that President Samuel Doe had been killed. Unlike reports of the assassination of Prince Johnson, this time it was true. Doe had come with a small armed force to ECOMOG headquarters in the Freeport area for discussions with the commander when the building was stormed by Johnson's INPFL, and a battle followed, in which most of Doe's entourage were killed. Doe himself was savagely tortured before being killed, and within days gruesome video recordings of his slow death were on sale in the streets of Monrovia. Quick off the mark in offering a verdict, Earl Caldwell in the *American Daily News*, told readers:

> 'Doe's days were always numbered. A part of it was the blood on his hands. He did not just overthrow the government; he rounded up the leaders and had them all shot. The violence he started; he was never able to shake.'[1]

The BBC's Elizabeth Blunt, reporting three days after news of the killing first broke, told listeners that despite the arrival of ECOMOG there was 'little sign of an end to the violence in the Liberian capital.' In the vicinity of the main city barracks and the Barclay Training Centre, Prince Johnson's force appeared to be 'making a determined attack on the remains of Doe's beleaguered army',[2] which was desperately trying to retreat to the relative safety of the Executive Mansion. At the same time ECOMOG, anxious to put in place the interim government as soon as possible, needed to obtain firm assurances from Johnson that its forces would not be attacked. And, as Blunt pointed out, the INPFL leader was 'a very volatile and erratic sort of man.' But there could be no doubt that Doe was dead. He had been captured by Johnson's INPFL, taken to Redemption hospital and there tortured and killed. His entourage, consisting among others of his Defence Minister, Brigadier General J. Boimah Barclay and about 60 soldiers, had also been slaughtered.[3]

***

The circumstances of Doe's assassination have never been fully explained, leading to a number of theories, including those of a conspiracy between ECOMOG and Johnson. Although much has been written about this subject,

DOI: 10.4324/9781003219309-15

and while some of the circumstances of the killing suggest at least the possibility of collusion,[4] on the balance of probability it seems unlikely.*

***

Two days after Doe's assassination, on 11 September, a delegation from Liberia's new interim government led by Levy Zangai, leader of the Liberian Action Party, set out from Banjul for Liberia to establish itself in Monrovia. When safe to do so, the new government in its entirety would travel and, led by Amos Sawyer, would then administer Liberia until the outcome of general elections scheduled for October 1991. But the process was already being burdened with complications and contradictions. On the previous day Johnson had proclaimed himself Liberia's 'Interim President', as did one General David Nimley, commander of what was left of Doe's presidential guard (barricaded behind the walls of the Executive Mansion). Charles Taylor had already declared himself president some weeks previously.[5]

Taylor, for his part, appeared to be concentrating his energies on a quick military victory, responding to news of Doe's death by declaring, yet again, that he would launch a final assault on Monrovia, 'even if it means leveling the whole city.'[6] ECOWAS Executive Secretary, Dr Abbas Bundu, countered angrily saying Taylor had always declared that he was fighting to liberate his country from Doe's dictatorship and 'now that Doe had left the scene, why was he continuing to fight'?[7]

Nigeria was especially frustrated by Taylor's attitude for, although he had neither attended nor been represented at the Banjul conference, he now quite unexpectedly announced his agreement with its outcome, giving the green light to a ceasefire and an interim government. ECOWAS officials, unused to the ways of the INFL leader, hoped the crisis was now firmly on the way to being resolved and ECOMOG's intervention no longer necessary. Nigerian President Babangida, however, casting a watchful eye on developments, declared that in view of the situation on the ground the time had not yet come for a withdrawal of ECOWAS troops.[8] But even the astute Nigerian leader could never have envisaged that it would take well over another decade before such a withdrawal could take place.

Babangida was not unaware that, in addition to Taylor's refusal to lay down arms (despite his current protestations to the contrary), there was at least one ECOWAS member state (and probably a second) actively working against a resolution. This was Blaise Compaoré's Burkina Faso, which had formally condemned the deployment of ECOMOG. Nigerian diplomatic sources were claiming that Taylor had recently spent time in Ouagadougou, Burkina Faso's capital, and that not only had he procured more weapons, but Burkinabe troops were now assisting him on the ground. Whatever about such claims, Lieutenant Colonel Gabriel Ochiedu, head of the Nigerian contingent, made no such allegations, at least publicly. Instead, he told journalists that Taylor's rebels were 'maintaining a provisional ceasefire with ECOWAS' as they faced one another

---

*   The LTRC makes no reference to the issue of collusion.

north of Monrovia, adding that he had met NPFL rebels on two occasions and 'was able to explain to them the aims of the peacekeeping force.'[9]

***

In Bong Mine, with the opening up of a new food aid programme, sponsored by CRS, John Feeney had decided to re-engage in distribution work. On 14 September he attended a meeting convened by the agency where people were appointed to oversee the programme. They seemed to him, he told his diary, 'to be a good group, capable without doubt and hopefully honest.'[10] Three days later he noted the 'good progress being made in taking a census for the CRS programme.' Hopefully it would succeed and would 'be a great help in preventing starvation.'[11] A few days later the programme swung into action. The ship bearing rice docked in Buchanan and the unloading started. Committee members from Bong Mine who had come to Buchanan 'were highly impressed by the manner in which the rice was being stored.' However, on 29 September, when Feeney and committee members went to unload rice which had been brought to Bong Mine from Buchanan by NPFL lorries, there was disillusionment.

> There were only two trucks instead of three. There were only 500 bags of rice instead of 750. A great disappearing act was performed last night, and it was not performed by the local residents.[12]

And Feeney had no doubt who was to blame!

The Bong Mine pastor had another concern. With frequent killings being carried out by the NPFL he was particularly worried about the behaviour of his 'guests' – those to who, at great personal risk, he had given refuge.

> I am very annoyed with my 'guests.' I know that they are eating much better than those who are living in so-called Freedom. To avoid detection I have made it a rule that nothing must go in or out of their room without my knowledge. This morning I saw the catechist taking food into them. He admitted that he had taken a letter from one of them to a friend on the outside. As a result, food was sent in. It looks as if they have no realization of the seriousness of their situation or of what might happen to me and them if it is discovered that I was harbouring 'dangerous criminals.'

***

On the military front, a month into the ECOMOG mission, progress had been slow but sustained.[13] Both the NPFL and the INPFL had been pushed out from metropolitan Monrovia and ECOMOG had also taken suburban areas such as Bensonville, Carysburg, Paynesville, Johnsonville and Spriggs Payne airfield. Some elements were now approaching the Firestone Plantation. The so-called Armed Forces of Liberia (AFL), remnants of Doe's army, were still holed up in the Executive Mansion and the Barclay Training Centre area, from which ECOMOG was now trying to prise them. There was fighting too between Taylor's and Johnson's forces to gain control of the waterworks near

White Plains and the hydroelectric dam at Mount Coffee. Johnson's forces were to succeed in both objectives, but the fighting had left both plants badly damaged and requiring major repairs. Outside Monrovia, despite setbacks, Taylor's forces were by no means in retreat, bolstered by heavy armaments and ammunition from Burkina Faso channelled through the Ivory Coast. ECOMOG was using fighter jets based in Lungi (Sierra Leone) in an attempt to destroy this weaponry. And there was no let-up in atrocities, with daily killings of Ghanaian and other West African nationals interned by the NPFL in the Tubmanburg military barracks.[14] In Monrovia itself, however, life at last was beginning to show a semblance of normality. MSF teams had returned – bringing with them the medicines they had salvaged when St Joseph's hospital was evacuated – and were now requesting the Spanish religious brothers to return and re-open the hospital.

Taylor, clearly no longer on the verge of conquering Monrovia, was now taking more frequently to the airwaves of his rebel radio station in Gbarnga, requesting a round-table conference between the warring parties at a neutral venue. Nobody responded, perhaps because the Banjul-brokered interim government was expected daily in Monrovia. Vehemently rejecting its legitimacy, Taylor was maintaining that he was the true president, properly installed in his chosen capital, Gbarnga. In this capacity, he had convoked national elections for 10 October and the installation of a new government on 15 October. In point of fact, a government was to be installed six days later, on 21 October. It was not to be Taylor's but the Banjul-conceived interim government under Sawyer, known as the Interim Government of National Unity (IGNU).

***

There were now signs that the various non-governmental groups in the U.S. concerned with Liberia's crisis were focusing less on political advocacy and engaging more in relief advocacy and even direct relief work. The AFJN's well-briefed *Information* news-sheet, edited by Ted Hayden, outlined the scope of the current relief effort and the problems that it was encountering. It reported that the CRS was willing to 'rush food to Liberia', but ships were still 'unwilling to dock there because of the uncertain situation.'[15] Even 'Liberia Watch', whose primary concern was the safeguarding of human rights, became preoccupied with the practicalities of relief work. Its executive council meeting on 6 November reflected this change of emphasis, urging members to approach Congress, the UN, as well as the general public, to increase the scale of relief aid. It also called for greater co-ordination of relief efforts within the U.S. and to this end urged all engaged in such work to 'associate with the Coalition of Liberian Organisations in the United States' which now had obtained a tax-exempt number and was incorporated. Already the Coalition had sent two shipments of food to Liberia and a third was planned to arrive for Christmas.

***

On 14 November 1990 ECOMOG's official status as a peace-keeping monitoring force, already dubious, was blown out of the water. On that day five Nigerian aircraft bombed the port of Buchanan. Within hours a spokesperson for Taylor was heard on the BBC claiming that civilians had been killed and a ship in the harbour carrying relief supplies and medicines had been damaged.[16] ECOMOG confirmed that the raid had taken place while the ECOWAS political ambassador in Sierra Leone, Joshua Iroha, defended the attack saying weapons destined for the NPFL were being brought in through the port in containers.[17] Agence France-Presse was less restrained about the ships contents and fate, reporting that the aircraft had destroyed a vessel 'loaded with weaponry.'[18] On the following day other NPFL targets nearer Monrovia were attacked by bombers dispatched from bases in Sierra Leone and by ECOMOG field artillery.[19]

***

The bombing of Buchanan and its designation by ECOMOG as a war zone was to have serious repercussions for those expatriates engaged in food aid distribution. First to suffer were the CRS team which was accused of spying and taken at gunpoint to NPFL headquarters. There 'they were stripped, insulted and slapped' until they were eventually released.[20]

The Catholic missionaries were next. Jennings described what happened.

> This morning a force of NPFL burst into the mission and our house. They were suggesting that we were involved with the enemy and guiding the planes into the port area. They wanted to take us for questioning to NPFL headquarters. We agreed to go but only to see Dr Mané (the NPFL military commander)[21]. In the event Fr Kilcoyne went with them and I was placed under house arrest.[22]

As it transpired, the leadership was apologetic and Kilcoyne was taken around to the town checkpoints to apprise fighters that he was 'persona grata.' However, as Jennings told his diary:

> the tour around the town was misunderstood by the people who began shouting 'spies, spies, down with spies.' They thought we were under arrest and were being paraded for spying.

Jennings and Kilcoyne remained in their house that day but decided that in the present chaotic circumstances it would be prudent to leave Buchanan for some time. At a meeting with parishioners after Sunday Mass they were strongly encouraged to act on this decision. And so, on Monday 19 November they set out for LAC (to which the Sisters had earlier fled), jeered on the streets as they passed and enduring repeated accusations of being spies at checkpoints along the road. From LAC they made their way to Gbarnga and then on across the Ivory Coast border to Danané. Finally, on Friday 23 November they set out by plane from Abidjan bound for Ireland.[23]

***

The ECOMOG bombing campaign of Buchanan's port area, which had commenced on 14 November, quickly escalated. On 17 November the NPFL claimed that Nigerian fighter planes had 'carried out a sustained bombing raid' on its Gbarnga-based radio station.[24] Neutral sources reported renewed air attacks on the port of Buchanan and on military installations in the town.[25] Reports on the bombing campaign and its outcome were now coming thick and fast. Particularly alarming was an Agence France-Presse claim, on 19 November, quoting American diplomats to the effect that the 'air raids last week on Buchanan had resulted in a large civilian death toll, mainly women and children.' The sources further claimed that 'the Nigerian pilots were indiscriminate in their targets and unleashed bombs which caused massive destruction.'[26]

The U.S. reprimand about the Buchanan port bombings was not the only adverse reaction received by ECOMOG. Sawyer, president of the IGNU, awaiting security clearance before going to Monrovia, declared on Ghanaian radio that ECOMOG should 'now go on the *defensive*[27] in the war against Taylor. In ECOWAS circles there was 'consternation and shock' at this pronouncement leading Sawyer to 'clarify' his statement. He said that he had asked ECOMOG to tentatively maintain a defensive posture so as to facilitate current peace-making diplomacy which was reaching a delicate stage. At the same time, he took care to say that he was not asking ECOMOG 'to permit the landing of arms at Buchanan or the stockpiling of arms in churches in Gbarnga (Taylor's headquarters).'[28]

Whatever about Sawyer's competence in military matters his credentials as a political scientist and politician dedicated to peaceful means and the pursuit of democracy were unassailable. It was not widely known until he spoke on Ghanaian radio that for some time he had been engaged in talks with Taylor, trying to persuade the NPFL leader to attend an ECOWAS peace conference, scheduled for Bamako, capital of Mali, at the end of November.[29] It was true, Sawyer said, that according to the Banjul Peace accord the leaders of the factions and the president and vice president of the IGNU would be ineligible to run for the highest office in the elections scheduled for 1991.[30] However, ECOWAS was now prepared to offer Taylor the next most influential post for which he was entitled to run, namely that of Speaker of the Legislative Assembly. He was also being offered approximately 50% of the seats in the Assembly. The incentive for the NPFL leader was clear, namely that the pursuit of a political course rather than a military one, was more likely to succeed.[31]

***

Yet, on the ground, the NPFL was still capable of dealing death, shelling the ELBC radio station in Paynesville – now the voice of the IGNU and ECOMOG – and killing four Nigerian soldiers. The AFL remnant too was dealing death, making occasional forays in search of food and plunder, also launching attacks on the NPFL with, it appeared to some neutral observers, ECOMOG backing. Reporting from Monrovia, the young freelance reporter, Scott Sterns,[32] described how a battalion of AFL soldiers was supported by ECOMOG artillery as it drove rebels 'toward the VOA transmitter near Kenema Beach, 12 miles east of the capital.' And Prince Johnson, too, was receiving help, 'awaiting ECOMOG ground support before moving from positions north of the water treatment facility towards his long-desired goal of taking the strategic crossroads at Kakata, 25 miles north.'[33] Allegations that ECOMOG took sides – mainly against the NPFL – were to plague the force throughout the years of the civil war.

Sawyer, for his part, still under advice from the ECOMOG commander not to return to Monrovia for his presidential inauguration, was visiting the heads of state of three countries which had contributed contingents to ECOMOG.[34] He was now confident that the forthcoming Bamako conference would succeed.[35] Meanwhile, in the Bushrod Island suburb of Monrovia, a rather curious scene was unfolding. Here Liberian IGNU member, Ambassador Gabriel Farngalo, (one of a number who had already arrived in the capital) was cutting the ribbon to the Duala market building which was re-opening, with a voluble Prince Johnson in attendance. 'Ask not what the interim government can do for you', Johnson declaimed to the gathering, 'but what you can do for the interim government.'[36]

It was at this point that Emmanuel Bowier briefly re-emerged from the shadows. No longer a Minister since July when imprudently he had advised President Doe to step down, Bowier had taken the wiser course of going into exile. Surfacing in Dakar, Senegal, on 20 November he made a passionate appeal to the warring factions to lay down their arms, put aside personal ambitions, 'reason together' and to 'forgive, forget and compromise in the interest of the country and future generations.'[37]*

***

As the deadline for the Bamako conference approached, while insisting he would attend, Taylor staged a show of strength, going on the offensive against ECOMOG and shelling Monrovia's Freeport. It was the first time in some weeks that NPFL forces had taken the initiative. During the shelling a number of children were reported to have been killed. But Taylor, calling up the BBC's Robin White, absolved his soldiers of the allegation. In contrast to his broadcasts on the eve of ECOMOG's arrival, he now appeared back to his suave, assured self. When White asked him why he was shelling the port he replied:

> Well Robin we have confirmed intelligence reports that there was a stockpile of arms there being used by the enemy, so this is just a decapitating exercise to reduce the capabilities of the enemy. I would love for my people to receive relief supplies through both ports, and I hope we can come to some understanding to stop the senseless war.[38]

When told that children had been killed in the bombardment, Taylor questioned the credentials of the journalist who had made the 'outrageous' claim.

---

*   Bowier later re-emerged as a clergyman, wrote a book and became a prominent religious leader. He also gave extensive testimony to the Liberia Truth and Reconciliation Commission.

When told of eyewitness evidence that children had been killed while taking refuge in a yard, he would have none of it, angrily proclaiming 'I would never kill Liberian children!' All his endeavours, he added, were directed 'to stop this war, sit down, and begin the talking.' It was for that very reason, he said, that he was determined 'to go to Bamako over the next several days to begin the peace process.'[39]

***

On 26 November 1990, courtesy of a Burkina Faso Fokker-28, Taylor, true to his word, landed at Bamako airport with a delegation of forty, some armed with rocket launchers. The presence of this heavily-armed group led to an immediate protest to the Malian authorities by General Joshua Dogonyaro, the current ECOMOG commanding officer, whereupon the delegation was escorted to a military camp some ten miles from the capital and later, after tense discussions, disarmed.[40] Given his long record of abstention – he had already failed to attend four ECOWAS conferences – there was much speculation as to why Taylor had decided to attend. Apart from ebbing military fortunes, diplomatic pressure and the persuasiveness of the argument that the NPFL would benefit more from a political strategy, there was the fact that a recent ECOWAS mission to Libya had obtained a promise from Muammar Qaddafi to suspend the supply of arms to Taylor.[41]

Despite considerable optimism concerning the outcome of the talks – a ceasefire looked certainly achievable – the atmosphere was tense when the various parties (which included 13 ECOWAS heads of state and the current OAU President, Uganda's Yoweri Museveni) began to gather. The NPFL delegation was noticeably nervous – not surprising in the light of what had happened to Samuel Doe at ECOMOG headquarters in Monrovia. Angry claims were made by the delegation that Nigerian ECOMOG aircraft were currently bombing NPFL positions in Lofa County on the Sierra Leone border and at Cape Mount north-west of Monrovia.[42] However, Woewiyu assured journalists that the NPFL would not walk away from the talks, due to commence on Tuesday, 27 November, under the chairmanship of Mali's President Moussa Traoré.[43]

Further unsettling the conference organisers was the unexpected arrival of Ivory Coast's 84-year-old president, Félix Houphouët-Boigny, described by Mali radio as 'the doyen of African leaders' and suspected by ECOWAS officials of supporting Taylor. But others hoped that his presence might be helpful in persuading the NPFL leader to agree a ceasefire. And indeed, Malian sources, anxious no doubt that a conference held in their capital should succeed, were saying that Taylor already had 'privately agreed to a ceasefire.' Another important powerbroker in West Africa to attend the meeting was Flight Lieutenant Jerry Rawlings of Ghana, who arrived with a high-powered delegation which included his head of security and Foreign Minister. Ghana had already made it clear to ECOWAS that, while supporting ECOMOG's military actions, it would prefer to see a political solution to the conflict. And to this end Ghana had participated in the delegation which visited Qaddafi in Libya seeking support for the peace initiative.[44]

During the course of the Bamako conference Nigeria was the only country to take a strong stand against the NPFL. This came as no great surprise. From the first mention of an ECOWAS peace-keeping force Nigeria, leading those in favour of its dispatch, had been a particular object of Taylor's venom. The tough terms set out by ECOWAS for a peace accord, adopted at the 27 August Banjul summit, which included a prohibition on the principals to the conflict standing in presidential elections, further reflected Nigerian influence. Less than two weeks before the dispatch of ECOMOG, as already mentioned, NPFL forces had attacked the Nigerian embassy in Monrovia and subsequently harassed Nigerians who crossed their path. And in the run up to Bamako the intensification of ECOMOG's military operations and particularly the bombarding of NPFL targets by Nigerian aircraft, raised Taylor's verbal attacks on Nigeria to fever pitch. Now at Bamako, while most other ECOWAS member states proffered the 'carrot' to Taylor, displaying an accommodating disposition, pointing out the benefits of pursuing a political strategy, Nigeria continued to represent ECOWAS's threatening disposition, wielding the 'stick' of retribution, offering no concessions.

***

Tuesday 27 November, the opening day of the conference,[45] was declared a public holiday in Mali, to mark what President Rawlings called this 'last chance summit.'[46] Early that morning Taylor met in secret for over three hours with Presidents Traoré and Joseph Saidu Momoh (Sierra Leone). The full summit, attended by representatives of 16 nations, convened late in the afternoon. A few days earlier ECOWAS had achieved a major success in Monrovia, namely the swearing in of Liberia's interim government (IGNU) – with a full attendance of ministers, led by Sawyer.[47] In recent days ECOMOG too had enjoyed success, pushing Taylor's forces some 40 miles inland.[48] Bamako, however, was already on the road to failure when at its opening session, as a precondition for a ceasefire, Taylor called for the abolition of the IGNU and immediate elections.[49]

By this very time, fresh from his inauguration, interim president Sawyer was on a helicopter (courtesy of the U.S. embassy) flying to Freetown and destined for Bamako. His government had been excluded from the conference, although Gabriel Baccus Matthews, designated Foreign Minister, had been given observer status. Now, however, the Malian Foreign Minister was arguing that Liberia's newly installed interim government should be represented at the highest level.[50] Sawyer, he said, was in agreement with him that while immediate new elections at the present time were unrealistic, the interim president might bring to the conference proposals which would enable a higher level of NPFL participation in the peace process. These might include the allocation of cabinet positions in the IGNU and a wider system of representation in the interim legislative assembly. Whether this was a major exercise in appeasement in the hope of saving the conference and Mali's reputation, or a brilliant stroke, making it impossible for Taylor to turn his back on the conference, remained to be seen.

In fact, there was very little time to wait. For early in the afternoon of the second day, 28 November, before Sawyer had arrived and much to the amazement of observers, Taylor, in the presence of Presidents Traoré and Dawda Jawara, along with representatives of AFL and the INPFL, signed a ceasefire agreement which pledged the parties to a peaceful resolution of the conflict.[51] Trumpeted by ECOWAS as an unparalleled success, the outcome was greeted with relief by the international community. However, more sanguine observers, who had been watching the Liberian crisis develop over a decade and who were well aware of the personalities involved, regarded it, at most, as a timid step in the right direction rather than the 'Big Breakthrough for Peace' dominating press coverage.[52] And when the terms of the accord were revealed there were certainly good reasons for withholding any overwhelming endorsement.

According to the terms of the accord all signatories unanimously agreed to a ceasefire. They also agreed to the replacement of the IGNU within a year by a second more representative interim government, charged with the task of preparing the way for national elections. The modalities for forming this second interim government would be drawn up within 60 days by Liberia's three warring factions and representatives of political parties and interest groups, at an 'All-Liberia Conference' to be held in Monrovia. This conference would also settle the modalities for monitoring the ceasefire. Taylor wasted no time in informing journalists that, furthermore, the conference would involve the preparation of an interim constitution which, among other things, would decide who exactly was eligible to stand for election. Thus, might be cast aside the prohibition against contesting presidential elections directed against Taylor, Johnson and other faction leaders – formerly central to the ECOWAS strategy. For, according to Taylor, the All-Liberia Conference had the authority to dispense with Sawyer, place himself or any other faction-leader in charge of the second interim government and permit all to stand in the election for a substantive government. In hindsight ECOWAS weakness on this issue was to prove a critical mistake.

***

Reuters Nicholas Kotch, for one, had no illusions about the outcome of the Bamako conference. Reporting from the garrison town of Kati, ten miles from Bamako, where Taylor's delegation was housed, he found the NPFL leader cock-a-hoop. Taylor, he said, had gone into the talks in an 'apparently weak position.' Libya had promised ECOWAS it would halt its arms supply while ECOMOG had been 'stepping up its air and ground attacks.' However, many delegates now believed that bolstered by several ECOWAS leaders Taylor had 'achieved most of his goals.' Emerging from the summit he had announced that he would do deals with the INPFL and AFL, but there would be 'no place at the top table' for Sawyer.[53] He had told journalists 'Amos Sawyer is not one of the principal players in this game', and calling him 'President Sawyer' was a 'downright joke.' The final communiqué, Kotch concluded, gave Taylor every reason to be upbeat. It had refused to endorse Sawyer's interim government and 'did not require Taylor to surrender his arms or his authority over the 90% of Liberian territory he claimed to control.'[54]

***

The fragility of the ceasefire was exposed on Friday, 30 November, scarcely three days after the agreement was signed, when an outbreak of fighting between Johnson's INPFL and the AFL occurred in the vicinity of the Executive Mansion.[55] ECOMOG responded by re-doubling its patrols and setting up additional check-points all over the city.[56] The outbreak underlined yet another weakness in the Bamako accord, namely its failure to spell out the modalities for disarming the factions, something which was to be left to the 'All-Liberia' Conference in which those factions were major participants. As long as the three main militias were heavily armed, prospects for a meaningful peace seemed distant. And the extent to which ECOWAS had bent over backwards to accommodate the NPFL leader – as well as the attitude which produced such an outcome – was further outlined on 1 December, when Bundu, its executive secretary, on a visit to Lagos, declared that Taylor 'could not be neglected in the formation of the next interim government', to be formed after the disbandment of Sawyer's interim administration.[57] In fact, this disbandment appeared to be imminent, for Bundu said that the All-Liberian Conference would be taking place 'in about two weeks' to settle differences over the formation of the next interim government. 'What we are trying to do now', he went on, 'is to get Professor Amos Sawyer in a meeting with Taylor so that together they can work out a government for Liberia.' This was a very different Dr Bundu from the one who on 11 September had castigated Taylor's continuing use of violence and cast serious doubts on the NPFL's leader's integrity.[58]

Whatever the attitude in ECOWAS, on the ground ECOMOG, under the formidable Major General Dogonyaro, faced with the reality of lawless and heavily armed factions, determined to disarm elements of Johnson's forces and those of the AFL. On 1 December ECOMOG arrested scores of INPFL and AFL soldiers and took them to its headquarters in Monrovia where they were relieved of their arms. Dogonyaro explained that the arrested soldiers had been in defiance of an IGNU order 'for all soldiers to return to their bases and barracks.'[59] And he further justified his action by stating that the Bamako Accord had 'empowered ECOMOG to commence disarming the factions.' Moreover, Taylor's NPFL, too, would be disarmed in the city following the IGNU's direction that 'only the peace-keeping force would be maintaining Monrovia's security.' However, disarmament had not been mentioned specifically in the cessation of hostilities declaration signed at Bamako. The most that can be said for Doganyaro's invocation of Bamako in the context of disarmament, was that he saw it as an integral element in fulfilling his mission to establish peace and order.

***

In Bong Mine Feeney was recording the arrest of a woman suspected of being of the Mandingo tribe. 'If she is Mandingo, the poor lady's fate is sealed.' Luckily, however, she was able to prove that she was of the Kpelle tribe. 'But since they thought she was Mandingo her husband must have thought likewise.

So they tortured him unmercifully for harbouring her.' His postscript to the journal entry was equally unmerciful.

> Revolutions usually have their quotas of intellectuals, philosophers, drea-mers, poets and idealists, but where is our supply of such individuals here? To find them one would search in vain. All that could be found would be greedy murderers lusting for blood and vengeance. Sadistic killers and looters. And yet there are those who would let them have the country for the sake of 'Peace.'[60]

*****

In mid-December, deeply disappointed at the Bamako Accord, Archbishop Francis held a conference of all diocesan staff in Monrovia. There he deplored those decisions taken at Bamako which had in effect signed the death warrant of the Sawyer interim government and gave the faction leaders full rein to participate in politics without giving anything in return. In preparation for the conference Francis produced a paper giving not only a valuable review of the developing crisis over the past decade but also an account of what had gone on behind the scenes in attempts to avert an enduring tragedy. In particular Francis analysed the role played by the Liberian Council of Churches during this traumatic period, a role which though significant, had not made the impact so greatly desired by its leaders. When Francis put pen to paper it was clear that he no longer had any doubts about the nature of Liberia's collapse.

> There is a great body of young persons who have learned the 'power' of the gun, and lack respect for any moral code. There is also a group of adults whose only desire is to gain power and in that process they know no restraints. They desire power for power's sake, without reference to any moral code; they violate with impunity the fundamental rights of our people regardless of the consequences.[61]

In developing his theme he pointed to the upsurge of 'tribalism and nepotism' during the Doe era. It was no surprise that when Taylor came on the scene he found fertile ground for carrying out his real intentions. Those intentions were simple. He wished to 'overthrow the Doe regime and become president of Liberia.' Every other professed intention by Taylor - his desire to bring peace, to restore democracy, to achieve true development - was designed, cynically, to help him accomplish his personal ambition. And this still remained the case. Nonetheless this was the man who consistently received the support of the heads-of-state of the Ivory Coast, Burkina Faso and Libya, and of a substantial number of Americo-Liberia exiles in the United States who wished to 'revenge the death of Mr Tolbert, or to revenge the loss of their status and properties.' Very few if any, the archbishop concluded, were concerned about the plight of the Liberian people.

Archbishop Francis was to become Taylor nemesis, largely because from an early stage of the insurgency he recognised the nature of Taylor's project, understood his methodology, and never flinched from proclaiming it locally and internationally. In this he took enormous personal risks. On the other hand he championed Sawyer, seeing in him perhaps the only Liberian leader with the moral capacity and personal integrity to prevail against the evils enveloping his country. In his paper, preparatory to the mid-December conference, he described Sawyer as the only person capable of bringing unity to the Liberian people, because he had had 'no part in the unfortunate crisis' and was 'a man with a clean record, a man devoted to constitutional government.' Francis's greatest hope at this time was that at the All-Liberia Conference, Sawyer would be confirmed in his position as head of the interim government or made head of any new version of that institution.

Notes

1   12 September 1990.
2   FBIS-AFR-90-177, 12 September 1990 (aB1109202290 BBC World Service, Elizabeth Blunt, speaking to Catherine Davis, host of '24 Hours' programme).
3   Ibid.
4   See Adewale Maja-Pearce, London Review of Books, 6 February 2020.
5   Barry Turner, ed., The Statesman's Yearbook 2003: The Politics, Cultures and Economies of the World (Palgrave Macmillan), 1041.
6   Ibid.
7   Ibid.
8   Ibid.
9   Ibid, quoting official Nigerian news Agency, NAN.
10   'Journal', 28.
11   Ibid, 29.
12   Ibid., 36.
13   A.T. Michael Francis to S. John Murray, 3 October 1990.
14   See, Asa Waltan, 'Addressing falsehoods and misconceptions of the past. The Liberian Truth and Reconciliation Commission reinterpreting Liberia's past', MA thesis, Historiska institutionen, (Stockholm, Sweden) 2014, 147.
15   11 September 1990.
16   FBIS-AFR-90-222, 16 November 1990 (AB1511175890 London BBC World Service).
17   Ibid.
18   Ibid, 16 November 1990 (AB1611153090 Paris AFT in English).
19   Ibid (AB1511202490, London BBC World Service, 'Focus on Africa', 15 November 1990).
20   A.B. A. Jennings, 'Personal diary', 37–38.
21   Mane was Senegalese.
22   Ibid., 39.
23   A.B. Buchanan Mission Diary, Summary: November 1990-June 1991, pp. 2–5.
24   FBIS-AFR-90–223, 19 November 1990 (AB1711210090 Gbarnga Voice of the NPFL).
25   Ibid.
26   Ibid (AB1911134290 Paris AFP, 9 November 1990).
27   Author's italics.
28   Ibid. See also Africa Watch, 'Liberia, Waging War to Keep the Peace'; 'The ECOMOG intervention and Human Rights', Reports, June 1993, vol. 5, no. 6.
29   FBIS-AFR-90–223, 19 November 1990. (AB1911100690 Monrovia Radio ELBC).

30 See, Human Rights Watch, Report: Events of 1991, published 1992, 75.
31 FBIS-AFR-90–223, BBC 'Focus on Africa', 16 November 1990.
32 Sterns was to have a distinguished career as a VOA State Department correspondent and White House Correspondent, also as a contributor to the BBC, UPI and Associated Press.
33 Ibid.
34 FBIS-AFR-90–220, November 1990. See Transcript of AFP in French; transcript Monrovia Radio ELBC.
35 FBIS-AFR-90–223, 19 November 1990 (AB1811134590 Dakar PANA in English and Monrovia Radio ELBC).
36 Ibid.
37 Ibid.
38 FBIS-AFR-90–225, 21 November 1990 (AB2011193290 London BBC World Service, 'Focus on Africa').
39 Ibid (AB2011193290 London BBC World Service, 'Focus on Africa', 20 November 1990).
40 AFJN Information, 28 November 1990 (Nicholas Kotch, Reuter News Report, Tuesday).
41 Ibid.
42 Ibid.
43 Chairmanship of ECOWAS had passed from Gambia to Mali during 1990.
44 Edward Ameyibor, Inter Press Service International News, 28 November 1990.
45 It took place at Bamako's Friendship Hotel.
46 Reuters News Report, Bamako, 27 November 1990.
47 Sawyer had been able to enter the capital through Spriggs Payne airport which was now firmly in the hands of ECOMOG.
48 Inter Press Service International News, Wednesday, 28 November 1990.
49 Xinhua, English Language News Service, 27 November 1990. See also Abiodun Alao, op. cit., 81, for discussion of the Bamako accord.
50 FBIS-AFR-229, 28 November 1990 (AB2711184890 BBC World Service, Scott Sterns, 'Focus on Africa').
51 Ibid. (AB2811154290, Bamako Domestic Service in French, 28 November 1990). See also, FBIS-AFR-90–235 (AB0512213890 Lagos Domestic Service, 4 December 1990).
52 Xinhua English Language News Service, Lagos, 29 November 1990.
53 Reuters News Reports, 29 November 1990.
54 Ibid.
55 Xinhua English Language News Service, Via News Net, 1 December 1990.
56 Ibid.
57 Ibid.
58 FBIS-AFR-90–177, 12 September 1990 (AB1109201790 Paris AFP).
59 Xinhua English Language News Service, Via News Net, 2 December 1990.
60 A.T. 'Journal of a Missionary', 55.
61 Office of the Archdiocese of Monrovia, Memorandum from Archbishop Michael Francis to the Conference on Liberia, mid-December 1990.

12 Liberia as a two-state entity

The Monrovia enclave rule by an interim government of national unity, and 'Greater Liberia' (capital: Gbarnga) ruled by the rebel government

As 1990 came to a close, for the first time ECOWAS had the necessary military and diplomatic force to impose a solution. The NPFL had been driven back in the field, its arms supplies drying up because of diplomatic pressure on donor countries. Strong action by ECOWAS at this point could and would have gained immediate and meaningful international support. The ECOWAS failure to grasp the opportunity, already evident in its willingness to compromise with Taylor at Bamako, was to prove calamitous for Liberia. Perhaps part of the explanation was that a number of West African leaders saw something of themselves in Charles Taylor, a charismatic, unelected, despot. The ECOWAS five-member Standing Mediation Committee, it is true, had sought a more severe regime, excluding Liberia's warlords from participation in future presidential elections and providing for a single interim government led by neutral elements. However, as the process came nearer to a conclusion there was a discernible softening of the line against Taylor. The NPFL leader, recognising where concessions were best sought, appeared to relish his elevation to the status of a quasi head of state at Bamako and became more intransigent in negotiation.

***

With the signing of the ceasefire and the All-Liberia Conference in prospect, a sense that the civil war was now over began to gain ground. Persistent reports that Liberia was generally calm reinforced this belief. However most of these emanated from within the relatively peaceful ECOMOG-controlled Monrovia enclave which accounted for a mere 10% of the country's geographical area. It was a very different story in the remaining 90% — the so-called 'Greater Liberia.' Those with an inside knowledge of what was happening there were very much in a minority; and were sometimes regarded as discordant voices by those who hoped that the nightmare of civil war was over.

The perception that the war was effectively over led to a flurry of activity by various international aid and development agencies, governmental and voluntary.[1] 16 December saw the first UN Disaster Relief flight from Freetown to Spriggs Payne airfield. A World Food Programme vessel was on its way to San Pedro (Ivory Coast) with a cargo of rice. Another ship, the *Steel Trader*, had already arrived in Monrovia's Freeport with a relief cargo from Freetown. In

DOI: 10.4324/9781003219309-16

addition, the Swedish government offered to provide a 200-bed hospital and technical staff while MSF-Holland and UNICEF had finalised plans for a measles vaccination programme. Public utilities were also being attended to. The White Plains water plant was now working at 30% efficiency thanks to the combined efforts of MSF-B, the Liberian Water and Sewage Company and UNICEF.[2] Official U.S. government relief assistance to Liberia was largely channelled through non-governmental agencies already working in the field, such as the International Red Cross, the Liberian Red Cross, Catholic Relief Services, Médecins Sans Frontières, and Action Internationale Contre la Faim. Direct aid was on a much smaller scale, largely mediated by the Office of U.S. Foreign Disaster Assistance, which dispatched two 'Disaster Relief Teams' to the region; and through the State Department Bureau for Refugee Programmes. Now, in the wake of Bamako, U.S. humanitarian assistance intensified.

***

The provisions for monitoring the ceasefire agreed upon at Bamako were patently inadequate. They stipulated that the combatants should remain where they were on the day the accord was signed. Subsequent discussions on the modalities of monitoring were to take place under the supervision of ECOWAS, not in Bamako but in Liberia at the so-called All-Liberia Conference. With regard to these there was merely an expression of hope that they would be completed within 60 days.[3] Moreover the Bamako agreement produced no timetable for disarmament, not even a notion as to how it was to be accomplished. This proved to be a major weakness in the ECOWAS attempt to resolve the crisis at this point.

One matter on which all warring factions were agreed was that the interim government of national unity (IGNU) led by Amos Sawyer should be taken out of circulation as soon as possible and replaced by a second interim government which would become an instrument of their policies and ambitions. To this end they agreed to hold peace talks in one another's territory, to which neither Sawyer's government nor ECOWAS would be invited. The first meeting was scheduled for early January at Johnson's INPFL enclave in Monrovia, the next in mid-January in NPFL-held Buchanan and the third on 21 January at the Armed Forces of Liberia (AFL) enclave in Monrovia. The purpose of the meetings was to 'decide on the details of the ceasefire agreements arrived at during the two sets of negotiations in Mali and Gambia.'[4] This would prepare the way for the All-Liberia Conference which would replace the current interim administration with one acceptable to the warring factions. Such independent action had been greatly facilitated by the failure of the Bamako agreement, even implicitly, to recognise the Sawyer government. The failure by ECOWAS to support its own creation was tantamount to a declaration of 'open season' on the IGNU. As for the scheduled meetings between the warring factions, unsurprisingly they never took place. It was clear that the appetite for power and the willingness to use every means to achieve it remained as fresh and as driven as ever, while the will of the regional and international communities to challenge had given way to a tired acceptance of compromise and accommodation. The reality was that Liberia's civil war was by no means over. In fact, it was only beginning.

***

In the last week of December Lee Cahill, in his capacity as Regional Superior responsible for the welfare of his Irish SMA colleagues, was compiling a report on the situation in Liberia for a forthcoming Society* meeting scheduled for June 1991 to be held at Tenafly. It was a prescient if depressing document.

> Liberia as we have known it is finished. The institutions and the communities - industrial, ecclesial, social – have been devastated and uprooted by a guerrilla war, with its consequences of killing, looting and destruction.[5]

The landscape of Monrovia and its hinterland, he continued, was badly scarred by the effects of civil war and there was great confusion as the various war factions still struggled for control. Liberia, as a country, was now composed of two political entities, one, comprising Monrovia and its hinterland of some 30-miles radius, which the ECOWAS-devised IGNU occupied alongside the AFL and the INPFL: and the other, the vast territories of Greater Liberia.

In terms of Cahill's duties as Regional Superior, covering the entire country, negotiating one's way across the two 'republics' had become something of a nightmare. Resident permits, re-entry permits, letters of authorisation and official stamps had to be acquired both in Monrovia and Gbarnga (capital of Greater Liberia) in order to travel over and back across the 30-mile partition between the two territories. The officials at either side were 'absolutely convinced of the total rightness of their position' and contemptuous of documentation from the other side. Most people, Cahill added in his report, were asking him whether he thought the war was really over; and despite expressing hope, he was unable to answer in the affirmative. Deep down there was a general awareness that the worst was yet to come.

In the last weeks of 1990 two U.S. Congressmen, Howard Wolpe and Donald Payne, undertook a 'fact-finding' visit to Liberia and the region. Visiting refugee centres in Liberia and adjacent countries they returned to the U.S., reporting to a congressional subcommittee that the Liberian crisis required an 'immediate legislative response.' Another member of the U.S. legislature to take a special interest in Liberia's plight was Senator Edward Kennedy. His first involvement in Liberian issues was a consequence of his chairmanship of the Senate subcommittee on Immigration and Refugee Affairs. Initially it took the form of efforts to prevent the summary deportation of Liberians living in the U.S, some 14,000 of who were reported to be refugees from the Doe regime. Up to late July 1990 these depended on 'a vaguely worded and poorly circulated cable' from Commissioner Gene McNary of the Immigration and

---

*   A meeting of all SMA Provincial and Regional Superiors with the General Council of the Society, held twice during the Council's six-year mandate.

Naturalization Service issued to local officials, asking that extension requests from the refugees be treated sympathetically on a case-by-case basis. There were strong allegations that this had not been done. Binalfer Nowrojee of the Lawyers Committee for Human Rights claimed that the mealy-mouthed response towards Liberian nationals could be attributed to 'elements of racism and neglect that typify U.S. policy in Africa.'[6] Whatever the truth of this, the Immigration Act of November1990, introduced by Senator Edward Kennedy, provided hope for Liberian refugees giving them 'Temporary Protected Status.' The dispensation was also granted to refugees fleeing conflict in the Lebanon and Kuwait. For Liberian exiles in the U.S., it was a blessing.

***

As Liberia entered the new year, relief agencies whose expatriate staff had taken flight during August 1990 continued to return, producing a plethora of reports on the situation. Each report, quite naturally, reflected the particular interest of the individual agency but, with this limitation, provided a useful account of the 'situation on the ground' in the areas visited, as well as details of the relief response. And more relief agencies were responding to the emergency. Oxfam had just arrived while the Lutheran World Federation had returned on 11 January. Another agency which had sent a four-person team to Monrovia early in January, following a ten-day visit to Sierra Leone, was the euphoniously sounding LICORE (Liberian Coalition for Relief, Resettlement and Reconstruction[7]). During that visit the LICORE team had provided 'medical, dental and social services to Liberian refugees in Sierra Leone and Monrovia.'

With a small handful of notable exceptions, the capacity of reports by international relief agencies and other concerned groups to provide an accurate assessment of the complicated political situation within Liberia and indeed the region, was limited. Typically reports were compiled by outsiders whose 'field trips' were of short duration and who had little experience or understanding of Liberia. Few ventured beyond the Monrovia enclave and most had only anecdotal knowledge of what was happening in Greater Liberia. Sometimes there was an additional factor, namely an overweening confidence that they had the 'solution' to Liberia's humanitarian problems, and that what was already in place was misguided or inefficient. It was not surprising therefore that many of the reports compiled in the wake of the Bamako Accord and ceasefire, declared the civil war was over, or as good as over, and that the task in hand, essentially, was to 'clean up the mess left behind by a year of hostilities'.

This lack of a keener political analysis by both voluntary and statutory agencies was unfortunate as it meant that in many cases much of the relief activity envisaged within Liberian borders and particularly in Greater Liberia, never took place. Activity envisaged for adjacent countries harbouring large numbers of Liberian refugees - more manageable and involving less risk - was much more successful throughout all phases of the civil war. Those few international organisations that succeeded in making significant humanitarian contributions within Liberian borders during the crisis were able to do so because of a sustained presence in the country, a willingness to respect local experience, and especially the courageous determination to give assistance beyond the relatively safe confines of the Monrovia enclave. It must be said that the number of agencies which met these standards was small.

***

Towards the end of January, while in Freetown, Cahill encountered Liberia's Pro-Nuncio, Archbishop Romeo Panciroli, who had been evacuated from Liberia over five months previously. When asked about plans to return to Monrovia the archbishop hesitated to commit himself. He would 'dearly have hoped' to be in Monrovia for 24 January for a Peace March but there were serious doubts about it taking place.[8] One Church leader at his post was Archbishop Francis. On 31 January 1991 he put pen to paper to write a report on the state of Liberia and of his diocese. It had been six weeks since he attempted a similar exercise. In the interim he found there had been little change. Despite Bamako, the NPFL was still refusing to recognise the existence and legitimacy of the IGNU and was focusing its energies on the All-Liberia Conference – now scheduled for mid-February – at which Taylor hoped to achieve sufficient dominance to control the formation of Liberia's second interim government. Johnson too was now publicly rejecting the IGNU, an institution which he had fulsomely supported at its inauguration.

And yet, Francis reported, in Monrovia and its hinterland the ceasefire appeared to be holding and there were even signs of a return to normality. Transport had returned to the streets, some shops and businesses had re-opened. The National Bank was functioning, and the commercial banks were due to open in a week. Police were again to be seen on the streets. Francis was unable to shed much light on the situation outside the Monrovia enclave. He did know that roads in NPFL-occupied areas were still closed rendering the large number of displaced persons in the capital unable to travel to their homes. This left Monrovia, normally a city with a population of some 300,000, swollen to over 500,000 people and that number was increasing as more and more refugees made their way to the relative safety of the ECOMOG-controlled enclave. It was projected, Francis wrote, that by the end of February Monrovia's population would have risen to 800,000 and perhaps a million by the end of April. Naturally this had caused a food shortage with an estimated 70,000 children malnourished and 'many, many people starving.' The social consequences of the war, principally though population displacement, were manifestly disastrous.

> Families have been broken up and, in very many cases, the whereabouts of other members are unknown… Thousands of children roam the towns and villages of our country, parentless and lost. Some of these – indeed thousands - have been taught to kill and have become killers. In Monrovia the situation is worst. Here thousands of young boys and girls, without parents or relatives – effectively orphaned – roam the streets.

***

By the end of January 1991 – 60 days since the signing of the Bamako Accord – there was no sign of the All-Liberia Conference taking place.

Frustrated by this and deeply concerned that there had been no movement on the tasks assigned to the conference, the SMC scheduled a new round of talks for Lomé (Togo), to be held on 12 and 13 February, under the chairmanship of the Gambia's President Dawda Jawara. Representatives from Burkina Faso, Mali, Togo, Ghana, Ivory Coast, Sierra Leone and Nigeria all attended. Sawyer was also present, representing the IGNU. The AFL was represented by J. Hezekiah Bowen, while the NPFL and the INPFL were represented, respectively, by Taylor and Prince Johnson.

The principal purpose of this gathering was to formulate and agree on a detailed plan for monitoring the ceasefire and to prepare the ground for the election of a new interim government. In the run-up to Lomé international pressure to co-operate mounted on the warring factions and, in particular, on Taylor. No less a body than the UN Security Council, as well as a tripartite communiqué from Nigeria, Senegal and Togo, called upon the factions to abide by the Bamako accord.

It appears that at Bamako the SMC had wanted a much tougher stand against Taylor, but had been overruled by the heads of state. In particular, they wanted to maintain the condition that no head of a warring faction could stand for election as future president of Liberia. Now, with the Bamako accord a shambles, and with ECOWAS under pressure to act, the SMC felt able to re-introduce this condition. This time, it was hoped, the heads of state would not weaken. At the commencement of the Lomé meeting Taylor, as customarily, adopted an intransigent posture on all issues, before appearing to soften his line under pressure from his old ally, President Blaise Compaoré of Burkina Faso. Eventually, but with bad grace, he signed yet another peace accord – 'mapping out the ECOWAS modalities for securing the ceasefire agreement.' These dealt with ceasefire violation reporting procedures, 'sensitization of troops on the ceasefire' and also called for disarmament.[9] With respect to the latter, the AFL would form an encampment at the Barclay Training Centre and Camp Schieffelin, both in Monrovia, while Johnson's INPFL would remain in their encampment at Caldwell. Taylor's troops would gather in their strongholds at Firestone, Naama, Salala, Ganta, Gbarnga, Zwedru and Toedi Mesurado. Weapons would be handed into ECOMOG 'reception Centres' adjacent to these encampments. Finally, with regard to the formation of a new interim government it was decided, for the second time, to entrust this task to the All-Liberia Conference which was now to be convened on 15 March.

As he had done at Bamako, as soon as Taylor appended his signature to the accord – an act performed with theatrical reluctance – he assumed the demeanour of a man 'betrayed' and 'cheated.' He told journalists that because his invasion of Liberia in 1989 had 'started the whole process', he should be allowed to be 'at the head of it.'[10] Now he was being excluded from contesting the presidential election. In addition, he declared his opposition to the provision, which he had signed, that arms and territory be yielded up to ECOMOG before the election of the new interim government.

It must be said that the ECOWAS heads of state were by no means sure that Taylor could be trusted and for this reason privately agreed to renew the ECOMOG offensive should he refuse to co-operate.[11] ECOMOG was in a position to do so, having now some 10,000 troops in Liberia, shortly to be increased by a contingent from Mali. Burkina Faso and Cote d'Ivoire, however, still refused to contribute to the force.

The Lomé meeting's final communiqué re-affirmed the SMC's approach to a settlement in forthright terms. In particular it declared that 'no leader of a warring faction should head the future interim government; and that whoever heads the interim government should not be eligible to contest the ensuing presidential and general elections.' In relation to the ceasefire agreement signed by the warring parties it reminded the factions that they had consented to confine their troops to positions determined in consultation with ECOMOG. While with regard to disarmament, they had agreed that 'upon the formation of the future interim government, that body would take appropriate measures, with the assistance of ECOWAS, to start the disarming of their troops.'[12] Finally the SMC directed the ECOWAS Executive Secretary 'to take all necessary steps to ensure that ECOMOG forces implemented effectively and speedily the ceasefire agreement and commenced the disarmament process, essential requirements for the convening of the All-Liberia Conference.

To most Liberians and the world at large, with the Lomé Accord, the peace process appeared to be back on track and all eyes now focused on the scheduled All-Liberia Conference which was to be moderated by the Inter-Faith Mediation Committee (IFMC). Many commentators now felt that the conference would endorse Sawyer's leadership and that the election of a second interim government, which the conference was to arrange, would see him re-affirmed as president.

∗∗∗

In the background to these events, receiving little coverage in the international media, a change of personnel was taking place within ECOMOG. On 27 February (1991) its commanding officer, Major-General Joshua Dogonyaro, was recalled by Nigeria's President Ibrahim Babangida. Doganyaro had indeed been an effective commander and leader. According to Stephen Ellis,[13]

> after Doe's murder he acted with exemplary decisiveness using aircraft and artillery to force Taylor's forces out of Monrovia. He had presided over the installation of the interim government, succeeded in disarming Prince Johnson's INPFL and getting the remnants of Doe's Armed Forces of Liberia back into barracks. In addition, he had encouraged international aid agencies to return to Monrovia and feed its population.[14]

Dogonyaro's replacement, Major-General Rufus Kupolati (February–September 1991) and his successor, General Isaac Bakut (September 1991–October 1992), were less effective. Both came from engineering units rather than infantry and confined themselves strictly to peacekeeping, 'maintaining the military stalemate and incurring less cost and fewer casualties.'[15] Why was Dogonyaro

recalled? There is a view that ECOWAS believed a more passive, conciliatory, commander would make more progress in negotiating with
Taylor. More likely he was recalled for political reasons. For although
Dognoyaro was the man who announced Babangida's coup d'état on
national radio, the Nigerian president feared a successful campaign conducted by him in Liberia might easily produce a political rival.[16]

***

On 25 February 1991 Cahill received a telephone call from Ireland informing him that the veteran SMA missionary, Mattie Gilmore, was already on his
way from Ireland to his mission in Liberia. A tall, spare, silver-haired 76-year-
old, with the expression of a surprised child, Gilmore, was a gregarious larger-
than-life figure from the West of Ireland. In the months before his dramatic
evacuation by U.S. Marine helicopter from Monrovia in August 1990 he had
stood out among his peers for the manner in which he approached the civil
war. Appearing to ignore its existence, armed with wide grin[17] and papal gesture, he travelled nonchalantly though checkpoints manned by nervous, trig-
ger-happy soldiers, confident that his white soutane and ebullient personality
would bring him safely through. From his SMA superior's point of view,
however, Gilmore was something of a loose cannon, unpredictable and
requiring close care. Now he was 'in the process of returning', having secured a
letter inviting him back from the archbishop (no superior now could stop him)
and having had discussions with Brother Joseph of Monrovia's Catholic Hospital, with a view to resuming his post as hospital chaplain. Although the
magnitude of the task of keeping Gilmore safe flashed before Cahill's eyes, his
first response was to express a wish to be in Monrovia to welcome him back
whenever he arrived. As it happened, Gilmore was to enter Liberia with the
details of his travel unknown to Cahill.

***

As the opening day of the All-Liberia Conference approached, ELBC radio
reminded the nation constantly that the principal task of the conference was to
elect an authentic broad-based interim government. And to this end an 8,000-
strong ECOMOG force would ensure 'law and order' and 'prohibit any irregularities during the poll and the counting.'[18] It also announced that 'Chairman
Ghankay Taylor' had declared his candidacy for the interim presidency,
although the BBC and other news agencies insisted that the recent accord
'excluded leaders of the factions from contesting the interim leadership elections.'[19] The reports about Taylor's intentions were true, for he had unambiguously declared his intention to contest the election, saying 'the Liberian
people were a grateful people and would give him the opportunity to serve
them as head of the incoming interim government.'[20]

J. Garsway Yameto a 'broadcast journalist from Liberia', but better-known as
one of Taylor's chief publicists, was afforded an opportunity on ELBC to offer a
'guest commentary' on this new development, under the headline 'Liberians …
Lets give Ghankay a chance!' He told the nation that

as architect of an uprising which liberated the people from untold sufferings he (Taylor) was justified in declaring his intention to run for the interim leadership. Without his vision and bravery ... Samuel Doe's murderous and disgraceful regime would still be in power.

Yameto concluded his broadcast with a rallying cry. 'Let us give credit where it is due by supporting Mr Taylor for a dynamic and progressive Liberia. Let's give Ghankay a chance!' That such a broadcast, effectively rubbishing a crucial element of the Lomé accord, was permitted to take place on national radio augured ill for the future of the All-Liberia Conference.

Nonetheless in the days leading up to the conference there was an air of anticipation that it might succeed; and already there appeared to be some straws in the wind pointing to a favourable outcome. For instance, the journalist John Momoh writing in *West Africa*, confidently reported that all major highways in Liberia were expected to reopen shortly 'in anticipation of the National Conference', a gesture which might signal that 'peace' was about to outweigh 'the sword.'[21] A Ghanaian colleague, Henry Mallet, writing from Lomé where he had covered the ECOWAS summit, seemed to have no doubt that Taylor was now willing to 'cooperate fully with ECOWAS in implementing the peace plan.'

***

The conference convened on the due date, 15 March, at the Unity Conference Centre, Virginia, Monrovia; it was to continue, with long periods of inactivity, until 20 April. In attendance were representatives of the rival rebel factions, six political parties and delegates from 14 civic, professional and religious organisations. ECOWAS — given the right by the participants — chose two key IFMC members to chair the sessions, namely Archbishop Michael Francis, and Muslim Council Leader Sheikh Kafumba Konneh. Nonetheless, having given ECOWAS the right to choose, Taylor was immediately unhappy with its selection of facilitators. He also expressed unhappiness at the composition of the conference, claiming it was unjust that only groups invited by ECOWAS were allowed to attend. And he demanded the participation of elected representatives from counties which he controlled who had been elected to the Greater Liberia legislature installed the previous November.[22]

On the opening day of the conference there was strong resistance from the NPFL delegation — led by Dr Toga Gayewea McIntosh — to the adoption of Archbishop Francis as a co-chairman. Taylor was not present, claiming knowledge of a plot against his life. Long disliked by Taylor and the NPFL leadership for his plain speaking, and widely recognised as the most formidable of the IFMC leadership, the attempt to block Francis's adoption was not unexpected. Nonetheless, amid disorder and uproar, the majority of representatives gave the archbishop their support and his chairmanship was duly confirmed. Despite this setback McIntosh declared that his delegation would 'not walk out of this meeting without an agreement on conditions for a lasting peace.' At the same time, the NPFL delegation continued to be disruptive and uncooperative. It objected strongly to the composition of committees established to allot credentials and draw up regulations for the conference. Little further progress was made on that day as the NPFL delegation persistently disrupted the proceedings; and eventually the talks were adjourned.

***

Frantic efforts were now made by ECOWAS officials to re-start the talks. Nigeria's Foreign Minister, Ike Nwachukwu, visited Taylor in Kakata in an unsuccessful effort to persuade him to attend the conference. ECOWAS Secretary General, Abbas Bundu, and the Togolese Foreign Minister, Yaovi Adodo, also visited Taylor appealing to him to come to Monrovia. But the NPFL leader refused claiming he had intelligence that Johnson was planning to assassinate him. Many who were well disposed to him, or over-awed by him, now began to see him in a different light; and attitudes among a number of conference delegates formerly inclined to placate tended to harden against him.

A week later, when ECOWAS and the international community were ringing hands in frustration, Taylor took to the NPFL radio airwaves to propose 'the creation of a 3-person ruling council to replace the IGNU and lead Liberia towards elections.' Next, speaking on air to the BBC's Robin White, he suggested that this projected ruling council should be composed of a representative of the IGNU, a 'neutral' person acceptable to both sides, and himself. The fact that Taylor was now proposing to recognise the interim ruling body – he had adamantly opposed its existence in any shape or form – appeared to many as a major concession. Nonetheless the conference, which reconvened to consider the proposal, refused to give its backing. Most of the delegates rejected the NPFL 'compromise' on the basis that the Banjul Accord had ruled out the inclusion of a faction leader in either an interim or an elected, substantive government and this had not changed at Bamako or Lomé. Now, despite the promise given on the first day not to walk out until a peaceful settlement had been achieved, MacIntosh led his delegation out of the conference. A few days later MacIntosh, who by all accounts was an honourable man, resigned his position citing differences with Taylor.[23]

It must be said that by this time there was a consensus among the delegates that Taylor should not stand for election as interim president and that they should proceed without him in forming an interim government. One delegate, Rev. Dixon Kumeh, put it in a nutshell: 'Everybody was supporting Taylor at the beginning', but now 'Taylor can never be president because of the widespread atrocities attributed to his supporters and his refusal to halt the fighting after Doe's death.' Sawyer echoed this view saying that there had been 'too much bloodletting' and that 'no one would feel secure with one of the military factions at the head of an interim government.'[24]

Kaye Whitman writing in *West Africa*, had some perceptive remarks to make on the NPFL leader's mind-set during this period. At a press conference in Ouagadougou, capital of Burkina Faso, which she attended Taylor appeared in a role which he relished, in 'presidential mode, fingertips pressed together as if in prayer.' Introduced as 'President Taylor' by his public relations chief, J. Garswa Yarmeto, his style was 'measured, considered, presidential.' He frequently included his trademark equation of 'we' with the 'will of the Liberian people.' His final offering at the press conference, noted by Whitman, was vintage Taylor, spoken with sincerity and conviction. Questioned as to whether he possessed a consuming ambition to be the incoming interim president he had responded:

> I do not seek to lead Liberia. There are so many qualified Liberians in my organisation who are very capable of leading this interim government and, if for any reason my organisation decides that I should step aside, I will do nothing to destroy that process because if I did, I would not care for my country. But if the Liberian people want it, I would have no choice but to continue.

Taylor's presidential posturing could not have been conducted with much comfort had ECOWAS remained firm on its peace plan's prohibition against faction leaders standing for election to interim and substantive office. However, the weakness and vacillation within ECOWAS and among many political commentators on this question, was to return to haunt Liberia and the region for a further decade. Some argued that Taylor's defiance of the ECOWAS prohibition would be to no avail since he would have to confront Sawyer in an election and would almost certainly be soundly beaten. This (mistaken) estimate, in their view, made his defiance of the prohibition something with which they could live.

Equally disturbing was the manner in which Prince Yormie Johnson was now being treated virtually as an equal by senior members of ECOWAS. President Babangida of Nigeria – it must be said, head of a military regime which had come to power by force – welcomed Johnson for man-to-man discussions during a visit to Nigeria. Johnson, using the expected statesman-like parlance, informed the media after the meeting that he had had 'fruitful discussions' with the Nigerian head of state. Whatever the content of their discussion – and no doubt Babangida had some hard things to say – the symbolism of the meeting was powerful. And quickly in its wake came reports that Taylor, despite his record of antagonism towards Nigeria, might soon 'pay a similar visit.'[25]

Concerning the profile of the incoming president, Johnson, at least, would not be one to defy the wishes of ECOWAS. The future president, he insisted, must be a neutral civilian who would have the authority to run the country and disarm the warring factions. If, however, those prohibited by the ECOWAS peace plan insisted on running for president – in particular Taylor – he would resist their attempts to disarm the INPFL. Finally, invoking images of that great statesman and leader, Cincinnatus, he announced, as if wearied of the great world, that he had no political ambitions and would return to school, not to study politics but to read theology.[*]

---

[*]   Johnson might not have gone back to school or studied theology but during the turbulent years following Liberia's first civil war – and fearing retribution from Taylor, now Liberia's president – he fled to Nigeria where he became a born-again Christian. Returning to Liberia in 2004 after Taylor's resignation he was elected

***

On 8 April the All-Liberia Conference reconvened in Monrovia but, almost immediately, collapsed. Sawyer roundly blamed Taylor who had 'remained stubborn throughout' and whose forces had continued to carry out incursions, not merely into ECOMOG territory but now, since the end of March, into Sierra Leone.[26] This latter incursion had been conducted in protest at the arrival of a new ECOMOG contingent of some 350 Sierra Leonean troops. Major General Dogonyaro, back in Nigeria, reacted to these developments by blaming those West African states who were continuing to support the NPFL rebels, specifying Burkina Faso and the Ivory Coast, countries, he said, which had 'done great harm to the people of Liberia.'[27] But he also explained that Taylor's attack on Sierra Leone,* was not only 'intended to derail the peace process and cause that country to pull out of ECOMOG' but was done in return for assistance given him by the Sierra Leonean 'Revolutionary United Front', which was bent on overthrowing the incumbent regime.[28] Dogonyaro was not the only Nigerian recommending a more forceful approach to Taylor and his NPFL rebels. The Nigerian Information Minister, Alexander Akinyele, called for a new ECOMOG offensive and the arrest of Taylor.[29]

Thereafter the NPFL leader turned his back on mediation and, instead, worked to consolidate his National Patriotic Government (NPRAG), which ruled Greater Liberia from Gbarnga. In his absence the All-Liberia Conference formed a new interim government, not unexpectedly under Sawyer. The IGNU thus formed was a truncated body whose authority had been intended to extend throughout the county but instead was limited to the Monrovia enclave. The All-Liberia Conference, a function of ECOWAS's weakness and lack of unity, was doomed from the day it first saw light at Bamako. Now it had fully run its doomed course.

Notes

1 UNDRO Situation Report No 20, 18 December 1990.
2 This analysis of the relief effort was prepared by UNDRO for the benefit of donor countries.
3 It was signed on 28 November 1990.

Senator for Nimba County (2005). Despite the LTRC's verdict (2009) that he should not be permitted to participate in public life for 30 years, he finished third in Liberia's Presidential Election of 2011 and was fourth of 20 candidates in the 2017 election.

* Dane F. Smith, (appointed U.S. Envoy to Liberia in 1995) describes Taylor's first contacts with the Sierra Leone rebel leader. After escaping from jail in America, Taylor 'made his way to Burkina Faso where he formed an alliance with Colonel Blaise Compaoré, soon to become Burkina's leader. Compaoré arranged for Taylor to go to Libya, where he was trained and financed by Muammar Qadhafi's government. There Taylor linked with Foday Sankoh, later to become leader of Sierra Leone's notorious Revolutionary United Front [RUF'] ('US-Guinea Relations during the Rise and Fall of Charles Taylor, The Journal of Modern African Studies, vol. 44, no. 3 (Sept. 2006), 421–422.

4 A.T. Mark Huband, UPI, Monrovia, 10 January 1991.
5 Report for Plenary Council, attached to Cahill to O'Reilly, 11 January 1991.
6 West Africa, 18–24 March 1991, 400–401 (Tunji Lardner Jnr, 'A Reprieve, But…').
7 Washington-based.
8 A.B. Note of telephone call to Cahill from Bishop Sekey in Tenafly, Thursday, 24 January 1991 at 4.50 pm.
9 West Africa, 25 February–3 March 1991, Peter da Costa in Banjul, 'Moving towards peace', 262.
10 Ibid. See also, Peter da Costa, 'Good Neighbours', Africa Report, 36, no. 6, Nov.–Dec. 1991, 22.
11 Peter Da Costa, 'Talking Tough to Taylor', Africa Report, (January–February 1993), 19.
12 A.T. 'Final Communique, Economic community of West African States' – Third Summit Meeting of the SMC, Lomé, 12–13 February 1991.
13 Ellis's view is shared by Felix Gerdes, in his Civil War and State Formation: The Political Economy of War and Peace in Liberia (Frankfurt/New York, 2013), 120.
14 Stephen Ellis, The Mask of Anarchy Updated Edition: The Destruction of Liberia and the ReligiousDimension of an African Civil War (Hurst and Co., London, 2006), 87–88.
15 Herbert Howe, op. cit., 168.
16 Felix Gerdes, Civil War and State Formation: The Political Economy of War and Peace in Liberia, Frankfurt/New York, 2013, 120.
17 Or occasionally a countenance of soulful gravity.
18 News Letter – National Patriotic Association of Liberia, USA and Canada (Somerset, NJ), vol. 2, no. 2, 25 February 1991 ('All-Liberia Conference Slated for 15 March 1991').
19 Ibid.
20 West Africa, 18–24 March 1991, 401.
21 Ibid, 400. See also ibid., 11–17 March 1991, 348.
22 Twelve of the 14 counties under his control had elected representatives at this time.
23 See, West Africa, 8–14 April 1991, 510–511.
24 Reed Kramer, Africa News, 1 April 1991, 'Longing for Peace in Liberia.'
25 West Africa, 18–24 March 1991, 400 (Henry Mallet from Lomé).
26 West Africa, 12 April 1991, 41.
27 Ibid.
28 Ibid.
29 Speaking in Washington.

13 The incursion of NPRAG forces into Sierra Leone and the signing of the Yamoussoukro accord

In Bong Mine the strain of isolation, insecurity and deprivation was taking its toll on John Feeney. So too was the giving of protection to persons who would be slaughtered if discovered and whose discovery would have the most serious consequences for himself. These two had lived secretly in the mission for the past nine months. For some time now Mike Moran (Regional Superior of the American SMA, contingent) had been urging Feeney to return to the U.S. on vacation. But Feeney could not contemplate such a step as long as he was giving protection to his 'guests.' Realising himself that something had to be done he began to make arrangements for sending his 'guests' to safety. Komina Nyodueh, who was currently a minister in Charles Taylor's government, based in Gbarnga, had as a youth wanted to become a priest. Feeney had encouraged him and opened the way for him to enter the seminary. Nyodueh did not persevere, but they remained friends. Now Feeney contacted Michael Flattery, pastor in Gbanga, and asked him to speak with Nyodueh about getting the 'guests' to safety. Flattery spoke to Bishop Sekey who in turn spoke with Nyodueh who 'promised that he himself would come to Bong Mine and take them away to safety.[1] Now, on 13 March 1991, Feeney was able to record in his journal that:

> at seven thirty last evening my friend, the former seminarian and now a (NPRAG) government minister, arrived with his own bodyguard to take away my guests. Thank God that they are now safe. The bishop was on the radio this morning with a very short message, 'Big John, the eagle has landed.'

Feeney was now free to take his leave from Bong Mine where things were going from bad to worse, owing to the virtual collapse of NPFL discipline.

> The trucks still keep coming (from Gbarnga) for the loot. There is a local population of forty to fifty thousand people and last February the Company imported supplies sufficient to last two years. Now it is all there for the taking.

DOI: 10.4324/9781003219309-17

Nor could there be any Holy Week ceremonies. 'We have no light, no transport and there is a very high degree of looting from ordinary citizens.'[2]

On 1 April Lee Cahill came to Bong Mine and took Feeney to Gbarnga where he was able to secure travel documents. Five days later he crossed the border into Ivory Coast and on the night of 6 April flew out from Abidjan for Rome. A week later he joined his family in Galway, Ireland. Badly in need of rest, Feeney was to remain on leave for the next eight months.

***

As April moved towards its close international attention shifted from the failed All-Liberia Conference to the incursions by the NPFL into Sierra Leone. Taylor continued to enjoy the freedom of the BBC airwaves, telling its wide international audience that he had absolutely nothing to do with the fighting over the border. What was happening, he said, was that dissidents within that country had commenced a rebellion against President Joseph Saidu Momoh, a dictator in the mould of former President Samuel Doe. And the U.S. offer of support for Sierra Leone's government was no more or no less than a repetition of what it had done in Liberia – propping up an evil dictatorship.[3]

The month of May saw increasing anxiety within the region about these incursions, and greater co-operation in repelling them. *The Washington Times* of 6 May reported that Sierra Leone forces, 'backed by troops from Guinea', had moved against 'the invaders', advancing on 'south-eastern border areas held by Taylor.' On the following day *The Times* published yet another bizarre story concerning Prince Johnson.

> Prince Johnson, who tortured President Samuel Doe to death in September, said yesterday he would like to build the slain leader a tomb, for despite his failings, Doe was one of the country's leaders. 'As such it is better to build something splendid befitting his honour as a president', he declared.

The IGNU, led by Amos Sawyer, and created to pave the way for a substantive government, scheduled presidential and legislative elections for 15 October 1991. Whether such elections had any possibility of taking place was doubtful. *The Washington Post* asked whether 'a war-torn nation led by an unpaid, all-volunteer interim government' could 'conduct free and fair … elections while half the population is either displaced or in hiding across the border?' Sawyer, however, determined to proceed, had already asked the U.S. to help with basic voter registration programmes, voting machines and ballot papers. He had also requested 'formal U.S. diplomatic recognition for his interim government', which the *Post* said was unlikely to happen. The U.S., it seemed, was taking into account the fact that ECOWAS countries had not yet given recognition to the interim government, 'out of hope that a deal could be brokered with Taylor.'[4] And lack of recognition meant that the IGNU did not have access to substantial funds lodged in the U.S. by the Republic of Liberia. The failure of the U.S. government and the international community to give formal recognition to Liberia's interim government was to facilitate the triumph of the warlords during the next decade and beyond. No less important was the failure of Banjul and Bamako to deal with the issue of disarmament and Lomé's purely aspirational solution[5] that all warring parties should effectively return to 'barracks' and there await disarmament. And yet the impression still remained widespread in the international media that Liberia's civil war was now over and that the task in hand was to deal with its aftermath.

***

In line with the importance (or lack thereof) of Liberia in the Bush administration's scheme of things, the State Department made few public statements on political matters relating to Liberia during these months, and those issued usually related to humanitarian matters. At this time, it should be understood, the Soviet bloc had begun to disintegrate and the Cold War, for which Africa had been one of the main battlegrounds, was effectively over. As a result American interest in the politics of that continent was no longer what it had been. U.S. government humanitarian agencies, however, maintained their commitment. By now the incursions into Sierra Leone by Revolutionary United Front (RUF) supported by NPFL had made their mark on the refugee situation. Owing to what was 'chaotic fighting' in the countryside along the border between the two countries, all existing relief activities had ceased. This had caused most of the refugees to flee further inland, to Freetown, or to neighbouring countries like Guinea; some had returned to Liberia or simply disappeared into the bush.

As a result of the fighting the number of Liberian refugees in Sierra Leone was now estimated to have dropped dramatically, from 125,000 to 20,000, these latter concentrated in urban rather than in rural areas.[6] Evidently some thousands of the remaining refugees were desperate to leave but found it virtually impossible to obtain transport. The official Sierra Leone government attitude towards them was still protective, but many locals were now growing suspicious, fearing they might be connected with the dissident forces bent on destabilising their country. Local militias in villages had been formed and were 'trying to ferret out rebels among the refugees.'[7] In Freetown refugees seeking assistance were being screened by police before being re-registered by the local Red Cross. Among those rumoured to be helping in uncovering rebels were ex-soldiers of the Doe regime. And now the authorities had chosen a single location for all Liberian refugees who wished to stay in Sierra Leone. This was an old airfield at Waterloo, near Freetown. Only those in Waterloo would receive assistance – the UN High Commission for Refugees estimated that perhaps some 20,000 might assemble there. MSF/F[8] had undertaken responsibility for medical care, CARE[9] for shelter, and UNICEF for water sanitation, while the League of Red Cross / Red Crescent Societies would provide food.

***

Edward Kennedy's interest in the Liberian crisis was to be further demonstrated in the closing months of 1991. The notion that, in addition to what already was being done by the Bush administration, the U.S. Legislature should enact substantial relief measures to assist Liberia, had first received mention from Hiram A. Ruiz. a senior policy analyst with the U.S. Committee for Refugees. He had declared that the U.S. response to Liberia's humanitarian crisis would 'determine the future of U.S.-Liberian relations for decades to come.'[10] In line with this thinking, on 7 February 1991 the Rehabilitation and Reconstruction Act of 1991, co-sponsored by Senator Paul Simon, was introduced to the Senate by Edward Kennedy. The measure proposed to make available $45 million for disaster assistance and $20 million for the estimated 780,000 Liberian refugees in neighbouring countries, as well as the local populations of the host countries. A further $27 million was to be made available for the purchase and transportation of an additional 40,000 tons of emergency food assistance, mostly rice. And the aid was to be administered by USAID using U.S. government and international non-governmental agencies.[11] As for the Brooke Amendment[12] which forbad economic or military aid to countries which had failed to repay loans[13], the Kennedy / Simon bill argued that in the case of Liberia the U.S. had moral and political imperatives which over-rode such strictures, citing among other things Liberia's historic and current special relationship with the U.S.[14]

***

Kilcoyne and Jennings returned from leave in Ireland to St Peter Claver's Church, Buchanan, on 19 May 1991. During their six-month absence Buchanan had been looked after by Fr Dominic Sumo from the nearby LAC mission who took up residence there from the second week of December. Having flown into Abidjan they were met by Cahill, who drove them across the border post over the Cavalla river near Lagatua and on through NPFL territory to Buchanan.[15] The journey was 'pretty uneventful', passing through quite a number of checkpoints but without problems. Kilcoyne confided to the mission diary his impressions of the Buchanan which he found on his return. It had become 'a strange place, with a strange feeling to it.' In contrast to six months previously its population now had swollen to almost 100,000,[16] tension had noticeably reduced, and there was 'a semblance of normality, with markets, bars, some video-shops using generators and so on.' The streets of the town were 'filled with young boys, many of them demobilised members of the NPFL who could be called up again in an emergency.' Looking to the future Kilcoyne noticed that while there was much 'shouting from both sides' there were also hopeful signs. CRS workers were able to 'pass fairly freely up and down to Monrovia' and the UN was 'thinking of opening up on this side as well – a very good sign.' One thing was certain, he wrote, '*nobody* here wants any more fighting.'[17]

***

The massacre of at least 600 people the previous July at St Peter's Lutheran Church – the toll no longer disputed – remained raw in the mind of Monrovia's small Lutheran community. The dead bodies had remained in the church for weeks as the fighting raged through Monrovia and when eventually they were recovered, counted, and buried in the adjoining churchyard, a sediment of human flesh remained. One of those who had walked among the dead in St Peter's just hours after the massacre was the American Evangelical Lutheran missionary, Bette McCrandall. Now, in May 1991, she was among those missionaries who returned to Liberia where she had worked since 1973. Sonia C. Groeneworld, writing in *The Lutheran* of 19 June 1991, had little illusion that more, and worse, was to come:

> The civil war has not yet ended. Liberia has existed in a fragile ceasefire since last November. Tension is widespread, even in the streets and markets of Freetown. The anxiety there reflects a growing fear that Sierra Leone would be pulled into Liberia's civil war. Dozens have already been killed in border incursions, allegedly by NPFL fighters... Liberians are 'waiting for the shoe to drop' at any moment.

Like other Churches the Lutherans, too, were doing what they could to alleviate hunger, displacement and the suffering of refugees, working through Lutheran LWR/CWS and Phebe hospital.

Another who had no illusions about the future was Archbishop Michael Francis. Gone was the mild optimism which he had expressed in February as the All-Liberia Conference approached. He now saw clearly that there could be no peace as long as Taylor remained free to pursue his objectives, unchallenged by ECOWAS or the international community. In his estimation Taylor was no different from Doe – both were 'big-man' despots, prepared to use any means to slake their thirst for power. The difference between them was that the well-educated, articulate and polished Taylor had a greater capacity for destruction than the naturally cunning, but otherwise limited, master-sergeant.

***

June 1991 saw an ominous development, rendering the Liberian conflict even more intractable, namely the emergence of another warring faction, the United Liberation Movement of Liberia for Democracy (ULIMO) whose raison d'être was an implacable opposition to Taylor and the NPFL. Drawn from former members of Doe's army, from Krahn tribesmen who had fled to Guinea and Sierra Leone, and from Mandingo elements, the faction was led by Raleigh Seekie,[*] a former government minister in the Doe regime. The movement was later to split, with the Mandingo element led by Alhaji G.V. Kromah[**] forming a separate faction. Before moving into Liberia, ULIMO had supported the Sierra Leonean army in combat against the rebel RUF. Having

---

[*]   He was from the Krahn ethnic group.
[**] Kromah attended St Patrick's Catholic High School for part of his education. George Boley, leader of the Liberia Peace Council militia, was also a product of the Catholic education system. John Feeney wrote of that system in his diary: 'For thirty or more years we have gloried in the superiority of our schools ... The products of these schools are now becoming known the world over because of their savagery and brutality ... Might it not be a good new beginning if ... we paid more attention to the *cura animarum*.'

crossed the border into Liberia a well-armed militia, ULIMO, was soon to win back significant northern territories from the NPFL.

***

On 16 July Hiram A. Ruiz gave testimony in Washington at a hearing of the Foreign Affairs Subcommittee on Africa. The greatest contribution the subcommittee could make, he said, was to approve H.R. 994, the 'Liberia Relief, Rehabilitation and Reconstruction Act' and start it on its way to enactment. This would require a firm determination from the Houses of Representatives since the administration had already pronounced the measure unnecessary on the grounds that the U.S. was 'already making significant contributions toward providing relief for Liberia.'[18] The Bill, in amended form, was passed into law in 1992.

Septimus M. Kaikai, Professor of Economics at Community College, Maryland,[19] was another who gave testimony at the 16 July hearing, speaking on behalf of the Sierra Leone community in the U.S. After an opening, cast in the staid, formal mould common at such sessions, he threw the UN's dictionary of diplomacy to the winds and spoke with passion. Subcommittee members were told that the invasion of Sierra Leone, which threatened regional stability in West Africa, was the work of that 'repulsive criminal and ex-convict', Taylor and his 'hoodlums.' Lacking respect for human life and internationally accepted norms, Taylor should not be permitted to 'heap injustice and carnage on innocent citizens.' Quoting Thomas Paine, Professor Kaikai declared that for Sierra Leoneans, these were 'times that try men's souls.' Taylor and his 'gang of terrorists' had invaded 'the breadbasket of Sierra Leone', disrupted the mining and agricultural industries and was now in the process of destabilising the entire sub-region.

Testimony phrased in a more traditional mould was given on the same day by Assistant Secretary Herman Cohen who admitted that the civil war in Liberia was now threatening regional security. He also confirmed that Taylor's forces were involved in Sierra Leone and on 23 March had moved 'across the border pillaging, occupying towns, and terrorizing local populations in the East and Northeast.' Defending criticisms of inaction throughout the crisis he noted America's considerable humanitarian response and its continuous dialogue with 'all Liberian parties to assist ECOWAS … in bringing an African solution to an African problem.'

Cohen's testimony did little to demonstrate that there had been any meaningful change in the U.S. hands-off policy towards Liberia. And with the end of Soviet attempts to make Africa communist, there seemed even less prospect. Cohen's attitude towards Taylor, markedly different from that of Professor Kaikai, was in line with that of the ECOWAS heads of state in treating Taylor as a *bone fide* leader of his people, equal in stature and status to any West African leader. Concluding his testimony, almost reverentially he declared that the Bush administration was especially calling upon Taylor 'to take that act of statesmanship which is the mark of true leaders and seek accommodation with his Liberian brothers and cooperation in securing the goal of democracy for all.'

The escapee from Plymouth jail had come a long way in the mind of official America.

***

In the last week of June yet another attempt by the regional powers was made to end the political impasse. This was spearheaded by Ivory Coast's President Félix Houphouët-Boigny under whose chairmanship a 'Committee of Five', all francophone members of ECOWAS (Burkina-Faso, Senegal, Guinea-Bissau, Togo and Ivory Coast), had recently been formed. This was a significant development, for up to this time Francophone West Africa had sat uncomfortable with ECOWAS policy on Liberia. Now the Francophones had stepped forward and were taking an active part in bringing about a resolution. A joint meeting between this body and the existing SMC took place at Yamoussoukro in Ivory Coast on 28 and 29 June where they met interim President Sawyer and NPFL leader Taylor. This was to be the first in a series of four meetings held at Yamoussoukro between June and October 1991 culminating in the Yamoussoukro Accord signed on 31 October.

This accord stipulated that the Liberian parties would work together for free, democratic elections across Liberia. Signatories for the NPFL, INPFL, AFL and ULIMO pledged to stop fighting, move their soldiers to designated locations and to embrace a disarmament process which was to take place within 60 days, commencing on 15 November 1991. In the interim, a group of which ex-U.S. President Jimmy Carter was the leading member[20], would visit Liberia with the purpose of reassuring former belligerents that the peace accord had international backing and that ECOMOG – the body implementing encampment and disarmament - was a truly neutral force. The accord also provided for the immediate withdrawal of all faction elements from Sierra Leone and the creation of a buffer zone on the Liberian border, supervised and staffed by ECOMOG troops. Finally, it stipulated that within a period of six months from the signing of the accord presidential elections would be held in Liberia. These would be organised and supervised by an Elections Commission with representatives from Senegal, Gambia, Guinea Bissau, Cote d'Ivoire and Togo. The Yamoussoukro Accord presented Liberia with a clear template for peace. But its success would depend upon ECOWAS's resolve to apply the template in its entirety and the willingness of those who had signed to embrace it.

In Greater Liberia things were also about to improve (albeit temporarily) for Liberia's principal Muslim ethnic group, according to a report in *West Africa*.[21] Taylor had 'removed the last … barriers to freedom of worship by allowing the Mandingo to worship in their mosques.' Until this time, accused by the NPFL of complicity with GOL, the Mandingo had been singled out, along with the Krahn, for special treatment. During the first nine months of the insurgency mosques had been desecrated, Muslims had been slaughtered while praying and there were horrific reports of 'dismembered heads being placed on copies of the Koran.'[22] At the time Taylor's Gio and Mano fighters had justified their actions claiming that 'it was Doe who had fired the first shot, by taking reprisals against their kith and kin in the wake of the foiled Quiwonkpa invasion of

1985.'[23] Although the pace of persecution had reduced during the first year of the invasion, the Mandingo population and other smaller Muslim populations, remained under siege. Christianity, however, the favoured religion of the invaders, had thrived.

But NPFL reprisals against the Mandingo had caused West African countries with large Muslim populations to revise earlier positive attitudes towards the invasion. Subsequent kidnappings and even assassinations of civilians by the NPFL – often Muslims from Nigeria, Ghana and Guinea accused of spying for ECOMOG – had further helped 'to create a dirty image for the rebellion.'[24] The dramatic scene at which the NPFL change of mind was communicated to the Mandingo population was described by one Mr Diallo, a beneficiary.

> One day Mr Taylor braved the heat of the sunny afternoon to summon a mass meeting at the Booker Washington Institute campus.... Dressed in a white, flowing Muslim gown beautifully laced with matching white designs and white hat, with a prayer bead in his hand, he presented himself to the crowd... 'I have come to tell the Muslims to open all the mosques.'[25]

Despite Taylor's declaration of good intent to Liberia's Muslim population, incidents of persecution continued unabated, leading eventually, as already mentioned, to an organised reaction. On 26 September 1991 *West Africa* reported that the Gulf States were supporting a Jihad launched by one Alhaji G.V. Kromah to avenge Muslims killed by Taylor and Johnson.[26] Kromah, initially based in Guinea, soon merged his forces with those of Raleigh Seekie, leader of ULIMO, and the combined group, retaining the title ULIMO emerged with Seekie as political leader and strategist, and Kromah its military commander.

***

There were, as always in Liberia, some curious chinks of light in the darkness. For example, that Prince Johnson had another side to him, emerged in an interview given by Bisi Iderabdullah who had founded an orphanage for child casualties of war.

> Her belief that, indeed, 'children are the future' led her to open the orphanage... Prince Johnson, impressed by Ms Iderabdullah's work and dedication, has helped to support Imani House... He also sponsors 240 children in another orphanage also on Bushrod Island.[27]

And sometimes the chinks of light were succeeded by surges of full-blown hope. For example, the fourth round of talks scheduled for late October at Yamassoukro gave rise to a groundswell of optimism. Evidence that the combatants were disposed to come to an agreement went beyond ULIMO's pledge of a ceasefire for the duration of the talks. On the day before they were due to start, former President Carter, who had landed in Lagos, told Nigeria's President Babangida that Taylor's troops must be disarmed and placed in encampments, and all roads must be re-opened, only to be informed that Taylor had already conceded all these issues.[28][29]

The talks, which lasted two days (29–30 October), appeared to validate this optimism. Reputable newspapers such as the *Manchester Guardian* were reporting by early November that the fighting was as good as over. Quoting AP in Yamoussoukro, it told its readers that Taylor had 'agreed yesterday to surrender control of territory held by his fighters to a West African intervention force.'[30] This, the readers were told, had occurred at the close of an all-night summit. The bones of the peace accord signed by 11 West African countries, along with Taylor and Sawyer, was that elections would be held in six months and that a force of 7,000 ECOMOG soldiers would henceforth control Taylor's territory, as well as supervising 'the encampment and disarmament of all warring factions within 60 days.'[31]

As part of the flurry of diplomatic activity and buoyed up by the seeming progress at the Yamoussoukro summit, Sawyer travelled directly to the 46th Session of the UN General Assembly where on 3 October he delivered a statesman-like address to the assembled delegates. Strikingly he showed no reluctance to face up to the shameful reality which Liberia had become. 'We Liberians', he declared:

> are embarrassed by the fact that we have used up so much of the time, resources and energy of our West African sub-region on a fratricidal conflict. We permitted ourselves to degenerate to a stage where we not only became the problem-child but posed a serious threat to the nations of that region. As I speak to you today, more than 800,000 of our people, some 30 percent of our population, are refugees in neighbouring countries. Worse still, from our territory, an invasion was launched into Sierra Leone, thereby re-paying the people of that friendly country with ingratitude for their sacrifices and hospitality.[32]

However, at last, after almost two years of civil war, Sawyer saw signs of hope. 'For the first time in our crisis all sides seem convinced that we have now begun the final stretch in the journey to a lasting settlement.'

Sawyer's address conveyed the impression – widely shared within the international community – that as far as Liberia was concerned the crisis was over. The evidence was there in the details of the accord signed by all parties at Yamoussoukro IV, the result of a lengthy and tedious process, pursued with determination by the regional body with the strong support of the international community. 'Liberians', he declared, 'at long last, have reached a consensus on a strategy for settling the Liberian conflict.'

***

Yamassoukrou IV (as it came to be called) was formally ratified on October 31 bringing large numbers onto the streets of Monrovia and other towns, celebrating and 'weeping with joy at news of the accord' which at last had set a 'timetable for disarmament and elections.'[33] But few could deny the inherent fragility of the accord. Neither ULIMO nor the INPFL had been represented at the talks.[34] There were also claims that Taylor's signature, so critical to its success, was coerced. *Africa Confidential*, a well-informed and usually reliable journal, reported that 'strong-arm' tactics had been used to get 'an increasingly isolated Charles Taylor to agree to disarmament and elections.'[35] Backroom arm-twisting and Nigerian exasperation, it was claimed, had forced Taylor to accept the plan that ECOMOG would move throughout Liberia, disarming various militias, including Taylor's, within 60 days, beginning on November 15.[36] In any case, the euphoria was quickly evaporating in the face of fresh outbreaks of fighting between the NPFL and ULIMO. One of them was observed by Barbara Ann Muttra, an American Sister, who travelled weekly from Monrovia to Klay parish bringing CRS food.[37] Fighting in the area, she recorded, was now endemic as ULIMO attempted to wrest control of the Bomi-Cape Mount area from the NPFL. Passing through checkpoints had become 'a nightmare.'

Aware, no doubt, that achieving a genuine ceasefire would be easier said than done, Yamoussoukro IV had made provision for a new round of talks to deal with 'outstanding issues' and it was hoped that these might yield something tangible in relation to the new violence. Optimism again soared when ULIMO declared it would suspend hostilities during these talks scheduled for 29 October. Also, during a recent visit to Greenville, Sinoe County, Taylor was reported to have apologised for the 'excesses' of his troops during the 'liberation struggle.' This might not have been unrelated to the fact that five days earlier he had formally announced that he would stand for Liberia's presidency.

***

Against this background of wildly swinging moods of hope and despair, efforts were being made to implement the timetables laid down by Yamoussoukrou IV. On 15 November the first of a series of technical meetings took place to agree the modalities for disarmament and encampment. A joint tour of the designated encampment sites by ECOMOG and the NFPL was agreed. Also discussed were the ancillary requirements such as food, medical services and housing, which 'would make encampment and disarmament possible and practicable.' Five days later the technical committee met again to discuss the re-opening of roads and Robertsfield international airport.[38] And to further facilitate disarmament and encampment, it was agreed to reserve airtime for ECOMOG on Gbarnga NPFL radio, as well as on ELBC radio in Monrovia.

One significant player who was sure that progress was being made was the recently appointed ECOMOG commander. When delivering the third Charles Gbenyon memorial lecture,* Major-General Ishaya Bakut, who had replaced

---

*   Gbenyon, a young television journalist, had been at his post in the government-owned ELBC when the station was occupied by rebels during the abortive Qui-wonkpa coup. Accused of facilitating Quiwonkpa's broadcast to the nation and supporting the coup, Gbenyon was murdered. An account of the killing is to be found in LTRC, *Final Report*, Chapter 3, 16.

General Rufus Kupolati* on 28 September 1991, voiced his belief that encampment and disarmament of the warring factions would be completed on schedule. The exercise, to be completed within 60 days, had commenced on time and was 'moving gradually in carrying out its mandate.'[39] Nor did this Nigerian General believe that the reported RUF incursion into Sierra Leone would halt the peace process. A buffer zone along the Liberian-Sierra Leonean border, he said, was being created with the co-operation of the Sierra Leonean government and the NPFL.

Notes

1 A.T. 'Journal of a Missionary', 72.
2 Ibid, 82.
3 Liberia News, 24 April 1991 (CRWM, Grand Rapids, MI).
4 The Washington Post, 8 May 1991.
5 No modalities as to how disarmament and demobilisation would be accomplished were specified. See Veronica Nmoma, 'The Civil War and the Refugee Crisis in Liberia', Journal of Conflict Studies, vol. XVII, no. 1, Spring 1997, 9. https://journals.lib.unb.ca/index.php/jcs/article/view/11734/12490 accessed 3 January 2020.
6 A.T., Dina Esposito of the Bureau of Refugee Programmes, US State Department and David Barrett, Centers for Disease Control, 'Briefing Concerning Trip to S. Leone, Guinea and Cote d'Ivoire' (with note by Stephen Price, AFJN).
7 Ibid.
8 MSF France.
9 CARE, an international humanitarian relief agency.
10 West Africa, 21–27 January 1991, 49 (Chris Simpson and Rubi Ofori, 'Liberia's Experience').
11 James Butty, West Africa, 18–24 February 1991, 224.
12 Brooke Amendment to the Foreign Assistance Act, 1969.
13 In 1989 USAID had applied this to Liberia, then $7 million in arrears.
14 Senator Kennedy released report on refugee crisis in Liberia on 11 February 1991.
15 A.B. John Kilcoyne, Tony Jennings to John Quinlan, 26 May 1991 (St Peter Claver's Church, Buchanan).
16 Ibid.
17 Ibid.
18 A.T. Statement of Hiram A. Ruiz, Policy Analyst, U.S. Committee for Refugees, on 'Continuing Humanitarian Needs of Liberians', to hearing of the U.S. House of Representatives Subcommittee on Africa, 16 July 1991.
19 Professor of Economics and Chairman Business, Social Sciences and Human Services Division, Cantonsville Community College, Maryland.
20 'The Carter Center, Access to Justice Project.'

---

*   Abiodun Alao characterises Rufus Kupolati as very different from his predecessor, Joshua Dogonyaro. 'More calm than Dogonyaro, Kupolati believed … that he was expected to carry out traditional peacekeeping and to open a line of communication with all the warring factions, especially with the NPFL. Thus, throughout his command in Liberia, Kupolati did not fire a single shot. He even relaxed some of the military decisions made by Dongoyaro, especially the placing of an embargo on the Buchanan port, and he allowed members of the NPFL direct access to his office. This created subtle tensions between him and the president of the IGNU, Professor Amos Sawyer' (op. cit., 68).

21 John Momoh, 'Life Under Taylor', West Africa, 22–28 July 1991, 1204.
22 Ibid.
23 Ibid.
24 Ibid.
25 Ibid.
26 West Africa, 26 September 1991, 28.
27 Washington Times, 7 May 1991.
28 Carter had been involved in the negotiations through his foundation which was represented at Yamoussoukro.
29 West Africa, 4–10 November 1991, 1857.
30 The Guardian, 1 November 1991 (AP in Yamoussoukro, Ivory Coast).
31 Ibid.
32 A.T. 'Address by H.E. Dr Amos C. Saywer, President of the INGU, to 46th session of the UN General Assembly, 3 October 1991.'
33 Independent, 2 November 1991 (Reuters: Monrovia, 'Liberians celebrate peace deal').
34 Africa Confidential, 22 November 1991 (vol. 32, no. 23).
35 Ibid.
36 Ibid.
37 See A.T. Toni to Pat, 9 (or 5) November 1991 (from Gardnersville carrying CRS food to Garry Jenkins).
38 FBIS-AFR-91–226 (Gbarnga Radio ELBC, 20/11/1991).
39 FBIS-AFR-91–236, 9 December 1991.

14 Large-scale rebel rearming threatens attempts to implement Yamoussoukro agreement

As the last month of 1991 progressed, anxiety concerning the continuing closure of roads increased. On 10 December Sawyer called on Taylor to 'show concern for the suffering people by reopening the roads this Christmas season.'[1] Taylor was quick to respond to this, declaring on NPFL radio that the Yamoussoukrou accord was 'on course' and denying that he had ever placed obstacles in the way of ECOMOG to encamp and disarm his soldiers. But the fact remained that by mid-December not a single NPFL soldier had encamped or been disarmed. And the roads remained closed.

Meanwhile there were other straws in the wind indicating that the situation was deteriorating. Two days before Christmas the UN announced the indefinite suspension of its relief work in Grand Gedeh County following an NPFL attack on one of its workers. The worker was Sean Devereux, a young, former lay missionary from England, head of the UN's Zwedru office. On 13 December he had been assaulted for refusing to release food to Taylor's forces. The suspension of aid, it was announced, would continue until the NPFL committed itself to abide 'by agreements previously signed with the UN to protect relief workers from harassment.'*

Further disturbing intelligence emanating from the Ivory Coast claimed that Taylor was continuing to import arms; and in such volumes and of such quality as to suggest a renewal of hostilities and a final push on the capital. The arms and ammunition, it was said, were coming in through Abidjan, the Ivorian capital.[2] And there were also reports of shipments of vehicles, heavy artillery and other weaponry reaching Taylor's forces through the ports of Buchanan and Harper. Whatever the truth as to scale, it was clear that far from disarming, the NPFL was consolidating its military position and equipping itself for further action. The reports, which came mainly from Liberian sources, were also to be heard from BBC correspondents on the World Service network.[3]

---

* Devereux was assassinated on 2 January 1993 at Kismayo port, in war-torn Somalia, while working with UNICEF. He had publicly criticised the local warlord and the Mogadishu-based U.S. marines for failing to intervene as an orgy of ethnic cleansing swept through Kismayo. He was 28 years old.

DOI: 10.4324/9781003219309-18

The atmosphere of uncertainty was further compounded by the erratic and occasionally murderous behaviour of INPFL leader Prince Johnson. He announced as a Christmas offering the release of all NPFL prisoners in his custody and a decision not to press charges against six (NPFL) commandos engaged in armed robbery, captured and handed over to the interim government for trial. Johnson's Christmas day statement also expressed the hope that Charles Taylor would reciprocate by releasing all INPFL prisoners in his custody. In the same statement, however, Johnson, who declared himself tired of fighting, accused the rebel leader of wanting to conquer by force rather than by democratic election. He also attacked the interim government for placing an economic embargo on Taylor-held territory, prohibiting the export of fuel oil, kerosene, cigarettes and alcohol, although not medicines and food.

Sawyer had explained the background to this embargo in a press conference. As matters stood, there was no freedom of movement on roads and no sign that the NPFL would remove its numerous checkpoints. The only people allowed to travel freely into the capital were NPFL members. And it had come to his notice that 'truckloads of luxurious items', were being taken up-country to NPFL leaders, whereas the few impoverished inhabitants who had managed to come from NPFL territory to buy goods in Monrovia were charged exorbitant import duties when re-entering Greater Liberia. The embargo, he hoped, would put a stop to such excursions.[4]

But it was clear that the imposition of the embargo had a deeper significance, marking the point at which the IGNU ceased to believe that conciliation was the best course in persuading the NPFL to honour Yamoussoukrou IV. Not that great hope was any longer held out for other approaches to succeed. The peace process, Sawyer told the same press conference, had been stalled for months by the NPFL which had devoted its energies to building up 'a vast military arsenal.'[5] And already a sense of impending doom loomed over Monrovia as reliable reports of the large-scale NPFL military build-up filtered into the capital.

Responding to Sawyer's press conference (which had been widely reported in the international media), Taylor took to the NPFL airwaves denying emphatically any troop or armament build-up in his territory.[6] He was, he said, 'committed to the peace process and would personally ensure the disarmament and encampment of the NPFL forces.' His press secretary, J. Garswa Yarmeto, repeated these denials in a BBC interview, rejecting claims that the NPFL was recruiting and training fighters, importing arms from Burkina Faso via the Ivory Coast, or preparing for a final push on Monrovia. On the contrary, the NPFL, he said, was 'committed to the Yamoussoukrou accord', and Taylor would accept the verdict of the forthcoming general elections.[7]

Tom Woewiyu, erstwhile NPFL Defence Minister, now leader of the Gbarnga parliament as well as Minister for Defence, also took to the air waves. The primary purpose of his broadcast, made on 26 December second anniversary of the NPFL's invasion, was to announce Gbarnga as the capital of Greater Liberia and seat of government. But Woewiyu also addressed other issues. In non-conciliatory mood, he declared that the economic embargo would not force the opening of the roads and that the writ of Taylor's government would continue to run over every piece of territory won by force of arms. Also, rehearsing a familiar rhetoric, he blasted ECOWAS for interfering in Liberia's affairs.

***

At the very point when it seemed that the Yamoussoukrou accord was falling apart, Taylor, as was his wont, surprised the world by declaring he would meet with ECOMOG 'to iron out differences.' There followed within twenty-four hours a meeting of the technical committee with Woewiyu representing the NPFL and Ghana's Brigadier R.K. Agbemenu leading the ECOMOG delegation. On the agenda was 'the opening of roads, subsequent encampment, disarmament, and the creation of the buffer zone between Sierra Leone and Liberia.' Liberians listening to their radios late that evening heard their programmes interrupted by a 'news flash', and the voice of an announcer saying that after several hours of deliberations there had been a 'major breakthrough' and that the following matters had been decided. First, the ECOMOG field commander and 'President' Taylor would meet in Kataka on 2 January 'to issue a joint press release on the date of the opening of the roads.' Second, inspection tours of encampment sites by ECOMOG would resume on the same day. And finally, in the interests of transparency, 'the press, both local and international', would be invited to Kakata for the meeting between the principals after which there would be a press conference.[8]

Inevitably this sudden display of reasonableness by Taylor made its way on to the international airwaves through a compliant BBC World Service. On 28 December NPFL radio gleefully re-broadcast an interview aired earlier that day on 'Focus on Africa' between Taylor and the BBC's Robin White. Taylor was in vintage form denying that the roads were closed, asserting that everything was perfectly normal – apart from some small difficulties on the road at Kakata – and that he would be meeting with the ECOMOG field commander on 2 January to iron out these. For his part, Amos Sawyer naively attributed Taylor's change of heart to the success of the economic embargo. The ban, which he said had been confined to 'luxurious items', had now begun to yield 'fruitful results.'

True to his word Taylor met General Bakut on the scheduled day. Later that evening Robin White asked the NPFL leader on air how the meeting had gone? Taylor was his buoyant self, describing what had transpired as 'a major breakthrough':

> We have agreed that the Mamba-Klay Road [between Monrovia and Kakata], along with the Tubmanburg road, will open... On 10 January we are going to have the international press present when we put into place the various combined checkpoints (manned) by ECOMOG and NPFL and then the roads will be open formally. We also have extended an invitation to the ECOMOG group to send at least three or five liaison

officers to the Ministry of Defence in Gbarnga so as to avoid any type of misinformation or lies or deception on what we are doing or not doing. Robin, we have also extended them the invitation ... to assign ECOMOG personnel at the Port of Buchanan, because there have been a lot of lies and rumours that we have been bringing in arms; and this is not true.

In the same interview Taylor's mask of equanimity and benevolence slipped briefly when asked about his relationship with the IGNU. The 'closure' of the roads, he said, had been greatly exaggerated by the IGNU for propaganda purpose.[9] Concerning the lie spread by the IGNU that the NPFL did not want elections and were doing all they could to prevent them from taking place, he could prove that the opposite was the case.

We are going to do everything possible to get these elections going... Robin, we want these elections... These guys are Marxist-Leninist trained... They sent them to Romania, Bulgaria. Sawyer was the head of that group at the university.

***

A token that the promises made were genuine was given on the very day of Taylor's meeting with General Bakut when ECOMOG forces were permitted to move into the interior of Greater Liberia on an inspection reconnaissance, reaching as far as Voinjama, some 240 miles northwards, near the Guinea border. And there was further encouraging news when on 4 January (1992) Liberia's Interim Elections Commission – in which both IGNU and the NPFL were represented, and which had been languishing since its formation in October - was finally sworn in. The commission was to start its work 'immediately.' It seemed as if Liberia was in the early stages of a sea-change; the stormy winds which had threatened to engulf the bark of the republic had suddenly abated, replaced now by a gentle breeze bearing her safe to harbour.

The reality, however, was that while Taylor had embarked on a policy of fence-mending with ECOMOG, his attitude towards the IGNU remained uniformly hostile. In a 'special speech to the nation', given at Harbel, he warned that there were 'politicians in Monrovia bent on provoking the NPFL to war.' For his part, he praised General Bakut and assured the nation of his desire to co-operate with the ECOMOG field commander.[10] He also described the current chairman of ECOWAS (President Diouf of Senegal) as 'a fair and mutual man.'[11] Moreover, belying his earlier claims that the roads were already open, he declared that his NPRAG intended 'to open the road to Monrovia next month if technical details are finalized.'

Sawyer, for one, was not convinced by Taylor's seeming compliance with Yamoussoukrou IV. Speaking during an interview with Ivorian television on 6 January, he pleaded with the Ivory Coast government to stop the flow of arms through its territory. If this could be accomplished, he insisted, Taylor would be compelled to end the war. Aware of the Ivory Coast's leniency towards, if not outright support for, Taylor he expressed the hope that Félix Houphouët-Boigny would 'soon realize that Mr Taylor is not for peace' and that he and his associates were 'amassing fortunes from gold, diamonds and other resources.'[12]

Another cause for concern was the position of ULIMO in relation to the post-Yamoussoukrou situation. In an interview with the BBC from Conakry (Guinea) Alhaji Kromah, the ULIMO spokesperson and military commander, declared himself unimpressed by Taylor's promise to open the roads. Taylor, he said, had been playing for time and would continue to do so, while he amassed wealth. But ULIMO would put a stop to this shortly by launching a major offensive against him.[13]

Finally, on 7 January, some days after his return from his meeting with Taylor in Gbarnga, General Bakut addressed the unfolding situation on the BBC programme, 'Network Africa.' When asked why the deployment of ECOMOG troops in Greater Liberia, scheduled by the Yamoussoukrou accord to start on 15 November, had not taken place he gave it as his opinion that not enough time had been allowed for 'confidence-building measures' to convince the various stake holders that the accord must be implemented. The NPFL soldiers, for example, would need to be convinced before they would agree to hand in their arms. There were also, the General added, some new developments in the period after the accord, which complicated its implementation. For example, there was the emergence of ULIMO, followed by border clashes with the NPFL. But Bakut was now confident from his discussions with Taylor and from the NPFL leader's subsequent pronouncements, that ECOMOG would be able to deploy in Greater Liberia.

***

On 6 January, in pursuit of the IGNU's economic offensive against Greater Liberia, the Liberia Central Bank issued new five-dollar banknotes, calling for all old five-dollar bills to be submitted for exchange by 17 January. This caused panic in Monrovia, leading to long queues at banks. On the following day Taylor declared on radio that within NPFL territory only the old notes would be valid and warned that citizens found holding the new banknotes would be arrested. Prince Johnson also had his say, declaring himself absolutely opposed to the interim government's currency measure. He would, he said, gather all the new banknotes found on his soldiers and burn them 'in the presence of journalists.'[14]

Days later, Johnson was back in the news when it was reported that he had executed three of his associates, including his deputy chief of staff, and wounded a fourth. No reason for the executions was given. However, Johnson had a track record in such matters having executed several of his men, including one senior associate, in July and again in October 1991. After Sawyer had publicly condemned these extra-judicial killings, a contrite Johnson dutifully assured the IGNU leader that he would refrain from such actions in the future. An INPFL spokesperson later explained that the men had been executed because they had been found in possession of IGNU

banknotes, prohibited by Johnson for those encamped with him in Caldwell. And Johnson was in the news for another reason when, despite his
recent opposition to the new banknotes, he announced that his faction was
throwing in its lot with the IGNU 'with immediate effect ... in the spirit
of peace and unity.'[15] Johnson, it will be recalled, had broken with the
interim government some months previously accusing it of corruption and
of failing to bring unity.

The INPFL leader was not the only one guilty of erratic behaviour. ULIMO,
which had withdrawn to Sierra Leone when the Yamoussoukrou accord was
struck, and which had entered a truce with the NPFL in October, was again
flexing its muscles. On 9 January ELBC radio quoted a statement from Paul Allen
Wie, ULIMO General Secretary, accusing General Bakut of colluding with
Taylor. Bakut, according to the statement, had said that ULIMO was 'preventing
the swift implementation of the peace process.'[16] This was a 'blatant lie.' And
Bakut was now acting with Taylor, so that the latter would become president of
Liberia. They had devised a scheme whereby NPFL rebels, dressed in ECOMOG
uniforms, would advance on Monrovia and would be admitted by ECOMOG
units to take control of 'key points' in the city. ULIMO, Wie declared, did not
want to go back to war with Taylor but war was the only language which Taylor
understood! Wie might well have been asked whether ULIMO itself spoke any
other language, for avenging slaughters perpetrated by Taylor's NPFL was central
to its existence. Wie's notion of NPFL rebels dressed in ECOMOG uniforms was
entirely fanciful. But there was an element of truth in the suggestion that General
Bakut's relationship with Taylor was very different from that of his predecessors,
and most notably General Joshua Dogonyaro.*

***

The re-opening of the roads, such as it was on 2 January, brought considerable excitement and new hope to Liberia, although Sawyer was quick to
point out that at the heart of the peace process lay the issue of encampment
and disarmament; and that currently there was no sign of either taking place.
The Monrovia populace was greatly encouraged by the arrival of many vehicles
from Greater Liberia bearing travellers in search of food and commodities;
while Greater Liberia was happy to see a flow of travellers into its territory,
many of them in search of missing family members.[17]

As January moved towards a close the recently sworn-in Liberian Election
Commission travelled to the U.S. to study 'electoral law and 'electoral
machinery' and to seek assistance for its work. The most worrying difficulties
confronting the commission were the non-existence of both an electoral roll
and a population census, and the lack of equipment required to conduct a
poll. Voter registration, too, needed to be undertaken, which would require
commission offices in Liberia's 13 counties. Dr Patrick Seyon, the commission's co-chairman told the briefings that at least U.S. $22 million would be
required to set things right.

---

* See p. 150.

In addition, the 'more stable political environment' so earnestly sought in order to proceed with implementing Yamoussoukrou IV and its provision for elections, was still far from being established. For one, the emergence of ULIMO, whose raison d'être was the destruction of Taylor's movement, had greatly complicated ECOMOG's task in bringing about peace. On 14 January Raleigh Seekie, political leader of ULIMO, described the recent re-opening of the roads as a 'smokescreen' concealing the fact that Taylor had no intention of encamping his troops or of allowing them to disarm. At much the same time Taylor's Foreign Minister, T. Ernest Eastman, called for yet another Yamoussoukrou summit to discuss the issues of encampment and disarmament. This was necessary, he said, because of the threat to NPFL territory from ULIMO forces ranged across the border. The implication was that while such a threat existed there could be no question of abandoning arms or retreating into camps.

There was news, too, of the movement of some 3,000 refugees into the Ivory Coast as a result of the conflict between ULIMO and the NPFL. Hostilities between the two militias were to be renewed early in April with ULIMO steadily making gains. By August the NPFL had been pushed out of Cape Mount, Bomi County and Lower Lofa Counties. To many it seemed that a day of reckoning was approaching for Taylor.

Prince Johnson's INPFL also continued to prove a thorn in the flesh of peace-making, sounding unwelcome notes and occasionally resorting to arms against enemies real and imaginary. Peter Naigow, who had represented the INPFL at the Banjul conference and later had served for a time as IGNU vice president, disclosed during a private visit to the U.S. that Johnson's much trumpeted return to the interim government was now stalled. Johnson had signalled his wish to return on condition that he would again be given the right to nominate the IGNU's vice-president and would himself be given the post of Speaker of the House. But Sawyer's government would hear nothing of it.

In contrast to the resistance experienced by Johnson in his efforts to gain re-admission to the interim government, Sawyer's welcoming arms appeared wide open to the NPFL. Not that he had changed his mind about the prospect of NPFL's compliance with Yamoussoukro. Rather he was engaged in a last, desperate attempt to salvage the accord. Addressing the interim legislative assembly, he offered the NPFL the post of vice president, formerly the 'property' of Johnson's INPFL. In addition, he offered Taylor a number of prominent cabinet portfolios as well as the post of Speaker of the House for himself. And as a further incentive he offered a temporary lifting of the economic embargo on Greater Liberia which, he promised, would be abolished once disarmament and encampment had taken place.

But such overtures were to be unrewarded. As February came to a close, it became clear that NPFL forces had no intention of encamping or disarming. And even the small measure of progress which had been reported was turning out to be illusory. ECOMOG's commander, General Bakut, had said on 9 February that disarmament would be completed on schedule. However, with four days remaining not a single act of disarmament had taken place. Moreover, apart from a small number of ECOMOG soldiers deployed in Buchanan, no ECOMOG soldier had crossed into Greater Liberia. Again, the two highways from Monrovia into Greater Liberia which had been declared open by Taylor, were no longer safe, with bands of NPFL soldiers roaming free and mounting checkpoints. Few Liberians now dared to travel on them. And when challenged about the failure of his movement to disarm, Taylor had a ready answer. ULIMO rebels were poised to attack, and the NPFL had to defend itself.

***

Since the outbreak of the civil war, it will be recalled, Fr Mattie Gilmore had managed to steer clear of trouble, cheerfully negotiating checkpoints that others might have approached with foreboding. His good fortune was to run out in the second week of February 1992, when he travelled over the border into Greater Liberia to visit Fr Larry Collins[18] in Zorzor. His public transport taxi was stopped at the first checkpoint exiting Gbarnga. Caught in possession of banned Monrovia 'Liberty' currency (a sum of LD $20, equivalent to U.S. $2.40) hidden in a sock, he was detained, stripped and interrogated for over 30 hours, then charged with the crime of 'economic sabotage.' Released on a bail bond of LD $10,000 (U.S. $1,183, paid by the Mission), he was forbidden to leave Gbarnga for four weeks, pending trial. During this period, in effect under house arrest living with the local pastor, Michael Flattery, his health began to deteriorate, and he was permitted by the NPFL to enter the Lutheran Phebe hospital. There he was visited by Lee Cahill on a number of occasions. Finally, when told informally that the matter would be taken no further, Cahill was able to take the much-weakened veteran missionary back to Monrovia.

Seraphino dal Pont, the Italian Consolata priest from Italy, was another missionary who fell foul of the NPFL at this time. Pastor of two parishes in Margibi County – St Pius, Harbel/Firestone and St Christopher, Kakata – he had a number of brushes with the NPFL authorities before he was eventually imprisoned. On 3 April he was arrested in Harbel for having in his possession a copy of the archdiocesan monthly magazine in which an article showed Taylor and the NPFL in an unfavourable light. Released on bail of LD $10,000, two weeks later he was rearrested and charged with espionage while driving in the vicinity of Robertsfield airport en route to celebrating Easter liturgies in a nearby church. While in custody a further charge – possession of illegal banknotes – was lodged against him. He was to spend three weeks enduring extreme conditions in a Kakata prison before being deported from Greater Liberia.[19] As in the case of Gilmore, Seraphino's bail of LD $10,000 was confiscated.

During the Doe regime Archbishop Francis had occasionally been criticised by some of his clergy for 'remaining silent.' It is true that during the first six months of the regime he made few public pronouncements on political matters. But restraint was not a noticeable feature of his personality and thereafter he was outspoken whenever he felt human and civil rights were being violated. It will be remembered that in speaking out against President William Tolbert in the wake of the Rice Riots he ran the risk of provoking presidential anger and the wrath of the True Whig Party. In speaking out during the regimes of

Samuel Doe and Taylor he ran the very real risk of assassination. In the after-math of Yamoussoukrou IV, at a time when Liberia was drifting back into uncertainty and insecurity, and the resumption of civil strife seemed imminent, Francis again spoke out. On 10 April he issued a statement, carried in several Monrovia newspapers, targeting increasing lawlessness in Greater Liberia.[20]

Harassment of Church personnel, in the view of Francis, was not a random occurrence but rather had the character of an orchestrated campaign. He had been especially incensed by Seraphino's detention 'in inhumane conditions' and at the time had demanded either he be brought to trial or released 'uncondi-tionally from the dungeons of the NPFL.'[21] Francis' claim, that the NPFL's entertained a special animus against his archdiocese, was not without merit. Cahill had his own view on why this might have been the case, pointing to certain divisions within the Church not only in relation to pastoral policy but, more significantly, in attitudes towards Taylor and the NPFL.

> Bishop Sekey asks me (on the occasion of the Seraphino trouble, which occurred within his diocese) if there is anything I can do to curb Michael Francis from his high-profile image. Michael (Francis) asks me if I can get Sekey to do something for religious and lay personnel who suffer in Greater Liberia. The apparent alliances of Michael Francis and President Sawyer on one side and Bishop Sekey and Charles Taylor on the other still hold in popular opinion.[22]

In short, the animus was less against the Church than against those of its leaders who spoke out against Taylor and the NPFL; and principally Michael Francis.

Nor was this divide confined to leadership level.

> There is evidence of how easy it is for Church personnel to form overt or covert allegiances to the parties in control of their respective areas. This divisiveness is perhaps most evident in the Archdiocese of Monrovia … itself now having within its own confines all four[23] factions…[24]

Cahill himself was clearly on the side of the archbishop, summing up his feelings in a report to the SMA international leadership. Incidents involving the NPFL and the mission, he wrote, 'which ranged from the abusive to the very frightening', had already taken place during 1992 involving Gilmore, Jenkins, Feeney and Flattery, all members of the SMA, and also Salesian Fathers, St Louis Brothers, Franciscan Missionaries of Mary, Consolata Sisters and, of course, Fr Seraphino. 'There had also been arrests, detentions, internment, sham trials and (in Seraphino's case) deportation. In all this, Michael Francis spoke out. Bishop Sekey did nothing.'[25] For Cahill this was the nub of the issue.

However, in his defence it must be said that Bishop Sekey's diocese was exclusively within Greater Liberia, its seat in the very town where the NPRAG was located. In fact, the bishop's own residence was side by side with the main NPFL barracks in which Taylor often lived and from where he directed military operations. It must be said, too, that Taylor had exercised his charm with considerable success on those likely to cast him in a poor light, including international journalists and broadcasters. He also exercised his charm on missionaries and some succumbed to it albeit temporarily. Archbishop Francis, to his credit, was quicker than most to see through Taylor's veneer, just as he had seen through the posturing as 'Saviour of the Nation', by Taylor's predecessor, Samuel Doe. And there was also the age-old dilemma whether to face tyranny with patience in the hope that it would pass or to confront it openly and suffer the consequences. Whatever the case, Cahill's criticism was accurate, to the extent that Liberia's three bishops did not always, or in fact often, speak with one voice on political issues.

***

The deterioration in NPFL discipline which emerged in the closing months of 1991 and opening months of 1992 was directly related to the emergence of ULIMO. That militia was every bit as ruthless as the NPFL and well-equipped into the bargain. The success of its initial incursions into NPFL territory had given it a measure of confidence and led to bolder attempts to gain ground. This had shaken the NPFL creating an atmosphere of uncertainty which frequently escalated into hysteria. ULIMO fifth columnists and infiltrators were perceived to be everywhere and those suspected, even on the flimsiest grounds, were shown no mercy. This caused a sense of outrage among the general population, which occasionally threatened to undermine NPFL control. A typical example of such occurrences is recorded in the Buchanan mission diary for the last week of March.

> Early in the morning there was terrible tension in the town. The NPFL picked up nine people as suspected ULIMO infiltrators. They brought them to the Benson River Bridge and shot all nine – 2 Fanti and 7 Bassa. All the Bassa people took to the streets and marched through the town in angry protest. Schools and businesses closed. The Bassa people demanded that all Mano and Gio NPFL and civilians must be taken out of Grand Bassa County. So, there was terrible tension and confusion all day.

NPRAG vice-president (Thomas Zote) and NPFL chief of staff (Isaac Musa) hastened to Buchanan to pacify the protesters but with little success. Finally, on 25 March, after Taylor came in person and negotiated with Bassa and Fanti leaders, it was announced that the nine executed 'had been cleared of ULIMO involvement by the proper authorities', and henceforth 'anyone suspected of involvement with ULIMO would be interrogated by concerned citizens and not the NPFL.' As for those who had perpetrated the killing of the nine, they 'would be brought to Gbarnga for interrogation.'

***

As 1992 progressed there was a noticeable hardening towards the NPFL mainly among ECOWAS Anglophone members. As already noted, no sooner had the ink dried on the final Yamoussoukrou communiqué than the implementation of the accord began to run into difficulty. On his return to Liberia Taylor claimed that he had signed the accord under duress and declared that as long as ULIMO continued to operate against his forces he would neither encamp nor disarm. Numerous efforts to secure compliance were subsequently made. Taylor was cajoled, coaxed and threatened. At times these efforts, more driven by a desperate desire to achieve a peaceful resolution than by a cold appraisal of what was possible, seemed on the point of yielding results. However, now the reality began to dawn within ECOWAS Anglophone circles that the NPFL was never likely to abandon its control over Greater Liberia, nor its ambition to overrun the remainder of the country and impose its leader as president. Only *force majeure* could put a stop to Taylor's march. Eventually, between 27 July and 29 July (1992) an ECOWAS summit meeting was convened in Dakar with the object of persuading the NPFL to implement Yamoussoukrou and if this failed to compel compliance. It was the last throw of the dice to save the accord. Held under the chairmanship of President Abdou Diouf, chairman of ECOWAS since early 1992, the summit signalled a critical moment in Liberia's history, setting the scene for a period of incredible violence.

Part of the background to the toughening of attitudes was the treatment meted out to ECOMOG, especially its Senegalese contingent, by the NPFL when attempts were made to implement encampment and disarmament. It must be said that the Senegalese presence in Liberia, dating from September 1991, had been largely an attempt to appease Taylor who repeatedly expressed doubts about ECOMOG's neutrality, complaining about the dominance of a hostile Nigerian contingent. At Yamoussoukrou IV he had requested the deployment of Senegalese troops in the buffer zone to be established along the border with Sierra Leone. This had been acceded to. However, it soon emerged that the NPFL had no intention of treating the Senegalese any different from other ECOMOG contingents.

In April the Senegalese had been deployed in Lofa County to commence the process of encampment and disarmament. But on 28 May they were ambushed by NPFL when purchasing food at a market in the border town of Vahun. A gun-battle ensued after which six Senegalese soldiers were taken hostage. On 8 June NPFL Radio in Gbarnga announced that these had been killed.[26] One consequence of the incident was the withdrawal of the Senegalese from Lofa County to Monrovia on 14 June. The full contingent, 1,800 strong, was to withdraw completely from ECOMOG in mid-January 1993.[*]

---

[*] Abiodun Alao, op. cit., 68, notes the speculation that it was the closeness between Bakut and the NPFL which explained 'significantly the success that attended NPFL's attempts to embarrass ECOMOG, as exemplified by the arrest and humiliation of ECOMOG soldiers who had been deployed to Taylor-held territories for the disarmament stipulated under Yamoussoukrou IV.' Aloa also remarks that 'NPFL members held Bakut in warm affection', and that in his discussions with NPFL members 'Bakut was rated as one of the finest Nigerian officers posted to Liberia.'

It was this atrocity which spurred the leading Anglophone ECOWAS members – already deeply frustrated – to act. At the Dakar summit they sought to restore the self-respect of the organisation by dealing forcibly with a situation which was plainly no longer amenable to diplomatic solution, or half-hearted threats of military force. Taylor had cocked a snook at ECOMOG and got away with it and not all ECOWAS leaders were prepared to tolerate such behaviour. One such was 25-year-old Captain Valentine Strasser, Sierra Leone's head-of-state, who had come to power through a military coup the previous April following his country's poor showing against Taylor's invading troops. He told the other heads-of-state that the time had come to match force with force. What followed fell short of Strasser's expectations but still represented a toughening of attitude, the summit issuing an ultimatum calling on the NPFL and ULIMO to implement Yamoussoukrou IV in full within 30 days. If this deadline was not met the communiqué threatened to devise new measures to make the factions comply. These would be drawn up by a joint gathering of the Standing Mediation Committee of ECOWAS and the Francophone 'Committee of Five' already scheduled for Cotonou in mid-October (1992).

Neither encampment nor disarmament took place. Nor did the ECOWAS threat to force compliance. At the root of the failure lay the continuing divisions within ECOWAS on the Liberia question. Ivory Coast and Burkina Faso remained steadfast in their support for Taylor while other member states, with the exception of Nigeria, Ghana and Sierra Leone, were largely indifferent, leading to a lack of resolve in the organisation as a whole. Well aware of these divisions, Taylor paid no attention to warnings and threats. On the contrary, he was already secretly preparing a major offensive which, he hoped, would soon make his dream of the presidency a reality. Sawyer's assertion that Taylor was heavily re-arming and recruiting was to prove accurate. Burkina Faso air force planes were landing at Robertsfield international airport (under NPFL control), carrying modern and advanced weaponry. Further military materials were reaching him by road from Burkina Faso, granted free passage through Ivory Coast.[27]

Taylor's ambitions were threatened by events which took place early in August 1992. At that time the fragile ceasefire brokered between ULIMO and the NPFL but frequently breached, was finally shattered when ULIMO troops went on the offensive, crossing from Sierra Leone and driving the NPFL from the border area. Amidst bitter fighting and atrocities on both sides, about 30,000 civilians fled southwards to Monrovia, while many more took refuge across the border. Some 580 ECOMOG troops, who had supposedly been monitoring the buffer zone and other areas where there had been skirmishes between the two factions, were instructed to withdraw to Monrovia. The NPFL, having had the worst of the fighting, accused ECOMOG of supporting the ULIMO offensive and refused the retreating soldiers safe passage, disarming and beating them, and prohibiting the transport of supplies from Monrovia. This humiliation continued into September when eventually an internationally brokered solution, involving U.S. President Jimmy Carter's International Negotiation Network group, was achieved and the ragged, malnourished and demoralised ECOMOG troops were finally able to reach Monrovia.[28] Henceforth, to justify his refusal to encamp and disarm his troops, at every opportunity afforded him, Taylor declared that the ECOWAS force could no longer be considered neutral but was out to destroy him.

Cahill summed up the situation despondently, in a diary entry, reflecting that within the 300 miles, as the crow flies, between Monrovia and Freetown there were now at least eight military groups: the Sierra Leonean national army, the Sierra Leonean rebel group RUF, the NPFL, ULIMO, INPFL, AFL and ECOMOG. And all efforts to resolve the crisis had failed. Numerous international summit meetings had been held and peace accords and ceasefire agreements had been signed at Banjul (October 1990), Bamako (November 1990), Banjul (December 1990) Lomé (February 1991), and Yamoussoukrou (October 1991). All had failed and now Liberia seemed on the edge of a precipice and ready to plunge into its depths.

Notes

1 FBIS-AFR-91–247, 24 December 1991 (AB2112193591 Paris AFP).
2 FBIS-AFR-91–248, 26 December 1991 ('NPFL Said Importing Arms Through Abidjan'; Monrovia Radio ELBC).
3 See ibid.
4 West Africa, 20–26 January 1992, 120.
5 Ibid.
6 Ibid.
7 Ibid.
8 Ibid, 2 January 1992 (A132912095591 Monrovia Radio ELBC).
9 FB1S-AFR-91–251, 31 December 1991 (AB3012145091 Gbarnga Radio ELBC).
10 Abiodun Alao, op. cit., 68, writes of Bakut that his 'alleged closeness to Charles Taylor' was one of the main criticisms of the General. 'He interpreted his assignment as to ensure harmony by working closely with the NPFL. This, however, earned him criticism from the AFL and IGNU.'
11 FBIS-AFR-91–251, 31 December 1991 (AB3012145091 Gbarnga Radio ELBC).
12 FBIS-AFR-92–004, 7 January 1992 (AB0601163592 Monrovia Radio ELBC)
13 FBIS-AFR-92–005, 8 January 1992 (AB0701210592 BBC World Service, 'Focus on Africa').
14 A.T. See Archbishop Francis, Report to Propaganda Fide, 1992.
15 A.T. FBIS-AFR-92–03 (AB0901204592 Monrovia Radio ELBC, 9 January 1992).
16 Ibid.
17 Ibid.
18 Laurence (Larry) Collins, nephew of Liberia's first Catholic bishop, John Collins, was the longest serving missionary at the time, first setting foot in Liberia in 1954.
19 A.G. (General Archives of the Society of African Missions, Rome), 1376/94. 11/2–47, 10 April 1992 ('Archdiocese of Monrovia: Position Statement of the Archdiocese on the harassment of Catholic personnel').
20 Ibid.
21 Ibid.
22 A.T. and A.B. EPC documentation, June 1992, 'Report from Liberia', 4 June 1992. See also Cahill's Report to R.S. Meeting at Winneba, 20 September 1992 and Cahill's Report to EPC, 11 November 1992.

23 AFL, INPFL, ULIMO, NPFL.
24 Ibid.
25 Ibid.
26 African Concord, 10 August 1991.
27 AB., Enda Byrne (Caritas), Report, 26 November 1992.
28 See, African Concord, 10 August 1992. c.f., Testimony by Leonard H. Robinson Jr
    (African Bureau, Deputy Assistant Secretary) to House Sub-Committee on Africa,
    19 November 1992.

Section 5

The Slaying of the Innocent

15 NPRAG forces commence a 122-day assault on the capital (Operation Octopus)

In the early hours of Thursday 15 October 1992 Taylor's forces commenced an assault on Monrovia, the so-called operation Octopus, which was to last for some 120 days, and which had as its objective the replacement of the interim government (IGNU) by the government of Greater Liberia (NPRAG) and Charles Taylor's accession to the office of president. Preparations for this assault, as seen above, had been underway for some months. The fact that ULIMO managed to make substantial gains within NPFL territory in those months was no accident. Taylor had no intention of fighting a war against ULIMO. For him the big prize was Monrovia. Conquest of Monrovia would mean destruction of Sawyer's interim government and the assumption of power by the NPFL under his leadership. Justifying his action, Taylor told the world that he was responding to an unprovoked attack by a combined ECOMOG and ULIMO force.

***

It so happened that in the week before Octopus the SMA Superior General, Patrick Harrington, and the American Provincial, S. John Murray, were visiting Liberia to promote a 'Policy Document for post-Civil War Liberia' which had been drawn up some weeks previously by the Rome-based General Council. On 14 October, a day before the meeting was scheduled, some 15 SMA missionaries, mainly from Monrovia and its hinterland had gathered in the Regional House[1] on the outskirts of Monrovia. Members based outside this area were unable to travel because of increasing tension along the border with Greater Liberia. The Regional House, it should be noted, was situated adjacent to the ocean about three miles along Monrovia's principal highway to the interior – leading to Kakata, Gbarnga and the north-east. About three miles further along this road was the town of Paynesville and a further three miles marked the border line between ECOMOG and NPFL's forces.

At 4.10 am on the morning of 15 October 1992, while still dark, the confreres were awakened by the sound of heavy shelling coming from NPFL lines. 'A number of us', according to Cahill's diary, 'watched thirteen shells exploding within a 500-yard radius of the house, all within a matter of minutes.' After that the shelling became sporadic and by 6.30 am, after the sun had come up and all had fallen silent, Cahill took advantage of the lull to find out what was

DOI: 10.4324/9781003219309-19

happening. Driving in the direction of Paynesville he noticed people in flight all along the roadway coming against him, carrying packs of belongings and food, making their way into the city. He also observed 'convoys of heavy ECOMOG artillery, moving from the town through Paynesville towards the front.'

Back in the Regional House the meeting scheduled for 9 am commenced on time but against a background of renewed heavy artillery in the distance. The meeting proceeded through the morning 'relatively undisturbed' and, after lunch and siesta, reconvened at 16.15. But not for long. 'We were into that section of the SMA policy document dealing with the contemplative dimension of missionary life when we were "lifted out of it" by a nearby explosion.' The meeting came abruptly to an end with its participants rushing out onto the balcony to find the sea directly in front erupting with showers of shells. 'Over the next hour', the diary entry continues, 'at least ten of these shells landed within 500 yards of the house and at last we began to realize the seriousness of the situation and the danger to our own lives.' For as the drama first unfolded, the reality of what was occurring was obscured by amazement and wonder. It took a while before the recklessness of remaining on the balcony became apparent. Later, in a safer location, the confreres surmised that the shelling was probably intended for the airport which was adjacent to the Regional House.

As it grew dark the sound of explosions petered out and then ceased. The guns were to remain silent for some days, but it was clear to all that Liberia was entering a new, terrifying, phase of civil war. That night Harrington and Cahill walked the beach for some two hours, rarely speaking, the immensity of what was happening being borne in on both. For Harrington, the Society's great endeavour to contribute to Liberia's reconstruction in a post-war situation, was clearly now in shreds. There would be no reconstruction but instead the continuing destruction of civil war. The meeting did not reconvene. Over the next few days those gathered dispersed, proceeding cautiously, through heavy security and empty streets, to their various mission stations. As for Harrington and Murray, they made their way across bush tracks onto the airport compound, walking along the runways to reach the terminal, where they managed to secure seats on a small aircraft bound for Freetown.

In Monrovia ECOMOG began to muster all its resources in an effort to push the NPFL forces back. During the first 36 hours they enjoyed some success with the front moving in the direction of Kakata. By 17 October extremely nervous civilians in Kakata, Gbarnga, Tapita and Buchanan were leaving in droves for the safety of rural villages.[2] Taylor, on the other hand, was again on NPFL radio telling the world that the NPFL was responding to an unprovoked attack on its positions by ECOMOG, in league with ULIMO.[3]

The growing conviction that ECOMOG was gaining the upper hand was reflected in a message from Cahill to his Irish superiors, sent late on 22 October. This managed to reach its destination courtesy of a Salesian amateur radio enthusiast in Monrovia and an equivalent enthusiast in Cork, local newspaper man Tony Burke. The message gave some detail of the grounds for optimism. During the early hours of that day several ECOMOG aircraft carrying reinforcements had landed at Spriggs Payne airport. It was true that during the night there had been a lot of gunfire, and shells had again fallen in the vicinity of the Regional House and airport, but now all was quiet, and an 'air of optimism' was discernible among the few confreres still there. Information on the situation in Buchanan followed a similar pattern. During the night the port area had been shelled from the sea by ECOMOG ships but now there was calm. Cahill had been in contact with some of the confreres in Greater Liberia by radio and all were well and hoping that the worst might be over. It was not to be.

The mood of optimism quickly dissipated. By 24 October, courtesy of a radio link between the Catholic hospital and the St John of God headquarters in Bilbao, Spain,[4] Cahill was informing his Cork superiors that the war, was now nine days old and even though there had been 'some OK days', they were becoming fewer. 'Last night and this morning' had been 'particularly unnerving' and fear and panic were taking hold. Among Catholic institutions already badly affected was the Rehabilitation Centre for physically disabled children at Pipeline, run by Spanish Sisters. Pipeline, a northern Monrovia suburb, was in the eye of the storm having been overrun by the NPFL and now under counter-attack by ECOMOG. Fearing for its safety the entire institution – comprising the sisters, the nursing staff and 25 children – was in the process of evacuating to the Catholic Hospital.'[5]

Many of the parishes in Monrovia and its hinterland were now experiencing the ravages of war.[6] The three on the western side of the city – St Mary's Bushrod, Holy Family Caldwell and St Edwards Logantown – were in the midst of a firefight, partly because that area, under the control of Prince Johnson, was coming under attack from the NPFL. Gardnersville parish, in Monrovia's northern-central suburb, had been completely overrun by the NPFL. James Hickey[*], its pastor, had managed to make it into the city two days previously and had eventually reached the Regional House. However, there was no information on the whereabouts of the five American sisters of the ASC congregation living in the parish.

In Greater Liberia the picture was one of increasing desolation. There had been no word for over two weeks of John Feeney (he had returned to Bong Mine in December 1991). In Kakata the mission and school had been closed and large numbers of the population had fled following intense aerial bombardment by ECOMOG a week previously. Among those who had abandoned the town was Sister John Joseph C.I.J., elderly principal of St Christopher's school. Buchanan, a NPFL stronghold, had been bombarded by ECOMOG from air and sea, and many people had fled. Nearby LAC mission was still functioning, so far unaffected by the fighting, but tension had reached new levels of intensity. Gbarnga town had been bombed by ECOMOG on 22

---

[*]   James Hickey had been deported from Liberia by the Doe regime in April 1987. In the changed circumstances after the assassination of Doe in September 1990 and the installation of the INGU in October 1990, he was able to return in December of that year.

October, leading to an exodus. Again, great tension prevailed there and Bishop Benedict Sekey, dwelling in close proximity to NPFL headquarters, was 'very sparing in use of his radio.' Ganta, too, was almost 'a ghost town', although the Medical Missionaries of Mary sisters were still at their posts in the Leprosy and T.B. Rehabilitation Centre. Yekepa, further north, was also witnessing a hae-morrhage of its population because of a fear of ECOMOG bombing. The mission there, under Chris Brennan of the SMA's Irish Province, was still functioning. Larry Collins in distant Zorzor was uncontactable, presumably because his radio had been confiscated by the NPFL.

Cahill transmitted a dispatch on the situation to Cork, on 28 October, again courtesy of Brother Benjamin Cornago in Bilbao. This link was to prove a vital line of communication, Cahill transcribing and then faxing his dispatches to Bilbao from where they were forwarded to Ireland. In this message, Cahill described the situation on day 12 of Operation Octopus. Paynesville, Congotown, Gardners-ville, the Freeport, Logantown, Caldwell and Bushrod all now knew exactly 'what shelling and bombardment are like.' ECOMOG forces remained strongly con-centrated in the Paynesville area, leaving a measure of security which allowed Gerry Sweeney, its pastor, to stay at his post. However other missionaries had been forced to flee. Frank Hynes and most of the people of Logantown had left their area when ground-based shelling intensified, augmented by salvos fired from warships in the port area. James Hickey, now safe in the Regional House, gave details of his exit from Gardnersville. He had been trapped there for a number of days and 'was lucky to get out, managing to bring with him to the hospital a woman and child, both suffering from bullet wounds' incurred while sheltering in his compound. But nothing had been heard of the five ASC sisters in Gardnersville for over a week. In the meantime, the NPFL remained in control of the area. The occupants of the Regional House, which now included Fr Guvvala Balaswamy,[*] continued to be rocked by frequent episodes of gunfire and shelling. And there were further unwelcome developments noted by Cahill.

> Last night we had our first taste of the new infamous NPFL rockets, three of them landing right between us and the Catholic hospital. Yesterday three of them landed about half a mile from the mission on Old Road, killing four civilians.[7]

One of those caught up in the chaos and confusion was Garry Jenkins[8] at Tubmanburg mission, about 15 miles north-west of Monrovia. On 22 October he had managed to flee with his mission staff into the suburb of Bushrod island. On the following day the NPFL broke through ECOMOG lines at Cald-well and there followed, well into the next day, a ferocious battle in the vicinity of Bushrod island. Jenkins and his staff were caught in the middle, sheltering in St Mary's convent. Late on Saturday afternoon, when the

---

[*]   An Indian associate of the SMA, linked with the British Province and working in Bong County. Another Indian associate was Fr Gnanapragasam Aarokiasamy.

fighting abated, the party decided to move out of hiding and make for the city centre. En route, they encountered an eerie silence, with no traffic moving and very few civilians. At various points they were stopped by soldiers, interrogated, and searched. In areas under ULIMO control they were closely inspected for NPFL insignia. Eventually, exhausted, and frightened, the small group reached the city proper, finding it overflowing with refugees and in complete chaos. Just as night fell, they arrived at the safety of the archbishop's residence on Ashmun Street.

Cahill's dispatch of 28 October also gave details of the wider situation. Radio messages from the mission stations in Greater Liberia described thousands of civilians fleeing Katata, Buchanan and Gbarnga – towns that had been hit by ECOMOG aerial shelling – and also Ganta, Sannequellie, Yekepa and Tapita, further north. In Monrovia, although there had been significant NPFL advances, these were unlikely to continue. This was because areas infested by the NPFL were now almost completely devoid of civilians – they had fled into the city centre – allowing ECOMOG, along with ULIMO and AFL forces, the opportunity to launch counterattacks without being impeded.

On 29 October another dispatch from Cahill expressed a growing concern for the ASC Sisters in Gardnersville. They had been unaccounted for since 20 October; and no investigation could be made in Gardnersville which was currently inaccessible, 'the one place in the city at the moment which is fairly well gripped by the NPFL.' Moreover, John Feeney at Bong Mine and Larry Collins in Zorzor had not made contact in recent days. In Feeney's case it was hoped that a food convoy projected by CRS for Bong Mine on the following day would locate him. All other SMA mission personnel, Cahill was able to assure his anxious superiors, had been in contact and were in good spirits. So too were the MMM sisters in Ganta and the FMM's in Gbarnga. But the Sisters of St Joseph of Chambéry (CSJ) in St Christopher's parish, Kakata, had been compelled to leave and were now in the Ivory Coast. So also the CSJ sisters (including the intrepid Irish woman Joan Margaret Kelly) had to abandon Voinjama and were now taking refuge in the St Louis convent, Gbarnga. Elsewhere the Salesians, based in Monrovia and Tappita, were secure, while the Brothers and Sisters at the Catholic Hospital were at their stations, tending to increasing numbers of wounded. The Christian Brothers in Yekepa, too, were secure and made 'good company' for Chris Brennan, the young Irish SMA who was on his own in the parish, church and house.

Cahill was not the only source for information going to Ireland. Brennan, who had access to a local amateur radio operator, was in touch with the Cork radio enthusiast Tony Burke. And Jim Lee, secretary to Bishop Francis, whose scheduled flight out of Monrovia had been cancelled, had managed to make one extended telephone call in which he briefed Cork on the situation. His interlocutors were Hugh Harkin, the Provincial secretary and Kieran O'Reilly, the councillor responsible for Liberia. They in turn remained in regular touch with the anxious families of the various Irish missionaries briefing them on developments and offering them some reassurance.

On 30 October (day 15 of the siege) Cahill reported to Cork that the daily arrival of 'at least 4 Kabo Airline jets bringing in troops and supplies to Spriggs Payne airport, had strengthened ECOMOG's position and again placed the NPFL on the back foot. Apart from the Gardnersville and Upper Caldwell suburbs, the city of Monrovia was now in ECOMOG hands. The previous night had been 'relatively good', interrupted only by the sound of gunfire and shelling from Gardnersville. Incursions by NPFL commandos into Logantown, Bushrod and other parts of the city which had caused chaos and fear during the previous week, were now at an end, 'at least for the moment' and the battle was now being fought mainly by heavy artillery. Every day Taylor was to be heard on NPFL radio from Gbarnga. His broadcasts had become increasingly incoherent as he raged at enemies real and imaginary. Particular venom was reserved for Nigeria's president, General Ibrahim Babangida, whom he accused of waging a so-called 'peace-keeping war' in order to win a seat for Nigeria on the UN Security Council. Already on at least four occasions, so Cahill reported, Taylor claimed to have taken Monrovia and on three occasions he announced that his forces had overrun Spriggs Payne airport. In a recent broadcast he had asked all ECOMOG soldiers to 'wear white helmets and to wave white flags.'

In the midst of the confusion there was still no word of the missing ASC nuns and concern was deepening. Aware of rumours circulating about their fate, Taylor took to the air on Friday, 30 October, to deny that they were prisoners of his forces. He believed, he said, that they were 'alive and staying with stranded orphans and other refugees in Chocolate City', an eastern suburb of Monrovia. Some days previously, the orphans in question had been evacuated from the fighting in Gardnersville under a truce brokered by a U.S. official. In that instance three buses were able to enter Gardnersville to collect hundreds of children from their orphanage, taking them to Chocolate City for safety. Anxious to set everyone's mind at rest, Taylor continued that he would brave ECOMOG bombings of the area 'to rescue the nuns' should it be necessary.

***

The early hours of Saturday, 31 October (day 16 of the siege) were to bring shocking news, quickly transmitted to Cork by Cahill.

> Our worst fears seem to have been confirmed regarding the five ASC sisters. Bishop Sekey informed us on the radio this morning that two aspirant sisters from the convent in Gardnersville reached Gbarnga and reported that three of the sisters had been killed outside their convent, and the other two somewhere up the road from there.

There was no room for doubt. The five ASC sisters, all American citizens, from the state of Illinois, were Barbara Ann Muttra, Joel Kolmer, Shirley Kolmer, Kathleen McGuire and Agnes Mueller. The Kolmers were first cousins.

***

A native of Springfield Illinois, and first professed as a sister with the ASC in 1943, Barbara Ann Muttra had been due to celebrate her Golden Jubilee[9] in religious life within a matter of months. She had enjoyed an adventurous life. Qualifying and then ministering as a nurse she had worked first in hospitals in the U.S. and then in CRS refugee camps during the Vietnam war, before going to Liberia in 1971. Her career there, over 21 years, had been largely devoted to a healthcare apostolate.[10] At the time of her murder she had been operating a clinic at Klay, 15 miles west of Monrovia, and behind NPFL lines. To reach this clinic from her convent in Gardnersville required braving a series of ECOMOG and NPFL checkpoints daily.

Mary Joel Kolmer, born in Waterloo, Illinois, in 1934, had joined the ASC in July 1957. Volunteering for Liberia in 1982 she worked in parish ministry and religious education until 1985 when she took on a new commitment as 'Director of Aspirants', responsible for young Liberian women who came to the Gardnersville convent with a view to joining the ASC. A creative, artistic woman, at the time of her death, in addition to her other posts, she managed both the elementary and high school run by the archdiocese in Gardnersville.

Her first cousin, Shirley Kolmer, also from Waterloo, had taken her first vows with the ASC in 1947. Possessing intellectual gifts and leadership qualities which were obvious to her fellow-sisters, she had served on the ASC Provincial Council before going to Liberia in 1977 to take up a Fulbright Scholarship at the University of Monrovia. A year later, elected Provincial Superior, she returned to America, resuming her mission in Liberia at the end of her mandate in 1983. At the time of her death she was principal of St Patrick's High School – the archdiocese's premier school for boys - while residing in the Gardnersville convent.

Kathleen McGuire, born in December 1937 in Ridgway, Illinois, first professed her vows in July 1956, and then worked in the U.S., variously as a teacher in elementary and high schools. In 1990 she volunteered for Liberia and there assisted Shirley Kolmer at St Patrick's High School, as well as helping victims of trauma. On the day of her death she had felt ill and had remained in her convent instead of travelling to school.

Finally, Agnes Mueller, born in November 1929 at Bartelso, Illinois, first professed her vows in July 1948. Qualifying as a nurse she served for 18 years at St Vincent's Hospital, Taylorville, and St Clement Hospital, Red Bud, Illinois. In 1968 Mueller undertook a very different apostolate, that of religious education. There followed (1983–87) further service of the congregation as 'Formation Director' for aspirants and novices. She went to Liberia in 1987, working there in the pastoral field and with a special interest in women's literacy.

The religious community to which these women belonged was international, founded in Italy in 1834. Over the next century it had spread beyond Italian shores to Brazil, China, Guatemala, South Korea, Vietnam and the U.S., where by the 1970s its 400 members worked in St Louis, Missouri, Columbia, Pennsylvania, Ruma, Illinois and Wichita, Kansas. The congregation had a strong hands-on ethos, providing local communities with a wide range of education and healthcare services and paying special attention to the needs of the poor. Significantly, ASC sisters did not confine themselves to projects run by the congregation but helped to staff schools and hospitals and other community activities run by local dioceses.

The congregation first undertook a missionary apostolate after almost a century of existence, in 1933, when a group of sisters went to China. Further missionary outreaches took place to the Belgian Congo (1956) and Tanzania (1969). In 1971 in response to a request from Liberia the ASC's American Province opened a mission in that territory. The request had come from the Cape Palmas Vicariate[11] in south-eastern Liberia, staffed by the American SMA Province. Its bishop, Nicholas Grimley, commissioned his colleague, Philip Bagnasco, who had worked in Cape Palmas, to seek out a congregation of American sisters for the educational apostolate. The vicariate already had two sisterhoods at work in education. The Bernadine Sisters of Villanova, Pennsylvania, had come in 1956, while the Sisters of the Child Jesus of Vancouver came in 1966 to work in the town of Pleebo. Grimley planned to extend the education apostolate and commenced building schools in four other towns. And it was to staff 'one (or more)' of these, that the appeal was made to the ASC at its Ruma headquarters.

***

The first public statement on the killings came from Archbishop Michael Francis, on the same day the news broke, when he told an inquiring Reuter's correspondent that the sisters had been murdered by fighters loyal to Taylor. Confirmation that the NPFL was directly involved, he said, had come to him that very day through eyewitnesses. Although he did not identify them, he was referring to two ASC aspirants who had been taken from the convent by NPFL soldiers, brought to Kakata, but had managed to escape, eventually reaching Gbarnga and Bishop Sekey's compound. He, in turn, at some risk – his compound adjoined Taylor's headquarters – passed the information to Archbishop Francis by telephone.

The Vatican's *Osservatore Romano* office also reported the killings on 31 October, citing Archbishop Francis as its source. A Vatican Radio news bulletin announced that in addition to the five sisters, the four Liberian aspirants living in the Gardnersville convent had been killed. In fact, there had been five aspirants and all had been spared.[12] Quick off the mark, on the same day, the NPFL denied any involvement. John Richardson*, one of Taylor's senior aides, emphatically told his BBC World Service interlocutor that the bishop was misled:

> I don't know where the bishop gets his information. Did he find the bodies? If this (killing) took place it was not in any area controlled by NPFL.

---

*   According to the LTRC 'John T Richardson, code-named "General Octopus", was the mastermind behind the planning and execution of "Operation Octopus", assisted by General John Teah, NPFL Commanding General' (LTRC, Consolidated Final Report, vol. 2, 61). Richardson is also listed in the report among the 116 Liberians designated 'Most Notorious Perpetrators', 352.

In any case, he added, at the time of the killings Gardnersville had been occupied by Senegalese troops belonging to ECOMOG; and he could assure the public 'that these nuns were never in our area' and that the NPFL never had 'secure control of Gardnersville.' This information was manifestly false on all counts.

Taylor also took to the airwaves later that Saturday night. Broadcasting from Gbarnga, he declared that what had happened to the nuns was 'unclear' and insisted his forces had never controlled the area around their convent. In the U.S., Taylor's press spokesperson, J. Garswa Yarmeto*, who at the time was receiving medical treatment in Newark, New Jersey, was emphatic. 'We categorically deny having had anything to do with the murder of the five nuns.... We are completely innocent.' The NPFL, he confided, had 'no knowledge' as to who had killed the nuns.[13]

Further details of what had happened began to filter out of Monrovia, most of it based on Archbishop Francis's statement and a homily delivered by him to an overflowing congregation of deeply shocked Liberians in the cathedral on Sunday 1 November. Francis had told the correspondent that Barbara Ann Muttra and Mary Joel Kolmer disappeared on the evening of 20 October when they left the convent to accompany a sick child** to the Catholic Hospital. They had been killed along the road. The other sisters, last seen in their convent on 22 October, 'had been killed outside the gate of their residence.'

The State Department's first reaction came on Friday 1 November, in a statement expressing shock and dismay, condemning 'this cowardly act', and declaring the killings had taken place 'apparently several days ago in an area under the control of forces loyal to Charles Taylor.'[14] Another State Department briefing, given on 7 November, was quick to point the finger at that bugbear of U.S. foreign policy, Libyan leader Muammar Qaddafi. He, it was said, had been funnelling weapons through Burkina Faso to rebel leader Taylor in an effort to install a radical government in Liberia 'and perhaps exert influence on the entire region.'[15]

Consequently, the U.S. administration was currently recalling its ambassador from Burkina Faso to protest against that country's involvement. In further official and unofficial briefings State Department officials explained that Libya had been active in the conflict from the time of Taylor's invasion but had recently 'increased its arms shipments using Burkina Faso as a transit point.' This had created the scenario which enabled Taylor to launch Operation Octopus, which in turn had led to the killings of the Sisters. The State Department skilfully steered clear of anything which might have suggested that

---

*   Like Emmanuel Bowier, Doe's spokesperson and Minister for Information, Garswa Yarmeto also turned to religion, going to the U.S. in 1999, studying at a Divinity College, and later founding his own ministry.

** In virtually all subsequent accounts the Sisters, accompanied by the convent watchman, were described as taking medicine to the watchman's home in nearby Barnersville where there was a sick member of the family. There is no mention of an attempt to take a sick child to the Catholic hospital. Such a journey would have been impossible in the chaotic circumstances of that period.

U.S. policy bore the least responsibility for what had happened. With Libya and Burkina Faso to blame what need was there of further analysis!

Meanwhile Taylor continued his broadcasts from Gbarnga, saying that the Gardnersville suburb of Monrovia had been 'really no man's land' and concluding that 'it is anybody's guess what has happened to those nuns.' In one broadcast NPFL radio had little doubt but that the sisters had been killed by 'fleeing Nigerian soldiers.' Later Taylor was to repeat the claim that the area had been controlled by Senegalese troops, adding that they were, 'a bunch of Moslems and they are the ones who killed the Catholic nuns.'[16]

***

Lee Cahill's first dispatch to Cork in the wake of the news of the Gardnersville killings, sent on 2 November, described the latest developments in Operation Octopus. On day 18 of the siege ECOMOG planes had attacked Taylor's headquarters in Gbarnga. In Monrovia Spriggs Payne airport was still under attack from NPFL mortars, missiles and rockets; and there had been civilian casualties. Nonetheless, Cahill had managed to take Jenkins to the airport and put him on a flight out to safety. Jenkins had been badly shaken during the blitzing of Bushrod island some days previously and was deeply distressed at the killings of the sisters. For the previous two years he had worked closely with Muttra, whose clinic at Klay was located in his parish of Tubmanburg. It had been a hazardous evacuation. While waiting to board a plane to Abidjan an incoming flight from Nigeria drew heavy fire from NPFL guns to which an accompanying ECOMOG jet replied with rockets. Everyone in the airport took cover on the ground. Eventually, after an hour the incident was over, and Jenkins' plane took to the air. He was to reach London on Tuesday 3 November.

Yet the overriding thoughts of all the priests and sisters and the Catholic community were with the slain ASC nuns. On 1 November, All Saints Day, the churches everywhere had been packed, and the Catholic mission was receiving sympathy from all quarters. On the following day, the feast of All Souls when the dead customarily are remembered, a Requiem Mass for the sisters was celebrated in a crowded cathedral, with large numbers unable to gain access, thronging the adjacent streets. The general sorrow was rendered even more intense by the fact that the human remains of the Sisters could not be given the dignity of shelter and reverence in the sanctuary of the cathedral. No one was sure where the bodies lay, and this would remain the case as long as Gardnersville was occupied by the NPFL.

As for the two aspirants who had surfaced in Gbarnga and brought news of the sisters' slaying to Bishop Sekey, Mike Moran (American SMA Regional) identified them as Joetta Sorwood and Rebecca Byeh.[17] They had escaped from the NPFL in Kakata making their way to Bishop Sekey's residence in Gbarnga. There, after listening to their account, the bishop confided them to the care of Sister Miriam O'Brien, a St Louis Sister, Director of the Pastoral Centre adjacent to the bishop's house. Their account was eventually written down and brought to Danané by a colleague of Miriam O'Brien's at the Centre. It then made its way to Ruma, Illinois, courtesy of the Jesuit Refugee Centre in Danané. There was no news of the other aspirants (Helena Koplah Tweh, Bethshela Goe and Agatha Jley Blamoh) who, in Moran's view, 'must have been behind the lines in Greater Liberia, since they did not come to the Requiem Mass.'

The transcription of the aspirants' account makes chilling reading.[18] According to the written eye-witness statement:

> On Tuesday, 20 October, Sisters Barbara-Ann Mutra and Joel Kolmer took the convent 'security man', to visit a sick member of his family. They did not return. Three days later, on 23 October, a group of NPFL soldiers appeared at the gate under the command of 'C.O. Devil.' Sister Kathleen and the Lebanese man[*] went out to meet them. The soldiers asked for the car keys. Having received the keys C.O. Devil shot Sister Kathleen in the arm, and she fell to the ground. The same bullet hit the Lebanese man who died on the spot.[19] Then C.O. Devil fired again, hitting Sister Kathleen in the neck and killing her. Next, he ordered the other Sisters and the Aspirants to come out from the house. He directed them to walk out onto the road but insisted that the Sisters stay separate from the Aspirants. Sister Shirley begged him to spare their lives. But he ignored her and killed both sisters on the road, just outside the gate and fence.

The group of soldiers then drove the distraught aspirants away. Minutes later they saw the bodies of Sisters Barbara and Joel on one side of the road, and those of the ECOMOG soldiers and convent watchman on the other side. The bodies of the two sisters were covered with a piece of cloth and were already decomposing.

According to the aspirants' account, the soldiers did not harm them but transported them some 60 miles to the Kakata district, where the NPFL had a large military base located on the outskirts of the town. Aspirant Helena asked for permission to buy a pair of slippers, which was accorded. She went alone and never came back. The soldiers found a room in the vicinity of the barracks for the other aspirants but it was too small to accommodate all three. For this reason Bethshela had to stay in another place separated from Rebecca and Joetta. They did not see anything of Bethshela subsequently and soon managed to evade their captors, eventually reaching St Christopher's parish church, Kakata. There an elderly man advised them to see the bishop, giving them money for transport to Gbarnga.

***

> The two reached the mission at 9:30 pm on the same day (Friday). They came to the bishop's place and related the whole event with great fear and with tears. Then the Bishop brought the two Aspirants to Sr Miriam Therese O'Brien, who took charge of them.

[*] The Lebanese was a businessman – one of a number of Lebanese and their families who had taken refuge in the Convent compound.

In the dark days following news of the killings fighting intensified, rendering several suburban areas of the city chaotic and lawless. However, Taylor's forces were gaining no new ground and there were signs that the tide was beginning to turn. The fighting and shelling was still concentrated mostly on the outskirts of the city, in the vicinity of Pipeline, Jacob town (near Gardnersville) and New Georgia.[20] People could walk up as far as the boundaries of St Anthony's parish (Gardnersville) from the Freeport side of the city and as far as Double Bridge from the Red Light side. Caldwell, which had been under threat, was now secured by ECOMOG and traffic from Monrovia was moving out as far as Klay and Tubmanburg. Planes, too, were still landing in Spriggs Payne, while Air Ivoire, which had recently cancelled its flights, announced that it was to recommence operations immediately.

In short, Taylor's plan to overrun Monrovia seemed to be stalled. Moran was able to report on 6 November that in the previous three days no incoming shell had landed within the metropolitan area. And although there had been 'a lot of indiscriminate killing of civilians, mainly by the NPFL, AFL and ULIMO factions, ECOMOG seemed to be growing in strength and exercising more control.[21]

In the same report Moran re-asserted that there was little doubt as to who were the perpetrators of the Gardnersville killings. The eyewitness accounts invoked by Archbishop Francis at the Requiem Mass in the cathedral, had left little room for doubt. As for the sombre issue of the recovery of the Sisters bodies, Moran explained that this had not been possible since Gardnersville remained inaccessible. And although U.S. embassy staff and 'Church officials' had appealed to Taylor for safe passage to enter the area, the situation was not encouraging. Already, on 30 October three ECOMOG soldiers who had entered the convent area in search of the nuns — then missing — had been ambushed and killed.

***

As early as 3 November Archbishop Francis, while still pointing the finger at the NPFL, was widening the list of those he deemed responsible. On that day in an interview given in Monrovia he declared that the Reagan and Bush administrations had to share some of the responsibility for reducing Liberia to the state which allowed the murder of the nuns to occur. The Reagan administration had given half a billion dollars to President Samuel Doe in the first four years following his coup, 'more than they had given in the entire history of this country.' Furthermore the U.S. had ignored the fact 'that most of the money lined the pockets of Doe and a clique from his Krahn tribe while he oppressed a nation of 2.3 million people, killing opponents and winning U.S. approval for rigged elections in 1985.' In return for turning a blind eye, Francis continued, the U.S. had been given 'carte blanche to use Liberia as a CIA listening post through Voice of America installations and the Omega navigation plant', enabling them, among other things, to monitor Soviet satellite communications. An account of the interview was published by the *St Louis Post-Dispatch*, on 6 November, and it is unlikely that the archbishop's trenchant views would have gone unnoticed by the State Department. Whatever the case, it was at this time that the State Department gave its defensive briefing outlining the reasons for the recall of its ambassador from Burkina Faso and implicating Libya in the crisis.

***

In the meantime, the war raged on. Militarily, ECOMOG, whose forces had increased from some 7,000 to 12,000 soldiers since the commencement of Octopus, at last appeared to be going on the offensive, slowly pushing back rebel forces and attacking their supply lines. On 16 November ECOMOG aircraft bombed a large NPFL arms arsenal at the Firestone plantation near Harbel, killing some 200 people according to Gbarnga radio, or 38, according to a neutral source. At much the same time Associated Press was estimating that since the commencement of Octopus on 15 October some 3,000 people, mainly civilians, had already died.[22] The results of war were plain for all to see. In Monrovia and its hinterland casualties floated on the surface of swamps while the limbs of those buried in shallow graves broke surface. Dr Ruth Tshabalala, the World Health Organisation's director in Monrovia, informed a meeting of medical personnel that 'masses of bodies' were now littering the suburbs. The dead, she said, lay 'in dozens and in tens of dozens.'

In the midst of the chaos and confusion rumours, some true most unfounded, abounded. It was said that ECOMOG's Senegal contingent was preparing to withdraw because of frustration at the ineptitude of other contingents in fighting the rebels. There was a rumour too that four U.S. ships carrying marines were on their way to 'liberate Liberia.' But over-arching this anarchic canvas was the civil war's second signature atrocity. The first had been the massacre of some 600 refugees seeking sanctuary in St Peter's Lutheran Church, by Doe's forces, on 29 July 1990. This, the second, was the savage slaying by the forces of Taylor of five non-Liberian women, who had come to serve the people, but now lay dead, their bodies unclaimed and unburied.

***

Apart from some anodyne, exculpatory statements by the State Department when the slayings were first reported, reaction from the Bush administration was subdued, virtually absent. Within the U.S. legislature, however, it was another matter. On 19 November the House of Representatives Subcommittee on Africa convened a hearing on 'U.S. policy in Liberia', inviting Sister Mary Margaret Kopisch ASC (a member of the Provincial leadership team) to give detailed information on the killing of her five fellow sisters.

Deputising at the hearing for Assistant Secretary Herman Cohen, Leonard H. Robinson resolutely distanced the U.S. from any responsibility for the crisis. 'The lion's share' of the blame, he told the gathering, was to be attributed to Taylor and the NPFL, who had refused 'to implement the accords signed at Yamoussoukro and Geneva.'* And the remaining guilt rested with the 'other

---

*   The reference to Geneva was to 'an informal consultative meeting of the ECOWAS Committee of Five' which took place there during 6–7 April 1992, at the Ivorian President's winter home. Changes to the timetables laid down at Yamoussoukro IV (30 October 1991) for ECOMOG's deployment and the completion of disarmament were agreed, and other matters were briefly touched upon. A short time later Taylor claimed that he had signed under duress and described the talks as a 'rat-trap' set to catch him (see Adekeye Adebajo, op. cit., 103).

warring factions', each demonstrating 'a willingness to resume hostilities.' Taylor was guilty of repudiating

> the 7 April Geneva accord within hours of signing it; executing six cap-tured Senegalese ECOMOG soldiers, humiliating 625 ECOMOG troops sent to supervise encampment and disarmament; murdering five American nuns...conscripting boys as young as 10 years old and sending them drugged into battle...[23]

However such crimes would not result in U.S. intervention because this was a regional crisis which must be resolved by the region – 'through the leadership of ECOWAS.' Nowhere in his statement did Robinson admit any responsibility, much less guilt, on the part of the Reagan or Bush administrations. Centrally, he ignored U.S. recognition and support of the calamitous Doe regime, justified at the time by claims that the coup leader was no better or no worse than most other West African leaders, but in reality driven by an appraisal of America's strategic interests which took precedence over any moral consideration. Nor did Robinson make any reference to Liberia's historic and moral ties with the U.S.

A question from the floor of the hearing about the role of Burkina Faso in supplying arms to the NPFL gave Robinson an opportunity to describe how busy the U.S. had been about that issue. Assistant Secretary Herman Cohen, he said, had met President Blaise Compaoré in 1990, exacting an assurance that the flow of arms and other materials would cease. Unfortunately this assurance had not been honoured; nor was a further assurance obtained by Robinson himself in March 1991, and others secured by American officials at the First African-American summit[24] (April, 1991) and at Compaoré's house in Burkina Faso.[25]

***

Sister Margaret Mary Kopish was the member of her congregation's council given special responsibility for the Liberian mission. Her most recent visit to Liberia had taken place in January 1990 and she had been due to travel there again on 20 November. Speaking calmly, Kopish gave a matter-of-fact account of what was known about the killings of the five sisters. This was the first authoritative chronological account, drawn from an intensive investigation of the circumstances, which included interviews with the two aspirants who had witnessed the events at the Gardnersville convent.[26]

Kopish's testimony not only cut through the rumour and conjecture sur-rounding the tragedy but also captured something of its true horror. It uncon-sciously portrayed a group of blameless women suddenly thrust into the heart of evil. What is most frightening about the account is its matter-of-factness:

> Our convent house is located about 8–10 blocks from the Gardnersville mission. The Sisters were at the mission church on Tuesday, 20 October, for morning worship. That afternoon, two of the Sisters, Joel Kolmer and Barbara Ann Muttra, set out to take medicine to an ill member of their watchman's family. On the way they picked up two ECOMOG soldiers

who stopped them for a lift and were later ambushed by NPFL forces. All persons in the vehicle were killed. Their vehicle was taken, and their bodies were left on the side of the road.

When the other Sisters went to Mass next morning they reported [to the pastor, James Hickey][27] that the two [Sisters] had not returned home the night before ... The fighting intensified on Wednesday afternoon and Thursday. It was on Friday, 23 October, that NPFL soldiers appeared at the convent gate and demanded the keys for the other convent vehicle. When Sister Kathleen McGuire and the Lebanese watchman went to the gate, the soldiers received the keys and then shot Kathleen in the arm. That same bullet killed the Lebanese man and then another shot was fired and hit Kathleen in the neck and killed her. The soldiers then told the two remaining Sisters, Shirley Kolmer and Agnes Mueller, and the four aspirants to walk out of the compound and directed the Sisters to stay apart from the others. Shirley begged that their lives be spared, but they were shot, both Shirley and Agnes. Early reports, a week following these incidents, stated that the bodies were still outside the convent gate in the road.

Although no mention is made of it, beneath the layers of the account is evident the deep sense of anxiety which must have encompassed the Gardnersville convent on the night that Joel Kolmer and Barbara Ann Muttra failed to return, and which was to become more profound on the following days. Unable to move outside the convent because of the intensification of the fighting, it was now impossible to make contact with the outside world, a world which, in any case, had become chaotic. Three days later that chaos was to arrive within the convent compound, when the Sisters were robbed, set apart and shot without mercy. There was little more to be said about the actual events of that week, Kopish told the hearing, apart from an expression of pride at the lives of these sisters, and a wish that the bodies might be returned so that a 'proper Christian burial' might take place.

In concluding her testimony, as might have been expected with a congregation of Sisters known for a strong social conscience, Kopish focused on what steps needed to be taken to address Liberia's current crisis. Flying in the face of the U.S. administration's analysis that Liberia was a regional problem which must be solved by the regional powers, Kopish called for a concerted international response, one in which the United Nations, 'working in close collaboration with ECOWAS', would take the central role and in which the U.S. must play a meaningful part. Her recommendation stopped short of a call for the deployment of U.S. soldiers but only just. It appealed for U.S. assistance with the deployment of 'UN observers, fact-finders and peace-keepers.' It also called for the provision of significant humanitarian aid through the enacting of the U.S. Liberian Relief, Rehabilitation and Reconstruction Act and the intervention of the Legislature's Foreign Operations Subcommittee and Appropriations Committee. The private sector, too, those 'large American

210 Liberia's First Civil War

corporations involved in the rubber and diamond … industries in Liberia', should also play their part. 'It should not be too much to hope', she concluded:

> that at this time, when even the lives of five American religious women have been given for the welfare of the people of Liberia we would, as a nation and as members of the world community, move swiftly to channel needed human, material, and financial resources to restore peace and rebuild Liberia.

Kopish's testimony was followed by expressions of condolence from various members of the legislature while the State Department's representative (Robinson) was commended for remaining at the hearing for the duration of her testimony, something curiously described as 'unusual.'

There followed, as promised, the testimony of those representing various political and social strands of Liberian society. Speaking on behalf of the NPFL was Taylor's Minister for Foreign Affairs, Momolu Sirleaf,[28] formerly a journalist jailed by the Doe regime. He blamed Liberia's crisis on ECOMOG which, he claimed, was waging an unjust war, 'introducing chemical-warfare and bombing schools and hospitals.' There existed, he said, secret documents which showed that the U.S. approved these cluster bombs 'to flush out Taylor.' Was there not, continued Sirleaf, a plot hatched by ECOMOG to assassinate Taylor driven by the Senegalese who had suffered humiliation and losses and wanted revenge? And had not the State Department been approached by ECOMOG for approval of such an enterprise? In such circumstances, therefore, when there was incontrovertible proof of ECOMOG's partisanship, he concluded, 'only UN intervention could save Liberia; only that organisation could stop the genocide.' Sirleaf had come a long way from his crusading anti-corruption journalism in the pages of *Footprints*.

Sirleaf's testimony, which brought echoes of the daily rantings of Taylor on Gbarnga radio into the solemn halls of the U.S. Congress, must have been dispiriting for the ASC nuns attending the hearing. Asked by one of the congressmen about the deaths of the five sisters, Sirleaf simply repeated what Taylor had been telling Liberians since news broke of their slaying: namely that the NPFL did not control Gardnersville at the time of their disappearance and so could have had nothing to do with whatever had happened to them; that claims of NPFL involvement had originated with Archbishop Francis who was not in a position to know anything; and that the NPFL were concerned for the sisters and were praying for them.

Notes

1 A house in which the Regional Superior, responsible for the welfare of his confreres, resided and where meetings took place. Missionaries visiting Monrovia from long distance were accommodated there.
2 A.B. Cahill to Quinlan, 17 October 1992.
3 Ibid.
4 His contact was Brother Benjamin Cornago, Hospitallers of St John of God.

5 A.B. Cahill to Harkin, SMA House, Monrovia, (Fax), 24 October 1992.

6 Ibid, To Harkin, 24 October 1992.

7 Ibid, 28 October1992.

8 Garry Jenkins is a member of the British Province of the SMA. He is currently (as at 2021) the longest serving Catholic missionary in Liberia having arrived there in 1972.

9 50 years.

10 Operating clinics and educating primary healthcare workers.

11 Cape Palmas was erected as a full diocese in 1981.

12 A.T. Mike Moran to S. John Murray, 5 December 1992 (Fax).

13 The Washington Post, 1 November 1992.

14 The statement made the point that 'these innocent women had no role in Liberia's civil war and were in the country to work with orphaned children and other victims of the conflict', a fact that made the killings 'all the more repugnant.'

15 See, St Louis Post-Dispatch, November 1992.

16 AFJN Information (Washington DC), 15 November 1992.

17 A.T., Moran to Tenafly, 2 November 1992.

18 It was placed on record by Sister Mary Margaret Kopish in her testimony to the congressional hearing on 19 November 1992.

19 The wife of the Lebanese man was one of the many witnesses to these killings.

20 Ibid, 6 November 1992 (Fax).

21 Ibid.

22 AFJN Information, 20 November 1992 (quoting AP, Monrovia, 16 November 1992).

23 Testimony by Leonard H. Robinson Jr, 19 November 1992.

24 A meeting of Africans and African-Americans held in Abidjan, 16–19 April 1991 (organised by the Rev. Leon Sullivan).

25 A.T. Notes on Hearing of House Subcommittee on Africa, 19 November 1992. See transcript of hearing, https://babel.hathitrust.org/cgi/pt?id=uc1.31210009418847; view=1up;seq=35 (accessed 31 January 2018).

26 Their written eyewitness account of the killings had reached the Ruma ASC headquarters courtesy of John S. Murray, in Tenafly. It had been smuggled out of Liberia on 7 November 1992.

27 Author's insertions in brackets.

28 A crusading journalist during the Doe regime and publisher of the frequently suppressed New Footprints, he was twice arrested (See pp.). Later, a Taylor loyalist, he served twice as Foreign Minister in IGNU governments, nominated by Taylor's faction (1993–94, 1995–96).

16 Francophone members of ECOWAS and the UN begin to play a more active role in securing a political settlement

The initial ECOWAS response to the Octopus offensive reflected the composition of that body. A meeting comprising the Francophone 'Committee of Five'* together with the ECOWAS Standing Mediation Committee, which took place in late October, concluded without any meaningful progress apart from scheduling yet another meeting to take place in Abuja on 7 November 1992. The Anglophone nations, led by Nigeria and Sierra Leone, had pushed for a major military offensive against the NPFL, while Francophone Ivory Coast and Burkina Faso sought UN intervention. The projected Abuja meeting, to be attended by the heads of states of nine nations, was a crisis summit taking place against a sobering awareness that the diplomatic path to a solution which ECOWAS had ploughed for over two years was now on the point of collapse. This was reflected in the measures agreed. When the meeting took place sanctions against member states engaged in supplying arms to the warring factions – in the air since the previous July – were formally imposed. The meeting also requested the UN Security Council to assist in applying these embargoes not only to offending member states, but to the international community. Perhaps most significant of all was a request to the Security Council for the appointment of a special representative 'to cooperate with ECOWAS in the implementation of the ECOWAS peace plan.'[1] Such an appointment, if made, would at last ensure a direct involvement (however limited) by the world's policing body. Another measure – one which was to cause much controversy - was an authorisation given to ECOMOG to use force in preventing the shipment of arms to the NPFL and in implementing encampment and disarmament. This measure, in a more definite fashion than that heralded earlier by the bombing of Buchanan port in November 1990 altered ECOMOG's status as a 'peace-keeping force' to that of a 'peace-enforcement body', although a formal declaration of the change was still lacking.

On 19 November 1992 the UN Security Council responded to the ECOWAS request for assistance with Resolution 788, imposing an embargo on the export of arms to Liberia (except to ECOMOG contingents) and, a day later, appointing Trevor Livingston Gordon-Somers[2] as the 'Special Representative

---

* See p. 173.

DOI: 10.4324/9781003219309-21

of the UN Secretary General for Liberia.' He would be expected to visit Liberia and make recommendations to Secretary-General Boutros Boutros Ghali on what might be done to support the ECOWAS-led peace process. The UN, it must be said, already had a representative in Liberia since December 1990 (Mr Ross Mountain) whose role was to co-ordinate the UN's numerous humanitarian aid programmes. Gordon-Somers role would be predominantly political.

The ECOWAS imposition of a ban on the export of arms to the NPFL and its endorsement by the Security Council was to prove largely ineffective. Although ECOMOG was now empowered to stop the flow of military supplies, it lacked the resources to do so, its energies being fully concentrated on pushing the NPFL out of the Monrovia enclave back into Greater Liberia. The appointment of a 'Special Representative', too, appeared to long-finger the UN's response to the crisis, his role being to observe and recommend courses of action. On the other hand, it indicated that, however tentative, the UN had taken a step towards a greater level of involvement.

While weak in action, the UN (through its General Assembly, Security Council and General Secretariat) was strong in rhetoric. The Security Council communiqué, expressing much regret at Liberia's failure to implement Yamoussoukrou IV, appealed to the warring factions to accept that accord as the best option for bringing about peace, and urged member states to continue humanitarian assistance for displaced persons and refugees. It also fulsomely commended ECOWAS for its 'untiring efforts' towards brokering a peace, condemned the violations of the various ceasefires as well as the attacks on ECOMOG and called on all parties to respect 'international humanitarian law.' It was clear that at this stage the UN, much like the U.S., had no stomach for a substantial involvement in the crisis. It would support ECOWAS diplomatic and military initiatives as best it could and continue to address the humanitarian crisis through its many agencies[3] but did not regard the Liberian civil war as a threat to international peace. The regional instability currently manifesting itself as a result of the conflict, if not to be ignored, was of insufficient importance to merit a more robust response.

***

NPFL discipline continued to deteriorate. In Buchanan few of those who had welcomed Charles Taylor as liberator now had any illusions. Robberies, destruction of property and the random killing of civilians, had become commonplace and the people were tired. The Catholic mission was not immune as Jennings was to find out on 18 November (1992).

> About 10 or 12 members of the NPFL came demanding the pick-up. I refused to give them the keys. They beat up our security man badly. Then one of them took a bottle of water and threatened to break it on my head. Still I resisted. After about two hours they left, saying they would return in the morning. Sure enough they did come back and this time were much more aggressive. When I refused, one of them pointed his gun and said he

would shoot me. He then walked into my bedroom and took the keys. Finding that he could not start the engine – it had been disconnected as a safety measure – he pushed the vehicle out onto the road and was trying to reconnect it when lo and behold who should arrive but 'Jack the rebel', a senior officer[4]. He arrested the culprits and took them away. Later that day we parked the pick-up in one of the empty containers to keep it out of sight.[5]

* * *

On the night of Sunday 29 November news reached the ASC community in Ruma that, at last, the bodies of three of the missing sisters had been recovered. Earlier that day ECOMOG forces had managed to push the NPFL out of the vicinity of the Gardnersville convent. The grim discovery had been made hours later by Mike Moran and two representatives of the U.S, Embassy, wearing bulletproof vests and escorted by ECOMOG soldiers. This had been the third attempt to enter the area. Four bodies had been found lying outside the convent gate – those of Shirley Kolmar, Kathleen McGuire, Agnes Mueller and the Lebanese businessman. All had died of bullet wounds. The bodies were brought to the American embassy where a UN pathologist, at the request of the embassy, commenced forensic tests with a view to confirming the identities of the deceased and paving the way for repatriation.

On the following day, a statement by Mildred Gross, the ASC Provincial Superior, expressed gratitude that the remains had been recovered and hope that efforts to reach those of Barbara Ann Muttra and Mary Joel Kolmer might be successful. In the meantime arrangements were being made to repatriate the remains of those recovered, while medical and dental records were being assembled in Ruma to confirm their identities, since the bodies had lain unclaimed since 20 October. Gross also took the opportunity to explain that all five sisters had already brushed with death during the height of the civil war violence in 1990. Luckily on that occasion they been evacuated in time and returned to the States. However, following the Yamoussoukrou IV and subsequent ceasefire, they had decided to return to Liberia.

* * *

Shirley Kolmer, Agnes Mueller and Kathleen McGuire had died on 23 October. Their remains had been recovered some seven weeks later on 29 November. Now, at last, on 5 December, they were to be repatriated and laid to rest. On that day their remains were brought from St Joseph's Catholic hospital to Spriggs Payne airport. There the caskets were blessed by Archbishop Francis in the presence of as many of the priests, sisters and Catholic laity who could make their way to the airport. The caskets were then loaded onto a U.S. Air Force C-130 cargo plane which set out on the first phase of the long journey back to the U.S. After refuelling in Spain, the aircraft proceeded to Germany where the caskets were transferred to a larger aircraft for the transatlantic flight to Dover Air Force Base, Delaware. At about 9.30 on the evening of 7 December the aircraft finally reached its destination. After the passengers disembarked and the cargo was unloaded the caskets were placed in the middle of the plane and a brief service was conducted by an Air Force chaplain. In attendance were Gross, her assistant, Margaret Kopish, two members of each deceased Sister's family and S. John Murray of the American SMA Province. Four representatives of the U.S. State Department were also present. After the ceremony the caskets, covered in blue tie-dye cloth, were carried from the plane by an honor guard of Air Force soldiers and placed in a hearse for transportation to a morgue. Four days later, on Friday, 11 December, the Sisters' remains were flown to Lambert International Airport, St Louis, Missouri. The last stage of this sombre journey saw the caskets driven in hearses to the ASC American headquarters at Ruma – to the place from which each of them had set out for their mission to Liberia. It was a day of quietness and sadness, on which the deep resources of faith in the ASC community were called upon as never before.

There was little peace in Liberia on the day the remains of the ASC Sisters departed that country. Moran was to report that on that very day a salvo of NPFL rockets landing in the Logantown suburb of Monrovia – the parish of Frank Hynes - killed nine people and injured 16 more. Each of them, too, belonged to a family and a community and those who died were also grievously mourned. To history they remain among the nameless victims of Liberia's civil war.

The Sisters burial Mass took place on Sunday, 13 December. Archbishop Francis, who had arrived in the U.S. some days previously, was chief celebrant. After the Mass the Sisters were laid to rest in the cemetery within the Ruma convent compound. 'The general feeling', Murray noted, 'was one of relief that the bodies had been returned but there was also sadness because the bodies of Barbara Ann Muttra and Mary Joel Kolmer were not yet recovered.'

***

By the end of the second week of December the tide for the NPFL was ebbing sharply. On the previous weekend ECOMOG launched an offensive, driving Taylor's troops beyond Paynesville on the northeastern side of the city. Shelling by the NPFL was now sporadic, even rare, and the spirit of Christmas began to be experienced. Over the previous ten days ships had continued to enter Monrovia's Freeport and unload cargo. Rice was being widely distributed and food was no longer scarce. The water supply was fitful but adequate and new wells were being sunk.[6]

The NPFL was also under pressure in Bomi county and early on the morning of 9 December (1992) ULIMO troops entered Bong Mine. John Feeney described the course of events.

> Everything was very unsettled. Eight people were executed by the NPFL and a number were beaten unmercifully, all supposed to be connected to ULIMO. At 3 am the following morning the whole area exploded with the sound of gunfire. Twenty minutes later the mission house was shaken from its foundations as a rocket-propelled grenade made smithereens of the

church roof. The gunfire continued all day and ULIMO soldiers became as plentiful as ants while the NPFL fled for their lives. Hundreds of people fled with them. Unfortunately ULIMO are doing the very same thing as NPFL. They have killed a lot of people because of their supposed connection with NPFL.[7]

And there were also acts of tribal vengeance.

Poor Stephen Gondu. He used to serve Mass and never harmed anybody. He was of the Gio tribe. Two Mandingo soldiers caught him and cold-bloodedly put a bullet in his head.

Nor was the mission exempt from the zeal of the new invaders.

On the night of 13 December I was suddenly awakened when my door was shot open and I was ordered outside. There were ten soldiers looking for rebels and guns. They ransacked the whole house and took away some of my clothes, my money and food. An hour later six others burst through the house. They took away nearly everything that the others hadn't taken. A delightful night indeed.[8]

***

The discovery of the remaining missing bodies – those of Barbara Ann Muttra and Joel Kolmer – was first reported on 21 December. Moran described how accompanied by a U.S. Embassy 'military person' and protected by ECOMOG they found the burnt-out car and human remains. The car was completely overturned but Moran was able to identify its number plate.[9] Later that day he was able to assure S. John Murray by fax that he was confident the remains were those of the sisters, 'corresponding almost to the letter' to the particular descriptions he had been given. Murray could now pass on this information to Gross at Ruma. Like those of the three sisters already lying in the Ruma cemetery, the remains of Sister Barbara Ann and Sister Joel were borne to the Catholic hospital where they would await repatriation to the U.S. early in the new year. Already a tentative date for their burial – 17 January – had been set. Some days after the news became public Murray noted that no U.S. newspaper, radio or television station had reported the recovery of the bodies.[10]

On the day of Moran's sombre trip to recover the remains of the two sisters there was an influx into the Gardnersville area of thousands of former inhabitants, not to stay – the area was still regarded as unsafe – but to see the conditions of their homes. Many were to discover those homes no longer existed or were damaged beyond repair. But some were surprised to find their property almost intact. Moran reported that the High School was the 'most damaged of the archdiocese's seven buildings in Gardnersville.' The new Health Center was the 'least damaged.' As for the convent, it was being used by ECOMOG.

***

Particularly distressing for the ASC Sisters and their families were reports, circulating not only in Liberia but also in the U.S., that the murdered sisters might have been molested or mutilated. Some radio stations had gone so far as to contact Ruma headquarters in Illinois in connection with this speculation and a call had been received also from the State Department. S. John Murray was able to address these concerns authoritatively having received information from Moran to the effect that the speculation had no foundation. Moran had been among those who found the bodies, had formally identified them and was present at the time of the initial autopsies. He was able to assure Murray that, in the first case, the sisters had been shot in an ambush and left at the scene and, in the second, they had been shot outside the convent gate in the presence of witnesses, who testified that they had neither been beaten, tortured or molested in any way prior to their deaths.'[11] As for the sisters first killed, there was no contrary evidence from the observations of those present when they were found or from the subsequent autopsies. Initially Murray had decided not to release this information out of delicacy but when rumours began to take hold and when consulted by Mildred Gross, he decided to break his silence. Gross was greatly relieved to receive the information which she passed on to her community and to the families of the slain sisters. On the day the bodies arrived in Ruma for burial, she was to write to Moran thanking him for sharing details about the condition of the bodies with Murray. 'We have tried to be honest and open with the families through this entire process', not an easy undertaking in the circumstances, but the families had 'appreciated that approach.' Moran's sombre testimony, however difficult to bear, was at least the truth and had helped her and the families.

***

The year 1993 opened in a military and political stalemate and growing despair. Instead of disarmament there was entrenchment, with the various rebel factions showing no disposition towards complying with Yamoussoukrou IV and its subsequent variations. Taylor confidently addressed the nation in a press conference broadcast from Gbarnga on New Year's Eve. Calling on his fighters to 'stand firm and united', he shrugged off suggestions from reporters that the economic blockade of Greater Liberia imposed by ECOWAS, might bring him down. 'Blockades and embargoes never succeed in subduing a people.' It was simply a matter of tightening belts and growing more food.[12]

In Gbarnga cathedral, on the instructions of Bishop Sekey, the New Year's Eve celebrations were muted, as was befitting a Church in mourning in the wake of the Gardnersville killings. In Monrovia and its hinterland a deeply shocked Church was attempting to re-assert itself against a background of sporadic violence.[13] Early on New Year's Day fighting erupted at the front, near Robertsfield, leading to the deaths of two NPFL soldiers. On that same day Moran travelled to Gardnersville to celebrate the first Mass since the deaths of the sisters, while Jim Lee celebrated the first Mass in Pipeline district since its priests and sisters had been driven out. Gardnerville's war-scarred church was relatively full for the occasion. At Pipeline no more than a dozen managed to attend. Yet in both locations the people saw something of the real meaning of new beginnings. By now ECOMOG had consolidated its recaptured positions on Monrovia's outer ring, although isolated attacks, such as the one on 1 January, continued to occur. Further afield, ULIMO was making steady gains at the expense of the NPFL. Kakata was believed to have fallen to them and, like any location where NPFL and ULIMO had been engaged in fighting, was said to be largely destroyed. Other locations where impending battles looked likely were Harbel, Gbarnga, Voinjama, Buchanan and Zorzor.[14] While such battles were not imminent the people in those areas knew they stood in deadly danger; for, going on the past record, if war came, it would be waged without mercy.

***

Nothing had been heard for some weeks of John Feeney in Bong Mine (still in the hands of ULIMO). But now came good news that he was safe and had just arrived in Monrovia.[15] He had been sheltering in a parishioner's house after the mission, church and school had been looted when an ULIMO detachment came for him and escorted him to Monrovia. 'The trip', he confided to his diary, 'was an extremely hard one but I'll keep the details to myself.'[16] It seems that he was first marched in the direction of Tubmanburg, kept there overnight and then on the following day marched most of the way to Monrovia.[17] On the day after his arrival a local newspaper ran the headline: 'Catholic Priest rescued by ULIMO' causing Moran to comment wryly in a message to friends in Tenafly that 'having finished taking all his property of value, ULIMO decided to take him.' By way of explanation he conjectured that 'a number of the big people in the organisation' knew Feeney and were 'concerned that nothing should happen to him.'[18]

But it was not a conventional rescue.

Moran also wrote of another visit to Gardnersville — a week since he had celebrated Mass there — where he found continuing instability and anxiety.

> The people are returning and trying to get their lives back into some sort of shape, but the area is badly damaged and vulnerable.

However, he was heartened by the actions of Archbishop Francis, defiant as always, who was determined to restore Gardnersville mission and had already set in motion the repair of schools, church and mission house. He had also set a deadline of 8 February for the schools to re-open.

***

As noted above, the first serious political and diplomatic engagement by the UN in Liberia's crisis occurred on 20 November, 1992, with the appointment of Trevor Gordon-Somers as the 'Special Representative' of the Secretary General. Tasked to evaluate the situation and report back, Gordon-Somers first visited Liberia and the region in late November and early December 1992. During an initial fact-finding visit to Greater Liberia he met a Taylor proclaiming himself the victim of savage aggression by ECOMOG acting in collusion with the IGNU, ULIMO and the AFL. It will be remembered that since Octopus had stalled, Taylor had repeatedly alleged that ECOMOG was no longer neutral, a view which UN officials had consistently rebutted. Now, in a BBC interview given in Ghana, Gordon-Somers made it clear that the UN was still unwilling to accept such a construction. Yet there existed a body of evidence to the contrary.

On 18 January 1993 Monrovia Radio ELBC announced Gordon-Somers had again set foot in Liberia. He was there for the second time to meet with all the principals, including Taylor, Amos Sawyer and Major General Adetunji Olurin,[19] the recently appointed ECOMOG field commander. He would then go to Ivory Coast to confer with Félix Houphouët-Boigny before returning to New York to finalise his report. At a press conference before travelling, he referred to the instruction from Secretary-General Ghali that his role was not to replace but to work with ECOMOG. The UN, he said, considered ECOWAS and the UN as partners in implementing the UN peace initiative. During his meeting with the NPFL leader in Gbarnga Taylor again highlighted the 'victimisation of his people' by ECOMOG. And to make his point he conducted Gordon-Somers on a tour of ruined hospitals, schools, churches and food depots all which, he claimed, had been destroyed in ECOMOG bombing raids. When Gordon-Somers continued to insist that ECOMOG was a wholly neutral source, the NPFL leader became deeply angered. Nonetheless when appearing together at a joint press briefing at the end of the visit, Taylor declared his government's wholehearted commitment to a ceasefire, while alluding to some shortcomings in the Security Council's Resolution 788, principally its failure to extend the arms embargo to ECOMOG.[20] It appeared to some observers that Taylor's attempt to 'run rings around' the UN Representative was not wholly successful.[21]

***

Consistently in his dealings with the UN Taylor represented himself as the victim of plots to destroy him hatched by ECOMOG, ULIMO and the AFL. He considered himself not 'more sinned against than sinning', but in fact a sinless victim. Hence, he was not a little angered when Gordon-Somers' report to the UN Secretary General was finally published.[22] The UN's special representative, according to Taylor, had reported the NPFL's complaints about ECOMOG bombing rather than reporting the bombing as an 'established fact.'[23] This anger was to linger.

On 26 March, with the report finally tabled, the Security Council considered all aspects of the Liberian crisis. The result was the passage of Resolution 813 which re-endorsed the terms of Resolution 788, condemned the continuing attacks on ECOMOG and called on the combatants to 'respect strictly the provisions of international humanitarian law.' In addition, the UN Secretary General was mandated to investigate the feasibility of convening all parties to the conflict with a view to recommitting themselves to the provisions of Yamoussoukrou IV. This was an important development, marking an intensification of the UN's formal diplomatic engagement in the peace process. He was also asked to investigate how the UN might best assist ECOWAS and, in particular, to consider the possibility of sending UN observers to Liberia. This latter was perhaps the most significant development, signalling a willingness to move beyond rhetoric and engage on the ground beyond the current deployment of relief personnel.

***

Reference has already been made to the growing divisions within ULIMO. On 8 February, 1993, Alhaj G.V. Kromah announced that ULIMO would now throw in its lot with the IGNU and transfer all its conquests to that interim government. On the following day Raleigh Seekie declared that Kromah was no longer a leader of the movement and had no right to make any decisions on its future. Hot on his heels General Roosevelt Johnson (a Krahn), the current chief military commander of ULIMO, left the BBC's Robin White in no doubt where he stood:

> The military position is that we are not going to turn over our territories to the IGNU. We are fighting to liberate the Liberian people and we believe that ECOMOG is there as a neutral body to make peace. As for any turning over of our territory, the modalities will be worked out between us and ECOMOG, but we are not going to turn them over to the IGNU.[24]

Within a relatively short period the split was complete with two ULIMO militias, one known as ULIMO-K (mainly Mandingo) under the leadership of Alhaji G.V. Kromah with its headquarters in Tubmanburg; the other known as ULIMO-J (mainly Krahn) under the leadership of Roosevelt Johnson with its headquarters in Freetown, Sierra Leone. Soon came allegations from Seekie that Kromah had made efforts to have him assassinated.[25] Some months later, in June, Seekie was alleged to have returned the favour when two ULIMO-K commanders, Colonel Apollo Swen and Colonel Frederic Batti were arrested in Tubmanburg.[26] The officers, it was said, had been promised four vehicles each, 1,000 bags of rice, and $200,000 if they assassinated Kromah.

At much the same time new anti-Taylor factions were springing up like Hydra's heads while Taylor continued to maintain that he remained unchallenged.[27] Janet Fleischman[28] who assessed the situation during a March visit to Liberia on behalf of Human Rights Watch, was alarmed at the growing number of militias.

> At least two 'warlords' who broke off from NPFL have surfaced in Lofa County. And a shadowy [anti-NPFL] group called the Nimba Redemption Council has recently emerged in Nimba.[29]

Moreover, according to Fleischman, the activities of the ULIMO factions gave little hope that their proclaimed objective of removing the NPFL and returning Liberia to its people was any more real or sincere than the stated objectives of Taylor.

> ULIMO is now behaving like the NPFL, limiting the free movement of people and goods in its territory. It denied 'Africa Watch' a pass to travel to its areas without an ULIMO escort and it has established checkpoints where there is large-scale harassment. Summary executions, beatings, arbitrary arrests are the order of the day. ULIMO has accelerated the Liberian crisis by affirming people's worst fears – that there would be more warlords and more warring factions.

Certainly the task of securing encampment, disarmament and demobilisation was daily growing more challenging and the prospects of the combined ECOMOG-UN initiative ever achieving these objectives, steadily receding.

***

As February entered its second week ECOMOG announced that, having set fire to buildings and also to the nearby Firestone rubber plantation the NPFL had been driven out of Harbel. Ten days earlier it had reported the fall of Robertsfield international airport. NPRAG's spokesperson, Tom Woewiyu, speaking on the BBC, countered that, although both locations were under attack, neither had fallen.[30] As for the fires in Harbel, Woewiyu had a ready answer. The weather and ECOMOG were to blame!

> This is the dry season. ECOMOG has been launching long range barrel-missile rounds into Harbel. Aircraft have been dropping cluster bombs and firebombs all over the rubber plantation and the dry leaves catch fire …

Despite Woewiyu's denials, however, there could be no doubt that the NPFL was firmly on the back foot, under pressure from ULIMO-K and other militias, with ECOMOG pushing on relentlessly, in control of Robertsfield airport and with Firestone surrounded. The loss of Kakata to ULIMO-K, taken with earlier losses of territory and threats of more, meant that it was now virtually impossible for the NPFL to move personnel and materiel between Buchanan, Firestone, the Robertsfield area and Gbarnga. Moreover, the NPFL grip on Buchanan was perilously close to being lost.[31] A constant procession of ECOMOG heavy weaponry could be observed going up the roads from Monrovia toward Kakata and Robertsfield.[32] And there were now signs that, for his part, Taylor was withdrawing his heavy artillery to defend Nimba County from where his insurgency had started.[33] Even Gbarnga, Taylor's capital, was under threat. Sister Miriam O'Brien who had just returned from that town to Ireland for medical attention, described large numbers fleeing, terrified that an attack by ULIMO-K was imminent. And in Greater Liberia generally, she reported, sanctions were biting severely while, more ominously,

Taylor's rebel movement was beginning to fragment. She, along with many others, was of the view that Taylor now had no prospect of victory.[34] This was the second occasion when such a scenario was widely accepted within Liberia and further afield.* It proved to be a misjudgement, not because of any surge in NPFL military fortunes but because of a lack of resolve within ECOWAS, the UN and the international community.

***

By the third week of February Tony Jennings noted in his diary that fighting in the approaches to Buchanan, which included shelling from the sea, was becoming more frequent and that it was only a matter of time before ECOMOG reached the town. At the same time within the town's bounds the NPFL was getting 'more out of hand', more 'dangerously aggressive', to the extent that he felt he had no alternative to moving away for a period.[35] He would depart on 6 March, travelling with two parishioners, Dr and Mrs Jaya-suriya[36] whose three daughters already had been evacuated to Man (Ivory Coast). He would avoid Nimba County as much as possible before reaching Ganta. From there he would cross the Ivory Coast border to Danané and finally, via Man, proceed to Abidjan. The avoidance of the straightforward route through Nimba was dictated by the advance of two new anti-Taylor militias in that county, the larger being the so-called 'Nimba Redemption Council' which had recently capture the Logantuo border post and the towns of Karnplay and Yekepa.**

Jennings committed an account of this perilous journey to his diary.

> On 6 March we left Buchanan at 2.00 am estimating that we should be in Man by 10 am if all went well. We took the back road to the north of Gbarnga only to find many NPFL checkpoints with soldiers demanding money and threatening us with prison or death if we refused. It took us almost nine hours to reach Ganta, a journey of 143 miles. We continued our journey to find more and more aggressive checkpoints. At the Liberian border post we were pestered with demands for money for over two hours. When we finally crossed the border, some twelve hours after leaving Ganta, we were tired, hungry and mentally shattered, but thank God, still alive.[37]

First of all, Jennings would rest in Man and, when sufficiently recovered, would fly back to Monrovia to see whether it might be possible in calmer conditions to get back to Buchanan. In fact it was to be almost six weeks before he would again set foot in his mission and only then as a consequence of ECOMOG's finally wresting control of the town from the NPFL.[38]

---

*   The first occasion when NPFL military fortunes were at a low ebb occurred as 1990 came to a close. See p. 154 below.
** This faction was led by Karpeh Dwanyen, son of David Dwanyen, who had been executed by the NPFL.

***

On 5 March came news that Nigeria had increased the size of its contingent in Liberia from 8,000 to 10,000 to compensate for the withdrawal of the Senegalese troops the previous January. The total ECOMOG strength now stood at about 14,000 – representing a three-fold increase since Octopus.[39] In Liberia and further afield a consensus was growing that Taylor and the NPFL were on the verge of defeat, that there would be a last ditch stand by the rebel leader in Nimba County but that eventually the reinforced ECOMOG assisted by ULIMO-K, by the Nimba Redemption Council and by a second local anti-Taylor militia, would prevail. ECOMOG was already warning Nimba inhabitants not to let Taylor use their county for a 'last stand.'[40] And now, with persistent military setbacks, and the view that military defeat for Taylor appeared to be a foregone conclusion, even Taylor's staunchest supporters appeared to be losing heart.[41] But the causes of disillusionment with Taylor in Nimba went deeper than fear of defeat. The county's traditional leadership was now stirring, having being bypassed by Taylor who had chosen for his project a new leadership corps, of younger men in whom the desire for revenge against Krahn and Mandingo was 'especially pronounced.'[42]

***

It was at this juncture that the Holy See's gaze turned towards Liberia and a belated attempt was made to influence the course of events. Bishops Sekey and Dalieh arrived in Monrovia joining Archbishop Francis in welcoming the arrival from Rome of a high Vatican official, Cardinal Roger Etchegaray, the French head of the Pontifical Commission for Justice and Peace, who was accompanied by the Papal Nuncio to Liberia and other places, Archbishop Luigi Travaglino.[*] They had come on a peace mission. Not everyone was overjoyed at this development. Cahill, for one, was unimpressed. Taylor had once before received a reprieve from defeat by the intervention of diplomats. Now, when he was virtually surrounded and cut off from outside help, he might be given another opportunity to escape. 'Our fear is that he [the cardinal] wants to meet Taylor … the last thing the vast majority of Liberians want. Under no circumstances should Taylor be handed a platform again.'[43] But there were other reasons for Cahill's lack of enthusiasm. The cardinal would 'be told in no uncertain terms' how the missionaries felt about the higher echelons of Church leadership, coming in the door after being absent from Liberia throughout the war and now undertaking a nonsensical task.' The fear was that the cardinal, a Frenchman, had been 'got at' by Taylor's supporters in the Ivory Coast, in France and even in the Vatican, to undertake his peace mission.[44]

Etchegaray arrived on Sunday 17 April, bringing a message from Pope John Paul, and saying that he intended to spend two days seeing what the Vatican

---

[*]   Archbishop Luigi Travaglino had replaced Archbishop Romeo Panciroli on April 4, 1992. Since his appointment he had never set foot in Liberia, either to present his credentials or visit the Church. Instead, he took up residence in Freetown, Sierra Leone.

might contribute to the search for peace. During his visit he celebrated a Mass for 800 chosen attendees (including President Sawyer) in the Sacred Heart Cathedral, visited Gardnersville and centres for displaced people, and held talks both with Sawyer and the ECOMOG commander, the Nigerian, Major General Olurin.[45] He was then scheduled to fly to Ivory Coast, in order to 'cross into the shrinking enclave controlled by Charles Taylor.'[46]

***

On Wednesday 21 April, with the Vatican's peace mission to Liberia still ongoing, Cahill gave a somewhat more positive view of the proceedings. Etchagaray had impressed him by his energy, intelligence, and amiability. The cardinal had 'made a good impression on all, including the government and the other Churches.' On the next day, when Etchagaray was on his way to Gbarnga with Gordon-Somers and a mediator from the Organisation of African Unity, Cahill told his diary:

> We all hope that in meeting with Taylor they will not be giving him a platform. However we know their message to him is uncompromising. The only message for him is summed up in two words: Yamoussoukrou IV.[47]

Whatever about the cardinal, Taylor did not disappoint, delivering, to the delight of the international media, a statesman-like address of welcome to the 'Papal Delegation.' In his address he declared the Yamoussoukrou accord a beautiful framework for peace and expressed his willingness to meet Sawyer in a neutral place 'to bring lasting peace to Liberia', his readiness to 'begin negotiations for a ceasefire that would lead to genuine elections', and his preparedness to 'disarm to a neutral peace-keeping force.' He also expressed a wish for 'neutral observers.'[48]

Cahill was deeply disappointed with the visit which fulfilled his worst expectations and confirmed his initial instinct about the affair. Despite the fact that Gbarnga was 'holding its breath' in the expectation of an ECOMOG attack, Taylor had kept the Papal Delegation 'waiting and hungry for nearly 4 hours', after which they just 'played up to him' and 'made idiots of themselves.'[49]

***

The widely shared view that Gbarnga would be overrun, and Taylor defeated, received a setback on 13 May when the NPFL mounted a series of attacks on Kakata where ECOMOG had a Brigade headquarters. Although these attacks were repulsed there were several ECOMOG casualties. NPFL raids on the environs of the town were accompanied by the usual killings of civilians deemed hostile.

> In those villages which have no military presence ... the NPFL carried out horrific atrocities on civilians ... beheadings, rapings and inflicting the kind of horrible mutilations that have been associated with Cambodia at its worst. The evidence brought to hospitals is so raw; survivors, terribly mutilated ...[50]

News of atrocities could always be denied by perpetrators, attributing them to hostile factions or to ECOMOG. But internationally the NPFL's reputation plummeted when ECOMOG revealed that it had intercepted an internal radio conversation between Taylor and henchman John Richardson, in which the former was reported as saying, with regard to refugees in his territory: 'kill the men, rape the women … and to hell with them.'[51]

And allegations of misconduct and worse were not confined to the NPFL and ULIMO-K. A report by the Jesuit Relief Services 'Liberia Working Group', published on 1 June, painted a deeply disturbing picture of ECOMOG.

> The question is delicate, since for some years they have been left without significant support from the international community. However ECOMOG are now subject to several serious and urgent criticisms. They are impeding the just provision of humanitarian aid to the larger part of the country. They threaten civilian populations by bombing and artillery. They do not operate as neutral peacekeepers. They have armed some factions which now need to be controlled. They appear to be one of the protagonists. They do not control the looting and at time even participate in it.[52]

***

Notes

1 Comfort Ero, 'ECOWAS and the Sub-Regional Peacekeeping in Liberia', The Journal of Humanitarian Assistance (Feinstein international Center), 25 September 1995 (http://sites.tufts.edu/jha/archives/66 - accessed 28 October 2012).
2 A Jamaican diplomat.
3 United Nations Development Programme, the Food and Agriculture Organisation, the United Nations Population Fund, the United Nations Children's Fund, the World Food Programme, the World Health Organisation and the UN Refugee Agency. The United Nations Special Co-ordinator's Office to manage these agencies opened in Monrovia in December 1990.
4 George Duana.
5 A.B. A. Jennings, 'Personal Diary', 50–51.
6 Ibid.
7 A.T. 'Journal of a Missionary', 102.
8 Ibid., 103.
9 Moran to the author, 7 April 2020 (email).
10 A.T. S. John Murray's circular to members of the SMA American Province, 13 December 1992.
11 A.T. Moran to S. John Murray, 14 January 1993.
12 Reuters, Stanton Peabody, Monrovia, 1 January 1993.
13 A.B. Cahill to Quinlan, 3 January 1993 (Fax via Spain).
14 Ibid., 7 January 1993 (Fax via Spain).
15 A.B. Cahill to Quinlan (Fax via Spain), 5 January 1993.
16 A.T. 'Journal of a Missionary', 105–106.
17 A.B. Cahill to Quinlan, 5 January 1993.
18 A.T. Moran to Brendan Darcy, 9 January 1993.

19 Olurin commanded Ecomog from October 1992–October 1993.
20 FBIS-AFR-93–011 (AB1801201293 London BBC World Service, 'Focus on Africa', 18 January 1993).
21 FBIS-AFR-93–4417, 28/1/1993 (AB2701123593 Gbarnga Radio ELBC).
22 In mid-March.
23 Richard Carver, Liberia: What Hope for Peace? (WRITENE, 1 October 1994) 94.
24 FBIS-AFR-93–027, 11 February 1993 (AB1102070293 London BBC World Service, 'Focus on Africa').
25 A.T. Liberia Working Group, 'Newsletter', June 1993 (Jesuit Refugee Service, Rome).
26 FBIS-AFR-93–122, 28 June 1993 (AB2506182893 London BBC World Service, 'Focus on Africa').
27 A.B. Cahill to Quinlan, 4 March 1993.
28 An Associate of 'Africa Watch' and African specialist, she was later (9 June 1993) to testify before the US Senate's Committee on Foreign Relations.
29 Janet Fleischman, 'Africa Watch' Report, May/June 1993 (Human Rights Watch, Washington DC).
30 FBIS-AFR-93–026, 10 February 1993 (AB0902204093 London BBC World Service 'Focus on Africa').
31 A.B. Cahill to Harkin, 15 February 1993 (Fax).
32 Ibid.
33 Ibid.
34 A.B. Memo of telephone conversation with Sr Miriam O'Brien (Harkin, Quinlan), 26 February 1993.
35 A.B. Diary, 54–55.
36 Of Sri Lankan origin the Jayasuriya family was very much part of the Buchanan community before the civil war. Dr Jayasuriya worked in the government hospital during the 1980s and later ran a private clinic. He was doctor to the mission until compelled to leave with his family in 1993.
37 Ibid., 56–58.
38 A.B., Cahill to Quinlan, ibid., 6 April 1993 (Fax).
39 Ibid., 'Nigerian ECOWAS Envoys leave for Ivory Coast (quoting Reuters, Lagos, 5 March 1993).
40 Lindsay Barrett, 'The Nimba Equation', West Africa, 1–7 March 1993, 325.
41 Ibid.
42 Ibid.
43 Cahill to Cork, 15 April 1993 (Fax).
44 Ibid.
45 AFJN Bulletin, 18 April 1993, quoting Reuters, Monrovia.
46 Ibid.
47 Ibid., 21 April 1993 (Fax).
48 A.T. 'Statement of the Hon. Charles Taylor delivered to His Eminence the Lord Cardinal, Roger Etchegaray and to the other members of the Papal delegation', dated Gbarnga, 21 April 1993.
49 To Harkin, 25 April 1993 (Fax).
50 A.B. Cahill to Harkin, 14 May 1993 (Fax).
51 Ibid.
52 Liberia Working Group, Newsletter, June 1993 (Jesuit Refugee Service, Rome).

17 The appointment of a UN Special Representative amid continuing atrocities

On the night of 5–6 June one of the worst atrocities of the civil war occurred when some 600 displaced persons taking refuge in an abandoned Firestone rubber plantation complex near Harbel (called 'Carter Camp') were massacred. The raiders, it was reported, escaped by river with about 200 prisoners, who were forced to carry rice stolen from UN relief supplies. At first it was assumed that the NPFL had committed the outrage. One of those who brought news of the massacre to the international community was Augustine Mahiga of the UN High Commission for Refugees who had witnessed the aftermath. *The New York Times* reported his estimate of 300 dead and 755 wounded.[1] Survivors told Mahiga that the killings began just after midnight and lasted for two hours. Women and children were the main victims.[2]

The massacre was quickly linked to Taylor's recently reported telephone conversation with Richardson. Taylor, *The New York Times* stated, had been 'heard ordering his commander to unleash a "reign of terror" on refugees at the front lines' and although Taylor had vigorously denied any such conversation 'Mr Mahiga and others' who had 'listened to it said they recognized the rebel chief's distinctive baritone voice.' Survivors had told Mahiga that NFPL soldiers had come to the complex in search of food 'just after midnight Saturday, a day after the UN had distributed rice in the area.' They 'collected the rice, then went on an orgy of killing and mutilation … going from house to house killing entire families.'[3]

Early reports from many sources, including the usually reliable Reuters agency,[4] blamed the massacre on the NPFL. Amos Sawyer, too, was quick off the mark saying, 'we have seen the crossing of the line from rebellion to terrorism by the NPFL.' The public was reminded that in addition to the intercepted phone call with Richardson, Taylor had recently announced a change of strategy, abandoning 'open confrontation' and adopting 'guerrilla tactics.' And it was noted that since this statement civilians in hinterland villages had been subject to armed attack and summary executions. Taylor responded in the tried and trusted NPFL manner denying any responsibility and blaming other factions, in this case the interim government's army (AFL). Speaking on the BBC by satellite telephone he described the massacre as 'another attempt' to give his army 'a bad name.' The atrocity had been carried out, he said, 'as a pretext for an offensive against him by

DOI: 10.4324/9781003219309-22

AFL troops and another rebel faction (ULIMO), with the consent of ECOMOG.'[5] Tom Woewiyu, described in a Reuters report now as 'a senior military official in the NPFL', claimed categorically at a news conference in the Ivory Coast that under no circumstances were NPFL soldiers involved in the Harbel massacre. 'Last Saturday and Sunday, on the day they're talking about, they (ECOMOG) bombed all day in Gbarnga and other parts of the country and when the bombing is going on nobody moves…'[6] But given the NPFL's long record of denying involvement in atrocities, most recently the slaying of the ASC Sisters, few believed these professions of innocence.

Some sources, however, were unable to verify the claims that the NPFL had perpetrated the outrage. The U.S. State department, for one, was reticent. Questioned two days after the massacre, a spokesperson declared himself unable to point the finger 'until more facts are known.'[7] This reticence was to prove wise.

***

Probes into the Harbel massacre soon multiplied. On 10 June, despite Sawyer's initial claim of NPFL culpability, the IGNU set up a commission to investigate whether AFL troops might have been involved, while the UN awaited the preliminary report commissioned by Gordon-Somers. The IGNU's investigation was prompted by increasing evidence implicating its own military force, the AFL. Although initially survivors had blamed the NPFL some were now saying that the attackers wore military fatigues similar to those of AFL soldiers. Others were asking how the attackers, who had arrived by bus, managed to enter the compound without being challenged by the two AFL soldiers on guard. Neither had been molested and both vacated the camp while the massacre was being conducted. Moreover the fact that the attackers so readily identified themselves as NPFL suggested an intention to implicate that faction. At first the IGNU was only prepared to admit that the AFL guards were guilty of negligence. But the growing chorus in the local and international press and on BBC World Service broadcasts, in which survivors were widely quoted, prompted Sawyer to reassess his government's position.[8]

Although by far the gravest, the Harbel massacre was by no means the only outrage committed in June 1993. *West Africa* reported the NPFL beheading and disembowelment of some two dozen civilians in Maribi County and the use of their mutilated bodies as roadblocks.[9] It also reported a large NPFL attack on Fassama town in Bopolu district during which 21 persons were killed and 530 were abducted.[10] There was a raid, too, on Belle Yalla in Lofa County in which 22 were killed and 150 abducted. Further attacks were recorded in neighbouring towns and villages in which 200 civilians were killed and an additional massacre at Bernard Farm. These attacks were part of the new NPFL strategy outlined by Taylor and called 'Surgical Guerrilla Military Operations.'[11]

***

Efforts by Gordon-Somers to obtain the further implementation of the Yamoussoukro Accord, were rewarded when representatives of the IGNU, NPFL, ULIMO-K and the AFL gathered in Geneva on Saturday, 10 July 1993, under the auspices of ECOWAS, the OAU and the UN. Facilitating the proceedings as chairpersons and mediators were Gordon-Somers, Canaan Banana, former president of Zimbabwe, and Abbas Bundu of ECOWAS.[12] Representing the IGNU was Foreign Minister, Gabriel Baccus Matthews, Minister for Justice, Philip Banks and Information Minister, Lamini Waritay. ULIMO-K was represented by Alhaji Kromah, the only faction leader present. The NPFL delegation was led by Foreign Affairs Minister Momolu Sirleaf, and included J. Laveli Supuwood, Justice Minister in NPRAG and the ever-present Woewiyu, its Defence Minister.

Militarily on the verge of defeat, with ECOMOG and its allies in the ascendant, the NPFL desperately needed now to fight on the political front. Not that the NFPL delegation let this show. On the contrary it took every opportunity to create difficulties in the early stages of the conference, while Taylor, from a distance, was noticeably disruptive, interrupting sessions with phone calls to Sirleaf and setting out uncompromising positions in broadcasts delivered on Gbarnga radio.[13] Thus the deliberations got off to an inauspicious start with the NPFL delegation refusing to recognise either the IGNU or ULIMO-K and asserting that NPRAG alone was the legitimate government of Liberia. Next it questioned Bundu's role as one of the three co-chairman of the talks – claiming he was biased through his association with ECOMOG which it alleged was no longer a neutral force. This was followed by a demand that the first item for discussion should be an immediate ceasefire instead of the issue of disarmament which had been given priority on the agenda.

But this recalcitrance on the part of the NPFL was posturing; and the various objections, apart from one, were never pursued. Despite grumbling about the lack of legitimacy of the other factions, the NPFL delegation never threatened a walk-out, and participated fully in the various discussions, plenary sessions and working groups. Calls for the exclusion of Abass Bundu were countered by the shared view of the others – ultimately accepted by the objectors – that, since the current talks were about implementing Yamoussoukro IV brokered by ECOWAS, that body could not be excluded. The objection concerning agenda priorities was passed on to two working committees set up to consider 'military and political matters.' It was regrettable that ECOWAS and the UN representative did not show firmness on this issue. Before the meeting convened Taylor had agreed to everything in the proposed agenda apart from 'the prerequisite of disarmament and encampment of his forces.' In this he was now allowed to get his way, entering into the talks without making this commitment and agreeing only to a ceasefire scheduled to commence on August 1. Gordon-Somers and the other diplomats might have thought that the NPFL could be persuaded to change its position. More likely, their enthusiasm for talks outweighed their determination to remain firm on this crucial issue.

For those within ECOWAS, like the Nigerians, who at this point saw Taylor's military defeat as the only solution, his refusal to commit himself on the issue of disarmament 'heightened their determination … to force him into submission.'[14] However the NPFL leader could count on the restraining influence of ECOWAS francophone members and on the UN's determination to seek only a diplomatic solution. Buoyed up by the fact that the talks had gone ahead in spite of his refusal, Taylor made even greater demands. On the meeting's fourth day, speaking on Gbarnga radio, he threatened to wreck proceedings unless all territory lost by the NPFL since Operation Octopus was returned.[15] Aware that this would cause consternation in Geneva, he must have been gratified, if not surprised, when on the very next day, 17 July, the med-iators declared that a ceasefire had been agreed and that 'a comprehensive political settlement' was now possible within a matter of days.[16] This, the world was told, at last had been achieved. All that remained was a gathering in Cotonou (seat of the ECOWAS presidency) of all the principals to the conflict together with ECOWAS, the OAU and the UN, to deal with what were described as 'the very few matters still outstanding'; and sign off on what hen-ceforth would be called the 'Cotonou Accord.' This duly took place on 25 July. Significantly, Taylor did not attend, the NPFL being represented by Enoch Dogolea, a vice president of the NPRAG.

The Cotonou Accord declared that during a transitional period, pending elections for a substantive president and legislature, Liberia would be governed by a 'Council of State', tasked with preparing the ground for 'free and fair democratic elections' which would take place within seven months. This body would be seated within 30 days of the signing of the accord and 'concomitantly with the commencement of the disarmament process.'[17]

The accord was essentially a re-run of Yamoussoukro IV, scheduling a per-manent ceasefire to commence on 1 August, to be followed on a fixed time-table by encampment, disarmament, demobilisation, and finally the holding of elections. The difference lay in the measures taken to ensure implementation. Four thousand additional ECOMOG troops, including contingents from outside the West Africa sub-region, were to be drafted in. And signalling the first practical involvement of the UN in the crisis, a group of UN military observers was to be deployed, to be known as the UN Observer Mission in Liberia (UNOMIL). Joint ceasefire monitoring committees – consisting of ECOMOG and faction members - had been tried before and had failed. This time, however, a UN contingent would join in the process. It would operate under the supervision of the UN Special Representative who in return would report to the UN Secretary General. The ECOWAS-UNOMIL objective was formally defined as securing encampment, disarmament and demobilisa-tion, a subsequent electoral process and the supply of humanitarian aid. Evi-dence that the UN meant business was signalled by a Security Council Resolution (No. 856), signed on 10 August, directing the Secretary General to dispatch an advance group of 30 UN military observers to Liberia. A fur-ther Resolution (866), signed on 22 September, was to formally establish UNOMIL.

An earnest of the problems facing this new co-operative model of UN intervention became evident on 9 September when Boutros-Ghali, briefed the Security Council on his plans for UNOMIL. On that occasion, he stated that should ECOMOG fail to meet its commitment to significantly increase the number of its troops – as provided for in the Cotonou Accord – there was very little chance of succeeding and he might be compelled to recommend the withdrawal of the UN Observer Mission. Co-operation with ECOMOG, he declared, was therefore crucial and to this end a formal agreement, detailing its modalities, would be drawn up. This was done in November with both parties appending signatures.

Evaluations of the prospect for success varied. It was pointed out by some that Taylor had already broken 20 agreements and was unlikely to adhere to this most recent accord. Trevor Gordon-Somers was more optimistic, saying that he expected the Security Council would approve the dispatch of UN observers to oversee the ceasefire. A jubilant Momolu Sirleaf who had nego-tiated so effectively on behalf of the NPFL in Geneva, told the world 'that this time we have come to the conclusion of the war.'[18]

But already there were ominous signs for the future. Three days before the accord was signed Sawyer had denounced a clause inserted in the text by Taylor after the final session in Geneva had taken place to the effect that dis-armament, encampment and demobilisation of NPFL troops would not be entrusted to ECOMOG but to the new troops recruited from other OAU member states. And he had managed to insert yet another clause stipulating that ECOMOG should play no part in providing for his future security; rather all arrangements would be determined by the NPFL in consultation with UN monitors.[19] Sawyer sought the removal of these insertions on the grounds that ECOMOG was effectively the instrument of ECOWAS, the regional body which had pioneered the peace process and was central to its successful com-pletion. Such a body, he declared, should not be side-lined after 'such a painful exercise in trying to restore peace.'[20]

Moreover, as soon as the text of the accord was published it became clear that many issues had not been fully negotiated. For example, the accord agreed on the formation of a transitional government prior to elections to be held within six months but had not determined the composition of that government's executive. The NPFL sought a triumvirate of rotating two monthly presidents in a five-man State Council, two members of which would be neutral persons. The IGNU wanted Sawyer to remain president but with two vice presidents, one from ULIMO-K the other from the NPFL. ULIMO-K wanted a president chosen from a short-list of nine names to which each party would contribute three.[21] The Cotonou Accord left this critical political question unresolved. In addition, there was a doubt that Taylor, who had not signed the accord in person, 'could repeat his well-known ploy of refusing to accept it by raising procedural questions concerning the interpretation of the terms.'[22]

On 1 August – the day on which the ceasefire came into force – an ebul-lient Taylor announced on Gbarnga radio that the war was over, warning that any of his soldiers found shooting at ECOMOG would be 'held personally responsible.' He also announced that he would run against Sawyer in the forthcoming election.[23]

***

On 5 August UPI reported the arrest in Washington DC of a State Department secretary and a journalist.[24] They were charged with 'wilful communication, delivery, transmission or retention of documents relating to the national defence to persons not entitled to receive them.' The secretary was 47-year-old Geneva Jones who worked in the Bureau of Politico-Military Affairs while the journalist was one Dominic Ntube, a 'permanent resident alien of Cameroon.' Next a Washington DC radio station[25] reported that the espionage of which they were accused related to Liberia and that Ntube had been caught 'funnelling information to Mr Charles Taylor's NPFL.' Mark Fritz[26], writing in the *Boston Globe*, immediately recalled that *West Africa, New African* and *Africa Confidential* had recently published leaked cables sent to the State Department from a number of U.S. embassies in Africa. On 5 August Reuters reported an FBI source to the effect that cables about U.S. military operations in Somalia and Iraq had also been leaked.[27] Jones, whose office had dealt with 'strategic military policy', had apparently 'taken dozens of classified documents in her purse or between the pages of newspapers.' These she passed on to Ntube and to one Fabian Makani, 'an illegal alien from Kenya' who worked in Silver Spring near Washington DC. Jones, it was reported, had confessed to passing on documents for some 18 months. In all the FBI had recovered 'several thousand classified State Department documents and 39 secret Central Intelligence Agency documents from Ntube's residence.'[28] There was little consolation in the announcement by Sondra McCarty (spokeswoman for the State Department) that Jones's clearance to view top-secret material had been suspended at the time of her arrest. Jones and Ntube were formally arraigned in a federal court charged with espionage.[*]

***

In Liberia nominations to the Council of State, which according to the Cotonou Accord would be installed as interim government of the entire country before the end of August, were being submitted. The nominees by the parties were all non-controversial citizens, prominent in their own right. Dorothy Musuleng-Cooper, formerly NPRAG education spokesperson and generally well-respected, represented Taylor's government. Bismarck Kuyon, speaker of the IGNU, was nominated by Sawyer while ULIMO put forward Mohammed Sheriff, a former UN Paris-based official. The two unaligned members were Robert I.E. Bright, a former chairman of the True Whig Party, and Gustav Barnard, a labour minister in the Tolbert government. After a weekend of discussions in Cotonou by the interested parties under UN supervision, the interim government was formed according to the provisions laid down in the accord. The five members of that government, it was determined, would now choose a president and two vice presidents from among themselves while in seven months elections for a substantive president and legislature

---

[*]   Jones pleaded guilty to 21 counts of theft and two counts of unlawful communication of national defence information. She received a sentence of 37 months imprisonment.

would be held. In the interim, according to the accord, encampment and disarmament would take place.

On 15 August Cahill reported to his superiors in Cork signs warranting
optimism. The ceasefire appeared to be holding. Moreover, the aid route into
Greater Liberia from Monrovia had been tested and appeared to be operating
satisfactorily. The first convoy – small in size – had successfully reached
Gbarnga on the previous Monday, and a second had travelled to Weala on
Friday. Neither had experienced any harassment from the NPFL. Now a much
larger convoy was planned to carry much needed food aid to Yekepa by train
from Buchanan. 'If this goes off without a hitch, a huge step will have been
taken', Cahill told his Irish superiors.

***

The last few days of August brought a body blow to the peace process when
Nigeria's interim government ordered the immediate withdrawal of its troops
from ECOMOG. The decision was related to a period of instability in Nigeria
following the resignation of President Babangida and the installation of an
interim government pending a return to full democratic rule.* The announcement had been made by Interim President Chief Ernest Shonekan who directed Defence Secretary, Sani Abacha, 'to work out a withdrawal plan
immediately so as to bring the boys home before the end of the tenure of the
interim national government.' Shonekan's rationale was that with the Cotonou
Accord the Liberian civil war was now over and the return of the soldiers
would help create a better climate in Nigeria.[29]

Hot on the heels of this calamitous development came disturbing reports
from ECOMOG that NPFL forces were preparing for a new offensive. On 30
August an ECOMOG spokesperson said a 'large group of heavily armed rebels
was massing near Monrovia' and it was feared that this was a 'prelude to an
attack on Liberia's capital.' Appearing to give substance to this was the fact that
the NPFL representative on the Council of State had not yet taken her seat.
Such reports created great nervousness in Monrovia. But the NPFL was quick
to deny the allegations and scotch the rumours. On 1 September Joe Mulbah,
NPRAG Information Minister, spoke with Robin White on the BBC World
Service, categorically dismissing ECOMOG's allegations and claiming that
'since the Cotonou Accord was signed none of our troops ever fired a shot and
all have remained in their positions.'[30] As for the Council of State, he told
White, the NPFL had 'a high-powered delegation' consisting of Mrs Musuleng-Cooper and thirteen others, escorted by supporters, poised to travel to
Monrovia in a convoy of buses at the weekend where they would attend the
inauguration of the Council of State 'as per the Cotonou Accord.'

But Sawyer, for one, remained unhappy, complaining to Gordon-Somers
that nothing had happened in the crucial area of encampment and disarmament, despite the accord's stipulation of such action preceding the inauguration

---

*   In the event, there was to be no return to democratic government, General Sani
      Abacha seizing power three months later.

of any government. Not a single member of the 30-strong UNOMIL team, which was to work with ECOMOG in overseeing encampment and disarmament, had set foot in Liberia even though six weeks had elapsed since the signing of the accord.[31] Nor had a single member of the additional OAU reinforcements to assist in these steps which, if reports about the imminent withdrawal of Nigerian troops were true, was doubly depressing. Unless progress on military matters caught up with political developments, he concluded, there would never be peace.[32] And there could be no question of any inauguration of the new interim government until this happened.

As the day scheduled for that very inauguration approached, tension in Monrovia reached fever pitch. Bus-loads of NPFL 'officials' and their supporters had been promised by Taylor while Tom Kamara, IGNU spokesperson, announced on radio that 'no one is going to take power with guns...'[33] The crisis was averted by a decision of the chief negotiator, Benin's President Nicephore Soglo, to postpone the swearing-in ceremony due to take place in Cotonou before formal inauguration of the interim government in Monrovia.[34] The reason given was the delay in recruiting additional forces for ECOMOG.

***

On 10 September the three-person panel of inquiry appointed by the UN Secretary General to investigate the Harbel 'Carter Camp' massacre, headed by a former Kenyan attorney general, Amos Wako, reported its findings. It found the AFL guilty of the crime. '[35] This panel had concluded that:

> at about midnight armed soldiers attacked and systematically massacred and mutilated the bodies of nearly 600 Carter Camp residents, mainly women, children and elderly persons. Some 45 bags of rice and beans and other loot were removed, apparently carried by 100 or more survivors abducted by the attackers. About 1,100 terrified survivors managed to escape the massacre and fled in all directions.[36]

The report had no doubt that the perpetrators of the massacre were AFL soldiers. Originally these had taken on the role of protectors of the refugees, who were mainly from the Bassa tribe. Quickly their behaviour had become more threatening than protective as they preyed on the refugees, stealing whatever wild food they had managed to harvest from the bush and selling it in the Harbel market. Although in receipt of some food aid at the distributions made by the World Food Programme (WFP), they harassed the food distributors, stole rations from the refugees and looted camp supplies. Within a short time the extent of food stolen escalated tenfold. Efforts to put a stop to this culminated in a decision by the WFP to exclude the soldiers from all future food distributions. This policy was to be introduced for the next distribution, due on 5 June. In the dark of the night, after that distribution had taken place, Carter camp was invaded by disgruntled AFL soldiers, members of the so-called Black Beret brigade who were stationed nearby. Among those named in the investigation as chiefly responsible were the AFL Harbel commander, Major Nelson Paye, a 23-year-old private Zarkpa (Zagba) Gorh, who was described as the 'permanent camp commandant' and a Lieutenant Kollie.[37] Finally, the report stated that shortly after the massacre ECOMOG was in a position to identify the perpetrators but chose to remain silent.

The verdict of the Wako panel was strongly opposed by the IGNU which declared 'no new evidence has been uncovered by the panel of inquiry to render invalid the conclusion reached by investigations conducted by the interim government. But now, in the light of the Wako findings, the AFL, army of the Sawyer-led IGNU, was being implicated in one of the worst massacres of Liberia's civil war. The IGNU response was to arrest the three soldiers mentioned in the report but to continue its denials that the AFL was responsible for the massacre. No new evidence, it continued to insist, had been presented and it reiterated its belief that the NPFL was to blame.[38] The three soldiers had been arrested, it explained, not because they were guilty but for their own protection. Should a legal basis for a prosecution against them be found, then they would be charged and tried.

Commentators pointed out that the IGNU already had a track record in protecting AFL soldiers accused of misbehaviour, banditry and killing. For example, in April five AFL soldiers had been arrested for killing the British technician, Brian Garnham. None of the five was charged with murder. Instead all were court-martialled for a variety of disciplinary offences and in the five months which had elapsed since their trial no verdict had been issued.[*] Thus, ECOMOG's silence about the identity of the perpetrators of the Harbel/Camp Carter massacre, caused commentators to invoke the alliance between that force and the AFL in their battles with the NPFL.[39]

Nonetheless, the Liberia Truth and Reconciliation Commission (LTRC), while reporting the massacre, does not express a view on the identity of the perpetrators.[40] Moreover Stephen Ellis, one of the most respected historians of the Liberian civil war, was to write that a number of reports claimed the massacre was 'at least partly the work of the NPFL' and that some of the NPFL Marines, the unit commanded by the fearsome Nixon 'Striker' Gaye,[41] had admitted carrying out the killings.'[42] Ellis concluded that 'the most plausible explanation for the massacre is that it was carried out by elements in the NPFL as a means of getting world attention and increasing the pressure for a ceasefire, which was now in the NPFL's interest.' Lansana Gberie also attributes responsibility for the massacre to the NPFL. Highly critical of the LTRC he nonetheless invokes testimony given before that body by one M. Allen Nicholas, a.k.a. 'Mission Ant', a former child soldier, who said, 'he was one of dozens of NPFL fighters under the command of 'Jack the Rebel' (George Duana) and 'Christopher Varmoh [Vambo] a.k.a. 'Mosquito', who carried out the Carter Camp killings. And he also mentions

---

[*]   The LTRC makes one reference to the killing of Brian Garnham. 'January 1993: AFL soldiers found responsible for extrajudicial execution of Garnham, manager of a research laboratory.' (LTRC, Consolidated Final Report, vol. 2, 227).

testimony by General Zigzag Marzah, a former NPFL commander, which attributed the killings to Yeaten, Varmoh, Joe Tuah and others.[43] James Kokulo Fas-
uekoi's excellent article on the 20th anniversary of the massacre does not shed new
light but makes the point that the IGNU's rejection of the Waco Report 'was
quite logical and convincing to the point that members of the WACO commission left Liberia almost in shame with little or nothing to celebrate', and that 'many
people including journalists who were quite familiar with the political dynamics of
the war equally took serious exception to the WACO Report.'[44] To this writer it
is clear that there is still no conclusive, corroborated evidence on the identity of
the perpetrators of the Carter Camp massacre.

* * *

In early September 1993 an uneasy peace prevailed. There were rumours of
fighting between the NPFL and ULIMO in Grand Gedeh County and on the
Ivory Coast border, strongly denied by both sides. Momolu Sirleaf told a press
conference in Abidjan that what was being reported were 'squabbles' between
factions within ULIMO.[45] An ULIMO-K spokesperson at Kromah's Tubmanburg headquarters gave some substance to this, suggesting that the
ULIMO-J faction led by Raleigh Seekie, not a party to the Cotonou Accord,
and with its headquarters in Sierra Leone, might have been involved.

Elsewhere there were no reports of fighting although the armies faced each
other at the front.[46] There were reports too that there was some fraternisation
between these troops.[47] At the same time, relief convoys continued to enter
Greater Liberia and a second relief train destined for Yekepa was due to travel
on 8 September. Setting out two days behind schedule, it carried 700 tons of
beans and rice. This was the largest shipment since the 23 August train shipment of 500 tons of meal and milk to Gbarnga. Both shipments were the work
of the Catholic Relief Services under the direction of the energetic American
priest, Ken Vavrina. He was already planning a further and even larger shipment of 1,000 tons to the south-eastern port of Harper for the distressed of
Harper and Grand Gedeh County.[48] As against this, the failure of the UN to
get monitors on the ground to oversee the ceasefire and participate in the task
of disarmament did not bode well for Liberia's fragile peace; nor did the delay
in recruiting additional OAU troops to commence the all-important process of
encampment and disarmament. Efforts to secure these additional forces continued to be frustrated. Egypt's offer to send a contingent was rejected by
Charles Taylor on the grounds that its diplomatic recognition of the IGNU
amounted to taking sides.[49]

Nonetheless efforts were being redoubled to overcome the many obstacles. Early
in September a 'team of experts' from the American State Department and the
Department of Defence visited Liberia to determine 'logistics, air and sea, as well as
communications facilities required by ECOMOG for the extra battalions.'[50]
Among the countries listed as likely to make troops available were Tanzania,
Uganda and Zimbabwe. There was also positive movement on the issue of the
deployment of UN observers when in the first week of September Boutros Ghali
brought his detailed plans to the Security Council. The UN Observer Mission

would consist of 350 military observers comprising 41 six-man teams, 25 military observers at UNOMIL headquarters and eight observers at each of the four regional headquarters.[51] The communications network, made up of civilian personnel, would require 25 persons, while a 20-member medical unit would also be required. In addition, 45 military engineers would be needed 'to work with ECOMOG and to provide accommodation and other facilities for UN personnel.'[52] On 10 October the Chief Military Observer arrived and by mid-December a total of 166 observers – still well short of the total complement – had joined him. Signalling a sensitivity to Taylor's animosity to ECOMOG, the Joint-Ceasefire Monitoring Committee, in which all parties were represented, was chaired by a UN delegate.

***

On 4 October Mike Moran, writing to Brendan Darcy from Monrovia gave good news about the Nigerian contingent. So far, no Nigerian troops had been withdrawn and he had been told by the contingent's chaplain that plans had been made to replace a number who were due for leave. But on other fronts the news was less encouraging. Although the ceasefire was holding, shops and businesses and schools were re-opening and the White Plains water plant was beginning to pump water, the people were still finding it extremely difficult to make ends meet. Each day at the SMA Regional house gate, up to two-hundred penniless people were to be found seeking money, food, clothing and the wherewithal to repair their homes. The political feeling in the Monrovia enclave was that most people wanted the IGNU 'out' and its successor, the Liberian National Transitional Government (LNTG) 'in.' That, at least, would represent 'progress' for the peace process. In Greater Liberia Moran reported 'lots of hungry and desperate people.' Even rebel soldiers, reputedly, were turning themselves in to ECOMOG 'because they have little food and no ammunition.' Nonetheless the humanitarian situation there would have been much worse had not food shipments managed to reach into the territory via the Monrovia–Kakata highway and the Buchanan–Yekepa railroad. At the same time the NPFL, 'on its uppers' in the months leading up to the Cotonou Accord, was now beginning to flex its muscles militarily as well as diplomatically, acting aggressively in Lofa and around the Firestone-Harbel area. The AFL, in contrast, well used to flexing its muscles where civilians were concerned, had suddenly become 'most courteous' at checkpoints, 'perhaps worried about its future with the cessation of the IGNU.'

***

News of the emergence of yet another military faction came in the closing weeks of October, when Cahill, visiting Buchanan, reported heavy fighting in the River Cess area 'between a new group and the NPFL.'[53] The new faction bore the unlikely name: Liberia Peace Council (LPC)[54]. Milling crowds of refugees were pouring into Buchanan to get away from the fighting. Buchanan mission, as in the past, would once again be involved in catering for refugees, distributing aid brought in by CRS. Tony Jennings and John Kilcoyne were still on leave although due back shortly, but the Consolata Sisters had returned to their convent.[55]

On 24 October Archbishop Francis led a 'Memorial Mass' in the cathedral for missionaries killed during the civil war. Those remembered included the five ASC sisters and Damian Kwashie, the Ghanaian priest killed in July 1990. In the course of his homily he called upon those with 'notorious human rights records who have been appointed to serve on the new transitional government, to resign for the sake of genuine peace.'[56] Since he did not mention anyone by name, there was some speculation about who exactly he had in mind. Few had much doubt that he was referring to a NPFL army officer, Isaac Musa[57], who on 22 September had been nominated by Taylor in place of Mrs Musuleng-Cooper. Musa, according to Francis, in a report written for Propaganda Fide[58] a month later, had been responsible for thousands of deaths.[59] The elevation of this ruthless man to the State Council reflected Taylor's dissatisfaction with Musuleng-Cooper's refusal to take a 'hard line.' Francis also addressed the recent hostilities in south-eastern Liberia which had signalled the emergence of the LPC. Commenting on the title of this new faction, he ruefully asked 'how can people using the name of peace bear arms?' Francis concluded his cathedral homily by addressing what he considered the central issue standing between war and peace, that of disarmament. He asked the congregation to 'imagine what we will be placing ourselves in if we install a new government while the warring factions are still bearing arms' adding that any structure built on such a foundation was destined to founder sooner or later.

***

Further progress in the implementation of the peace accord took place at a meeting of all parties in Cotonou (3–5 November) to arrange the composition of the incoming LNTG, the transitional government which would replace the IGNU, an institution which would now last seven months after which elections for a substantive government would take place. Thirteen of the 17 cabinet posts were duly allocated. However, the first setback in what up to now had appeared to be a seamless process occurred when agreement on the remaining four posts – the critical ministries of Finance, Justice, Defence and Foreign Affairs – could not be concluded. Nonetheless the composition of the Electoral Commission and the appointments of Speaker of the Legislature and Justices of the Supreme Court were settled; and it was agreed that outstanding issues would be dealt with at a later meeting. For his part, Boutros Ghali was able to inform the Security Council that preparations for the critical phases of disarmament and demobilisation were now 'well under way.' Those phases would commence, he added, as soon as the additional ECOMOG contingents arrived. At the same time, he had to explain the failure to meet the timetable laid down in the Cotonou Accord which required disarmament to commence 'within 30 days of the signature of the agreement, concomitant with the establishment of the transitional government.' He did so by invoking the view, shared by all parties, that the timetable was 'highly ambitious', requiring not only the formation of UNOMIL but a significant increase in ECOMOG strength, both complicated objectives. There was another factor which he did not mention: whether there was sufficient will within ECOWAS and his own organisation to accomplish disarmament in the face of repeated refusals to comply by the factions?

***

In the last days of November Archbishop Francis submitted another report[60] to his Propaganda Fide superiors in which he introduced an idea and a phrase which was to become something of a mantra for him in the years ahead. 'The peace process', he declared, 'in spite of setbacks, is irreversible.' This conviction, in the face of the continuing nightmare, was essentially an act of faith rather than the outcome of rational analysis. At root it was an expression of faith that in the end goodness would prevail. Such a faith would help the embattled archbishop to persevere. It would stiffen his resolve and bolster his courage. Not that Francis had now decided to abandon rational reporting. His expression that the peace process was irreversible was followed by a forensic analysis of events since his last report. However the mantra occasionally impacted on his judgement leading him to see hope where the evidence pointed in another direction.

In his report Francis recounted how, when forced into hiding and facing defeat, Taylor had successfully sought UN intervention in the form of peace conferences first at Geneva and then at Cotonou. The result was the accord signed on 25 July 1993. And yet the transitional government had not yet been seated and no disarmament, encampment or demobilisation had taken place. The delay had been caused by the non-arrival of new ECOMOG troops and by Taylor's refusal to disarm to ECOMOG. But the 'expanded ECOMOG' was due to arrive by the end of November and Francis was confident that 'although there have been hurdles on our way to Peace, Peace will come.' Manifestly, Francis's ardent desire for peace had affected his usually sharp judgement for earlier, on at least two occasions, facing military defeat, Taylor had managed to save himself by persuading ECOWAS and the international community that he was ready to make peace. On both occasions this ploy, which gained him valuable time to re-consolidate and reinforce, had succeeded. Now again, pressed on all sides by opposed militias and a strengthening and more aggressive ECOMOG he had managed to change the nature of the battlefield. He had signed the Cotonou Accord, just as he had the four Yamoussoukro agreements and several previous to that, with no intention of abiding by its terms.

Notes

1   6 June 1993 (quoting Michelle Paul, AP, Abidjan).
2   Ibid.
3   Ibid.
4   7 June 1993.
5   Star-Ledger (New Jersey, USA), 7 June 1993, (AP report from Abidjan, Ivory Coast).
6   Steve Weizman, 'Liberia Rebels say their headquarters bombed', Reuters, Abidjan, 8 June 1993.
7   Star-Ledger, Reuters, 7 June 1993.

8 See, Isaac Bantu, West Africa, 21–27 June 1993, 1039; See, Moran to S.J. Murray 15 June 1993.

9 Ibid.

10 Reference is made to these atrocities in LTRC, Consolidated Final Report, vol. 2, 128, 224, 252.

11 Klaas van Walraven, 'Project Conflict Prevention in West Africa ...Lessons from the Intervention in Liberia', 1990–1997] (CPWA, 1999), 39.

12 See West Africa, 26 July–1 August 1993, 1292–1294.

13 Ibid.

14 Mark Huband, African Report, 15 July 1993.

15 AFJN Bulletin, 20 July 1993 (quoting Reuters, Monrovia, 15 June 1993).

16 A.T, document, 15 July 1993 (Geneva, UPI).

17 Article 14.

18 AFJN Bulletin, 20 July 1993 (quoting AP, 17 July 1993).

19 21 July 1993, (UPI Monrovia); see also, Lindsay Barrett, West Africa, 26 July–1 August 1993, 1294.

20 Ibid.

21 West Africa, 26 July–1 August 1993, 1292–1294.

22 Ibid.

23 Monrovia, 1 August 1993, AP.

24 AFJN Bulletin, 9 August 1993, quoting UPI, 4 and 5 August 1993.

25 Radio WTOP.

26 Mark Fritz, at this time a staff writer for Associated Press, won a Pulitzer Prize for his coverage of the Rwandan genocide in 1995.

27 5 August, The Boston Globe.

28 UPI, Washington, 4 August 1993 (AFJN Bulletin).

29 FBIS-AFR-93-169, 2 September 1993. (AB0109150093 Ghana Broadcasting Corporation).

30 Ibid.

31 FBIS-AFR-93-169, 2 September 1993 (AB0209114593 Monrovia Radio ELBC).

32 Ibid.

33 Stanton Peabody, Reuters, Monrovia, 2 September 1993.

34 Ibid., 3 September 1993.

35 Lansana Gberie, 'Briefing Truth and Justice on Trial in Liberia', African Affairs, 107/428, (Oxford University Press on behalf of Royal African Society, 2008), 460.

36 10 September 1993: 'Executive Summary – The Carter Camp Massacre – Results of an Investigation by the Secretary General's panel of Inquiry' (published in New York).

37 A.T. Reuters, Monrovia, 21 September 1993.

38 Ibid.

39 AFJN Bulletin, 25 September 1993, quoting Steve Weizman, Reuters correspondent in Abidjan, 20 September 1993.

40 The LTRC report makes note of a special inquiry committee tasked with investigating the Carter Camp Massacre and other massacres perpetrated at this period. However, there is no further mention of the matter (LTRC, Consolidated Final Report, vol. 2, 72, 202, 253).

41 Executed in August 1994 for leading a mutiny against Taylor.

42 Ellis, Stephen, op .cit., 100–101.

43 Lansana Gberie, op. cit., 460–461.

44 Liberia: Carter Camp – 20 Years After the Massacre, The New Dawn, 24 February 2012.

45 A.T. Stanton Peabody, Reuters, 8 September 1993.

46 The frontline extended from Vahun through Voinjama, Zorzor Salsyea, Bong Mine, Kakata, Firestone and Buchanan.

47 A.B. Cahill to Harkin, 7 September 1993 (Fax).
48 AFJN Bulletin, 11 September 1993 (quoting from Steve Weizman, 'Record Aid Shipment leaves for Liberian Interior', Reuters, Abidjan, 9 September 1993).
49 AFJN Bulletin, 11 September 1993. See FBIS-AFR-93-130, 9 /7/1993 (AB0607151993 Paris AFP).
50 West Africa, 6–12 September 1993, 1591 (from Ben Asante in Monrovia).
51 Anthony Goodman, 'UN Proposes 350-man observer mission for Liberia', 10 September 1993 (Reuters).
52 AFJN Bulletin, quoting from Reuters (n.d, September 1993).
53 Ibid., 21 October 1993 (Fax).
54 The Liberia Peace Council, founded by George Boley, had been drawn mainly from Krahn members of ULIMO and AFL.
55 A.B. Quinlan to Cahill, 24 October 1993.
56 Rufus Darpoh, West Africa, 24 October 1993, 1987.
57 Isaac Musa was among the 23 names listed as 'Dead Perpetrators' compiled by the LTRC. See LTRC Consolidated Final Report, vol. 2, 329 ('The list of 'Dead Perpetrators', represents perpetrators who the LTRC determines were responsible for various forms of human rights abuses … and war crimes but died before the conclusion of the LTRC').
58 The Congregation for the Propagation of the Faith which is responsible for the direction of the Church's missions worldwide.
59 A.G. November 1993 – Report on Liberia, 1 July–20 November 1993.
60 Covering the period 1 July – 20 November 1993.

18 ECOWAS and UN commitments increase in the region

It will be remembered that UN Observer Mission in Liberia (UNOMIL) had been established for a period of seven months and that an extension of its mission would be dependent upon reports submitted to the Security Council by the Secretary General, Boutros Boutros-Ghali. Under the terms of the mission, such a review was scheduled for 16 December, and unless the Secretary General could report substantive progress in implementing the Cotonou peace accord, the mission would be aborted.[1] Boutros-Ghali's report, submitted on 13 December, was generally positive. The Council of State had been selected although its installation – now more than three months overdue – had not yet taken place. The delay had been caused by the failure of disarmament to commence. This in turn awaited the expansion of ECOMOG forces to include contingents to which the NPFL had agreed to disarm. These forces were in the process of being recruited. Regarding the incoming LNTG which was to exercise its authority over all of Liberia, eleven out of 17 cabinet posts had been allocated. It seemed therefore that genuine progress had been made and that outstanding problems would soon be resolved. However the report did mention the emergence of two new factions, the Liberia Peace Council (LPC) in the south-east and the Lofa Defence Force[2] in upper Loffa, which had complicated the political scene. On the other hand, as of 11 November, there had been agreement on when disarmament should commence and on the 'roles and responsibilities to be entrusted to UNOMIL and ECOMOG.'[3]

In his concluding remarks Boutros-Ghali again expressed the view, widely shared, that the timetable laid down at Cotonou was over-ambitious. But he reassured the Security Council that there was 'every indication' disarmament would shortly begin and that the LNTG would soon be installed. In addition, he hoped in his next report to be able 'to provide more precise information on the timetable for elections' to be held during the first half of 1994.' He also noted that there had been no major violations of the ceasefire. Taking everything into account he therefore felt able to recommend that the Security Council 'should continue to implement the mandate entrusted to it under Resolution 866', although it was 'unlikely that the original timetable for elections would be met.' The assessment failed to mention that the cantonment centres where disarmament and demobilisation would take place, had not been inspected because the

DOI: 10.4324/9781003219309-23

militias – and primarily the NPFL – had refused access to both ECOMOG troops and UN observers. Nor was it true to say that there was 'every indication' that disarmament was imminent. If anything, the opposite was the case.

Within two weeks of Boutros-Ghali's statement, tensions within the transitional Council of State erupted. Its chairman-elect, Bismarck Kuyon, the IGNU nominee, had been replaced. This was directly related to the NPFL's earlier substitution of the well-respected Dorothy Musuleng-Cooper by Taylor's chief-of-staff, battle-hardened Isaac Musa. This had upset the balance of the Council which now required a stronger chairman. Kuyon, it appears, had been acting in a manner which suggested he was no longer a representative of those who had accredited him.[4]

Moreover, despite Boutros-Ghali's claim that there had been no serious breaches of the ceasefire, one body, not party to Cotonou, was continuing to fight and made no apologies for it. This was the LPC, whose activities, according to James Butty, were threatening to 'derail the gains made so far in the search for peace.'[5] This organisation was now claiming to have recaptured from the NPFL five of Liberia's 13 counties, including Grand Gedeh, Rivercess, Sinoe, Maryland and Grand Kru. It was also claiming to have captured and killed Nelson Taylor, elder brother of the NPFL leader, on 11 October in Sinoe County. And its chairman or leader, Dr George Boley, of the Krahn ethnic group, was addressing journalists, and anyone who would listen, in Washington DC about the reasons for the LPC's aggression and also offering its remedies for Liberia's problems. Boley, educated in a Catholic school, a graduate of the University of Akron, Ohio, formerly a member of the Progressive Alliance of Liberia and later adviser and Minister of State during the Samuel Doe regime, described the LPC as 'a non-ethnic, non-religious, non-partisan movement.' It had taken up arms, he said, because the NPFL had committed 60 violations of the Cotonou Accord in Boley's home county of Grand Gedeh. What was absolutely true was that Boley's movement had nothing to do with preserving the integrity of the Cotonou Accord but was hell-bent on revenge against the NPFL which had wrought havoc among the Krahn of Grand Gedeh County.[6]

***

Much refreshed by leave in Ireland, on Christmas Eve 1993 Tony Jennings and John Kilcoyne returned to Buchanan which for the past three months had been served by Fr Jonathan Aidoo and before that by Fr David Bansubu, chaplain to the Ghanaian ECOMOG contingent. On arrival they received 'a great welcome' but also experienced much 'sadness at the absence of so many familiar faces and by the colossal presence of so many displaced people.'[7] Jennings noted in his diary that there were now almost 2,000 displaced in the mission compound, most sleeping in shelters erected by Médecins Sans Frontières and Action Internationale Contre la Faim, while the mission community hall was being used for treatment of malnourished children and pregnant women. The town itself, which was catering for almost 40,000 displaced, was 'very peaceful, with ECOMOG in complete control.' However a short distance away on the

Rivercess road the NPFL and LPC were fighting one another, plundering villages, and making it impossible to reach many of Buchanan's outstations. Yet one by one Buchanan parishioners, who had fled *en masse*, the previous year,* were returning.

> Most had endured horrifying experiences. Many had been tortured and the women raped; all had seen people killed for no particular reason. Some of them spent over a year travelling through the bush, going from village to village and often sleeping in the open.[8]

***

On the previous Sunday Catholic members of the Nigerian ECOMOG contingent had held a 'harvest'** in Kakata for which Battalion Commander, Dominic Oneya, laid on an escort for all who wished to travel from Monrovia. Cahill had invited Mattie Gilmore to travel with him. Gilmore was not in the best of form. Recently the Spanish John of God congregation, which ran St Joseph's Catholic hospital in conjunction with the Sisters of the Immaculate Conception, had been joined by one of their priest members who would now become the 'official' chaplain. Having up to then had the field to himself, Gilmore was somewhat at a loss, despite the assurance of Brother Joseph (the superior) that the new priest would 'not be touching anything he had been doing for the past decade.'[9]

***

There was good news on the question of additional contingents for ECOMOG. On 23 December the first Tanzanian troops arrived and by 7 January some 500 of the expected 800 had landed. On the same day the first group of Ugandan troops, 150 in number, disembarked in Monrovia – they were expected shortly to take up positions in Buchanan – while a 10-man military delegation from Zimbabwe flew in 'to finalize arrangements' for the deployment of their troops.[10] But there still remained anxieties. Of the ten encampment sites selected only three had been inspected and equipped to receive demobilised fighters. In addition, ULIMO-K and the NPFL – both citing security concerns – had not yet accorded permission to UNOMIL to travel freely within Greater Liberia; while the failure of the factions to provide detailed information on the number and location of fighters, weapons and mines, remained a major obstacle to disarmament. Moreover, as the old year waned, Charles Taylor started questioning the interpretation of the Cotonou Accord with regard to disarmament. He told the BBC that Cotonou did not direct ECOMOG to undertake disarmament.[11] Instead it had given that right to the incoming transitional government once it was installed. And ECOMOG would have to await instructions from that government before acting on the issue. Sawyer, in contrast, said the accord should be followed to the letter and that the process of disarmament should begin in earnest before the

---

*   Many had fled during the bombing of Buchanan by ECOMOG in October 1992 and many more subsequent to fighting between ULIMO and the NPLF.

**   A Harvest = liturgical thanksgiving for a successful harvest at which a portion is given to the Church.

installation of the transitional government.[12] And he repeated that according to the accord, responsibility for disarmament was entrusted solely to ECOMOG with UNOMIL providing assistance.

***

One person not afraid to speak his mind on the developing political situation was Captain Valentine Strasser, the youthful Sierra Leonean head of state. He told journalists that according to the Cotonou Accord the warring factions were 'expected to disarm and encamp before the creation of a transitional government.' But 'instead they had shocked the world by spawning more factions.'[13] The Americans were also alarmed by the lack of progress. On 18 January a State Department spokesperson said that with the arrival of additional ECOMOG forces and almost a full complement of UN Observers, it was time for the Liberian parties 'to take responsibility and settle their political differences.' They should 'proceed immediately with disarmament and the concurrent installation of the transitional government.'[14] Concurrently a senior State Department officer declared that the administration would stop supporting the process unless an agreement on disarming was reached by February.[15] The Clinton administration's position, he said, was the same as that of the Security Council which would have completed another review of UN involvement by the same date. The U.S., it must be said, had contributed $31 million to 'put Tanzanian and Ugandan troops into Liberia to disarm factions.'[16] If they were unable to accomplish this, he added, 'then there would be no point in continuing support.'[17]

Efforts to speed up the peace process by exhortation and even threats and warnings, appeared to bear fruit when on 15 February a meeting in Monrovia's Riverview district, held under the auspices of ECOWAS, the UN and the OAU, and attended by the IGNU, NPFL and ULIMO-K, reached 'certain basic agreements.' The date of 7 March was set 'for the full deployment of ECOMOG and UNOMIL throughout Liberia and for the beginning of disarmament.'[18] In addition, all parties agreed to the installation of the LNTG 'concomitant with the beginning of disarmament.' It was also agreed that elections would be held on 7 September, six months later.

There was one caveat. Agreement on these issues was reached after assurances of support were given by UN Special Representative Gordon-Somers. And these assurances would have to be meaningful. Amos Sawyer explained what exactly was at stake in a letter to the UN Secretary General.

> As you may be aware, the ECOMOG Field Commander has, on many occasions, expressed the very serious problems of logistics facing the peace keeping forces. Without such logistics, which we are informed, include transportation and communication equipment, ECOMOG would be unable to deploy its forces throughout the country and begin disarmament, a condition for the installation of the LNTG.

At the meeting, recognising these facts, Gordon-Somers had given 'the necessary assurances' that ECOMOG's requirements would be met in time to carry out its expected assignment. In a word, meeting the deadlines of 7 March and 7 September was dependent on 'the delivery of the needed logistics,'[19] and nothing would happen unless everything was fully in place.

Also agreed at the Monrovia summit was the provision to ECOMOG by each of the factions of lists of their combatants and weapons. This was to be done within 48 hours. By 22 February lists had been handed in from the AFL and NPFL. ULIMO-K did not meet the deadline giving encouragement to a rumour then circulating that Kromah had been killed. Whatever about this rumour (which was unfounded) ULIMO-K was reported to have created havoc in Kakata the previous Tuesday when its units stopped and completely looted a UN relief convoy bound for Gbarnga.'[20]

***

As 7 March (1994) drew near, destined to see the installation of the LNTG and commencement of disarmament, excitement grew not only within Liberian borders but internationally. On 3 March, under the by-line of Mark Fritz who had followed the Liberia story for over a decade, *The Washington Times* published an encouraging article under the heading: 'Liberia's brutal civil war expected to end soon.'

> On Monday 7 March, tens of thousands of guerrillas are to come out of the bush and give up their guns in exchange for two T-shirts, a pair of slacks, sneakers, a bag of rice and a bus ride back to their villages. On the same day, a coalition government comprising the three main combatants is to convene with the sole purpose of steering the nation towards multiparty elections on 7 September. Even the main players seem driven by the collective will to end this ugly war, bending their positions into a series of 11th hour accommodations. Never has peace seemed so clearly at hand in Liberia.

Fritz was not the only one carried away by the excitement. Even the NPFL appeared to have been affected. Taylor's current chief negotiator, John Richardson, declared that disarmament was the 'easy part of the deal.' The real challenge would be making the new transitional government work. 'We want to give fighting up quickly and move into the political arena.'[21] In the meantime, older, often discarded, politicians who had managed to keep their heads down during the fighting, were emerging from the shadows to eye the Presidency. One such aspirant, Harry Moniba, had been a vice-president during the Doe regime, a man who now, according to Fritz, 'types deep into the night in his $100-a-day hotel room (his house was looted by the war) while rushing to complete a book that will outline his platform.' His slogan: 'I'm prepared, I'm capable, I'm willing and I'm available.'[22]

In the new mood however there remained a gnawing worry at the back of minds, caused by the fact that there had as yet been no agreement on the allocation of the four key cabinet positions in the incoming transitional government. Successive efforts to resolve this difficulty had failed.[23] A final attempt had been made on February 28 during a meeting of the parties held in the Virginia suburb of Monrovia. That meeting represented a last-ditch effort to give shape to the transitional government. Without it there could be no installation and the 15 February agreement would be worthless. However, sufficient was salvaged at the meeting to proceed when it was agreed that the appointment to the four key ministries should be made by the incoming LNTG, and that the leadership of that body should be shared. David Donald Kpormakpor (IGNU's nominee) was named Chairman, Thomas Ziah (ULIMO nominee) First Vice-Chairman and Isaac Musa (the NPFL's nominee) Second Vice-Chairman.[24]

Monday, 7 March, deadline for the commencement of disarmament and the installation of the government, would test whether Liberia had a genuine peace process. The LNTG was installed after a delay of five hours, owing to ULIMO infighting, its new ministers and their officials occupying by nightfall the defunct IGNU offices in the Executive Mansion.[25] Three days later the UN Security council voted to continue with its mission to Liberia until 22 October 1994. As for disarmament, a few days in advance of the LNTG's seating, ECOMOG had begun to deploy in ULIMO-held territory (in the west – near the border with Sierra Leone), while ECOMOG forces accompanied by UNOMIL moved over the border into NPFL-held Liberia. Troops from the Ghanaian contingent took over responsibility for Monrovia. AFL compliance was signalled by its commander, General Hezekiah Bowen.[26] On 8 March a total of 152 AFL fighters handed over their weapons, with 300 more on the following day. In all, UNOMIL estimated the AFL to consist of some 7,000 fighters. Although this was not impressive it did represent a beginning. Significantly, there was no response from the larger factions.

UNOMIL estimated the strength of ULIMO and NPFL at about 10,000 fighters each. By 9 March, 48 hours after the deadline, neither had begun disarming. However, both UN and ECOMOG officials played down the delay expressing confidence that both groups would commence disarmament by the weekend. ULIMO-K had not started, it was claimed, because of infighting within its ranks. The NPFL said it would start as soon as its security could be guaranteed. What exactly did this mean? The infighting within ULIMO referred to a challenge thrown down by its military commander, General Roosevelt Johnson, some days previously, to the political leadership of Alhaji G.V. Kromah.[27] The latter had been the recognised leader of ULIMO-K since the split with Raleigh Seekie, and it was he who nominated ULIMO's two appointees to the LNTG's collective presidency. The issue which sparked the crisis was Kromah's replacement of nominee Thomas Ziah, by Dextor Bah Taylor. Johnson objected to Ziah's removal telling journalists that Kromah was acting unilaterally and was therefore relieved of his duties as chief spokesperson for the movement.[28] The roots of the conflict within ULIMO were plainly ethnic. Kromah was a Mandingo, while those who opposed him were almost exclusively Krahn. As the conflict developed rumours began to circulate that Kromah had links with Muslim extremist groups and that he was being supported by Islamic troops from Guinea and Mali. Although Mandingo Liberians were well received in Guinea, and ULIMO-K received help, there is no evidence that either Malian or Guinean troops became involved. A further obstacle in the way of disarmament was the proliferation of sub-factions whose leaders had signed none of the agreements.[29] The Lofa Defence Front and the Bong Defence Front were the most recent, allied to Taylor and Kromah respectively. A third, larger sub-faction was George Boley's LPC, made up of Krahn formerly in the AFL and 'understood to be supported clandestinely by Bowen's forces.' At the very moment disarmament was to start this latter body commenced attacks on NPFL positions in the south-east, seizing control of coastal areas east of Monrovia and 'pushing Taylor back to within 19 miles of his Gbarnga capital.'[30]

And there were rumours too that there were significant differences on how disarmament should be carried out between Major General Inienger, ECOMOG's field commander (December 1993–August 1996) and his UNOMIL counterpart, Major General Oprande. That there were certain tensions between ECOMOG and UNOMIL could hardly be doubted. For example, ECOMOG officers resented the fact that UNOMIL – a body that, among other reasons, was brought in because of Taylor's distrust of ECOMOG – was empowered by the various agreements not just to observe the conduct of disarmament but to supervise it. And they also took exception to an earlier broadcast by Oprande in which he praised the 'good faith' of the NPFL for announcing that it would commence disarmament unilaterally. They accused him of naivety 'in failing to recognize that the NPFL wanted to avoid close monitoring of its positions and the location of its arms caches.'[31]

The 'infighting' within ULIMO-K turned out to be more serious than anticipated. On Thursday, 10 March, UPI reported at least 200 killed in Bong Mine and Katata during the previous week. This had rendered the Bong Mine area inaccessible as the priests from the territory, Frs Aarokiasamy and Balaswamy, discovered when they attempted to return after a meeting in Monrovia. Moran, for his part, writing to his Provincial in Tenafly on 10 March, reported that 'no real effort to hand over arms' had been made by ULIMO-K or the NPFL and that Taylor's government in Gbarnga was still in place.[32] On the very next day, however, Taylor made the following dramatic declaration to a group of journalists at his Gbarnga headquarters. 'At 1500 hours GMT tomorrow we are going to begin handing our guns to the Tanzanian forces, wherever they are.' And on the following day Reuters correspondent, Stanton Peabody, confirmed that Taylor had kept his word. And there was further good news, this time concerning the ULIMO-K tribal split. On the same day as the NPFL's act of disarmament ULIMO's military commander, General Roosevelt Johnson, declared on national radio that 'in the interest of `peace in Liberia' he still recognised Kromah as leader of the movement, concluding with a rousing declaration of allegiance to ULIMO-K and to the Cotonou Accord:' I pledge my loyalty to the organisation and call on all fighters to lay down arms.'[33]

The handing-over of weapons by the NPFL, trumpeted by Taylor as the beginning of disarmament, which took place in the central town of Konola, was a token gesture, never to be repeated. Regrettably, Taylor explained to journalists, because the NPFL was under attack from LPC militia, his forces would be compelled to keep their weapons in the southeast. A more realistic appraisal of what was happening appeared in the text of Archbishop Michael Francis Lenten Pastoral, issued on 27 March:

> Right now, two full weeks after the seating of the LNTG [with a mandate to govern all Liberia] the country remains partitioned, *de facto*. The writ of the transitional government extends no further than that of the defunct IGNU government. By now the extended ECOMOG was supposed to have been the only armed group in the country, deployed throughout the length and breadth of the land and responsible for security, effectuating a programme of disarmament and demobilization. In fact, ECOMOG has penetrated into the country no further than the Po River Bridge in one direction and Konola, in another. Token disarmament is all that has taken place to date. The three fighting factions are still maintaining an armed military capacity and remain in a posture of confrontation with ECOMOG.[34]

The sense of euphoria evident in the days leading up to the 7 March deadline - which had caused many Liberians, including Archbishop Francis, to see the peace process as 'irresistible' – was now showing itself to have been illusory. It had been born of weariness and desperation and a sense that if everyone hoped enough what was hoped for would materialise. The cold reality which was now apparent was that Liberia's crisis still remained and was deepening. The sincere professions of 'good faith' and true 'patriotism' by the chief faction leaders were a lie. They had signed the documentation setting up the LNTG and the programme of disarmament; and had gone as far as initiating participation in these affairs. But their real objective was political power, to seize it irrespective of the wishes of the people. For them this was 'irresistible.'[35]

***

By the end of the month, although ECOMOG commanders publicly professed to be encouraged by the level of compliance,[36] the disarmament of combatants had failed to proceed beyond token gestures. According to UN estimates, by the last day of the month less than 1,500 of the 60,000 fighters, had disarmed, and of the 556 weapons handed in, many were rusted and obsolete.[37]

On the political front the ingenuity for contriving reasons for non-compliance, noted in his letter by Francis, was already evident. The NPFL had challenged the LNTG's first decision, namely that all nominees for ministerial portfolios must undergo a confirmation process presided over by the Speaker of the Interim Legislature. Taylor declared that his nominees would stand aside from any confirmation process and that he would only recognise the LNTG when his nominees took up office. Of the ministries already allocated, Taylor's nominees occupied the most important. Through his control of agriculture, lands and mining, he was effectively in command of the nation's resources; the labour and internal affairs ministries gave him the capacity to manipulate appointments; while the information ministry gave control over the dissemination of information.[38] Regarding the outstanding ministerial appointments – Finance, Defence, Justice and Foreign Affairs – Taylor now announced his rejection of the method agreed at the frantic negotiations of 28 February. The matter should not be decided by a vote of the LNTG; instead his nominees for the Justice and Foreign Affairs portfolios, Messrs J. Laveli Supuwood and Momolu V. Sackor, should be inducted without delay. Thus, after almost three weeks of existence the LNTG cabinet could not be seated. By the same token when the proclamation calling for the dissolution of the IGNU and of all factions was promulgated on 14 March – in accordance with the Cotonou Accord – only the IGNU dissolved itself. By the end of the month all factions remained in place.

***

Meanwhile the internal strife within ULIMO-K, which appeared to have been resolved, broke out again with a vengeance on 25 March. This took the form of an attack on Tubmanburg, Kromah's Liberian headquarters, by Krahn fighters loyal to Roosevelt Johnson. This was eventually beaten off with heavy casualties among the Krahn.[39] And there was further disruption in southeast Liberia (Rivercess County) caused by hostilities between the NPFL and the LPC.[40] Compounding the disruption and impeding the work of ECOMOG and UNOMIL, the LPC was reported to be making further gains from the NPFL, now controlling not only Grand Gedeh County but Tappita, the key border town between that county and Nimba County.[41] Finally, the AFL which had trumpeted its willingness to disarm on numerous occasions, was now saying (through its leader Hezekiah Bowen) that it had no intention of disarming.[42] In Liberia, once again, after a brief interlude of hope, it was business-as-usual.

***

A new and significant variation in divisions within factions occurred on 20 April when a number of NPFL nominees to ministerial office in the LNTG took their seats without the approval of their leader. Taylor immediately took to the airwaves to deny the validity of their action, warning them that he could no longer guarantee their safety if they tried to return to Gbarnga and suggesting instead that they stay where they were, 'among the rats and the roaches.' Among those who had defied their leader were the hitherto most loyal Tom Woewiyu, appointed LNTC Minister for Lands, Mines and Labour, leading many to wonder how deep was the split.[43]

***

The closing week of April found Archbishop Michael Francis in Rome attending a synod of African bishops gathered to discuss the future of the Church on their continent. Among public statements issued was a plea calling on the Western world to stop selling arms to African countries – a practice that was greatly exacerbating the already grave problems of tribalism and ethnic rivalry. Michael Francis was given special prominence commenting on this issue. Frankly admitting that Africans were responsible for much of the chaos and dislocation, he also pointed the finger at outside influences in an eloquent if sometimes distraught *cri de coeur*.

> Where do we get our armaments from? Who manufactures them? Where does the money come from and where is it banked? We do not exonerate ourselves. The internal factors are there, unfortunately, but we also have external factors. We are dictated to – what we should eat, what we should wear, how we should sell our goods, at what prices, how many children we should have – all by external forces. Our fundamental rights are trampled upon when we have such structures imposed on us.[44]

Meanwhile, yet another review of Liberia's progress towards peace was scheduled by the UN Security Council for 19 May (1994); and UN officials again warned that UNOMIL would be withdrawn if 'acceptable headway' was not found to have been made.[45] U.S. Assistant Secretary of State for African Affairs, George Moose, also weighed in, warning that 'while we remain committed to the process we cannot maintain this support without a clear demonstration of the Liberian parties' own commitment to peace.'[46] Even as these warnings were being issued a new menace of violence had arisen in the Firestone-Harbel area. Here General Hezekiah Bowen, the AFL commander, accused NPFL forces of infiltrating AFL positions and announced that unless ECOMOG intervened there would be ethnic slaughter on a scale to rival that currently taking place in Rwanda. In response ECOMOG hurried two truckloads of soldiers to the area 'as a preventative and precautionary measure.'[47] This measure had little effect with gun battles raging in the vicinity of Harbel two days later and a number of incidents in which ECOMOG peacekeepers were detained by NPFL patrols.[48]

Despite these setbacks, Boutros-Ghaili was optimistic when he addressed the Security Council on 19 May. He told the members he was pleased that the Liberian parties had now 'succeeded in implementing one of the major tasks called for in the Cotonou Accord', namely the seating of the LNTG.[49] The selection of the four outstanding major cabinet posts – which had held up this crucial step for so long – had finally been resolved the previous Friday when the Foreign Ministry was awarded to the NPFL and the remaining three portfolios (Justice, Defence and Finance) were divided between the INPFL, ULIMO and IGNU. The Security Council responded positively, noting its satisfaction at the installation of the LNTG and agreeing to extend UNOMIL's mandate for a further period.[50]

As it had done on every occasion it had met, the Security Council also expressed its concern at the hostilities within and between the various militias and called on them to resolve their differences.[51] The meaningless nature of such calls, when not backed by effective action, was again evident as groups of survivors of yet another series of massacres began arriving in Monrovia. These had been perpetrated by the bizarrely named Liberia Peace Council against people suspected of supporting the NPFL and had been taking place systematically over some months.[52] Monrovia also received a small number of civilians evacuated from Tubmanburg by ECOMOG. Among them were the Indian

priest, Fr Aarokiasamy and the Liberian seminarian Charles Boyce. Also evacuated were 17 UN workers who had been held as hostages.[53]

***

Taylor, with his eyes firmly focused on the forthcoming election continued
to make demands. He called on the LNTG to set up an army of 5,000 men,
half of which would be drawn from the NPFL[54] — a demand which was firmly
rejected by the chairman of the transitional government, David Kpormakpor.
'While we are trying to take away the guns, it is proposed that we form yet
another army out of these same men and return the guns to them.' Furthermore, he declared himself doubtful that the all-important elections, scheduled
for 7 September, would take place on time because of the lack of interest in
peace among the warring factions. And he was worried that the U.S. government, the principal funding agency for UNOMIL, might, as it had recently
indicated, abort its support if by 30 June (the date of the next UN Security
Council review) some 30% to 50% of arms were not handed up.

In an effort to redress this darkening situation Kpormakpor's government had
asked ECOMOG to enforce disarmament only to be told that it lacked sufficient strength to use force. To compound Liberia's misery the Ghanaian government, noting that disarmament had stopped, and the planned elections
would not be 'feasible', signalled its intention to withdraw its troops 'unless the
warring factions quickly prove they want peace.'[55] Few had any hope that they
would.

Notes

1   Report by the UN Secretary General to the Security Council, on the UN Observer
    Mission, 13 December 1993.
2   Founded by Francois Massaquoi in 1993 to defend Lofa County from ULIMO.
3   Ibid.
4   West Africa, James Butty, 20–26 December 1993, 2293.
5   Ibid.
6   See Ibid., vol. 2, 224, 226, 234, 253, 257, which lists massacres of Krahn and
    Mandingo in Grand Gedeh County. The report recorded 4,010 deaths and 6,569
    violations perpetrated against the inhabitants of the county, mainly (but not exclu-
    sively) by the NPFL.
7   A.B. Cahill to Harkin, 1 January 1994 (Fax).
8   A.B. A. Jennings, 'Personal Diary', 65–66.
9   Ibid.
10 FBIS-AFR-94–005, 7 January 1994, reproduced in AFJN Bulletin.
11 18 December 1993. See also, FBIS-AFR-94–047, 10 March 1994 (AB0903180394
    London BBC World Service).
12 AFJN Bulletin, 11 January 1994.
13 West Africa, 7–13 February 1994, 206.
14 Bill Dodds, Our Sunday Visitor, 30 January 1994.
15 AFJN Bulletin, James Butty, 10 February 1994.
16 Ibid., 10 May 1994.
17 Ibid.
18 A.T. Sawyer to UN Secretary General Boutrous Boutrous Ghali, 19 February 1994.
19 Ibid.

20 A.B. Cahill to Harkin, 22 February 1994 (Fax).
21 Mark Fritz, The Washington Times, 3 March 1994.
22 Ibid.
23 West Africa, 'Dateline', 7–13 March 1994, 390.
24 Africa Confidential, March 1994 (vol. 35, no. 5).
25 A.T. Moran to S. John Murray, 11 March 1994.
26 Steve Weizman, 7 March 1994, Monrovia, Reuters. 'Liberian Army Chief tells men to Disarm.'
27 Ibid., 9 March 1994.
28 AFJN Bulletin, Ezekiel Pajibo, 'Implementation of Liberian Peace Accord, an Update.'
29 See, Africa Confidential, March 1994 (vol. 35, no. 5); Liberia Working Group, Newsletter, no. 11, September 1994 (Jesuit Refugee Service, Rome).
30 See, Human Rights Watch, Africa, vol. 6, no. 3, 1994, 'Introduction to Report on Human Rights Abuses by the LPC.'
31 Ibid.
32 A.T. Moran to S. John Murray, 22 March 1994.
33 A.T. Stanton Peabody, Reuters, Gbarnga, 12 March 1994.
34 'That we may be free.'
35 Ibid.
36 A.T. See, Ezekiel Pajibo, AFJN Bulletin 'Update', 30 March 1994.
37 See The Washington Times 31 March 1994; Ben Asante, West Africa, 21–27 March 1994, 497; A.T. Moran to S. John Murray, 13 May 1994.
38 West Africa, 4–10 April 1994, 589.
39 Ibid.
40 Tepitapia Sannah (Deutsche Presse Agence, Monrovia), The Washington Times, 31 March 1994.
41 Ezekiel Pajibo, AFJN Bulletin 'Update', 31 March 1994.
42 15 April 1994, Reuters, Monrovia.
43 A.B. Cahill to Harkin, 21 April 1994 (Fax).
44 AFJN Bulletin, 21 April 1994, Philip Pullella, Reuters.
45 Ibid., Reuters, Monrovia, 17 May 1994.
46 AFJN Bulletin, transcript of UPI report, 19 May 1994.
47 Ibid; UPI, 17 May 1994.
48 AFJN Bulletin, transcript of UPI report, 19 May 1994.
49 Ibid., Reuters, Anthony Goodman.
50 AFJN Bulletin, 23 May 1994.
51 See Ibid., 19 May 1994, Reuters (Goodman).
52 Ibid., 20 May 1994, Abidjan. Nick Simeone.
53 Ibid., Tubmanburg, Liberia, UPI.
54 Ibid., 8 June 1994.
55 AFJN Bulletin, Nicholas Kotch, Reuters, Tunis, 11 June 1994.

Section 6
Endgame

19 Internal tensions within militias produces chaotic conditions in Greater Liberia, but Civil Society emerges as a major player

As the situation worsened efforts to save the peace process intensified, bordering on the frantic. A forum held in Abidjan attracted representatives from 18 countries, 15 international organisations and 12 non-governmental organisations. Here the fact began to sink in that there was little or no prospect of disarmament and that the deadline for elections would not be met. Speaking at its conclusion Wilson Tarpeh, LNTG finance minister, simply said that the elections would have to be postponed because disarmament had ground to a halt. Up to that point both the LNTG and the UN had been slow to make such an admission, fearing the effect it might have on international support for the peace process. Now Trevor Gordon-Somers was telling the gathering there was 'no doubt that if the country is not gun-free you cannot have free and fair elections.' The UN, he added, would 'not repeat the Angolan experience of elections without peace.'[1]

More locally, ten Liberian political parties, meeting for two days in Monrovia, called on the UN 'to provide logistics and military hardware to enable ECOMOG enforce peace.' And they again pleaded with ECOWAS to formally empower ECOMOG to engage in peace enforcement, as the Cotonou Accord was being ignored by all the militias.[2] Another effort to mediate in the crisis was mounted by Liberia's Inter-Faith Mediation Committee, which held 'closed-door negotiations on June 16 with Roosevelt Johnson, leader of the recently victorious* ULIMO-J faction.'[3]

But instead of any reduction in hostilities the situation deteriorated further. On Sunday 19 June 1994 Gbarnga radio reported that Taylor's fighters had been ordered to occupy the Buchanan highway and blow up all bridges in order to prevent the Liberia Peace Council from bringing arms into south-east Rivercess County. This was followed on Wednesday, 22 June, by renewed fighting between the AFL and the NPFL which finally blocked the highway to Buchanan.[4] A week later ULIMO-K, under Alhaji G.V. Kromah, overwhelmed the north-western section of Brewerville – a suburb of Monrovia – after renewed fighting with Johnson's ULIMO-J.[5] Peace prospects faded further after ULIMO-K called for the immediate withdrawal of the Nigerian contingent on the grounds that it had supported Johnson's faction in the recent leadership contest.

★   Victorious in the recent battle against ULIMO-K, but not in the war.

DOI: 10.4324/9781003219309-25

The call came after ECOMOG troops had raided Kromah's empty house in Monrovia where it uncovered an arsenal of weapons.[6]

And further depressing news came on 1 July, when BBC correspondent Nyenati Allison reported that the UN was pulling out its observers from the Tubmanburg area. This followed the abduction some days earlier of six UNOMIL personnel by ULIMO-J claiming they had been responsible for the World Food Programme's decision not to allocate rice to their faction. The observers' compound, located in Tubmanburg, was thoroughly looted and those abducted were beaten, prohibited food, and locked up in darkness. Withdrawing from the area would mean that the large UN base, situated outside the town, home to some 16,000 refugees, would be disbanded.[7]

One of those who did not see much prospect of success in the numerous efforts to save the peace process was former Foreign Minister in the now defunct IGNU, Dr H. Boimah Fahnbulleh. He placed much of the blame on U.S. policy towards Liberia and specifically its refusal to grant formal recognition to the LNTG, just as it had ignored the IGNU. This had 'strengthened the intransigence and refusal of the NPFL to honor the Cotonou Accord' and had given out a signal that the international community 'lacked the political will to assist.'[8] The failure of the U.S. administration to give recognition had indeed proved to be a serious setback to the IGNU and had come in for harsh criticism from Archbishop Francis. That it continued to be the case with the LNTG was unfortunate, significantly weakening that interim government's standing.

On Sunday 3 July 1994, two days after Fahnbulleh's view of the peace process was broadcast, the ebullient South African bishop, Desmond Mpilo Tutu, arrived in Monrovia 'to mediate an end to the war.' He had a lightning schedule, first meeting with Amos Sawyer and then travelling to Gbarnga to visit with Charles Taylor. Finally, he would meet members of the diplomatic corps and representatives of the UN agencies and NGOs.[9] Whether the visit had any meaning in terms of the peace process is doubtful, but it certainly attracted much media attention.

Another former Minister also ascending a platform to save Liberia's peace process was Dr Togba Nah Tipoteh. He had just visited the U.S. and was now passing through London on a tour in which he advocated a campaign by Liberia's civil society to end the war. Speaking in London he concluded that the warring factions did not really want peace. Rather they saw their interests best served by a continuation of the war, because 'they know they cannot see the light of day in free and fair democratic elections.' The time had come, he said, for the Liberian people to take their destiny in their own hands instead of depending upon peacekeepers and other outsiders.[10] Tipoteh claimed to lead an organisation with over a million members, including women and student groups, trade unions and cultural groups.[*] Civilian movements, such as that

---

[*]   The movement, known as the 'Civil Society and Special Interest Groups', represented 32 national organisations including the National Bar Association, Liberian business organisations, women's organisations, trade unions, teachers unions, Liberians in the diaspora, and youth organisations.

headed by Tipoteh, it must be said, were in the process of becoming more vocal and were to play an increasing part in the movement to bring about peace in Liberia. They were to become especially influential during the final years of the war.

***

Archbishop Francis was also on the move, visiting Washington DC between 18–22 July, hoping to meet administration officials and members of Congress. But there was little hope of attracting serious attention since the international focus at this time was firmly on Rwanda, Sudan and Nigeria. While there the archbishop spelled out, to whoever would listen to him, his priorities for action by the U.S. He urged the denial by the U.S. of travel instruments to the heads of the warring factions and their surrogates; also that U.S. resident permits for Liberians implicated in the war should be revoked. He called, too, for an intensified diplomatic campaign to increase financial support for ECOMOG. Finally, he implored the U.S. administration to recognise the LNTG, a measure which would 'help build confidence not only within the interim government but also among Liberians who were confused about U.S. support for the peace process.'[11] However, there was little interest either in this message, or indeed in Liberia, among the higher echelons of the administration. U.S. policy remained as it had been since Samuel Doe took power in 1980. America would work in the background to bring stability and peace leaving the 'heavy lifting' to the regional body.

***

The downward spiral continued into September with yet another bizarre twist. Late in July *West Africa* had published an article by Tom Woewiyu critical of Taylor.[12] Now, on Wednesday 7 September, Woewiyu was on the BBC announcing that Taylor was no longer leader of Greater Liberia's government (NPRAG). Early on the morning of that day Bishop Sekey drove an ailing Christian Brother and Gbarnga's Catholic pastor, Michael Flattery, to Monrovia. The Brother would be taken to hospital while Flattery was due to fly out to Ireland. The bishop had travelled in order to ensure their safety following disturbances during the previous 48 hours within NPFL ranks in Gbarnga.[13] They reached Monrovia safely, 'notwithstanding the many checkpoints and unnecessary delays on the road.' But by evening the bishop found himself unable to return to Gbarnga because that highway had been closed. Evidently during the day NPFL discipline had completely collapsed when rumours spread that Taylor had gone into hiding in Ivory Coast.[14]

The principal source of dissension within the NPFL, as already mentioned, was the decision by three of Taylor's senior associates Woewiyu, Sam Dokie and J. Laveli Supuwood, to take up ministerial posts in the LNTG against his wishes. Woewiyu and Dokie were now calling for Taylor's removal and execution, accusing him, among other things, of summarily putting to death several leading Liberian citizens, including Jackson F. Doe who, it was believed, had won the 1985 elections rigged by Samuel Doe.[15] There were also others suspected by the NPFL leader of disloyalty, of going the way of former NPFL commander, Prince Johnson. One of these had been Taylor's chief of staff, 23-

year-old General Nixon Gaye who, accused of conspiring with Dokie to lead a mutiny, had been injured in a skirmish and died after interrogation.[16][17] The killing had been followed by a mutiny of NPFL troops in Konola, Margibi County. Although this had been quickly suppressed it showed Taylor that he had reason, more than ever, to be nervous about the loyalty of his troops.

Dissension within the NPFL was only one cause of the extremely dangerous situation in which the inhabitants of Greater Liberia now found themselves and which led to the closure of the highway to Monrovia. For it coincided with a new onslaught by the LPC and ULIMO-K on Taylor's stronghold of Gbarnga.[18] Fighting was concentrated on an area some 20 miles to the west and south of the town but its ramifications were felt throughout the territory.

Ganta itself was in 'great confusion', with 'big crowds' streaming in. Law and order in the town was quickly breaking down with one vehicle taken from the Leprosy Rehabilitation Centre, and Médecins Sans Frontières losing all its vehicles and radio equipment. Cahill's information came from Bridget Murphy of the Medical Missionaries of Mary who was able to reassure him that Larry Collins, the pastor, was 'alright, but very uncertain about what he will be doing.'[19]

The news from Sannequellie, still in NPFL hands, was also disturbing. The two vehicles belonging to the Brothers of St Louis[20] had been taken the previous day and currently the two Dutch Brothers and four FMM Sisters were 'on radio every few minutes.' The most recent transmission found the Sisters 'very upset' as NPFL soldiers had recently entered their compound, taken the convent vehicle and were currently looting the premises. Their last words were: 'we do not know what is going to happen.' And since that moment there had been no further contact. Cahill was also able to report that all UNOMIL communications equipment in Sannequellie had been 'silenced', although the six observers there had not been harmed.[21]

Yekepa was equally worrying. There had been no contact since 8 September, when David Gbemie, the catechist, had been on the air. In Buchanan, however, both Kilcoyne and Jennings were safe and had been frequently in contact.[22] As for Tappita, there had been radio contact with the Sisters (Consolata) on 10 September. They had told Cahill 'Very simply, "we're OK"' – a phrase that, according to an agreed code, implied that the situation was really bad. And there had been no subsequent contact with them.[23] Two days later, reviewing the overall situation, Cahill noted that 'utter confusion' seemed to be 'the order of the day.' There was still no word of the whereabouts of Louis Zeigler (he had replaced Michael Flattery as Pastor in Gbarnga) who had been missing for some time, while in Phebe (near Gbarnga) and Cuttington 'all relief agency vehicles and houses' had been looted and there was 'still no clarity' as to what was going on within the NPFL.[24]

Early on the morning of 13 September, Cahill was relieved when Gbemie came on the radio from Yekepa, speaking carefully because of the danger of interception but indicating that the situation there had deteriorated to the point where he and his family, and many others, were preparing to cross over the border into Guinea.[25] On the following day came news that the Sisters and

Brothers from Sannequellie had successfully crossed the border and had arrived in Danané in a 'washed out' condition. Also evacuated to Danané were all UNOMIL personnel from Ganta, Sannequellie and Yekepa. A day earlier they had moved out of Todee, after leaving Konolo some time before.[26]

***

In the midst of the chaos, efforts to save the peace process continued apace, to the extent that peace initiatives were now getting in one another's way. All followed a familiar pattern. Already on 24 August a newly-formed grouping - the Liberia National Conference - had convened in Monrovia attended by a consortium of Liberian political parties, military factions, interest groups, woman's groups and other civilian organisations and remained in session for the remainder of September and beyond. Bizarrely, with this conference in full swing, the Ghanaian authorities, prompted by Gordon-Somers and Jimmy Carter, decided to hold a peace conference to which only the NPFL, ULIMO-K and the AFL were invited. This duly convened at Akosombo, near Accra, producing yet another peace accord, signed on 12 September 1994, in which the three factions mentioned were given 'free rein' to shape Liberia's future. The signatures to this agreement were Taylor, Kromah and Hezekiah Bowen. The witnesses were President Rawlings, current chairman of ECOWAS and Gordon-Somers. According to the agreement the LNTG was in effect to be replaced by a military Troika formed of the three largest factions. Reuters reported that, extraordinarily, the new government would be charged with disarming warring factions and leading the country to elections.[27]

Needless to say, the Akosombo Peace Accord, such as it was on paper, superseded the Cotonou Accord, although it presented itself as an attempt to salvage it.[28] How all this was to be achieved remained something of a mystery until 16 September, when in the absence of progress a delegation of Ghanaian ministers arrived in Monrovia where they extended invitations for further talks in Accra. Among the invitees were the three faction leaders, Taylor, Bowen, Kromah), Bayogar Junius and Varney Sherman representing the Liberia National Conference, Sawyer of the defunct IGNU and Philip Banks and Isaac Musa of the LNTG.

The Akosombo peace conference had taken place a matter of days after the breakdown of order in Gbarnga, described above,[*] which in turn was followed by attacks on the town by the various factions and militias opposed to Taylor. At the very time the accord was being signed, the siege of Gbarnga had intensified led by Kromah's ULIMO-K, supplemented by dissident NPFL forces, some ULIMO-J fighters and two smaller militias. Not surprisingly, when the conference was over, Taylor was unable to return to his capital from Ghana and went instead to 'a safe destination.'[29]

***

In contrast to the NPFL leader, Bowen returned to Monrovia to face the wrath of that city's civilian population and a revolt within the AFL. And wrath there was! When news of the Akosombo Peace accord became public, it was

★   See p. 257.

greeted with scorn in the free Liberian press, rejection by the Liberia National Conference which was still in session, and dismay in the streets. An increasing number of voices began to call for the head of Gordon-Somers.[30] Writing to Cork on 13 September Cahill reflected the thoughts of many.

> Now we have real trouble on top of what is already there ... the three ugliest military groups [NPFL, ULIMO-K, AFL] determining the future of the country ... and others scarcely less ugly who were excluded from the meeting destined to oppose the Ghana solution in the only way they know ... by continuing the killing and devastation.[31]

Ezekiel Pajibo, following events closely from the U.S. but with excellent contacts on the ground, wrote that the Akosombo Peace Accord

> rewarded the very individuals who are the primary cause for prolonging the civil war... But even more insulting to the Liberian people, was to put the fate of their country in the hands of three individuals who have shown callous disregard for human rights, and no inclination whatsoever towards pursuit of justice and democratic governance.

***

During the night of 14 September 1994, two days after the signing of the Akosombo Accord, chaos enveloped Monrovia with the sound of explosions and heavy gunfire, and broadcast warnings to stay indoors. It took some hours of daylight before it became clear that the AFL – supposed allies of ECOMOG – had attempted a coup. Under the leadership not of Bowen but of one of his military commanders, the notorious Charles Julu*, AFL soldiers had occupied and were holding the Executive Mansion. However, efforts to occupy other buildings and installations, had failed. As the day wore on ECOMOG tightened its ring around the Executive Mansion. It was later to emerge that the AFL act of war was prompted by the Akosombo meeting. Incensed at the outcome a large group led by Julu set out to kill Bowen [a signatory of the accord] and take control of the country. Bowen had fled to the nearest ECOMOG base for protection, while from within the Mansion Julu was putting out statements that he was not only in control of Monrovia but of the entire country.[32]

Taylor, too, was under pressure, coming on the BBC to deny he had been overthrown and to claim he was still in Gbarnga and in full control of Greater Liberia. Neither claim was likely to be true. It was known that the opposition to him was led by a coalition of which Woewiyu was a part. Many former

---

*   Julu had a long track-record of violence as a military commander with the Doe regime. He is listed among the 'Most Notorious Perpetrators' in LTRC, Consolidated Final Report, vol. 2, 351. There are several further references to his brutality in the LTRC findings. See ibid., 47, 218, 294, 295.

NPFL had joined it, including Oliver Varney, a former military commander. But although Taylor and the NPFL had been driven out of Gbarnga, largely by ULIMO, he had never been defeated or overthrown. Some sources were claiming that Ganta, a town which was mostly deserted, was now in his hands and that he had set up his headquarters in the Sisters' Convent.[33] Mike Moran had different information. Writing to Terry Doherty on 22 September, he placed Taylor 'somewhere in Ivory Coast.'[34] The truth was that there continued to be conflicting information about the whereabouts of the NPFL leader since he left Ghana.

***

Politically and militarily the close of September contained little to justify Archbishop Francis's vision of an 'irresistible peace process.' Within days of the signing of the Akosombo accord a large ECOMOG convoy, some 100 soldiers strong, evacuating civilian and foreign aid workers from Gbarnga, was ambushed, leaving two Tanzanian soldiers killed and four missing. The attack by ULIMO-J militia[35] took place near Kakata. At the same time, a jubilant Kromah, leader of the predominant ULIMO-K, was boasting that he now controlled Taylor's capital.[36] Kromah's development into a fully-fledged warlord and the triumph of his faction over Roosevelt Johnson's was now virtually complete. No longer was his movement based solely on avenging the massacre of Mandingo by the NPFL. It too was fully engaged in the pursuit of political and military power. The location of Kromah's headquarters was uncertain, believed to be either in Guinea or in the northern town of Voinjama, near the Guinean border to where he had moved in March after being driven from Tubmanburg by Johnson. Since then Johnson's Krahn force had dwindled with many defections while Kromah's Mandingo force, receiving some support from Islamic states, had gathered strength. In contrast, the fortunes of Bowen, AFL leader and ally of ECOMOG, were sharply in decline. Although not implicated in the coup attempt by his deputy Julu, he was now directly subject to the anger of Monrovia's citizens because of the Akosombo Accord, and was becoming marginalised.[37]

Meanwhile, Gordon-Somers looked more and more beleaguered, his last toss of the coin – the Akosombo-crafted military dictatorship by a triumvirate of warlords – roundly rejected by the vast majority of Liberians. He had returned to New York and was not expected to revisit Liberia. In fact, the UN had begun the process of disengagement, reducing UNOMIL's strength from 360 to 100 and removing all UN observers from combat zones which now comprised most of the country, and entrusting their duties to 'Liberian committees, each made up jointly of militia representatives', with UN staff supervising their activities from long distance – from Guinea and the Ivory Coast.[38]

In Gbarnga from which the NPFL now had been expelled, the victorious factions were fighting one another to the death over the entrails of that town. Nonetheless the NPFL was showing signs of regrouping elsewhere. What was sure, Reuters' astute Steve Weizman reported, was that Liberia 'had not heard the last of them.' Further up-country the 'mayhem' was continuing.[39]

***

A further effort to rescue whatever was left of the peace process commenced on 12 November when President Rawlings, current Chairman of ECOWAS, convened a meeting of the triumvirate at Akosombo.[40] Rawlings, it seems, was anxious once and for all for a conclusion so that he could bring home a Ghanaian contingent which could claim to have achieved its mission.[41] The original Akosombo Accord, it will be recalled, had been rejected by the Liberia National Conference because it rewarded those responsible for the failure to implement previous accords[42] However a softening of attitudes now began to be discernible among some members of the Conference, a body in which almost 1,000 Liberians, mainly from the political classes but also from civil society, participated. And when the Conference finally concluded its business and disbanded in early October it was felt that with certain changes Akosombo might become more palatable. Among these, it was suggested, might be provision for a meaningful inclusion of the Liberian political classes and Liberia's vast refugee constituency in the process. Responding to this change of attitude from Monrovia the Ghanaian and Nigerian Foreign Ministers met with the three Akosombo signatories on 6 November 'to fine tune' what had already been agreed. The opening statement by the Ghanaian chair of Akosombo II was a call to the Liberian political classes to 'accept a modified version' of Akosombo I as a 'workable framework for resolving the Liberian crisis.'[43] The talks were to continue intermittently through October.

***

Moran's view of the overall situation, given in a letter to Hayden dated November 10, was again typically forthright and unembellished. People were confused by the current Akosombo discussions, while ECOWAS was running out of patience at the lack of honesty of some of its member states. The Ivory Coast was continuing to assist Taylor, now allowing him to set up bases in its territory. Thus the recent very violent NPFL assault on Pleebo had been mounted from the Ivory Coast.[44] Nigeria was supporting 'any group that vows to get Taylor', namely the LDF, the LPC and both varieties of ULIMO. All the factions seemed to be low on munitions at the present but were vigorously rearming. The first group to rearm would waste little time in launching attacks on its enemies. And, regrettably, Moran continued, Liberia's civil society appeared to lack the resolve to end the conflict

> because those with education enough to guide and direct or be in the forefront of a mass peace movement are benefitting from the situation and so are reluctant to put time into a peace movement. Many are working at the UN or some other NGO making good U.S. dollars and kept busy with the work, so that they cannot agitate a real move for peace. Instead they talk about peace and give seminars on the topic.[45]

Moran's judgement on civil society perhaps underestimated the capacity of that constituency to rise above self-interest. In fact already there had been signs that civil society was stirring in a new direction.[*] Usually reticent, Moran's final words to Hayden reflected the strain under which he and his fellow missionaries were operating. 'Being here still is not easy… not easy, psychologically and physically.'

***

On 9 December Cahill visited Kakata where he was told it was the first night in two years without gunfire. It was also the eve of a day Kakata was unlikely to forget for some time:

> On that night five ULIMO soldiers had gone to a Fula man's store and killed two men. By 2 am, at orders of the ULIMO high command, the five were captured. At daybreak civilians were summoned to the town centre. At 7 am in their presence, the first three were brought out, petrol thrown on them, and they were burned alive; the other two were then brought out and simply shot. But it left the town frozen all day.[46]

Monrovia was soon to experience its own day of savagery, described by Cahill:

> 16 December was a black day in Monrovia as the full extent of the atrocities in the Cow Field area of Paynesville became clear, namely the massacre of truly humble, innocent people, the majority being infants and children. It is still unclear as to who did the shooting, butchering and eventual burning of the victims, whose remains were carried through the city yesterday afternoon, with a huge, angry but controlled crowd accompanying them…The big suspicion is that it had been a Krahn operation …witnesses seem to be bearing this out. But, Taylor, too, has launched his 'Operation Grasshopper'[**], which, he claims, does NOT include Monrovia. So we'll wait and see. The next few days will be very important, as far as gleaning some kind of direction in the present events.[47]

Much later it was to transpire that the NPFL had carried out the massacre.[48]

Two days after the Cow Field massacre the talks in Ghana reconvened. Those representatives who flew out from Monrovia were under no illusion of the mood in the city having witnessed the quiet, dignified procession of citizens bearing the dead through the city on the previous day. The message was clear, namely, not to return unless they brought peace. The talks produced what came to be known as the Accra Peace Accord signed on 21 December 1994. This provided for a general ceasefire to commence on 28 December and a non-aggression pact to come into force immediately.[49]

***

Despite the signing of the Accra Peace Accord, the year 1995 began in confusion, with faction leaders frustrating the peace process at every turn in their determination to position themselves favourably for elections which

[*] See, p. 258–59.
[**] See p. 266 above.

inevitably must come. Chief among these was Taylor, hard-bitten, elusive, clever, contemptuous. But there were new elements, too, which had entered into Liberia's life during the closing months of 1994 and grew more vocal in the early months of 1995. Among them was the emergence of the plain people of Monrovia shouting loud for all to hear that they had had enough, collectively expressing strong sentiments of disgust and disillusionment at the failure of warlords and politicians to agree a peace.

The first manifestation of this new populism was the massive demonstration which followed the 15 December Cow Field massacre. It took place at a time when the identity of the perpetrators was as yet unknown and all factions were suspected. Its spontaneous, disciplined and non-violent nature coupled to its very size gave a sense that the 'ordinary people' had at last risen up and were drawing a line which no warlord or faction might dare to cross. It sent out a powerful message to the warlords, at that very time mired in fruitless talks in Ghana, that 'enough was enough.'[50] Within a month, the return of the faction delegates from yet another fruitless round of negotiations in Ghana, witnessed a second massive demonstration, but of a different character. Equal in size, it quickly developed into a riot, with undisciplined youth engaged in burning, looting and killings. The extent to which this belligerence was spontaneous was questionable, more than one observer noting that the violence was perpetrated by young and familiar-looking thugs, reminiscent of those found at checkpoints in Greater Liberia. It is true that any demonstration ran the risk of being infiltrated by unemployed youth and street children motivated by the prospect of loot but in this case more familiar sinister elements appeared to have been at work. At least this was the common perception at the time. For although the 15 December demonstration engendered a sense of power and purpose, that of 15 January left the city 'shocked and frozen' by a sense that the stranglehold of the factions remained intact.[51] Nonetheless, the experience of having, albeit for a brief period, cast off this stranglehold did not go unremembered, and after the initial disappointment and despair the stricken population began tentatively to assert itself, this time more cautiously, forming neighbourhood watch schemes and other community organisations.

A second feature of the early months of 1995 was a steady growth in the military and political profile of the NPFL. Early in January Taylor, claiming to be back in Gbarnga, was re-arming and taking the offensive, his forces stiffened by 'a cadre of mercenaries'[52]. His so-called Operation Grasshopper, in which the NPFL made lightning and extremely violent raids on easy targets, struck fear into people not only in remote villages but in the suburbs of Monrovia[53]. The Cow field massacre was a stark example of this tactic. Equally his use of child soldiers manning road-blocks – young boys who had hardly reached puberty and were commanded to 'kill and kill quickly' – struck terror into Liberians. Not that the overall situation was without some hope. There was always the possibility the unending negotiations might yield results and Rawlings appeared determined not to fail. In his pursuit of agreement he had already visited Conakry in Guinea, Lomé in Togo, Abuja in Nigeria, Monrovia in Liberia, and he was shortly to visit the U.S.

It was at this point that the continuous pattern of failure, as well as the extension of the conflict beyond Liberian borders, led the Clinton White House to fear that the West African sub-region was on the verge of serious destabilisation. Within Congress anxiety was also increasing and leading members of both houses were calling for action. It was against this background that early in 1995 the White House appointed a 'Special Envoy to Liberia', Dane F. Smith Jr, with instructions to assist President Rawlings in his efforts towards peace.[54]

The setbacks experienced by Rawlings had now led him to realise that Nigeria, with its new leader, Sani Abacha, would have to be centre stage in the peace-making process. Ibrahim Babangida who had ruled Nigeria until August 1993, had been implacably opposed to Taylor. But Abacha, who had seized power in November of the same year, might be more even-handed in his dealings with the NPFL leadership.[55] Consequently, in March 1995, during a visit to the U.S., Rawlings suggested that the next ECOWAS summit on the Liberia crisis be held in Nigeria in the hope that this might encourage co-operation between Abacha and Taylor. This was well received by the Clinton administration which instructed Envoy Dane F. Smith to assist in bringing it about.[56]

***

On the political front, although he had never set foot in Monrovia since the start of his insurgency and did not do so now, Taylor was orchestrating a self-publicity campaign in the city, addressing Monrovia through his radio broadcasts as if he was already the elected president. Newspapers and radio stations appeared to indulge him with almost statesman-like status and there was a sense that this most determined of warlords would become chairman of the LNTG whenever it was seated and would win the subsequent presidential election hands-down. There were, of course, setbacks to his image-making crusade in the public mind. When it became known that he had executed a batch of his closest aides – briefly revealing the old Taylor – press coverage became less benign. But such setbacks were temporary.

***

Cahill continued to visit his confreres when there was a lull in fighting. He was relieved to observe that Buchanan, where the mission compound was still home for 'a mighty number of displaced persons', was 'very calm', and that thanks to ECOMOG the mission had the benefit of electric light for three or four hours each evening.[57]

In Monrovia, the scene was 'one of waiting ... waiting for the current round of negotiations in Ghana to come to a conclusion.' Agreement on the composition of the Council of State had so far proved elusive. Seats had been allocated to Taylor representing the NPFL, Chief Tamba Taylor representing rural Liberia, Kromah representing ULIMO, and Oscar Jaree Quiah representing the Liberia National Conference. The stumbling block was the fifth seat, allocated to a Coalition formed by those parties which had been ignored by Akosombo I[58] but for which an agreed nominee could not be produced. Contending for this last seat were Bowen of the AFL, now regarded as pro-

Taylor, and Supuwood, the one-time Taylor minister but now bitterly opposed to the NPFL. Such was the profile of those already nominated to the Council, the destination of its final seat would be of critical importance for the election of Council Chairperson.

***

On 13 January 1995 news reached Monrovia that the latest round of talks in Ghana had ended with the destination of the fifth seat still unresolved.[50] Boley (LPC), Bowen (AFL) and Supuwood had been proposed. The Ghanaian facilitators had requested the first two step down, but Bowen had refused. Taylor was apparently seething at the outcome, claiming in a press conference that he was being victimised, and denouncing 'Nigerian interference.' The facilitators, at their wits end, had then ordered the Liberian delegates home with orders to agree a candidate among themselves within days.

Early on the morning of Saturday, 14 January, the paved road surface leading to Spriggs Payne Airfield was found covered with slogans denouncing the warlords who were due to fly in later that day. Within hours large crowds began to congregate while ECOMOG soldiers tried to keep traffic flowing. Sometime later, elements in the crowd began to block roads and set tyres on fire, before moving to ransack the houses of politicians and warlords and setting them on fire.[60] Among those selected for this treatment were Gabriel Baccus Matthews, Francois Massaquoi, Tom Woewiyu and J. Laveli Supuwood. The fact that no NPFL, AFL or LPC figures had been targeted suggested that these latter organisations, and principally the NPFL, had infiltrated and orchestrated what had begun as another populist demonstration against those deemed responsible for the political impasse. Taylor, for his part, was to be heard more frequently on the air waves, incandescent with rage at the obstructions being placed in his way to becoming chairman of the new State Council. This caused growing apprehension at what he might do since his present utterances recalled similar tirades before unleashing Operation Octopus in 1993.

On 21 January as faction delegates flew out of Spriggs Payne airport for yet another round of negotiations in Accra, fighting erupted in the vicinity of Gbarnga and River Cess and more and more people flooded into Buchanan. In Yekepa, some 155 miles away, David Gbemie who had returned to his mission, was at last able to come back on the radio. Things were quieter, he said, and tension had eased. And Ted Hayden, who had just flown into Monrovia for a visit, was on his way to Gardnersville to take up residence with James Hickey. The country was truly full of paradoxes. On the previous day, the African Cup of Nations encounter between Liberia and Senegal went ahead as scheduled at the football stadium in Monrovia. As it transpired, Senegal equalised with the last kick of the game.[61] Such snatches of 'normality' helped to ease tension and tantalise people that there was another world, another type of living available if only politicians and warlords had the inclination to grasp it. The atmosphere around the match was 'good-humoured' and it was, at least for a couple of hours, 'like old times.'[62]

***

In Monrovia all awaited news of the latest negotiations in Accra,[63] without expecting too much. What was certain was that a further failure to agree would lead to more civil unrest, a prospect for which it seemed ECOMOG was on full alert.[64] However, on 27 January came the encouraging news that the State Council membership had at last been agreed. The contended 'fifth seat' was to be allotted to the AFL's Hezekiah Bowen. It only remained for its members to select a chairman and it now looked likely that Taylor would be appointed.[65] But the NPFL leader, on the very cusp of success, was to be thwarted for when the delegates returned to Ghana to appoint a chairman early in February there was further dissension, and the talks broke up in disarray.[66]

Taylor, like a wounded lion, flew out to Burkina Faso to plot his next move while fear that he was about to seize power now gripped Liberia, with ECOMOG on high alert in Monrovia, Buchanan and Kakata. The latter town was increasingly under threat as the NPFL continued to press towards the coast, holding the Bong Mine/Kakata road and reportedly abducting civilians from villages around Todee. One sign of the ECOMOG alert in Kakata was the hoisting into firing positions of four heavy-calibre artillery pieces which had been lying idle on the ground for the past month.

Up-country the situation was equally threatening. Irish NGOs working with Save the Children Fund and MSF-Holland, had briefly entered Liberia from the Ivorian border and reported that the NPFL was now in control from the border to Totota, that the notorious SUBs (Small Boy Units) were manning all checkpoints, 'more numerous and younger than before', and wearing t-shirts with terrifying slogans, such as the notorious: 'the killing must be done quick.'[67]

On the other hand, the proverb 'it's an ill wind that blows nobody good', was being quoted in Monrovia, since the stalemate concerning the selection of the Council Chairman had put off the evil day when the Council would enter Monrovia to be seated. Few of the warlords, it was widely anticipated, would set foot without bringing large military escorts; and the arrival of armed rival factions might push the city over the brink. But now that day was approaching.[68]

***

In Buchanan, fear of NPFL infiltration was low-down on the scale of worries since, once again, the town was overwhelmed by refugees. The intensification of fighting between the NPFL and Liberia Peace Council in the LAC area had led to an influx which ran no risk of over-dramatization. In excess of 12,000 had arrived in the previous weekend creating a humanitarian crisis of frightening proportions and in which Kilcoyne and Jennings, assisted by Willie Brandon SMA British Province, were now fully immersed.[69] In Kakata the atmosphere was one of foreboding as the Guinea ECOMOG contingent, which gave the town a sense of security, had recently been transferred to reinforce another line of defence against the feared NPFL assault on Monrovia – the line from Mount Barclay across the bush to Duport Road (scene of the Cow Field massacre).[70]

In Monrovia an uneasy calm prevailed with warnings by ECOMOG of NPFL infiltration.[71] There could be no doubt that NPFL elements were in the vicinity and could strike anywhere. Cahill had 'grisly evidence' of this when travelling to Kakata on 10 February:

> At Gate 15 the (ECOMOG) checkpoint commander brought me to a terrified lad who had just escaped from the nearby bush where the NPFL were present. The commander lifted the boy's ragged shirt to reveal a back almost bare of skin, the result of whipping with wire lashes. On his chest were razor marks while his elbows and wrists bore the ugly signs of the now-so-familiar 'tapaving' used by all the factions – tying together of elbows and wrists with insulated wire which quickly cut deep into the flesh. This had all happened to him within the previous three days after he had been abducted by the NPFL from Paynesville, just behind the Omega Tower not far from the city proper.

***

In Cape Palmas, traditionally the mission of the American SMA, the Church continued to be a 'Church in Exile', with its centre of gravity across the Ivory Coast border in Tabou where Bishop Boniface Dalieh was now living and where its main thrust was the pastoral care of thousands of Liberian refugees. There the agony of displacement was now being compounded by difficulties in accessing relief supplies, not because they were unavailable but because of bureaucratic chaos and corruption. Infant deaths caused by lack of food were increasing and debilitated refugees and their families were compelled to walk long distances to receive wholly insufficient measures of food.[72] The atmosphere there had become quite fraught, and Bishop Dalieh was in receipt of death threats.

Notes

1 AFJN Bulletin, Nicholas Kotch, Reuters, 21 June 1994.
2 A.T. 26 June 1994, UPI, Monrovia.
3 Ibid., 24 June 1994.
4 Ibid., 22 June 1994.
5 UPI, Monrovia, 25 June 1994.
6 A.T. Steve Weizman, Reuters, 27 June 1994 (from Voinjama).
7 FBIS-AFR-94–098, 20 May 1994 (AB1905192394 London BBC World Service).
8 FBIS-AFR-94–129, 3 July 1994, Radio ELBC.
9 UPI, Monrovia, 3 July 1994.
10 25 July 1994, IPS, Julian Samboma (An Inter Press Service Feature).
11 AFJN Bulletin, 1 August 1994.
12 A.B., Cahill to Harkin, 10 September 1994 (Fax).
13 A.T. Bishop Ben Dotu Sekey, 'Report on Gbarnga Diocese', 16 October 1994.
14 A.B. Cahill to Harkin, 10 September 1994 (Fax).
15 Ezekiel Pajibo, New People Feature Service, 1 October 1994.
16 LTRC, Consolidated Report, vol. 1, 229, records: 'August, 1994 – The NPFL was reported to have executed up to 80 of its own fighters, without trial, and to have tortured and killed Lieutenant-General Nixon Gaye, an NPFL Commander, for leading a mutiny against Taylor. Gaye also appears on the LTRC's list of 'Dead Perpetrators.'

17 Liberia Working Group, Newsletter, no. 11, September 1994 (Jesuit Refugee Service, Rome).
18 Ezekiel Pajibo, op. cit.
19 Ibid.
20 A teaching order of Brothers from the Netherlands.
21 A.B. Cahill to Harkin, 10 September 1994 (Fax).
22 Ibid.
23 Ibid., 12 September 1994 (Fax).
24 Ibid.
25 Ibid.
26 Ibid., 14 September 1994.
27 AFJN Bulletin, Reuters, 18 September 1994.
28 Ezekiel Pajibo, op. cit.
29 Steve Weizman, Reuters, Monrovia, 29 September 1994; See also, Bishop Sekey, op. cit.
30 Ibid. See also, A.T. Ezekiel Pajibo, op. cit.
31 A.B. 20–25 July 1994 (Fax).
32 A.B. Cahill to Harkin, 15 September 1994 (Fax).
33 Ibid., 19 September 1994 (Fax).
34 A.T. Moran to Terry (Doherty), 22 September 1994.
35 LTRC, vol. II, Consolidated Final Report, vol. 2, 229.
36 Liberia Working Group, Newsletter, No 11, September 1994 (Jesuit Refugee Service, Rome).
37 Steve Weizman, Reuters, Monrovia, 29 September 1994.
38 Ibid.
39 Ibid.
40 A.T., Ezekiel Pajibo, 'Liberia's Quest for Peace, Update' 12 November 1994, AFJN.
41 Dane F. Smith Jr. 'US-Guinea Relations during the Rise and Fall of Charles Taylor', The Journal of Modern African Studies, vol. 44, no. 3 (Sep. 2006), 426.
42 Ibid.
43 A.T., Ezekiel Pajibo, op. cit.
44 Moran said it had been mounted from the Nyaakan area.
45 A.T. Moran to Hayden, 10 November 1994.
46 Ibid., 9 December 1994 (Fax).
47 Ibid., 16 December 1994 (Fax). See A.B., Report to Plenary Council, 23 February 1995.
48 See LTRC Consolidated Final Report, vol. 2, 221, 230, 252 (15 December 1994: Cow Field massacre of 48 civilians, while they were asleep, on Duport Road, Monrovia, by the NPFL).
49 Ibid., 22 December 1994 (Fax).
50 A.G. Cahill, Report to EPC, 23 February 1995.
51 A.B. Cahill to Harkin, 23 January 1995 (Fax).
52 See LTRC, Consolidated Final Report, vol. 2, 326–329. The report names 102 mercenaries who fought with different militias during the conflict, those joining the NPFL coming mainly from Sierra Leone.
53 Cahill to Harkin, 6 January 1995 (Fax).
54 Dane F. Smith Jr, op. cit., 426.
55 Ibid.
56 Ibid.
57 A.B. Cahill to Harkin, 11 January 1995 (Fax).
58 AFL, LDF, NPFL-CRC.
59 Ibid., 13 January 1995 (Fax).
60 Ibid., 14 January 1995 (Fax).

61 Ibid., 22 January 1995.
62 Ibid.
63 See New Democrat, 25 January 1995.
64 Ibid.
65 27 January 1995.
66 2 February 1995.
67 A.B. Cahill to Quinlan, 7 February 1995 ('Ann Cronin').
68 Ibid., 7 February 1995 (Fax).
69 Ibid. Also A.T. Moran to Darcy, 24 February 1995.
70 A.B. Cahill to Harkin, 10 February 1995 (Fax).
71 Ibid., 13 February 1995 (Fax).
72 SMA (American Province) 'Newsletter', 21 February 1995.

20 The Abuja Summit and the increasing role of Nigeria

Despite the danger of infiltration and manipulation by the factions, genuinely public protests and demonstrations, conducted with greater sophistication, continued to gain momentum in Liberia's capital. On 8 March 1995 Monrovia's citizens demonstrated their anger at the failure of the new Council of State to be seated by staying put in their homes. This 'stay-at-home' protest was widely observed. Not long after, four members of the projected Council entered Monrovia and held unofficial meetings making appeals to the fifth member, Charles Taylor, to join them.[1]

Reports of new massacres in Greater Liberia were coming in thick and fast. On April 9 came news of the massacre of some 80 civilians[2], mainly women and children, in villages near Buchanan where the NPFL and Liberia Peace Council were engaged in fighting. In that instance, the perpetrators used cutlasses to hack their victims to death.[3]

Yet there were also moments of hope and optimism. One such occurred during the Easter Tridium which missionary Lee Cahill conducted at Kakata.

> Although we did have the sad sight on Good Friday of nearly 700 unfortunate men, women and children, making their way into Kakata, after running the gauntlet of danger from Bong Mine: nevertheless under the full moon of Saturday night, our community in St Christopher's did have a really memorable Paschal Vigil, for the first time in years being actually able to march around the streets of Kakata, singing the Easter hymns.

And there had been some hopeful developments in the military situation:

> We were happy that ECOMOG has succeeded in driving ULIMO off the Tubmanburg Highway from Monrovia, without a shot being fired. Better still they have driven the armed ULIMO men out of Bomi (Tubmanburg) and have declared that they have now made Bomi the latest 'Safe Haven.' If this is to presage similar kinds of sorties, then there are possibilities for something better for Liberia.

DOI: 10.4324/9781003219309-26

And buoyed up by the experience of Easter and news of recent ECOMOG successes Cahill sounded a rare but heartfelt note of optimism, based on his faith in the Liberian people:

> I do not want to be regarded from my reports as presenting a situation which deteriorates by the day and leaves less and less room for hope. It is true that up-country there is a hell and in the secure haven along the coast there is another world where there seems to be possibilities for recovery. However, if anyone considers that the warlords hold all the cards and are blind to the heroism of the ordinary citizens, then they are missing the seat of hope for Liberia's future. To be frank, although we are tired and drained, bruised and battered, this Easter I have felt an optimism for Liberia unlike anything experienced in the last three years.[4]

***

In May 1995, fruit of the discussion between Rawlings and Clinton, a meeting organised by Presidents Abacha and Rawlings, took place in Abuja, hoping to break the stalemate concerning the structure of the Council of State. No progress was made, but for other reasons the meeting was to prove significant. Writing at the time of the meeting Dane F. Smith, U.S. envoy to Liberia, wrote that, although Taylor was not present, the meeting had brought Nigeria into the heart of the peace process and that the next challenge would be to bring Taylor face to face with Abacha. This was to happen on 1–2 June when, gratifying those who saw a change of attitude by Nigeria towards Taylor as the only solution to Liberia's crisis, the NPFL leader led a 76-person delegation to Abuja, spending four days in discussions with the Nigerian president.[5] The ground work for this development had been carefully laid since the beginning of the year by discreet contacts 'between Taylor's aides and officials of the Nigerian Foreign affairs ministry.'[6]

The rapprochement between the formerly hostile NPFL and Nigeria can be traced to the seizure of power by Sani Abacha on 17 November 1993. At that time Nigeria had been fruitlessly embroiled in the Liberian crisis for almost four years. For Abacha, achieving a settlement of the Liberia civil war would permit a return home of Nigerian troops and would strengthen his own position as Nigeria's leader. Abacha saw Taylor's accession to the presidency by democratic means as the only way of bringing the civil war to an acceptable conclusion. And he shared this view with President Rawlings. As for Taylor, with the growing pressure from militias bent on his destruction, such as ULIMO-K, ULIMO-J and the Liberia Peace Council, and with a larger and better-equipped ECOMOG standing in the way of military victory, the option of achieving the presidency through the political route became more attractive. In addition Taylor was urged to reconcile with Nigeria by a number of his regional supporters, Presidents Gnassingbé Eyadéma of Togo and Nicephore Soglo of Benin, and above all by President Blaise Compaoré of Burkina Faso who had financed Taylor's June visit to Abuja. In short, while Taylor's francophone supporters were no longer prepared to support victory through success on the battlefield, they would accept victory by the democratic process. At last, they were open to co-operation with the ECOWAS plan. The Ivory Coast leadership which had led the formation of the 'Committee of Five' demonstrated this when it introduced strong measures to prevent the further transit of military materials across its territory.[7]

***

On 17 August 1995 a meeting attended by UN, U.S. and OAU representatives, by envoys of most ECOWAS heads of states and, finally, by the heads of most of the factions (including Charles Taylor) convened in Abuja. This was the first time such a meeting was conducted in Nigeria, signifying at last that country's willingness to take on a leadership role in bringing peace to Liberia. On this occasion there was swift movement towards agreement, with a committee producing recommendations on the formation of the Council of State and on a timetable for subsequent steps. There followed the signing of a peace accord on 20 August 1995. The signatories were Taylor, Kromah, Johnson, Tom Woewiyu (National Patriotic Front of Liberia- Central Revolutionary Council), Francis Massaquoi (Lofa Defence Force), Chea Cheapoo (Liberia National Conference) and Dr George Boley (Liberia Peace Council).[8]

The terms of the accord were not unlike those endorsed at several earlier meetings. The Accord's formal title, reflecting the byzantine nature of the peace process, was 'The Abuja Agreement to Supplement the Cotonou and Akosombo Agreements as subsequently clarified by the Accra Agreement.'[9] There would be a ceasefire from midnight, 26 August, followed by the installation of the Council of State and, finally, the election and installation of a democratic government by the end of 12 months.[10] As for the vexed question of the Council of State's composition, the recommendations of the committee were accepted. It was to be composed of six members, with Mr Wilton Sankawulo[11] as Chairman. The other members – each with the rank of vice president - were Kromah, Taylor, Boley representing the Coalition, Oscar Jaryee Quiah representing the Liberia National Conference and Chief Tamba Taylor.

Unlike previous occasions the Council of State was quickly seated, the ceremony taking place on 1 September. Taylor had made a triumphal entry into Monrovia on the previous day, his first visit to the capital since 1989. He took up temporary residence in a property, Cahill noted, 'immediately next door to the archbishop.' Later he would move to a new house in Congotown. Regarding the allocation of Ministries, the agreements signed by the parties at Cotonou in November 1993 were re-affirmed, with some small variations to accommodate factions not party to Cotonou. In this respect Coalition members Hezekiah Bowen, Francois Massaquoi, Tom Woewiyu, Laveli Supuwood and Samuel Dokie were to be given ministerial or other senior government positions, while ULIMO-J would not be forgotten, receiving three minor ministries and a junior ministry.[12]

There were two provisions in the agreement which, perhaps, explain Taylor's acceptance of a position other than that of Council Chairman. Office holders in the transitional government wishing to contest substantive presidential and legislative elections were to vacate their posts three months before the poll took place; while the Chairman of the Council would be 'ineligible to contest the first presidential and parliamentary elections held pursuant to the Agreement.'[13] At the same time the speed of his conversion was directly related to his new relationship with Nigeria. To displease President Abacha by displaying recalcitrance during the negotiations would have placed that relationship in jeopardy.

***

In the new dispensation inaugurated by the Abuja Peace Accord and the seating of the Council of State, the faction leaders continued with their attempts to upstage one another and gain electoral advantage. Taylor was first off the mark, appointing his own people to posts assigned to other factions and mainly that of Kromah. The Council had to intervene to nullify these appointments. Outside Monrovia the ceasefire between the factions was generally holding, although there were skirmishes, Within Monrovia, however, the seating of the transitional government had brought 'a feeling of growing relaxation' which was beginning to spread beyond the Monrovia enclave.[14] Travelling the roads out of the city was less of a nightmare. In fact there was a 'happy easiness' now in travelling the Monrovia–Kakata road which lasted well beyond the latter town, as far as Konola. The road to Bong Mine from Kakata, too, was open for travel with ECOMOG providing security. And ECOMOG had begun to deploy beyond its traditional bases, albeit in small steps, but giving hope that a more substantial security might be offered Liberia's citizens.

***

However, as the weeks and months went by, the calm which followed the Abuja Peace Accord began to dissipate. Samuel Kofi Woods* put it succinctly:

> Six months have come and gone since the much-acclaimed Abuja Peace Agreement was signed; six months have come and gone since the seating of the faction-composed government; six months have come and gone since the faction leaders promised that the carnage was over and, once they took political power, they would disarm their fighters. Instead they have busied themselves with rearming on a scale that makes more destruction and territorial conquest inevitable.[15]

***

Although skirmishes between and within factions recommenced days after the transitional government took office, the first major breach of the ceasefire occurred in January 1996 when ECOMOG soldiers went to the Bomi and Lower Lofa region to commence the disarmament of the two ULIMO

---

*   Samuel Kofi Woods was secretary of the Catholic Commission for Justice and Peace. A distinguished human rights campaigner, he was to serve in Ellen Johnson-Sirleaf's cabinet as Minister for Labour (2006) and Minister for Public Works (2009).

factions. Their task was compounded by the fact that ULIMO-J was itself divided[16] between a larger faction, mainly Krahn, led by Roosevelt Johnson, and a smaller faction led by Armah Youlo and William Karyee.[17] In the event, the ECOMOG force was attacked and overwhelmed by forces loyal to Johnson, and dispossessed of its weapons and equipment. ECOMOG suffered severe casualties in the encounter with scores killed; numerous civilians also lost their lives.[18] This was to be the first in an escalating series of breaches which in a relatively short time reduced Liberia to a chaos equalling that which occurred when the NPFL launched Operation Octopus in October 1992.[19]

Consistent with the terms of the Abuja Agreement,[20] the Ceasefire Violation Committee conducted an investigation into the ECOMOG/ULIMO-J fighting. In its findings Roosevelt Johnson's ULIMO-J was cited for unprovoked attacks on the peacekeepers. There followed on 5 March a meeting of the Council of State which Johnson refused to attend. In his absence the four remaining members of the Council suspended him from his Ministry of Rural Development and also withdrew recognition of his leadership of ULIMO-J, transferring it to 'General William Karyee,' chief of staff of the weaker, less belligerent faction? In addition orders were given to ECOMOG to search Johnson's Monrovia property for arms and military equipment, an operation which was swiftly conducted, and which seized a large cache of weapons.[21]

On the following day, in retaliation for Johnson's demotion and the ECOMOG raid, ULIMO-J militia in Kakata, loyal to the Krahn leader, blocked the only route through the town and gateway to Liberia's interior. Two days later NPFL forces mounted 'Operation Restore Hope,' and striking at 2 am soon got the upper hand driving ULIMO-J out of the town. Later that day, after the fighting, Taylor made a rare personal appearance, holding an impromptu press conference, dressed in full combat gear, and toting an AK-47 rifle. 'We moved into Kakata,' he declared, 'to ensure that this highway remains open,' adding that he would, of course, turn over control of the town to ECOMOG.[22]

In the immediate aftermath of the fighting Kakata's NPFL liberators, brandishing assault rifles, roamed the town pillaging homes and shops accusing its civilian population of having supported ULIMO-J. Many died.[23] The survivors fled leaving the town virtually uninhabited by the time ECOMOG returned some days later to reoccupy its barracks. For their part, the defeated ULIMO-J militiamen, numbering over 225, having fled to nearby Todde and Goba town, declared themselves 'tired of fighting' and handed in their weapons to ECOMOG officers who arranged transport for them to the capital.[24]

Among those caught up in these events were two elderly nuns, Canadian members of the Congregation of Sisters of the Child Jesus,[*] who were taken from their Kakata convent by the NPFL and marched 10 miles through the

[*]   Sister John Joseph (Mary Aldina Hughes) and Sister Regina (Marie Regnier). Sisters of the congregation first came to Liberia in the mid-1960s.

Firestone forest.[25] Some days later, on making inquiries about their where-abouts, Cahill was informed that the two were being brought back to the Kakata area 'not only on the orders of the local NPFL commander but on Taylor's express orders.' Evidently, for the NPFL leader, anything to do with Sisters was a 'raw matter' since the deaths of the five ASC Sisters in 1992. And so it happened. 'The two old ladies arrived safely in unbelievable fettle, one aged 76, and the other 79 and with a heart condition to boot.'

***

On Wednesday, 20 March 1996, Monrovia, which had been designated 'a safe haven' in the Abuja Accord, witnessed a series of skirmishes between ULIMO-J and the AFL. There followed a series of assassination attempts on leading figures of both sides and by generally increased 'acts of banditry and lawlessness.'[26] One of those shot dead by Roosevelt Johnson supporters was Daweh Bawoh a prominent member of the ULIMO-K faction who was killed in the suburb of Sinkor near Johnson's residence. In reaction the Council of State declared Johnson removed from the Council and issued a writ for his arrest on charges of murder which it entrusted to ECOMOG for execution. Johnson responded by barricading himself in his residence under the protection of his armed supporters.

The attempt to arrest Johnson immediately led to cries of 'selective justice' by Johnson's followers and, also, independent commentators. They claimed that leaders of other factions whose members had perpetrated murders and banditry should also be brought before the courts. One vocal critic was Samuel Woods. He declared that the arrest of Johnson,

> should mark the beginning of the prosecution of all those who have either directly or indirectly supervised war machines or directly participated in the scores of murders and other heinous crimes committed since the genesis of our conflict. But if justice should remain selective then it would be highly counter-productive to our search for peace...[27]

The Inter-Faith Mediation Committee also threw its weight behind calls for 'even-handed' justice, demanding the setting up of a National Commission of Inquiry 'to probe the present incident involving General Johnson of ULIMO-J and all other past, present and future acts of a similar nature and character so that the alleged perpetrators can be brought to justice.'[28]

***

On Easter Sunday, 7 April, Archbishop Francis published his Lenten Pastoral Letter for 1996, which was read in all Catholic churches and covered in some local newspapers. This again was a passionate, honest, accurate and indeed powerful account of the current situation, delivered fearlessly and at no small risk. It was also remarkably prescient.

> Over seven months ago when the Abuja Accord was signed many well-meaning Liberians breathed a sigh of relief; for at long last it was thought

Peace had come to stay. And when the Council of State was inaugurated, everyone said that this was Peace Time…

The warlords had told us almost *ad nauseam* that if given political power they would give us peace … They told us that, as they were the ones who gave their soldiers the guns, they were the only ones who could disarm them.

Many Liberians had voiced reservations about all this, holding that disarmament was fundamental to the peace process, that it should come before the making of a government. They were shouted down and told they were a stumbling block to the ushering in of peace for Liberia.

We Liberians in our naivety believed the warlords. Were they not the ones who said they came to liberate us! What have we experienced? The destruction of lives, property and our country. How could anyone believe that these same men would this time do what was right? But we wanted *peace* and so we gave them, once more, the benefit of the doubt.

But since that day, now over seven months ago, what has been our experience? The ceasefire has been broken. Our government is factionalized and our institutions all but non-existent. Camps for the displaced have increased; many children, women and men – all civilians – have been killed; our young girls raped, our homes destroyed, our schools looted and destroyed, our Churches desecrated. Today, Monrovia is an armed camp … and we are living on a time bomb.

The time bomb was truly about to explode

***

Attempts to execute the warrant against Johnson led to the most serious outbreak of violence since the signing of the Abuja accord. The fighting started early on April 6 when police surrounded his residence located in Monrovia's Sinkor district. When Johnson's supporters refused them entry NPFL and ULIMO-K militiamen – formerly sworn enemies – joined with the police and a firefight broke out.[29] Efforts by ECOMOG to restore order were unsuccessful and within a few hours law and order had broken down in many parts of the city. There were killings on all sides and hostage-taking of civilians and ECOMOG peacekeepers, mainly by Johnson's forces which had fortified the B.T.C. barracks. The fighting continued for the next four days until a truce was brokered by ECOWAS mediators with help from the United Nations Special Representative, Anthony B. Nyakyi[30]. The truce led to the release of large numbers of hostages including civilians, foreigners and ECOMOG soldiers.[31] But, although ECOMOG tanks now patrolled the streets, they were too few in number to prevent a renewal of the fighting and, apart from relative peace in the western suburbs, chaos returned to most other parts of the capital with buildings looted and burned, and streets littered with bodies, evoking images of August 1990, when Liberia's capital was convulsed during the worst days of Operation Octopus.

***

Within hours of the commencement of fighting the State Department began to make contingency plans for 'a sizeable' evacuation of the estimated 480 U.S. citizens and other non-nationals, dispatching a military assessment team to Monrovia.[32] Reminiscent of Operation 'Sharp Edge' which in August 1990 evacuated some 2,500 U.S. citizens and other non-nationals, the resultant plan – to be implemented on the order of the State Department - included the dispatch of U.S. ships carrying helicopters and airplanes, to be available off-shore; and the reinforcement of the embassy guard by an elite force of marine commandos flown in from Lungi Airport, near Freetown.[33] Ordinarily some 200 U.S. citizens were attached to the embassy. Now, since the outbreak of fighting, in excess of 10,000 Liberian civilians had taken up refuge in the embassy annex while a further 224 non-nationals were in the wider embassy compound. The first airlift of U.S. citizens took place during the evening and night of 9 April.[34] By Thursday morning 371 evacuees of various nationalities had been flown to safety but, with an intensification of hostilities and the rea-lisation that there was little prospect of peace, the pace of evacuation increased thereafter.

By now the breakdown in law and order was in full flight. No radio station was broadcasting – all seven had gone off the air because of lack of power and fuel. The UN Observer Mission lost two helicopters to heavy machine-gun fire and its 16 members were evacuated.[35] Among buildings completely looted and no longer functional were those of UNICEF, UNHCR and the UN Devel-opment Programme. A mob had broken down the gate of the UN's main compound in Monrovia causing its staff to flee to the U.S. Embassy.[36] Even the walls of the U.S. Embassy compound had been breached although the group of attackers had been quickly driven off by Special Forces. And there were reports, too, that command structures within the militias and even within ECOMOG had broken down and that elements of the peacekeeping forces had joined in the looting.[37]

***

Commentary on the crisis in America was revealing. Herman Cohen, now senior advisor on Africa to President Bush, like Pilate washing his hands, roundly blamed the Libyans and the passivity of the UN.[38] Fondly recalling 'happier times between Washington and Monrovia' when the African country provided 'the fullest support' for U.S. foreign policy, he conjectured that Liberia's pro-U.S. stance might well have contributed to its own downfall since Libya, always on the lookout for ways to limit U.S. influence in Africa, had targeted Liberia, 'training and financing the Liberian rebel group which entered the country in 1989.'[39] And, perhaps letting his guard down, as an afterthought Cohen added that the 2,500 U.S. marines sent to Liberia's coastal waters to monitor the safety of Americans at that time, should have gone further. 'Just landing a company of marines would have settled everything'!

James Wood[40], another former Africa expert at the Pentagon, agreed with Cohen's unguarded comment, saying that the U.S. 'hands-off' policy towards Liberia was irresponsible and regrettably had been 'embraced ever since by the

Clinton administration.'[41] Chester Crocker, who had returned to academia,[42] was less critical, saying that the choice not to take the lead in ending the civil war when nobody else had stepped forward, was made deliberately.[43] The unilateral U.S. intervention in Panama in December 1989 had been met by 'widespread international indignation.' To have intervened in Liberia a few months later would 'almost certainly have produced a similar outcry' and would 'most likely have led to the installation of Taylor as Liberian president because his forces were the strongest militarily.' President Bush, he explained, was absolutely opposed to elevate a man who had fled Liberia after allegedly stealing government funds. James Bishop, ambassador to Liberia strongly concurred. 'Bush,' he said, 'didn't want the U.S. to be a party to seeing a convicted felon become the next president of Liberia.'[44] Ex-president Jimmy Carter, now a mediator in conflicts throughout the globe, and recently involved in Liberia, also had his say. He admitted that 'the prospect of elections that we were trying to bring about is now on the back burner for a long time.'[45] The current Chief of Mission in the Monrovia embassy, William Milam, shared this bleak assessment.

> The peace process, which began with the agreement in Abuja last August, is very clearly in bad shape; it is on the rocks. And if this violence continues it is going to be extremely difficult to put it back together.[46]

***

Late on Friday, 12 April, the Ghanaian Foreign Minister announced that after negotiations involving the UN's Anthony B. Nyakyi, Liberia's Council of State, aid agencies and ECOMOG's high command, the combatants had agreed to a ceasefire. The Council of State had authorised the cordoning off of the B.T.C. barracks by ECOMOG, a measure to which Johnson – inside the fortified barracks with his militia and large numbers of hostages and refugees – had agreed on the assurance that his own demands would be given immediate consideration. And to re-establish order in the city ECOMOG troops – some 12,000 were now in Liberia – would fan out setting up checkpoints.

What prospects of success had this new ceasefire? Just a few days previously a similar agreement had collapsed before the ink was dry. Throughout the current hostilities Taylor on rebel radio had insisted that his troops would only agree to a ceasefire if Johnson handed himself up to the authorities to face the charge of murder. Had he now changed his mind? There was little delay in answering this question. Initially NPFL militia appeared to be honouring the agreement. Taylor ordered a cessation of all looting and was reported as having executed two of his own soldiers who defied this order in Bushrod Island. However the respite was to be short-lived. By 14 April fighting had again flared up around the besieged B.T.C. barracks, and it was 'business as usual' throughout the city.

The U.S. military – winding down its rescue mission at the time – was now forced to re-activate it and widen its net.[47] Twelve additional sorties were quickly staged – among those evacuated was General Philip Kamah, chief of staff of the Johnson faction – and the flotilla due off Monrovia week later was advised of likely large-scale evacuations of Africans as well as foreigners.[48] Meanwhile Monrovia's terrified citizens

> were left to fend for themselves among drugged-out gangs of gunmen and looters running rampant as even the world's emergency groups abandoned the warring country.[49]

Nobody was immune from the random violence unleashed upon the population. Michael Francis had consistently expressed optimism about the future. In the midst of chaos he had never given up hope that somehow or other peace might come about.[50] However this optimism was to be shattered on 14 April, when three groups of attackers entered his house holding him at gunpoint, demanding money and vehicles. Taking his mother with him and accompanied by Jim Lee,[51] he made his way to the American Embassy and was airlifted to Freetown.[52] There he pronounced the current crisis as the 'worst in Liberia's history' and declared his intention to travel to the Vatican to lay Liberia's situation before the Pope. Francis abandoned Liberia with reluctance. 'In this situation, when your life is at stake' he told journalists, 'What can you do, where can you go'? After his departure his house was ransacked and left derelict.[53]

Tina Susman, an AP correspondent who stayed in Monrovia throughout the crisis, embedded in the American embassy, described the scene there on 15 April.

> The swimming pool is nearly empty. The abandoned tennis courts are littered with tree branches. Everywhere, haggard people sit with over-stuffed bags, eating rationed food and staring blankly. The once-gracious U.S. Embassy and its nearby residential compound have become crowded refugee centers, housing some 20,000 Americans, other foreigners and Liberians seeking shelter from the war. Their alternative: streets roamed by teenagers wielding automatic rifles and knives, cruising in stolen vehicles.[54]

***

Missionaries who had taken refuge in St Joseph's Hospital decided to weather the storm. One of their number, Joe Brown, Regional Superior of the Salesians, later explained that they had remained 'because we went through a lot of this in 1990 when all-out civil war erupted, and because the hospital had always been respected by the factions, owing to the care given to all victims.' They did so, mindful that in 1992 five ASC Sisters who had hitherto been considered 'respected,' had been dealt a terrible death at the hands of the NPFL. Brown, who had worked for 16 years in Liberia, remained a valuable source of information on missionaries caught up throughout the crisis. Based in the hospital where radio and fax contact with Bilbao miraculously remained intact, he was able to transmit vital information to his superiors in Stockport, England. They, in turn, kept other missionary headquarters up to date about their personnel.

Among Irish missionaries evacuated during the crisis were Mattie Gilmore, Larry Collins and Lee Cahill. They were taken to Freetown by U.S. Air Force helicopter on the morning of Thursday, 12 April. Two of their American Province colleagues, James Hickey and Frank Hynes, were evacuated on the same flight and arrived in Tenafly two days later. Interviewed for a local newspaper, Cahill compared Liberia's situation to the ravaged landscape depicted in Francis Ford Coppola's film 'Apocalypse Now.'

> Many of the people with whom we have been in touch over the years have been scattered, killed, or displaced. There are very few women you would meet, at this stage, who have not been raped. And when you meet child soldiers – 6,000 have been recruited by various guerrilla factions – they look as fresh as any nine- or ten-year-old, but they have the eyes of grown men.[55]

***

Friday 19 April saw the brokering of yet another ceasefire. An ECOWAS delegation headed by the Ghanaian envoy, Captain Kojo Tshikata, had conducted meetings in the U.S. Embassy with representatives of the factions. Conscious of the growing international criticism of its 'hands off' policy, the U.S. had assisted by transporting faction representatives to the embassy and had also sent the Deputy Assistant Secretary for African affairs, William H. Twaddell[56], and some military advisers to work with the U.S. ambassador. The U.S., it was agreed, would focus on 'bringing ECOMOG up to strength,' promising the force $30 million, while military advisers would work towards a more effective deployment of ECOMOG in Monrovia. In a crisis the U.S. administration was always ready to lend a helping hand. Its record for the longer haul in bringing peace to Liberia was less creditable.

However, this latest ceasefire agreement, accomplished 'more through exhaustion than design,'[57] was destined to go the way of others. During the first two days civilians, emerging from hiding places to repair their looted houses and businesses, found Monrovia a sorry spectacle, with burnt-out buildings, its 'streets littered with burnt-out vehicles and heaps of garbage.'[58] ECOMOG had managed to bring in reinforcements and its patrols were more evident on the streets especially in the vicinity of the B.T.C. barracks. Médecins Sans Frontières aid workers, (France, Belgium and the Netherlands), had re-entered the city and set up clinics to combat cholera, although people were reluctant to approach because of the general insecurity. And though the Council of State had called on civil servants to return to work, few responded out of fear for their safety.

One confidence-building measure negotiated was to be a meeting of the Council of State in the Executive Mansion, scheduled for 21 April. Taylor and Kromah both announced their intention to attend while Johnson had declared his opposition saying that, if necessary, he would prevent the Council from reconvening. On the morning of the appointed day Charles Taylor travelled to the Executive Mansion from his nearby residence, escorted by armed fighters.

Some hours later heavily armed Krahn issued forth from the B.T.C. barracks onto the streets 'setting up checkpoints at strategic highway bypasses and parading through the streets shouting war chants.'[59] They then ascended the hill to the Executive Mansion taunting Taylor and those already assembled there. Anticipating trouble Kromah had already fled the Mansion.[60] While Taylor's guard now opened fire, the NPFL leader and Professor Sankawulo, Council Chairman, were seen 'running to a waiting car, and ducking to avoid the bullets.'[61] Fighting soon extended beyond the mansion area in Sinkor, and the two-day old ceasefire was at an end.

***

In the meantime various international organisations and think-tanks were offering their recipes for peace. One was the International Contact Group on Liberian Issues[62] which issued a lengthy communiqué after a session held in Geneva on 26 April chaired by U.S. Assistant Secretary for African Affairs, George Moose.[63] Attending the meeting were representatives from Belgium, Britain, Canada, Denmark, France, Germany, Italy, Japan, the Netherlands, Norway, Switzerland and the U.S., as well as ECOWAS, the OAU , the UN and the European Community Commission. This mega-meeting presented a succinct, if obvious, analysis of what was needed if any real progress was to be made. In the first place, Monrovia needed to be a secure and safe city. Secondly ECOMOG needed to be properly reinforced. And thirdly faction leaders needed to return to the Abuja Peace plan. To these ends the gathering committed itself to encouraging involvement in peace-making and reconciliation by local, regional and international forces. In particular this could be demonstrated by honouring without delay pledges of financial support towards the peace process given at an UN-sponsored conference in October 1995.[64]

A more radical recipe for Liberia's ills, was given by James Keough Bishop, erstwhile ambassador to Liberia (1987–90), who had retired from the diplomatic service in 1993. Published in the prestigious *Christian Science Monitor*,[65] under the title: 'A Solution for Liberia – Send in the Marines,' it was clear that he considered the State Department's policy of 'quiet diplomacy,' which he had had to implement, wholly discredited. Reciting the debt which the U.S. owed to Liberia for 'entering World War I and World War II'* and critical help given during the 'cold war,' he gave his verdict on America's response.

> In 1989, when Liberia most needed U.S. help ... the U.S. dispatched a naval task force, but it sailed away after evacuating foreigners, leaving 150,000 Liberians to die in a power struggle between egotistic and greedy warlords. Humanitarian aid became a sop for America's lack of will to intervene, and even diplomatically, U.S. envoys were barred from

---

*   Liberia formally joined the Allied powers in the First World War on 4 July 1917. When America entered the Second World War Liberia permitted the stationing of troops and aircraft in its territory and supplied vital commodities such as rubber. Later, in January 1944, Liberia declared war on the Axis powers.

mediation efforts... When West African governments organised their own peacekeeping force, the U.S. provided only token support... while in August 1995, when West African diplomacy produced a settlement widely considered to have a chance of success, the U.S. again offered only token backing for the essential peacekeeping element...

***

In the wake of this latest failed ceasefire agreement ECOWAS scheduled a review of the situation by the ECOWAS Standing Mediation Committee in Accra on 7–8 May 1996. The committee was entrusted with the task of reviewing the composition of the Council of State and 'redefining the faltering peace process.' With regard to the composition of the Council of State it was true that one civilian member, Oscar Quiah, was in hospital and out of commission, while George Boley, representing the Liberia Peace Council, had abandoned Liberia during the recent hostilities and withdrawn from public life. But there were wider considerations for convoking such a review. It had become clear that the previous strategy of admitting the faction leaders to high office in the hope that, all of a sudden, they might become statesmen, had manifestly backfired. Taking advantage of their elevation they had continued to pursue – with the greater means at their disposal – those same objectives which had always motivated them. Taylor, enjoying the respectability conferred on him by ECOWAS and the wider international community, kept his eyes firmly fixed on the big prize. While Johnson, hitherto a minor player, on the back of his elevation to the Council of State, had grown stronger and appeared the greatest threat to Taylor's ambition.

In the run-up to the 7 May meeting, although the 'Big Gun' strategy was now being questioned and a radical reconfiguration of the Council of State was discussed, no one in diplomatic and political circles was prepared to grasp the nettle. The Council's Chairman, Professor Sankawulo, who had proved 'a virtual puppet' of Taylor's, might easily be replaced. So also might 'the aged Kissi patriarch, Chief Tamba Taylor,' a figurehead whose appointment had been a nod in the direction of tradition.[66] But few were prepared to contemplate the course which recent events had indicated, namely the replacement of the 'Big Guns' by men of peace. On the contrary, opinion expressed in the anti-NPFL media and in some political circles was that Johnson who had taken on the joint might of the other factions and defied ECOMOG, and whose arrest for murder was 'a dead issue,' should be reinstated on the Council of State.

***

The 7 May summit – the 14th multinational meeting of its kind – convened in Accra on the due date but with neither Taylor nor Kromah in attendance.[67] It concluded with yet another ceasefire agreement. At the meeting, ECOMOG had made it clear that unless the warlords removed 'weapons and fighters from Monrovia' and returned seized 'ECOMOG weapons and looted UNOMIL equipment and materials,' it would seriously consider withdrawing from Liberia.

Further fighting quickly ensued, but noticeably outside the Monrovia enclave. In fact, within the city and its hinterland there were signs of a sea-change taking place – the first indications that factions were returning to barracks or vacating the city. Why it should have happened is difficult to explain. But sheer exhaustion after a month of fighting was among the factors. Moreover the leadership of Johnson, whose activities had been critical to the current outbreak of hostilities, was now being challenged from within his movement and his authority diminished.[*] The ceasefire in inner Monrovia was to lead, in the following months, to a meaningful ceasefire in the metropolitan area and gradually further afield.[68]

At a hearing of the U.S. House of Representatives Subcommittee on Africa, held early in May, Assistant Secretary Moose, back from his efforts to bring about a ceasefire during the closing weeks of April, had given a depressing account of developments in Liberia. His deputy, William H. Twaddell, was able to bring better news to the next hearing of the subcommittee held on 28 June. The situation had improved after the restoration of the ceasefire on the last day of May; and a relative calm had descended upon Liberia's capital.[69] Considerable numbers of NPFL had withdrawn and those left behind were obeying ECOMOG's diktat of 'no guns on the street.' The standoff at the B.T.C. barracks had been resolved 'with the fighters of ULIMO-J having left the centre unarmed.' And ECOMOG, which had deployed throughout the city, was 'seizing arms caches and exerting its authority to keep the peace.' The situation was slowly improving for the civilian population with many of the displaced returning to their communities. The resumption of commercial air traffic into Monrovia on 17 June was a further sign of progress.[70]

Twaddell told the hearing, too, that the U.S. was seeking to deal with those 'collaborators in the international community' who were selling illicit arms and munitions to the various Liberian factions and facilitating their delivery. Breaking this vicious cycle was critical to ending the war. It was true that information about this trade was 'sketchy and full of gaps,' but it did lead to some conclusions. One was that almost all the weapons reaching Liberia were not dispatched directly but came through neighbouring countries. 'Arms reaching Taylor's NPFL most likely transited Burkina Faso and Cote d'Ivoire, while those destined for Kromah's ULIMO-K were likely to pass through Guinea.'[71]

As to how the factions financed the purchase of arms, he stated that:

> the primary source of funds appears to be from the sale of commodities from Liberia's trove of natural resources, principally diamonds, timber,

---

[*]   Members of ULIMO-J's executive council and some of its military leaders moved him aside, replacing him with a young student, William Kayree. They cited Johnson's 'inability to forward the peace process.' Johnson fled the county in May 1996, while other members of the Council of State, including Kromah and Taylor, gave recognition to this change of leadership (Tom Lansford ed., Political handbook of the World, 887; see also, Gabriel H. Williams, Liberia: The Heart of Darkness: Accounts of Liberia's Civil War and Its destabilizing effects in West Africa, 194).

gold, and rubber. At present, Taylor and his current ally, Alhaji Kromah, control most of the areas where these commodities are found, namely across the northern tier of the country and along the border with Côte d'Ivoire.[72]

He estimated that Taylor had 'upwards of $75 million annually' passing through his hands.[73] In ULIMO and Liberia Peace Council territory the raising of funds followed a similar pattern. Regarding the purchasers of Liberian commodities, Twaddell told the hearing: 'trade records indicate that most Liberian-origin diamonds probably find their way to Belgium, while buyers in France and Malaysia are the primary customers for Liberian timber.' And there was another source of revenue since the Abuja Accord of August 1995 which had in effect handed over Liberia's government to the faction leaders. About 90% of Liberia's revenues – some $16 million–20 million – came from its maritime registry.

Perhaps the most fascinating section in Twaddell's testimony was that which dealt with faction fundraising in the U.S.

> While the U.S. is not believed to be a major source of arms for Liberia or a principal recipient of illicit Liberian commodities, it is a fertile ground for activities that have contributed significantly to the coffers of Liberian faction leaders. Most of the Liberian faction leaders and their associates have spent many years in the U.S., often as students, temporary workers, even as permanent residents. They own property, own or operate businesses and, more importantly, they know how the U.S. system works and how to make it work for them.

There followed a detailed account of the ways – many of them ingenious and some of them illegal – in which funds for the factions were raised.[74]

***

On 5 June, after an absence of some eight weeks, Archbishop Michael Francis returned to Liberia.[75] Two weeks after his hurried exit to Freetown he had made his way to Rome to report on his archdiocese and on 3 May met the Pontiff in a private audience. Francis had then proceeded to the Netherlands to seek humanitarian aid from Caritas and to discuss the sufferings of the Liberian people with officials at the Dutch Foreign Ministry. His next port of call had been Aachen in Germany where he made the same pleas for help to Missio, Misereor and Holy Childhood[76] – all Catholic mission-aid organisations. He was also to visit Koln, Freiburg and Munich, where again he sought help from a variety of organisations including Caritas Germany and *Kirche im Not*. Everywhere he found people 'helpful, sympathetic and understanding.' He began his return journey to Liberia on 26 May, flying into Freetown. Nine days later he obtained a seat on a helicopter which landed at the ECOMOG base on Bushrod Island. From here he was driven to the nearby St Mary's parish which had escaped attack, owing largely to its proximity to the base. His own house at Mamba point had been completely looted and vandalised.

Francis found the physical plant of his archdiocese in tatters, his clerical and religious staff, both local and missionary, largely dispersed. Nonetheless, despite dislocation and the immense humanitarian suffering, the Catholic community was not totally leaderless. The torch of leadership had been taken up, as it had in the absence of Liberia's largely expatriate priests during 1990 and again in 1992, mainly by the catechists embedded in their communities. And so when Francis attempted to visit the various parishes – in many cases this was not possible – he was encouraged to find the Church still vibrant, indeed defiant in the face of apparently insuperable obstacles. Churches, parish houses, convents, schools and diocesan institutions might have been destroyed or wholly looted, but the people were resilient, gathering together under their catechists and lay leaders to pray and assist those more desperate than themselves and now joyfully assembled to welcome back their pastor. Francis's report on his visit recorded in detail what had transpired in each location.

Notes

1 Ibid., 10 March 1995.
2 Mentioned in LTRC, Consolidated Final Report, vol. 2, 230.
3 For details, see Liberia working group, Newsletter, no. 13, May 1995 (Jesuit Relief Service, Rome). See also, Amnesty International Report, 20 September 1995.
4 A.B. Cahill to Harkin, 17 April 1995 (Fax).
5 Dane F. Smith, op. cit, 427.
6 Julius Mutwol, Peace Agreements and Civil Wars in Africa: Insurgent Motivations, State Responses, and Third Party Peacemaking in Liberia, Rwanda, and Sierra Leone (Cambria Press, 2009) (Kindle version), Loc. 1924.
7 Ibid., Loc 2305.
8 Accords of the Liberian Conflict, 68–69. (Liberia Online Document Resources), accessed 26 May 2017. www.google.com.ng/search?q=Accords+of+the+Liberian +Conflict&oq=Accords+of+the+Liberian+Con-flict&aqs=chrome.0.69i59j69i60l2.5607j0j8&sourceid=chrome&ie=UTF-8.
9 Liberian Studies Journal, XX, 2 (1995).
10 Samuel K. Woods, Secretary, Justice and Peace Commission, National Catholic Secretariat, 'Briefing,' April 1996.
11 Author and academic, Wilton Sankawulo taught in the University of Liberia and at Cuttington University. During 1983–1985 he was Director General of the Doe Cabinet and later became 'Special Assistant or Academic Affairs' to the President. In this capacity he was one of those who tutored President Doe for the degree awarded by U.L. in 1989.
12 Liberian Studies Journal, XX, 2 (1995), 274.
13 Ibid.
14 A.B. Lee Cahill to Peter McCawille, 17 September 1995 (Fax).
15 Samuel K. Woods, op. cit., 3 April 1996.
16 See, West Africa, 8–14 January 1996, 7; 15–21 January 1996, 48, 51; 22–28 January 1996, 97ff.
17 Timeline of History. Liberia, 1996: 'Johnson's chief of staff, Armah Youlo, and a group of supporters deposed Johnson as leader of ULIMO-J.' www.timelines.ws/ countries/LIBERIA.HTML, accessed 22 November 2017.
18 Ibid., 7 January 1996.
19 1 January (Fredericka Jacob, Chronology – published 15 April 1996).

20 Section G, Article 8, Sub-Section 2.
21 Third Progress Report of the Secretary General on the United Nations Observer Mission in Liberia, S/1994/463, 18 April 1994. See National Catholic Secretariat, Justice and Peace Commission Report, April 1994.
22 Reuters, 10 March 1996 (reproduced in AFJN 22832906, 12 March 1996).
23 UPI, 10 March 1996 (reproduced in AFJN 22832906, 12 March 1996).
24 Ibid.
25 A.B. Cahill to Quinlan, Wednesday, 13 March 1996 (Fax).
26 Samuel K. Woods, op. cit.
27 Ibid.
28 Ibid.
29 Irish Times, 8 April 1996. Nicholas Phythian, 'Spectre of war haunts Liberia's election dream,' Abidjan, 10 April 1996 (Reuters).
30 A Tanzanian, Anthony B. Nyakyi replaced Trevor Gordon-Somers in December 1994.
31 A.T. Nyenati Allison, Associated Press, Monrovia, c. 10 April 1996. See A.T., J.A. Q. to Tenafly, 9 April 1996.
32 For the following see, inter alia, J.A.Q. to Tenafly, 9 April (Info on Liberia from T.J.). Other foreigners would be evacuated if Secretary of State Warren Christopher ordered it.
33 In five large M53 transport helicopters. These were to be used subsequently in the large-scale evacuations of civilians.
34 Nyenati Allison (Reuters), 10 April 1996.
35 A.T. Renn Karl to reporters in Freetown on 9 April 1996 (attached to John A. Quigley to Tenafly 9 April 1996).
36 Sylvana Foa, UN spokesperson, New York.
37 LTRC, Consolidated Final Report, vol. II, 261 mentions 'occasional reports of sexual exploitations, looting, torture or degrading treatment were made against ECOMOG… A little more than 800 violations were reported against ECOMOG.' None of those involved are identified, nor are specific incidences cited.
38 Talking to Reuters correspondent in Washington DC.
39 A.T. Jackson Kanneh, Reuters, 11 April 1996; J.A. Qto Tenafly, 11 April 1996, citing Hermann Cohen.
40 He was the Deputy Assistant Secretary for African Affairs at the Department of Defence in 1986–94.
41 A.T., J.A.Q. to Tenafly, 11 April 1996 (quoting James Wood).
42 See p. 55, note on Crocker.
43 Jackson Kanneh, Reuters, Monrovia, 11 April 1996 (in J.A.Q. to Tenafly 11 April 1996).
44 Ibid.
45 Nicholas Phythian, 'Spectre of war haunts Liberia's election dream,' Reuters, Abidjan, 10 April 1996.
46 He told a television interviewer by telephone.
47 A.T., J.A.Q. to Tenafly, 14 April 1996.
48 Ibid.
49 A.T., J.A.Q. to Tenafly, 14 April 1996.
50 See Tina Susman, 15 April 1996.
51 Jim Lee travelled on to Dakar and, finally, Ireland. He was the last member of the Society of African Missions to leave the city.
52 Ibid.
53 'Evangelization and the Church Today,' Fides, 17 April 1996 (Rome); The Tablet, 20 April 1996.
54 15 April 1996, Tina Susman, Associated Press Writer (from 'Maura Browne, to All,' Subject: 'American Embassy').
55 Cork Examiner, 15 April 1996.

56 Deputy to George Moose.
57 Nyenati Allison, AP correspondent.
58 AFJN Issue Papers, Paul Ejime, Pana Staff Correspondent, Lagos, 27 April 1996.
59 Jane A. Morse (US State Dept. Correspondence) 'US supports ECOWAS efforts to restore peace in Liberia,' 22 April 1996, State Department briefing, 370.
60 Thalia Griffiths, Reuters, Monrovia, 30 April 1996.
61 Ibid.
62 The Contact Group was an international forum particularly active during Liberia's second civil war. Currently the institution functions as the 'International Contact Group on the Mano River Basin'.
63 George Moose held this post during the Clinton presidency between 1993 and 1997.
64 AFJN Issues, Ezekiel Pajibo, 'Liberia's 13th Peace Accord in Tatters,' 10 April 1996.
65 26 April 1996.
66 A.T. 'Renewed War in Monrovia and its Consequences,' April 1996 (cutting).
67 See Africa Confidential, 10 May 1996 (vol. 37, no. 10). A summit of The Committee of Nine: Ghana, Nigeria, Togo, Benin, Burkina Faso, Côte d'Ivoire, the Gambia, Guinea and Senegal.
68 AFP, 9 February 1997.
69 Africa News Online, United States and Africa - US Wants To Cut Off Liberia's Factions (Africa News Service, 28 June 1996).
70 Africa News Service, 28 June 1996.
71 Ibid.
72 Ibid.
73 Ibid.
74 Ibid.
75 Report on the Archdiocese of Monrovia (Michael Francis), June 1996.
76 Ibid.

21 The implementation of Abuja II and the election of the former NPRAG leader as President

On 17 August 1996 a meeting was convened by ECOWAS, in Abuja, under the chairmanship of President Sani Abacha. In attendance were representatives of all six warring factions and a delegate from the Liberian National Conference. The purpose of the meeting was to assess the progress achieved since Abuja I and make whatever changes were necessary to make it a reality. This meeting, known as Abuja II, was to bring the first phase of the Liberia's civil war to a conclusion and open the door for the withdrawal of ECOMOG.

George Klay Kieh in his article 'Peace agreements and the termination to civil wars', lists what he sees as the principal reasons why Abuja II succeeded where sixteen previous peace accords had failed.[1] The electoral route to the presidency, he says, was at last attainable because Nigeria had signalled its willingness to allow it happen. Moreover, there was now unanimity among ECOWAS members, anglophone and francophone, that Taylor should under no circumstances be allowed to come to power through force of arms but might, if the people so wished, become president through the democratic process. Finally, Taylor was finding it difficult now to source weapons and materials because of the UN embargo and was besieged by rival militias. In such circumstances he had little option but to yield to the pressures placed on him to pursue the electoral route.[2]

Abuja II nominated a 57-year-old widow and mother of seven children, Ruth Sando Perry[*], as head of a new Council of State, effectively Liberia's third interim government, tasked with the organisation of elections for 30 May 1997. The new agreement, formally titled the 'Abuja Accord Supplement', rejected the notion that elections might be held before full disarmament took place. Instead it declared that there would be an immediate ceasefire, the completion of disarmament, the ending of all factional enclaves by the close of January 1997 and, finally, an elected government to be installed by 15 June of the same year. It also provided sanctions for any faction which breached the

---

[*] 'A Senator during the Doe regime, now a widowed mother of seven children, a teacher and activist in the Liberian Women's Initiative (LWI),' (Prosper Addo, Peace-Making in West Africa: Progress and Prospects, 26 [KAIPTC Monograph no. 3, November 2005]).

DOI: 10.4324/9781003219309-27

terms of the accord. These included travel restrictions, exclusion from the electoral process, and arraignment before a war crimes tribunal.[3]

On 3 September the new Council of State was installed in Monrovia. Its composition was the same as the previous Council with the exception of its Chairperson, Professor Wilton Sankawolo, who was excluded on the grounds that he had not acted independently during his term of office. Ruth Sando Perry, it was hoped, would provide the necessary independent leadership. She had been declared acceptable by all the faction leaders at the Abuja summit.[4] As it transpired, she was to vindicate the faith placed in her.

***

Apart from its introduction of punitive measures for non-compliant warlords, one encouraging sign that on this occasion ECOWAS meant business was its appointment of a new ECOMOG field commander. The Nigerian Lt. General John Victor Malu, who had served as ECOMOG chief of staff during the Octopus assault on Monrovia, had a track-record as a 'no-nonsense General,'[5] He had now replaced Nigerian Major General John Inienger who had been blamed for allowing Monrovia to be overrun by factions in April.[6] Another encouraging sign was the fact that the ceasefire in Monrovia and its hinterland was holding, although there were reports of sporadic inter-factional fighting further afield. In addition, ECOMOG, under its new commander, had commenced the process of opening roads into the interior with some success, allowing humanitarian aid to be brought to areas where famine was rife.

However, even from an early stage, it was apparent that the accomplishment of disarmament according to the schedule laid down at Abuja II would pose the major stumbling block to the peace process. In a briefing delivered on 11 September, Samuel Kofi Woods reported that 'full-scale disarmament' had not yet commenced. There had been some developments but nothing meaningful. On 9 September Alhaji G.V. Kromah (ULIMO-K), to show 'good-will', had yielded up to ECOMOG some '166,000 pieces of ammunition, 100 rocket-propelled grenades and other military hardware,'[7] But while statements of intent had been made by other leaders there had been no 'practical action,' Charles Taylor had issued an order on 25 August for the disarmament of 500 of his force but nothing further had happened.

***

The closing months of 1996 were dominated by an assassination attempt on Taylor which occurred in the Executive Mansion on 31 October. For some months Taylor had been claiming that the U.S. was determined to kill him.[8] The attempt took place as Taylor, accompanied by his bodyguard and entourage, arrived for a meeting of the Council. At least three people were killed. Some sources put the number at seven. Taylor accused the LPC and ULIMO-J under Roosevelt Johnson of involvement but he also alleged that 'that a foreign power had supplied the remote control used to detonate the explosion,' No one had any doubt that the U.S. was the power he had in mind.[9] General Malu won much praise for the promptness and firmness of ECOMOG's reaction to the assassination attempt, instantly flooding the city with troops and imposing a rigorously-enforced curfew.[10] In the interim the Council was suspended and was only to reconvene in January 1997 after extensive negotiations.[11]

***

While the appointment of General Malu had led to more effective peace-keeping in the Monrovia enclave, so too the nomination of Perry as Chair of the Council of State, was a positive development. Although historically associated with the Unity Party and, later, with Samuel Doe's National Democratic Party, she had always been independent-minded, and this made her acceptable to the other Council members. Not that those relationships were always cordial. For example, Taylor claimed that Perry was not pursuing with sufficient vigour those who had attempted his assassination. As Chair she was to maintain this independence. She was also energetic and worked hard to forward the peace process,[12] highlighting the need for humanitarian aid by visiting areas of greatest need, delivering an impassioned address to the UN General Assembly on 9 October 1996, at which she won much badly needed support for the Liberian peace process, and travelling throughout the country pleading with faction fighters to lay down their arms.[13]

Abuja II had stipulated that Council of State members aspiring to the Presidency should resign their posts by 28 February. By this due date Taylor, Kromah and Georgy Boley (re-emerged from the shadows) had met the conditions. However there were grave concerns as to whether other requirements for free and fair elections could be met. For example, the formation of the all-important Election Commission to be composed of seven members – three from the factions and four from professional civilian groups – was delayed by months of bickering and was only inducted on 2 April, two months behind schedule. How was this commission to organise the election in the short time remaining? Moreover the reconstitution of the Supreme Court (which would have to adjudicate on any election disputes) was delayed by bickering between the National Bar Association and the State Council (the latter refusing to liaise with the former) and was only installed at the eleventh hour. In addition, the Electoral Commission headed by G. Henry Andrews, opted for proportional representation as the fairest, most representative method of electing both legislature and president.[14]This, of course, would require a nation-wide education campaign to enlighten the populace on the intricacies of the system. A third concern was the repatriation of refugees and the return of the displaced to their homes in advance of the poll. And there was the overriding consideration that no fair or free election could take place unless there existed a sufficient level of disarmament to ensure reasonable stability in all parts of the country. It was clear by April that the conditions necessary for the conduct of the poll, scheduled for 30 May, could not be met, although genuine progress was being made.

The only party which resolutely opposed an extension of the election date was the NPFL now formally a political party under the title National Patriotic Party (NPP). Taylor fancied his chances of winning an early election and few disputed this given his organisation's wealth, the continuing existence of its command structure and its dominance of media. Taylor's resistance had its effect when

ECOWAS at last met to judge the issue. At a summit held on 21 May it readjusted the date of the election a mere 52 days, to 19 July and the date for the installation of the new government from 15 June to 2 August 1997.[15] Most other political parties had hoped that the elections would be delayed until October.

Intensive political manoeuvring was already well underway before the date of the election was pushed back. By February seven political parties, seeking to prevent Taylor acceding to the presidency, formed an alliance with a view to presenting its own candidate. But this alliance was soon riven with disagreement, and on election day its chosen candidate, Cletus Wotorson (Liberian Action Party), had only the support of two of the parties.[16] Among the other candidates for the presidency – there were seven in all – were Alhaji G.V. Kromah (All-Liberia Coalition Party),[17] Gabriel Baccus Matthews (United People's Party), George Boley (National Democratic Party), George Toeh Washington (a former ambassador) and Ellen Johnson-Sirleaf (Unity Party). Melanie Flowers in her authoritative study says that Johnson-Sirleaf was the favoured candidate of the U.S., while Nigeria favoured the election of Taylor on the grounds that there would never be peace unless he became president.[18]

In accordance with the new schedule for elections, official campaigning begun on June 16 and was immediately followed by outbreaks of violence involving opposing political parties. This largely took the form of attacks by faction supporters on electoral opponents and their supporters, some of a vicious character.[19]

More disturbing, perhaps, were allegations of wrongdoing against ECOMOG. Reports of harassment and intimidation by the peacekeeping force in the south-eastern region were frequent and were confirmed by Ruth Sando Perry, who had visited the area. ECOMOG soldiers, according to the reports, had been responsible 'for human rights abuses including cruel, inhuman and degrading treatment or punishments and even murder and also of widespread brutality against citizens,'[20] Most of these reported breaches of human rights took place in the context of searches for arms. There was no doubt that, since the more vigorous deployment of ECOMOG and the completion of the voluntary phase of disarmament, the security situation had greatly improved. Nonetheless, ECOMOG was well aware that not all arms had been handed in and that sizeable quantities remained hidden. To recover these ECOMOG had commenced a 'Cordon and Search programme,' It was in the course of implementing this that most of the violations of human rights occurred. ECOMOG, conducting searches forcefully, was to succeed in retrieving large caches of arms in faction-controlled areas. Had its approach been more light-handed it was unlikely that it would have yielded such results.

Responding to these criticisms the ECOMOG High Command maintained that the greatest danger to the peace process was the existence of large caches of weaponry within the control of the factions. And in order to eliminate this danger vigorous search and cordon operations were required. These were conducted in the territories controlled by the factions and posed grave risks to the soldiers. The implication was that the claims of abuses against ECOMOG were manufactured by those who were subject to such search methods.

That the operations were achieving success could not be doubted. On 23 April a large cache of arms under NPFL control was discovered in Butuo, a cache, according to General Malu, which was sufficiently large 'to start a small war' and which included Howitzer artillery guns, anti-tank guns and anti-air-craft guns. Seven days later ECOMOG discovered a drum 'stuffed with arms and ammunition' buried at a Rubber Plantation[21] in Bomi County,' This area had been under the control of the ULIMO-J faction of Roosevelt Johnson before its dissolution. On 7 and 17 May, respectively, ECOMOG uncovered arms in a part of Lower Lofa County earlier controlled by ULIMO-K while, in May, a large cache of arms and looted goods were found on the farm of NPFL-nominated Deputy Minister for Defence, Austin Clarke.[22]

***

With regard to disarmament General Malu, speaking to reporters in February, estimated that the number of fighters to be disarmed stood at between 30,000 and 35,000. By June some 20,000 guns had already been surrendered under the terms of its so-called operation 'Gathering Rust,'[23] This 74–day campaign (between 22 November 1996 and 31 January 1997) had seen the disarmament of 23,403 fighters. And during the extension of the operation for a further week a total of 989 weapons were handed in. In addition to this, Malu mentioned the collection of 2,103 guns from 3,567 fighters during March and July 1994.[24] The disarmament process, the General asserted, was still underway and by the middle of March it would be possible 'to tell people that Liberia is an arms free society,'

***

Despite this rich harvest of weapons recovered, the prospect of a return to chaos and violence was never far away. It was rooted in the fear that a considerable arsenal of weaponry still remained available to the factions. It was hard to conceive that Taylor and the other faction leaders, who had resisted disarmament for so long with such determination, had yielded up the very source of their power. Could it be true, as so often in the past, that when the factions signalled their willingness to comply with peace agreements and ceasefires, they had in fact no intention of doing so? The fear of a return to old days was enhanced by the failure of the members of the transitional council, despite the best efforts of Perry to work together. Until the middle of May the council had acted without a fiscal budget and it was only with the greatest difficulty that one was eventually produced – after ultimatums from the transitional legislative assembly – and thereafter little effort was made to observe its provisions. Spending on foreign travel, the furnishing of homes and offices and the purchase of costly vehicles continued as before and there was little left to pay civil servants, many of who were without wages for between six to twelve months.[25] Meanwhile the plight of the ordinary citizen remained precarious with starvation never far from the door.

Among voices raised against the continuation of corruption and the failure of the Council of State to govern were those of the three Catholic bishops. Their hard-hitting press statement of 10 April deplored the refusal of the factions to work for the common good, the pervasive lack of cohesiveness of the Council, the consequent lack of civil administration in many parts of rural Liberia, the sufferings of the people, and the underlying threat posed to the peace process. These concerns were repeated in a pastoral letter issued in June in the wake of a meeting of representatives of the three dioceses[26]:

> Nationwide elections are now scheduled for 19 July 1997. All of the conditions necessary for free and fair elections are certainly not in place. In the absence of these we fear that the forthcoming elections may not be free and fair. Our country had a very bad experience in the elections of 1985. We do not want this to happen this time.

***

Nonetheless international support for the peace process remained resolute and a determination to push Liberia over the line of free and fair elections was evident. This manifested itself in practical support for the election process. For example, in May 1997 a high-level European Union delegation made substantial contributions to ECOMOG and the Electoral Commission. The German government, for its part, contributed 85 vehicles to ECOMOG to assist with logistics and 'enable it increase its patrols and presence throughout the country,'

***

The long-awaited elections took place on 19 July 1997 at 1,864 polling stations under the watchful eye of 500 international and 1,300 local observers, and massive ECOMOG security.[27]The UN declared the elections 'free and fair,' Taylor triumphed, winning 75.3% of the votes, followed by Johnson-Sirleaf with a mere 9.5%. The perceived wisdom was that Liberians voted for Taylor in the belief that war would be resumed should he lose. The NPP swept the boards in the legislature elections, winning 21 out of 26 seats in the Senate and 49 out of 64 in the House of Representatives.[28] Regarding the outcome as a success ECOWAS declared its intention to maintain ECOMOG in position for a further six months to assist with the transition and help in the formation of a Liberian army, after which the force would withdraw.

In the immediate aftermath of the elections the Liberian Catholic bishops issued a pastoral letter – 'That We May Be One' – which reflected a new optimism. The tone of the letter was very different from that of 10 April. In that pastoral the bishops had expressed their concern at the 'lack of cohesiveness of the Council of State ... manifested in the unwarranted delays in critical decision-making, the delay in the payment of salaries and the dispensing of justice,' In this letter, however, the bishops praised all concerned for conducting the exercise with dignity and integrity and offered fulsome congratulations to Taylor on his success:

We wish to congratulate all Liberians for turning out in mass and voting for the leader of their choice. We are particularly pleased with the level of political maturity exhibited during the exercise. We congratulate Mr Charles G. Taylor, president-elect, Mr Enoch Dogolea, vice president-elect, the NPP legislative candidates and legislative candidates of other political parties that were elected...

The Pastoral's prescription for the future was careful not to point the finger for the ills of the past.

After over seven years of violence that has left us wounded, bleeding, discouraged, humiliated, dehumanized and traumatized, we look forward to a period of tranquillity and sanity to enable us to pick up the broken pieces, reconstruct and rehabilitate our lives, our communities and our nation. We are a divided nation – we need unity. We are a hurt people – we need reconciliation and forgiveness. Above all we need to love each other as we love ourselves – for it is in this Great Commandment that we can achieve Peace.

***

The election outcome, which saw Taylor and his party win 75% of the votes cast, came as no surprise to many, but others – observers of Liberia since December 1989 – found it difficult to understand. Why should people vote in such numbers for a man who had visited upon them such suffering, death, displacement and destruction? If the elections were rigged this might well have been the outcome, but both local and international observers had declared the poll to be free and fair.

Stephen Ellis, characterising the election as 'the fairest' in Liberia's history in which '80% of the eligible population voted', offers an explanation as to why three-quarters of the electors voted for Taylor.

In some cases people may have reasoned that a vote for Taylor was the best hope for peace, since they knew that if Taylor did not win the election, he was likely to re-start the war.[29]

Dane F. Smith Jr, the White House envoy to Liberia – closely involved in the course of events leading up to the election – agrees with Ellis. 'There was', he wrote, 'a common consensus that Taylor won the vote because Liberians were afraid that if he lost he would go back to the bush to resume the civil war,'[30]

Samuel Kofi Woods suggests that Taylor's victory was influenced by the circumstances in which the poll took place. For example, he notes that many of the provisions of the original Abuja Accord of 19 August 1995 and the amended accord of 17 August 1996 had not been fulfilled by the time elections took place and that this favoured a Taylor victory:

There was no demobilization of former combatants, the military command structure of the factions was left intact. The repatriation of refugees was not in any significant way implemented with the result that almost 15% of the electorate could not vote as they were not allowed to cast their vote in the refugee camps.[31]

He also alleges that Nigeria sought victory for Taylor. 'The Nigerian Foreign Affairs Minister did all he could to let Mr Taylor have his way ... he and the government of Nigeria were overtly supporting Mr Taylor to run for the presidency,' And eventually support for Taylor, led by Nigeria, came to dominate ECOWAS thinking. Underlying this was the conviction that 'if Taylor did not win the election Liberia would become like Angola, overwhelmed by war and chaos,' Another who recognised a shift in Nigeria's position on the NPFL leader was Archbishop Michael Francis. In his pastoral letter of Easter 1996 he had 'lamented a perceived shift of ECOMOG sympathy, especially on the part of the Nigerian contingent, towards Taylor and the NPFL,'[32]

Few now challenge the view that Nigeria's assumption of a leadership role in resolving Liberia's crisis from early 1995 (an achievement chiefly orchestrated by Rawlings with the support of the Clinton administration) created a trajectory which culminated in Taylor's victory in 1997. It led first to a rapprochement between Taylor and the Nigerian president and ultimately to an ECOWAS conviction that a strong Taylor presidency was the most likely road to the stability which would allow for ECOMOG's withdrawal. Abiodun Aloa supports this analysis dating the sea change which came over Nigeria to General Sani Abacha's seizure of power in November 1993 and his meeting in early June 1996 with Taylor in Abuja.[33] However there is evidence that pro-Taylor sentiment within ECOMOG (if not within ECOWAS) had already gained ground at an earlier date. Funmi Olonisakin, in his study of ECOMOG, notes that this change in relationships between Taylor and the Nigerians became especially marked and apparent to observers with the accession of General Bakut as ECOMOG field commander in September 1991.

> Prominent and ordinary Liberians alike, recalled how General Bakut's relationship with Charles Taylor transcended that between peacekeeper and warlord. Indeed the prevailing opinion in Liberia was that the somewhat personal relationship which developed between General Bakut and Charles Taylor prevented him from taking necessary precautions even when there were indications of an impending NPFL attack on ECOMOG and Monrovia.[34]

The attack in question was Operation Octopus.

***

Nigeria's leadership role in the Liberian crisis coincided with, and was enhanced by, a major change in international relations which occurred from 1991, namely the end of the Cold War. From the post-World War II period and especially during the 1980s U.S. policy towards Africa was primarily influenced by a fear of communism taking root, sharply focused on preventing the defection of allies to the Soviet bloc, and the weaning of left-leaning regimes from dalliance with communism. Thus, in the 1980s, with the advent of Doe's restless and venal regime, the U.S. paid special attention to a country which had been previously its closest ally on that continent. Now, with the Soviet communist threat greatly diminished America's attention to matters in Africa became desultory, superseded by pressing concerns in South America, the Middle East and a Europe convulsed by the break-up of the Soviet Union. In such circumstances Nigeria was able to become perhaps the pre-eminent force in shaping Liberia's future.

In his post-election briefing on behalf of the Catholic Church's Justice and Peace Secretariat, Woods listed other factors which, while not affecting the result, might have led to a closer contest. Firstly, many of the twelve political parties were ill-prepared for the election while Taylor had set his mind on the presidency for almost seven years and controlled not only most of the country but its resources. He had put the latter to good use. For example, his use of the electronic and print media was masterful:

> He set up a short-wave radio station which covered the whole of Liberia and West Africa and an FM station in Monrovia covering the metropolitan area. For twenty-four hours daily he poured out over the airwaves fear and disinformation. The population was intimidated - if they did not vote for him there would be no peace they were told in their different languages. He controlled six newspapers in which disinformation, and mudslinging articles were the order of the day. The rural population had no other voice to listen to nor any information of what was happening only what Taylor wanted them to hear. His use of media was a potent force in convincing fearful, intimidated, and illiterate people that Taylor was the only choice for peace and that the alternative was war.

The failure to secure demobilisation, according to Wood's briefing, was also a critical factor in Taylor's success.

> The former combatants were able to go from village to village intimidating the people that if they did not vote for Taylor their homes would be burnt down and they would be killed. For people who had experienced seven years of war the message was clear - he had done it before, and he would do it again, so the best thing was to vote for him... In the displaced camps people were given food, money, clothes and warned if they did not vote for Mr Taylor they would not be able to go home and worse still their homes would be burnt down.

Other factors which favoured Taylor were the registration process, with many of the registrars former NPFL members and large numbers of under-aged former child-soldiers permitted to vote. And there was also the lack of civic education required by the Abuja accords. Furthermore, it must be remembered that in the serious fighting which took place between April and June 1996, during which ECOMOG largely stood by, the factions fought themselves to a standstill. And during the stalemate which ensued in Monrovia, the NPFL retook much of the territory which it had lost to other groups in the rural areas.[35] But most of all it was 'fear psychosis' which led the masses to support Taylor, fear of what might happen if he was defeated. 'Highly traumatized after seven years of savagery, fear permeated the whole atmosphere in cities and towns, rural areas and refugee camps. They could not and did not vote freely,'

Finally, it must be said that an important factor in bringing the war to an end was the sheer exhaustion of the combatants after seven years of hostilities and, for some, much longer. War weariness can often prove an important element in bringing to an end conflict which appear intractable.* Warlords, governments and other parties at last became amenable to negotiating a peaceful solution. It is true that the solution which first emerged – the advent of Taylor to the presidency – was deeply flawed, but within a relatively short time a more enduring settlement was to follow.

***

The calculation by ECOWAS and by those who voted in the election that allowing Taylor to become president would bring stability and peace was to prove disastrously wrong. Although ECOWAS felt able to withdraw its forces towards the end of 1998,** Liberia was soon submerged in a new round of internecine strife. But the story of the second civil war, essentially a renewal of the first, is for another day. What may be said here is that the miscalculation made by ECOWAS, aided and encouraged by the U.S. and the international community, was to lead to a further six years of chaos and horror for the people of Liberia. Like Master Sergeant Doe, Taylor lacked the qualities of political leadership which might have given him a slight chance of success. Instead, like his predecessor, having finally achieved the presidency, his principal purpose thereafter was to cling on to it. The many he had offended during his bloody road to the Executive Mansion, sought to bring him down and increased in numbers and strength. Regional neighbours turned against him following his interference in the Sierra Leonean and Guinea-Bissau civil wars. The international community, discomforted by his destabilising influence on the region, also turned against him with a vengeance. He was eventually forced from office on 11 August 2003 and into exile. It took a further tortuous two years before Liberia was ready to hold a general election.

---

*   This author is reminded of the violent conflict in Northern Ireland which commenced in 1969 and was concluded only in 1998. War weariness, undoubtedly, was one of the significant factors in bringing this particularly intractable conflict to an end.

** ECOMOG was deployed in the region to combat the Sierra Leone rebel group and to bring to an end the Guinea-Bissau civil war. Its only intervention in Liberia occurred in 2003 when it was briefly deployed to stop the occupation of Monrovia by rebels. However, it was the UN intervention force, UNOMIL, which oversaw the conclusion of Liberia's second civil war.

Liberia's return to stability can be dated to the swearing in of a government led by Ellen Johnson-Sirleaf on 16 January 2006. That date too brought an inestimable measure of relief and security to the region.

Notes

1 Kieh, George Klay Jr, African Journal on Conflict Resolution, 2011/3, 19 August 2011, 'Peace agreements and the termination of civil wars – Lessons from Liberia', https://www.accord.org.za/ajcr-issues/peace-agreements-and-the-termination-of-civil-wars/, accessed 4 April 2020.
2 Ibid.
3 Samuel Kofi Woods, Catholic Justice and Peace Commission, 'Briefing Paper on Liberia', 11 September 1996.
4 Tina Susman, 23 September 1996.
5 Samuel K. Woods, op. cit.
6 Tina Susman, 23 September 1996.
7 Samuel Kofi Woods, op. cit.
8 Abiodun Alao, op. cit, 189–190.
9 Ibid.
10 The ACP-EU Courier, May/June1997 (no. 163), 'A Harvest of Guns,'
11 WFP Emergency Report no. 44 of 1996. (https://reliefweb.int/report/liberia/wfp-emergency-report-no-44-1996-liberia. Accessed 17 June 2017).
12 Africa, January-March 1997 (Revue de Presse – Press Review), transcript, Rick Wells, BBC World Service, 'Focus on Africa'; c.f. Adekeye Adebajo, Liberia's Civil War, 202–203.
13 Adekeye Adebajo, op. cit., 203.
14 The ACP-EU Courier, May/June,1997 (no. 163), 'Liberia the Bitter Sweet,'
15 Ibid., 'A Harvest of Guns,'
16 Melanie Flowers, Conflict Resolution: Peace Implementation in New Wars, 123.
17 All Liberia Coalition Party.
18 The ACP Courier, May/June 1997 (no. 163), 'Country Report'.
19 A.T. Samuel Kofi Woods, 'Briefing Paper on Liberia', June 1997.
20 Ibid., April-May 1997.
21 Factory 6 G3 Camp, in the Gutherie FN Rifles.
22 Samuel Kofi Woods, 'Briefing Paper on Liberia', April-May 1997.
23 The ACP-EU Courier, May/June 1997 (no. 163), 'A Harvest of Guns,'
24 Ibid. See also, Patrick L.N. Seyon, 'A Quick Fix for the Liberian "Humpty Dumpty"', Liberian Studies Journal, XXIII, 2 (1998), 6–7.
25 Samuel Kofi Woods, 'Briefing Paper on Liberia', June 1997.
26 Convened 9–11 June 1997.
27 Melanie Flowers, op. cit., 124.
28 Ibid.
29 Ellis, op. cit., 109.
30 Dane F. Smith Jr., op. cit., 427.
31 A.T. 'Report and Assessment on the July 19 Presidential Elections' (n.d).
32 A.B. John Kilcoyne, op. cit., p. 39.
33 Abiodun Aloa, op. cit., 70.
34 Funmi Olosakin, Reinventing Peacekeeping in Africa; Conceptual and Legal Issues in ECOMOG Operations (London, Boston, The Hague, 2000), 201.
35 A.B. Kilcoyne, John, op. cit., 7.

Maps

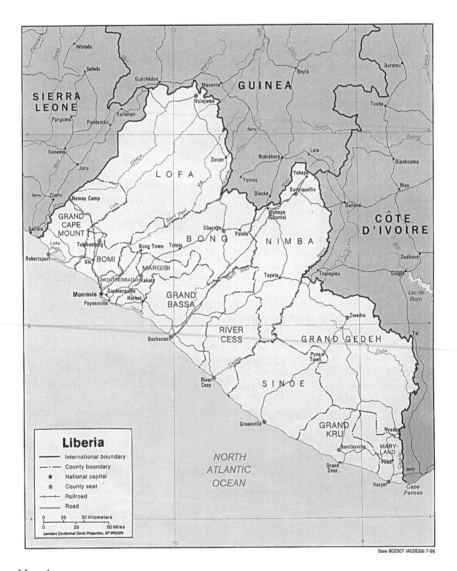

Maps 1

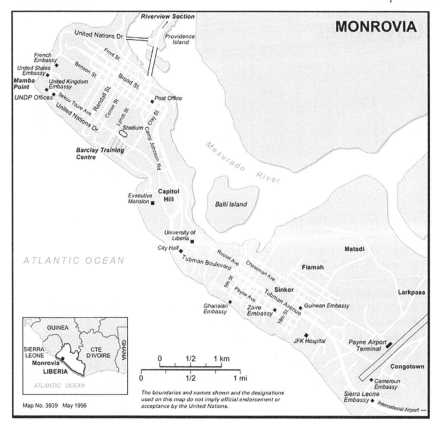

Maps 2

References

Addo, Prosper, *Peace-Making in West Africa: Progress and Prospects* (KAIPTC Monograph No. 3, November2005).

Adebajo, Adekeye, *Liberia's civil war: Nigeria, ECOMOG, and regional security in West Africa*, (U.S. and UK, 2002a).

Adebajo, Adekeye, *Building Peace in West Africa (Liberia, Sierra Leone, and Guinea-Bissau)*, (International Peace Academy, Occ. Papers Series, U.S. and UK, 2002b).

Advocates for Human Rights, *A House with Two Rooms: Final Report of the Truth and Reconciliation Commission of Liberia Diaspora Project* (2009).

Ahluwalia, D. Pal S., *Politics and Post-colonial Theory: African Inflections* (London and New York, 2001).

Allen, William E., 'Liberia and the Atlantic World in the Nineteenth Century: Convergence and Effects', *History in Africa*, Vol. 27 (2010), 7–49.

Ali, Taisier M., Matthews, Robert O., et al., *Civil Wars in Africa: Roots and Resolution* (McGill-Queen's Press, Montreal, 1990).

Alao, Abiodun, *The Burden of Collective Goodwill* (Taylor & Francis, UK, 2017).

Bekoe, Dorina A., *Implementing Peace Agreements: Lessons from Mozambique, Angola, and Liberia* (Palgrave Macmillan, UK, 2008).

Berkeley, Bill, *Liberia: A Promise Betrayed: A Report on Human Rights* (New York, 1986).

Berkeley, Bill, *The Graves Are Not Yet Full: Race, Tribe and Power in the Heart of Africa* (New York, 2002).

Blahyi, Joshua, *The Redemption of an African Warlord: The Joshua Blahyi Story a.k.a General Butt Naked* (U.S., 2013).

Collectif. 'Liberia, Sierra Leone, Guinee: la Regionalisation de la Guerre', *Politique Africaine*, N-088, 2003.

Dalton, George, 'History Politics, and Economic Development in Liberia', *The Journal of Economic History*, vol. 24, no. 4 (December1965), 569–591.

Dietmann, Susanne, *Radio Veritas in Liberia - Entwicklungspolitische Zielsetzungen und Inhalte* (Grin Verlag, Germany, 2005).

Dolo, Emmanuel, *Ethnic Tensions in Liberia's Identity Crisis*, (Africana Homestead Legacy Publishers, 2007).

Dunn, Elwood D., Beyan, Amos J., & Burrowes, Carl Patrick, *Historical Dictionary of Liberia* (U.S., 2001).

Edwards, James, *A Mother's Will: The Story of Liberia's Civil Wars and The Women of Liberia Mass Action for Peace Movement* (CreateSpace Independent Publishing Platform, 2012).

Ellis, George W., 'Dynamic Factors in the Liberian Situation', *The Journal of Race Development*, January 1911, vol. 1, No. 3, 255–276.

Ellis, Stephen, 'Liberia 1989–1994, a Study of Ethnic and Spiritual Violence', *African Affairs*, 94, 1995, 165–197.

Ellis, Stephen, *The Mask of Anarchy Updated Edition: The Destruction of Liberia and the Religious Dimension of an African Civil War* (Hurst & Co, London, 2006).

Fahnbulleh, Boimah H., *Across the Landscape: Selected Political Writings and Speeches on Liberia* (Universal Publishers, Florida, 2004).

Flowers, Melanie, *Conflict Resolution: Peace Implementation in New Wars* (UK and Germany, 2010, 2013).

Gberie, Lansana, 'Briefing Truth and Justice on Trial in Liberia', *African Affairs*, 107/428, 455–465 (Oxford University Press on behalf of Royal African Society, 2008).

Gerdes, Felix, *Civil War and State Formation: The Political Economy of War and Peace in Liberia* (Frankfurt and New York, 2013).

Gifford, Paul (Ed.), *The Christian Churches and the Democratisation of Africa* (Leiden, New York and Cologne, 1995).

Gifford, Paul, *Christianity and Politics in Doe's Liberia* (Cambridge Studies in Ideology and Religion, May2002).

Goodhand, J. & Atkin, P, *Conflict and Aid: Enhancing the Peacebuiling Impact of International Engagement: A Synthesis of Findings from Afghanistan, Liberia and Sri Lanka* (International Alert, UK, 2001).

Harris, David, *Civil War and Democracy in West Africa: Conflict Resolution, Elections and Justice in Sierra Leone and Liberia* (International Library of African Studies, 2014).

Hettne, B. ed., *The New Regionalism and the Future of Security and Development*, Volume 4, (Palgrave Macmillan, Gordonsville, U.S., 2000).

Heyns, Christof (Ed.), *Human Rights Law in Africa* (Leiden, Netherlands, 2002).

Higate, Paul & Henry, Marsha, *Insecure Spaces: Peacekeeping, Power and Performance in Haiti, Kosovo and Liberia* (Zed Books, London, 2013).

Hogan, Edmund M., *Catholic Missionaries and Liberia − a Study of Missionary Enterprise in West Africa, 1830–1950* (Cork University Press, 1977).

Howe, Herbert, 'Lessons of Liberia: ECOMOG and Regional Peacekeeping', *International Security*, vol. 21, no. 3 (Winter, 1996–1997),145–176.

Huband, Mark, *African Report*, July 15, 1993.

Huband, Mark, *The Liberian Civil War* (Routledge, UK, 1998).

Hyman, Lester S., *United States Policy Towards Liberia, 1822 to 2003: Unintended Consequences* (Africana Homestead Legacy Publisher, New Jersey, 2007).

Jimo, Emma, *ECOWAS Humanitarian Intervention in Liberia in the 1990s: The Politics, Legality, and Morality of using Military Strategy* (Academic/Research Papers, 2017).

Kieh, George Klay Jr, *Liberia's State Failure, Collapse and Reconstitution* (Africana Homestead Legacy Publishers, New Jersey, 2012).

Kieh, George Klay Jr, 'Peace agreements and the termination of civil wars – Lessons from Liberia', *African Journal on Conflict Resolution*, March2011, www.accord.org.za/ajcr-issues/peace-agreements-and-the-termination-of-civil-wars, accessed 4 April 2020.

Kilcoyne, John, 'The role of the Catholic Church during Liberia's Civil Crisis, 1990–1997, in the light of the Liberation Theology paradigm', Dissertation submitted to Middlesex University and Missionary Institute, London, May 1999.

Kotia, Emmanuel Wekem, *Ghana Armed Forces in Lebanon and Liberia Peace Operations (Conflict and Security in the Developing World)* (Lexington Books, Maryland, 2015).

Kufuo, Kofi Oteng, 'Developments in the Resolution of the Liberian Conflict', *American University International Law Review*, vol. 10, no. 1, Art. 4, 1996.

Liberia Truth and Reconciliation Commission, *Consolidated Final Report* (Government of Liberia, 2009).

Liebenow, J. Gus, *Liberia: The Evolution of Privilege* (Cornell University Press, 1969).

Liebenow, J. Gus, *Liberia: the Quest for Democracy* (Indiana University Press, 1987).

Liebenow, J. Gus, 'Liberia, Dr Doe and the Demise of Democracy', Part 1: 'The Anatomy of Subterfuge' (31 August1984, *USFI Reports*, Issue 17).

Lipschutz, Mark R, *Dictionary of African Historical Biography* (University of California Press, 1989).

MacKenzie, M. D., *Journal of the Royal African Society*, vol. 33, no. 133 (October1934), 372–381.

Magyar, K. P. *Peacekeeping in Africa: ECOMOG in Liberia* (Palgrave, UK, 1998).

Mailabari, Nuhu, *Why ECOWAS Peace Enforcement Intervention failed in Liberia* (LAP LAMBERT Academic Publishing, 2016).

Massing, Michael, *Best Friends: Violations of Human Rights in Liberia, America's Closest Ally in Africa*, May1986 (A Fund for Free Expression Report, New York).

Moran, Mary H., *Liberia: the Violence of Democracy* (University of Pennsylvania Press, 2008).

Mutwol, Julius Peac, *e Agreements and Civil Wars in Africa: Insurgent Motivations, State Responses, and Third Party Peacemaking in Liberia, Rwanda, and Sierra Leone* (Cambria Press, Amherst, 2009).

Nevin, Timothy D., 'The Uncontrollable Force: A Brief History of the Liberia Frontier Force, 1908–1944', *International Journal of African Historical Studies*, vol. 44, no. 2 (2011), 275–297.

Niagawoe, Tuoquellie Garlon, *The Result of Failed Leadership: The Republic of Liberia* (Xlibris Corp., 2010).

Obi, Cyril I., 'Economic Community of West African States on the Ground: Comparing Peacekeeping in Liberia, Sierra Leone, Guinea Bissau, and Côte D'Ivoire', *African Security*www.tandfonline.com/loi/uafs20, 2009. Accessed 20 February 2020.

Ohanwe, Augustine C, *Post-Cold War Conflicts in Africa: Case Studies of Liberia and Somalia* (Adonis & Abbey Publishers Ltd, London, 2009).

Olonisakin, Funmi, *Reinventing Peacekeeping in Africa - Conceptual and Legal Issues in ECOMOG Operations* (Kluwer Law International, The Hague, London and Boston, 2000).

Omeje, Kenneth (Ed.), *War to Peace Transition: Conflict Intervention and Peacebuilding in Liberia* (University Press of America, 2008).

Omeje, Kenneth, *Peacebuilding in Contemporary Africa: In Search of Alternative Strategies* (Routledge Studies in African Development, 2018).

Outram, Quentin, 'Its Terminal Either Way – An Analysis of Armed Conflict in Liberia, 1989–1996', *Review of African Political Economy*, no. 23 (ROAPE Publications), 1997, 355–371.

Quereshi, Moeen A., Yoshio, Mizoe & Collins, Francis d'A., 'The Liberian Economy', *Staff Papers* (International Monetary Fund, vol. 11, no. 2, July1964, 285–325)

Peel J. D. Y., *Letters from Liberia* (International African Institute, London, 2016).

Porte, Albert, *The Day Monrovia Stood Still* (Crozierville, Liberia, 1979).

Reno, William, 'Foreign Firms and the Financing of Charles Taylor's NPFL', *Liberian Studies Journal*, vol. XVIII, no. 2, 1993, 175–187.

Rodriguez, Roberto Miguel, Peace Operations In West Africa -ECOWAS Successes and Failures in Liberia, Sierra Leone, Cote d'Ivoire, Guinea and Guinea-Bissau

(2014). www.academia.edu/19708515/Peace_Operations_in_Africa_ECOWAS_Suc cesses_and_Failures_in_Sierra_Leone_Cote_dIvoire_Guinea_and_Guinea-Bissau.

Smith, Dane F. Jr. 'U.S.-Guinea Relations During the Rise and Fall of Charles Taylor,' *The Journal of Modern African Studies*, Vol. 44, no. 3 (September2006).

Tessler, Mark, 'Liberia's difficult march towards Civilian Rule', *UFSI Report*, 1983/no. 17.

Waugh, Colin, *Charles Taylor and Liberia: Ambition and Atrocity in Africa's Lone Star State* (London and New York, 2011).

Williams, Gabriel I. H., *Liberia: The Heart of Darkness: Accounts of Liberia's Civil War and Its destabilizing effects in West Africa* (Trafford Publishing, U.S., 2002).

Williams, Levi C., *A History of the United Methodist Church in Liberia* (Outskirts Press, U.S. 2014).

Wippman, David, 'Enforcing Peace - Ecowas and the Liberian Civil War', in *Enforcing Restraint – Collective Intervention in Internal Conflicts*, Lori Fisler Damrosch, Ed. (Council on Foreign Relations, New York, 1993).

Woods, Samuel Kofi, 'Bassa – a Human Tragedy. A one day preliminary fact-finding human rights report' (Catholic Justice and Peace Commission, February 6, 1995).

Woods, Samuel Kofi, 'Report of the Justice and Peace Commission of the National Catholic Secretariat', *Liberian Studies Journal*, XX, 2, 1995, 286–291.

Index